P9-DNF-496

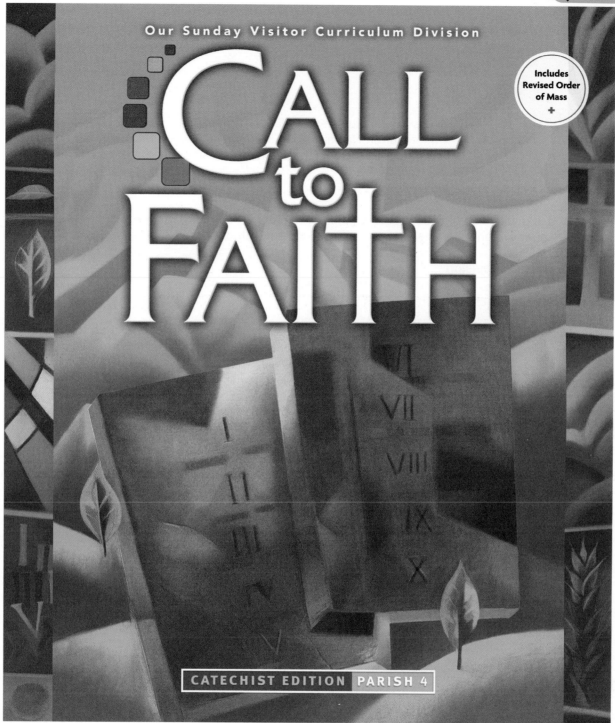

Our Sunday Visitor Curriculum Division

CALL to FAITH

Includes Revised Order of Mass ✠

CATECHIST EDITION PARISH 4

OurSundayVisitor

Curriculum Division

www.osvcurriculum.com

Nihil Obstat
Rev. Richard L. Schaefer

Imprimatur
✛ Most Rev. Thomas Wenski
Bishop of Orlando
December 14, 2007

The Imprimatur is an official declaration that a book or pamphlet is free of doctrinal or moral error. No implication is contained therein that anyone who granted the Imprimatur agrees with the contents, opinions, or statements expressed.

© Our Sunday Visitor Curriculum Division, Our Sunday Visitor, 2009 Edition.

Printed in the United States of America

Call to Faith Parish Grade 4 Catechist Edition
ISBN: 978-0-15-902292-4
Item Number: CU1388

5 6 7 8 9 10 11 12   015016   15 14 13 12 11
Webcrafters, Inc., Madison, WI, USA; July 2011; Job# 93367

CONTENTS

Opening Prayer

Sign of the Cross

In the name of the Father,
    and of the Son,
    and of the Holy Spirit.
                        Amen.

Let Us Pray

Oh God, Teacher and Giver of Life,
    we begin today a new journey,
    a journey of faith.
We are ready to learn from each other in this ministry,
    to support one another in love,
    and to work together as the Church.
Grant us your wisdom
    to deepen our understanding of you.
Grant us your love
    to grow in our love for each other.

Walk with us on this journey
    as we answer the call to faith
    and help others do so as well.
Lead us to make loving choices in everything we do.
Guide us with the witness of the saints,
    the words of Sacred Scripture,
    and the teachings of the Church.

We pray for these gifts,
    confident in your goodness,
    through Jesus Christ, our Lord. Amen.

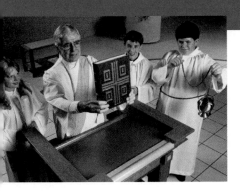

CALL to FAITH

Philosophy

Call to Faith is shaped around the following catechetical principles:

Conversion is central to catechesis. The aim of *Call to Faith* is to form participants into disciples who act with the mind and heart of Christ.

Catechesis is a lifelong process. Catechesis is gradual, systematic, and lifelong. We are touched and transformed by the living God and by the lived Tradition of the community throughout our lives.

Catechesis is the responsibility of all baptized members of the Church. The whole parish community (including parents, family members, catechists, and pastors) is called to hand on the faith through faith sharing and the witness of daily life.

Sources of Catholic Wisdom

Call to Faith is deeply rooted in Church Tradition. In its dependence on and faithfulness to both the *Catechism of the Catholic Church* and the *General Directory for Catechesis*, it remains true to the *magisterium*, or teaching office of the Church, and draws from the following sources of Catholic wisdom:

Scripture In *Call to Faith*, the treasure of God's word is highlighted and integrated into the program's instruction, reflection, sharing, and prayer. Throughout the program students, catechists, and families are provided with both the content and the tools necessary to explore the Scriptures and to enrich their faith.

Doctrine   Each lesson of *Call to Faith* draws on and instructs in Church doctrine in ways that help students, catechists, and families understand and appreciate the Church's teachings as they apply to life today.

Lives of Saints and People of Faith   *Call to Faith* takes seriously the importance of models and witnesses of faith as a factor in the faith development of both children and adults. The story of one person of faith whose life witnesses to the lesson theme is presented at the end of each lesson, and stories of other saints and people of faith are interwoven into the lessons when appropriate.

Cultural Customs and Celebrations   Many communities have customs and devotions that address or celebrate the faith. These customs and devotions involve the lived experience and wisdom of the Christian community, and they respect the context and the culture of the local community. The inclusion of many of these rituals and customs is a unique component of *Call to Faith* and assists parishes in making the curriculum their own.

Catechetical approaches in **CALL to FAITH**

Because of the many ways children learn, and because of the communal nature of the Church itself, *Call to Faith* uses a variety of catechetical approaches, which are designed to help you succeed and be faithful to the task of catechesis.

Content-centered catechesis

The presentation of the core elements of the faith is essential in religious formation and instruction. *Call to Faith* provides you with accurate and comprehensive content based on Scripture and the *Catechism of the Catholic Church*, as well as a teaching method that will help you effectively communicate the content to your students.

Catechesis in the whole community

Call to Faith is the first textbook series designed for use in a catechetical program that encompasses the whole parish community. Although these textbooks are designed for children of various ages, they are also specifically designed to be the basis for catechesis in the rest of the community. The *Pastoral Leader's Source Book*, which accompanies *Call to Faith*, provides resources that will extend catechesis to the entire faith community.

Blanket Donations

Liturgical catechesis

Call to Faith includes a generous amount of liturgical catechesis to help students and families become, as the Second Vatican Council's document on the liturgy expressed, "full, conscious, and active" participants of the assembly at Mass. *Call to Faith* students who learn by celebrating the rites and feasts, rather than by merely reading about them, are formed for life in the rich liturgical tradition of the Catholic Church.

Lectionary-connected catechesis

For Catholics, the Scriptures are proclaimed week after week in the Liturgy of the Word at Sunday Mass. The "Break Open the Word" feature in *Call to Faith* provides an ongoing opportunity to reflect on these Scriptures. Care is also taken to provide opportunities to reflect on the readings for the seasons and feasts of the Church year. Our Sunday Visitor Curriculum Division's website, **www.osvcurriculum.com**, serves the entire catechetical community in this effort.

 Visit **www.osvcurriculum.com** for weekly scripture readings and seasonal resources.

Generations of Faith &

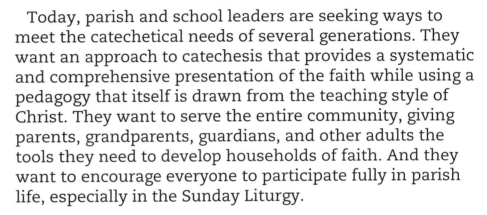

ouseholds of Faith

e first catechists in any young person's life
e family members. The home, known as the
omestic Church," is where young people
n grow in faith. *Call to Faith* partners with
rents and guardians to develop households
faith.

Family connections are made throughout the
program.

Complete Home Lessons for each chapter
available at **www.osvcurriculum.com**.

Additional family and community
connections at **www.osvcurriculum.com**.

Catholic Parent Know-How: Grade 4
and *Catholic Parent Know-How: Revised
Roman Missal* will help parents more fully
participate in their child's faith journey.

Take Out: Family Faith on the Go helps
parents build faith-filled families! Every
month, *Take Out* provides parents Catholic
insight and inspiration with Catholic
conversation starters, prayers, Sunday
Readings, advice from a Catholic child
psychologist, positive reinforcement for
boosting Catholic identity at home, and an
inspiring *Faith in Action* article.

sit **www.osvcurriculum.com**.

Today, parish and school leaders are seeking ways to
meet the catechetical needs of several generations. They
want an approach to catechesis that provides a systematic
and comprehensive presentation of the faith while using a
pedagogy that itself is drawn from the teaching style of
Christ. They want to serve the entire community, giving
parents, grandparents, guardians, and other adults the
tools they need to develop households of faith. And they
want to encourage everyone to participate fully in parish
life, especially in the Sunday Liturgy.

To help leaders meet these goals, Our Sunday Visitor
Curriculum Division has partnered with the Generations
of Faith Project of the Center for Ministry Development.
This partnership resulted in the all-new, systematic
catechetical program *People of Faith: Generations Learning
Together*. This program enables the parish community to
create a program of lifelong faith formation that is
centered in the events of Church life. It embraces all ages
and generations, promotes faith growth at home, and,
most importantly, promotes participation in Church life.

People of Faith: Generations Learning Together and *Call to
Faith*, working together, will provide you with an
innovative approach to lifelong faith formation that
engages all generations. All members of the community
are invited to learn and grow in faith together.

Lifelong Catechesis and *Call to Faith*

Call to Faith incorporates lifelong catechesis in its
curriculum. Through regular moments of faith sharing,
connections to the Sunday lectionary, and options for
family-centered catechesis and adult formation, *Call to
Faith* engages not only the specific learner but the larger
community of faith.

CALL to FAITH

Catechetical Process

Call to Faith uses a proven three-step catechetical process: Invite, Explore, Celebrate.

Invite   This step invites the learner into the catechetical process through simple and engaging reflections that draw out the life experience of the learner.

Explore   This step explores, in an age-appropriate way, the living Tradition of our Catholic faith as it is expressed in Scripture and doctrine. Through the use of a variety of stories, literary forms, and questions students enter more deeply into the chapter content and are helped to connect faith with their lives.

In order to show reverence for the word of God, Scripture is clearly labeled and set apart in each lesson. The "Words of Faith" feature included in this step helps build a common language of faith.

Celebrate   In this step, students celebrate what they believe through prayer celebrations that model the diverse ways in which Catholics pray. Prayers of praise, meditations, litanies, and celebrations of the word are included.

Music and song are included in each celebration. The *Call to Faith* music CD tracks are listed by chapter for ease of use.

Call to Faith Activity Process

Each chapter includes an integrated activity strand designed to lead the students from personal faith reflection to communal participation.

Let's Begin helps children reflect on their own varied experiences.

Share Your Faith helps children dialogue with others and act on their faith.

Connect Your Faith helps children connect with the faith life of the Church.

Live Your Faith helps children put their faith into action.

The Family Faith page also includes a "Live Your Faith" activity, emphasizing that it is in the family setting—the "domestic Church"— that students primarily live out their faith.

Call to Faith SCOPE AND SEQUENCE

	Grade K	Grade 1
Revelation	• God made the world. • God made people to be like him. • God made people to love him and others. Psalm 148:7–10, Genesis 1:27–28, 6–8, 1 Corinthians 13:4–7 CCC: 337; 356; 288	• God created everything. All that God made is good. • God knows and loves everyone. • God's world is a gift to you. • You can learn about God and his love from the world he made. • All creation is a gift from God. • Everyone must help care for God's world. Genesis 2:7–22, 1:5–25, 1:26–30 CCC: 282, 286–287, 290, 299, 355–361, 364; 32, 297, 301, 293–295; 2402
Trinity	• God shows his love through others. • When we pray, we are talking to God. • All people care for God's world. 1 John 3:1, 1 Thessalonians 5:16–18, Genesis 1:28–30, 6–8 CCC: 238; 278; 373	• The Holy Trinity is God the Father, God the Son, and God the Holy Spirit. • Jesus is the Son of God. • Jesus is both God and man. • Jesus, Mary, and Joseph are the Holy Family. • Jesus told stories, or parables, to teach about God's love. • The Bible is God's word written in human words. John 14:7-9, Luke 2:51–52, 15:3–6 CCC: 232–234, 240, 423, 458–459, 516; 464, 531–533; 105–110, 136
Jesus Christ	• Jesus is the Son of God and the Son of Mary. • Jesus taught us to live through his life. • All Christians are called to follow Christ. Luke 2:1–7, 6:27–36, 10:25–37, Mark 1:16–19 CCC: 422, 723; 561; 940–942	• Jesus' healing actions show God's power and love. • Faith is the gift of believing in God. • The Great Commandment is about love of God and others. • You are to love God above all else and love others as you love yourself. • Prayer is listening and talking to God. • Jesus taught his friends how to pray the Lord's Prayer. Luke 8:40–56, 10:25–28, Ephesians 5:18–20 CCC: 547–550, 153, 1814; 2052–2056, 2196; 2560, 2564, 2601, 2607, 2759, 2761
The Church	• The Church is a large family that belongs to God. • The Holy Spirit helps the Church family to love. • Each person has special talents to serve others. Colossians 3:12–17, Acts 2:1–4, Matthew 25:42–46, Luke 2:1–20 CCC: 751, 752; 253, 791; 910, 2447	• God invites everyone into his kingdom. • The Church is people who follow Jesus and say "yes" to God's call. • God the Holy Spirit is the third Person of the Holy Trinity. • The Holy Spirit fills people's hearts with love and guides the Church. • Saints are friends of God who can show you how to live. • People in the Church are called to live holy lives, as the saints did. Genesis 6:14–22, 7:1–23, Luke 14:16–23, John 14:25–26 CCC: 541–545, 551, 781–782, 768; 243, 685; 684, 688, 731–733, 828, 829, 1023, 825, 956
Morality	• Love one another as Jesus loves you. • God's rules help people make good choices. • Tell others when you are sorry. John 15:9, 11, Matthew 18:21–35, 19:18–19 CCC: 1825; 2472; 270; 1421, 2227, 1435	• Jesus' words and actions teach us how to love and serve God. • When you serve others, you are serving God. • The Ten Commandments are God's laws to help people love God and others. • God gives people the freedom to choose. • God always forgives those who are truly sorry and want to do better. • God asks that we forgive others and ourselves. John 13:4–17, Deuteronomy 10:12–13, Luke 18:9–13 CCC: 565, 459, 2825; 2053, 2058, 2067, 1730–1734; 982, 1431, 2840, 1446–1450
Sacraments	• The words and actions of the sacraments show the wonders of God. • Water is a source of life and also brings new life. • The bread becomes Jesus at Mass. Mark 8:22–26, 14:22–31, Acts 8:35–40 CCC: 459, 1749, 1131; 1, 1218, 1228; 1333, 1337, 1341	• God loves you so much that he sent his Son to save you. • Jesus died and rose to new life. • The Church has seven sacraments. They are signs of God's love. • Jesus gave the sacraments to remind people that he is with them always. • Your sharing in God's love and life is called grace. • Baptism is your welcome into the Church family. Luke 23–24, John 14:18–19, Acts 1:5, 8 CCC: 416–418, 422, 601, 654–655, 683; 1113, 1130, 1123; 1279, 1263–1270
The Kingdom of God	• God is great and we must serve him first. • The saints pray for us to God the Father every day. • To praise God for the wonderful things he does is adoration. 1 Corinthians 2:9, Matthew 25:35–39, Luke 24:1–12 CCC: 30, 1844, 223; 833, 958, 955; 54, 2639, 2097	• At Mass the Church family celebrates God's love. • Jesus gives himself to us in the Eucharist. • Heaven is being happy with God forever. • God invites all people to heaven. All who show love will go to heaven. • The signs of God's kingdom are justice, peace, and love. • Christians work here and now to help God bring his kingdom to its fullness. I Corinthians 11:23–25, John 14:1–3, 16:22, Romans 14:17–19 CCC: 1359–1361, 1374, 1325; 1024, 1023, 2819, 2818, 543–54

Call to Faith SCOPE AND SEQUENCE

	Grade 2	Grade 3
Revelation	• God is the creator of all that is good. • Jesus is God's greatest gift. Jesus is the Son of God. • God sent his Son, Jesus, to bring all people back to his friendship. • Jesus is the Savior and the Good Shepherd. • God tells us about himself through the Bible. • The Bible is God's word written by humans. Psalm 8:2, 7–9, Genesis 2–3, 6–9, John 10:11–14, Matthew 4:23–25 CCC: 290, 355, 422–464, 2415–2418; 430, 220, 389–390, 1441, 1846; 51–55, 80–82	• God created everything. All creation shows God's goodness. • God created humans in his image and likeness. • The Bible is the word of God written in human words. • The Church is the People of God gathered in the name of Jesus. • Children first learn about God's love through their families. • The family home is called the "domestic Church." Genesis 1:1–2:3, Acts 2:42–47, Luke 1:39–56 CCC: 315, 355, 293–301; 831, 836, 771; 1657, 1666, 2204–2207
Trinity	• You can call God "Father" because he created you and cares for you like a good parent. • You can trust in God because he loves you. • Jesus is the beloved Son of God. • Jesus is the Savior of the world. • The Holy Trinity is three Persons in one God. • The Holy Spirit guides the Church and helps you to be a disciple. Matthew 6:26–32, Luke 1–2, 2:41-52, 3:13–17, John 14:15–26, Acts 1–2 CCC: 355–356, 238–242; 461, 495, 437, 464–469; 685, 253, 1831, 1845, 731, 249–253	• The Holy Trinity is three Persons in one God. • Jesus, God the Son, taught about God the Father and God the Spirit. • The Mass is the Church's most important form of worship. • In the Mass the Church remembers what Jesus did at the Last Supper. • Prayer is the raising of one's mind and heart to God. • Prayer is an important part of a Christian's daily life. John 14:6–7, 16–17, Luke 18:9–14, 22:14-20, Matthew 6:5–8 CCC: 253, 240, 243; 234; 61, 69, 1083; 2559, 2659, 2688
Jesus Christ	• The Ten Commandments are God's laws to his people. • Jesus teaches you to love God above all things and to love others as you love yourself. • Conscience is God's gift that helps you know right from wrong. • Sin is a free choice to do what is wrong. • God is merciful and forgiving. • God will always forgive you if you are truly sorry. John 15:12, 18:17–18, 25–27, Luke 10:25–37, 15:11–32 CCC: 2060–2068, 2055, 1730–1731, 1847, 1996–2005, 1786–1789; 1428, 2839, 1846, 1870	• Jesus shared the good news about God's kingdom of justice, love, and peace. • Jesus is the Messiah, the chosen one, and Savior. • Jesus died and rose to new life to save all people from the power of sin. • The Church celebrates the Paschal mystery in all the sacraments. • The Church is the Body of Christ to which all members belong. • Church members continue Jesus' work when they help others. Luke 4:16–22, John 20:11–18, Matthew 25:34–40 CCC: 546, 1154, 2688; 613, 2099–2100; 521, 1267, 2427–2428
The Church	• Grace is sharing in God's life. • Sacraments are holy signs that come from Jesus and give grace. • In the Sacrament of Reconciliation, you receive God's forgiveness. • This sacrament also celebrates your friendship with God and the Church. • The Church year celebrates the life, death, and Resurrection of Jesus. • The Resurrection is the mystery of Jesus being raised from death. Genesis 6:14–22, 7:1–23, Acts 8:4–12, Luke 14:16–23, 7:36–50, John 14:25 CCC: 1131, 1996–1997, 1212, 1113–1130; 1849, 1440–1448; 1168, 1169, 1194	• The bishops are the successors of the Apostles. • The pope, bishops, and pastors lead and guide the Church. • The Holy Spirit unites the Church and makes its members holy. • Many cultures together make up the unity of the Church. • The Church's mission is to share Jesus' good news with the people of all nations. • The Church is catholic because it is everywhere and welcomes everyone. Matthew 16:15–19, 26:69-75, John 21:15–17, Luke 1:46–50, 1 Corinthians 3:5–9 CCC: 880, 884, 890; 813, 791, 957; 831, 830, 864
Morality	• The kingdom of God is love, peace, and justice for all. • Everyone is welcome in God's kingdom and the Catholic Church. • Jesus' disciples share in his life and in his work. • Followers of Jesus are to proclaim his good news to the world. • Prayer is being with God in your heart and mind. • Jesus taught his followers the Lord's Prayer. Luke 19:1–8, Matthew 6:5–9, 19:13–15, 28:20, John 15:4–5 CCC: 541, 543–544, 1826–1827, 2816; 1716–1717, 747, 902; 2762–2763, 2620, 2564	• Jesus' law of love is to love one another as Jesus loves each of us. • Jesus teaches that we should love and forgive our enemies. • God's gifts of faith, hope, and love help you live a good and moral life. • Christians are called by Jesus to be the light of the world. • The Holy Spirit and the teachings of the Church help you make good choices. • Your conscience and grace also help you follow God. Matthew 5:14–16, 43–48, Acts 9:1–30 CCC: 1822, 1825, 1970; 1813, 2105, 1697; 2041, 1496, 1444
Sacraments	• Mass is another name for the celebration of the Eucharist. • The assembly uses songs, prayer, and actions to worship. • In the Liturgy of the Word, God's word is read from the Bible. • We say what we believe about God and pray for the needs of the Church and the world. • The Eucharist is a memorial of the sacrifice of Jesus. • The Liturgy of the Eucharist is the second main part of the Mass. Acts 2:42–47, Matthew 13:31–32, 19:21–22 CCC: 1071, 1167, 1083, 1140–1144; 546, 1349, 1354, 101–104; 1357, 1374, 1356–1381	• Sacraments are signs that come from Jesus and give grace. • The Sacraments of Initiation are Baptism, Confirmation, and Eucharist. • The Sacraments of Healing are Reconciliation and Anointing of the Sick. • In these sacraments the Church prays for spiritual and physical healing. • The Sacraments of Service are Holy Orders and Matrimony. • These sacraments celebrate people's commitment to God and the community. Acts 2:38–41, Luke 8:40–42, 49–56, 1 Corinthians 4:1–2 CCC: 1229, 1271, 1272; 1421, 1514, 1531; 1534, 1535
The Kingdom of God	• Through the Eucharist, Jesus' followers are united with him and one another. • The gift of Holy Communion is received with reverence. • The Church's mission is to share Jesus' message of love and to spread the news of the kingdom of God. • All members of the Church share in its mission. • Heaven is life and happiness forever with God. • The Eucharist is a sign of joy and of what heaven will be like. Luke 9:10–17, 14:15–23, Acts 10:42–48, Matthew 22:2–10 CCC: 1358, 1390; 846, 791, 850, 849–856; 542–543, 545, 546	• God kept his promise to be forever faithful when he sent his Son, Jesus. • The Church continues to be a sign of God's covenant. • All members of the Church share in its mission to work for peace and justice. • The Church is a sign of the kingdom of God. • People who die in God's friendship live forever in God's presence. • At the end of the world, Christ will judge all people on the way they lived their lives. Matthew 10:5–14, Revelation 21:1–4, 22:13 CCC: 781, 1612, 813–822; 2046, 2443, 2448; 673, 681, 1041

Grade 4

- God loves and cares for all creation and has a plan for the world.
- All God wants you to know about him is in Scripture and Tradition.
- God's covenant with Abraham reveals that God is always faithful to his people.
- Sin is present in the world because of human choice.
- The Ten Commandments help you be faithful to God and his covenant.
- The commandments tell you ways to love God and others.

Jonah, Genesis 3, 12, 15, 17, 21, 37, 42, 44, 45, Exodus 2, 5, 14, 17–20

CCC: 302–308, 80–83, 50; 59–61, 385–389; 2055, 2060–2061, 577–580

- Every person is worthy of respect because he or she is created in God's image.
- Each person has a soul that will live forever.
- God created people for one another, and all must work for the common good. Such love of neighbor reflects the love of the Holy Trinity.
- No one can believe alone, just as no one can live alone.
- God has given you free will so that you can make good choices.
- Your conscience is the "inner voice" that helps you choose what is good.

Genesis 1:27, Acts 2:42–45, Luke 10:30–37

CCC: 355–357, 362–366, 1928–1933; 1905–1906, 1878, 1757; 1706–1786, 1704–106

- The Beatitudes describe the reign of God that Jesus announced.
- The Beatitudes show you how to live and act as a follower of Jesus.
- The Great Commandment is to love God with all your heart, strength, and mind and to love your neighbor as yourself.
- The Great Commandment sums up all the teachings of the Ten Commandments.
- The first three commandments are to honor, respect, and worship God.
- These commandments tell you to believe in, trust, and love God.

Matthew 5:1–10, 19:16–22, Exodus 32:1–20

CCC: 1716, 1720, 1723, 1078–1079; 2055, 2083, 2196, 2447; 2062, 2077, 2113

- Every person is called by God to a vocation.
- Through your vocation, you can help God increase his reign.
- The Church's holiness shines in the saints. All who live their love of God are saints.
- Mary is the perfect model of holiness, and she is called the Mother of the Church.
- Jesus gave the leaders of the Church the authority to interpret Scripture and Tradition for the faithful.
- The Holy Spirit directs the Church in teaching and guiding the People of God.

Jeremiah 1:5–8, Luke 1:46–50, Mark 8:27–30

CCC: 941, 2046, 2030; 828, 829; 85, 87, 940–943

- God created humans to live in strong, loving families.
- The fourth, sixth, and ninth commandments provide basic laws of family love and respect.
- All human life is sacred because it comes from God.
- The fifth commandment forbids anything that takes a human life.
- Because God is truth, his people are called to live in the truth.
- The eighth commandment forbids lying.

Luke 2:41–52, Matthew 5:43–45, John 8:31–32, 14:6

CCC: 2203, 2197, 2204, 2380, 2233; 2258, 2268, 2303–2304; 2465, 1741, 2467

- The Church year celebrates the Paschal mystery.
- The seasons of the liturgical year include Advent, Christmas, Lent, Easter, and Ordinary Time.
- The seven sacraments are signs, instituted by Christ, that give grace.
- The Sacrament of the Eucharist is at the heart of Christian life.
- God's forgiveness is offered to all who seek it.
- Reconciliation and the Anointing of the Sick celebrate God's healing love.

Ecclesiastes 3:1–8, Luke 22:17–20, 19:1–10, John 9:1–38

CCC: 1067, 1171, 1140; 1210, 1407, 1370; 1489, 1421;

- The commandments call you to be generous and to have the right attitude toward possessions.
- The goods of the earth are meant for the benefit of the whole human family.
- The Church's mission is to proclaim the Gospel and to work for the good of all.
- The Church is made up of people from many cultures united by belief in Christ.
- The Church teaches that at the end of time, all will be raised from the dead.
- All will come into the presence of Christ to be judged.

Mark 12:41–44, Matthew 25:34–40, 28:18–20

CCC: 299, 2402, 2407; 849, 1807, 942; 681, 682, 671

Grade 5

- True happiness can come only through communion with God.
- Religion expresses a relationship with God through beliefs, prayer, and practices.
- Humans share in the Creator's loving plan by caring for creation.
- God's providence is his care and plan for all creation.
- God communicates through signs.
- Through the signs and symbolic actions of the sacraments, God's life becomes truly present in your life.

John 4:7–29, Psalm 98:4–9, Exodus 3:1–15

CCC: 27, 28, 142–143, 153–155, 160, 162; 307, 302, 2404; 1147, 774, 1152

- The Trinity is the central mystery of Christian faith and life.
- Virtue is the habit of doing good. The theological virtues are faith, hope, and love.
- Prayer and worship are ways to show love for God.
- When we pray and worship, God fills us with joy, strength, and hope.
- The Great Commandment states that you will love the Lord, your God, with all your heart, soul, and mind and your neighbor as yourself.
- The cardinal virtues play a central role in helping people lead morally good lives.

John 1:32–34, 2 Samuel 6:1–15, Mark 12:28–34

CCC: 234, 1813, 253–255; 1083, 2638, 1082, 1071, 2565; 1804–1809, 1811

- The Incarnation is the belief that the Son of God became a human being.
- Jesus is both human and divine, truly God and truly human.
- God's kingdom is present and grows until God's reign comes in fullness.
- Jesus proclaimed the kingdom of God through his actions and parables.
- Through the sacraments, Christ unites his followers to his Passion, death, Resurrection, and Ascension.
- Jesus Christ is the Redeemer of the human race.

Luke 8:5–8, 24:5–9

CCC: 461, 464, 1701–1702; 763–769, 546–547, 567; 1076, 618, 654

- As members of the Church, we are all united in living out the mission of Christ.
- The Church is expressed in the images of the Body of Christ and the People of God.
- The Apostles proclaimed God's good news and cooperated with God's reign.
- Under the guidance of the Holy Spirit, the pope and the bishops continue the Apostles' mission to teach.
- Mary and the saints provide the Church with models of holiness.
- Canonization declares that a model Christian is enjoying eternity with God.

I Peter 2:4–5, Matthew 16:15–19, 28:19–20, Luke 1:30–31, 38

CCC: 811, 776, 775; 551, 85–86, 863; 1173, 828, 2013

- Evil is the result of humans' turning away from God's goodness.
- God sent his Son to redeem people from the power of sin and evil.
- The process of becoming Catholic is called the Rite of Christian Initiation of Adults.
- The Sacraments of Initiation are Baptism, Confirmation, and Eucharist.
- The Church receives God's forgiveness through the Sacraments of Healing.
- The Sacrament of Reconciliation includes contrition, confession, penance, and absolution.

Romans 5:19, 6:10–11, Luke 15:11–32

CCC: 311, 614, 1854–1863; 1232, 1233, 1212, 1231; 1421, 1491, 1527

- The wheat bread and grape wine become the Body and Blood of Jesus in the Sacrament of the Eucharist.
- In the liturgical assembly, the Holy Spirit strengthens the community.
- The word of God is conveyed through Scripture and Tradition.
- Jesus is truly present in the word as it is proclaimed and preached in the liturgy.
- The Eucharist is the source and the summit of the Catholic Church.
- The Eucharist closely unites Christ's followers to him and to one another.

Colossians 3:16, Matthew 26:26–28

CCC: 1374, 1141, 1378; 80–82, 1088, 108; 1324, 1372, 1398

- The vocations of ordained and married people build the reign of God and serve others.
- The Sacraments of Service are Holy Orders and Matrimony.
- Faith in the Resurrection is the source of hope in eternal life and happiness.
- Last rites of the Church include the Sacraments of Healing and the Eucharist.
- The Church's mission is to bring the good news to all people everywhere.
- Every baptized person has the responsibility of sharing the good news.

Matthew 9:35–38, 25:31–40, Luke 4:16–21

CCC: 1534, 1535, 1635; 989, 1525, 1024; 849, 863, 2820

Call to Faith

Grade 6

Revelation

- God reveals himself and his plan of salvation through Scripture.
- The most important truth of both Sacred Scripture and Tradition is that God is faithful and wants you to live with him forever.
- The stories of creation in Genesis reveal that God alone created the universe.
- God created humans in his own image to live in harmony with him forever.
- God fully revealed his faithfulness to humans by sending his only Son, Jesus.
- Humans have the ability to live in friendship with God.

Ruth 1:1–17, Genesis 1:1–30, 2:4-25   CCC: 51–55, 214, 108; 279–289, 355–361, 373; 396–411, 1730, 1468, 396

Trinity

- God calls you on a journey of faith toward salvation.
- The path toward salvation is paved with prayer.
- God rescued the Hebrews from slavery and sent his Son to save all people.
- The Passover and the Eucharist celebrate God's saving actions.
- The Ten Commandments are the laws of God's covenant with the Israelites.
- The Ten Commandments help you stay close to God and in right relationship with others.

The Book of Genesis, The Book of Exodus   CCC: 176–184, 2570–2572, 183; 62–64, 1150–1151, 430–431; 1961–1966, 1949–1953

Jesus Christ

- In Old Testament times, God chose leaders like Saul and David, who were anointed kings.
- God the Father anointed his Son Jesus to be prophet, priest, and king.
- The Bible teaches that true wisdom comes from trusting God and obeying his law.
- Jesus is the wisdom of God, sought in every age by those who are wise.
- Prophets of the Old Testament spoke for God, telling people to repent and obey God.
- Jesus is the Messiah described by the Old Testament prophets.

1 Samuel and 2 Samuel, 1 Kings, Job, Isaiah and Zechariah   CCC: 59–64, 695, 218–221; 156–158, 215–217, 1950; 2581–2584, 711–714, 702

The Church

- The Gospels are the good news of Jesus; they proclaim his life and teachings.
- The Gospels are interpreted by the Church through Tradition.
- Jesus laid the foundation for the Church through his life and teachings. He sent the Holy Spirit to help the Church fulfill its mission.
- The Holy Spirit continues to animate the Church today.
- The Church is one, holy, catholic, and apostolic.
- The Church is a community, united in faith, working together to share the Gospel.

Luke, Acts of the Apostles, 1 Corinthians 3:16, 12:12, Ephesians 1:22–23, 2:19–20   CCC: 124, 109–119, 772; 763–768, 849–854, 737–747; 811–813, 830–831, 823

Morality

- The Great Commandment allows you to achieve happiness and holiness.
- The Beatitudes and precepts of the Church help the faithful live holy lives.
- Working toward justice means respecting the dignity of persons and peoples.
- Justice is giving what is due to God and others.
- Your conscience helps you know when you have sinned.
- Through the sacrament of Reconciliation, God forgives sins and restores us to his friendship.

Matthew 17:1–8, 18:23–35, 22:37–40, Micah 6:8   CCC: 1716–1729, 2041–2043; 1939–1942, 2304–2306, 1807; 1777–1782, 1440–1445

Sacraments

- The mission of the Church is to proclaim the gospel in word and deed.
- Through the Sacraments of Initiation, Christians are given new life.
- All of the baptized are called to follow Christ by serving others.
- Ordained ministers serve God through preaching the word and through celebrating the sacraments.
- The Church celebrates marriage through the Sacrament of Matrimony.
- This sacrament helps a man and woman grow in love and holiness.

Acts 8:26–39, John 13:1–15   CCC: 849–856, 1212, 1285; 897–900, 1548–1553, 900; 1612–1617, 1646–1651, 2204

The Kingdom of God

- Members of the communion of saints can intercede, or pray to God for others.
- The communion of saints includes all holy persons, both living and dead, who are united in the Eucharist.
- Christ desires the unity of all his disciples.
- Ecumenism is the work of Christians toward unity.
- God will triumph over evil when Christ comes again in glory.
- In the new creation, God will reward good and punish evil.

Acts of the Apostles, The Gospel of John   CCC: 2634–2638, 946–948; 820–822, 813–819; 992–996, 1038–1041, 1042–1047, 991

SCOPE AND SEQUENCE

Grade 7	Grade 8

Grade 7

- God created the heavens and the earth, making humans in his image and likeness.
- God promised to restore the human race to his intended harmony and perfection.
- God is the author and inspiration of the sacred words of Scripture, recorded by humans.
- God continues to speak to us today through the Scriptures.
- We know God through Jesus Christ who is the sign of God the Father's love through the Holy Spirit.
- The natural and revealed laws help us choose what is good and to live as God's people.

Genesis 1:1—2:4a; 1 John 1:5; John 1:1–14; 3:16; Matthew 26:26–30; Exodus 20:1–17   CCC: 69, 315–319, 353, 410; 136–139, 521, 1802; 73, 1979–1983

Grade 8

- Humans can live in friendship with God because we have a soul, reason, and free will.
- God established a covenant with his people, promising to be faithful to them and to be their God.
- The Ten Commandments guide us in what it means to be and live in God's image.
- Scripture and the lived Tradition of the Church make up one source of revelation, or deposit of faith.
- Faith is both a gift from God and a free human choice and action.
- The Church is holy because her founder is holy and because the Holy Spirit lives within her.

1 Samuel 3:1–10; Mark 9:14–29; 1 Corinthians 13:1–13; Psalm 8:6–7   CCC: 44, 70–72, 228, 2080, 2081; 96–98, 176–182; 319, 353, 867, 2720

Grade 7

- The Trinity is a mystery, never totally understood by the mind, yet approached through faith.
- The love that the Father, the Son, and the Holy Spirit have for each other is a model for us.
- The Son of God has existed for all time, and through the Incarnation, became human.
- Jesus revealed his divinity through the working of miracles, which also reveal his human nature.
- The Holy Spirit gives the Church life and energy and unites us as the Body of Christ.
- The Holy Spirit guides the Church in her living Tradition and prayer.

Matthew 1:18–23, 28:16–20; John 1:1–21; 10:31–38, 14:15–17; Philippians 2:1   CCC: 261, 743, 1890, 2680; 479, 480, 483, 561; 747, 809, 2590, 2661, 2644

Grade 8

- Jesus' Transfiguration revealed his divine glory as the Son of God.
- The gift of grace helps us to know and love God.
- The Christian family (the domestic Church) has a special role in the establishment of God's kingdom.
- Through our Baptism we share in Jesus' mission as priest, prophet, and king.
- The gifts of the Holy Spirit help us live our Christian witness.
- The Holy Spirit lives in the Church, uniting, guiding, and giving her life.

Luke 9:28–36; 1 Peter 2:9–10, 15; 1 Cor 6:19–20; 2 Cor 6:16–18   CCC: 455, 2021; 804, 808, 942; 382, 747, 809, 1280, 1316, 1317, 1845

Grade 7

- Jesus is the second Person of the Blessed Trinity, at once fully human and fully divine.
- Jesus became human to show us how to live and reach our full potential as God's children.
- The Beatitudes reveal values of the kingdom and how to live in harmony with God and one another.
- By disobeying God the first humans introduced sin and suffering into the world.
- God promised a Messiah who would bring salvation and free his people from sin.
- Jesus conquered death and makes it possible for those who have faith to experience new life.

Luke 11:9–13; 1 Timothy 2:5–6; Matthew 5:3–12; 7:24–29; 1 John 4:10–11   CCC: 460, 479, 561; 1725, 1726, 1983; 70, 384, 415–419, 621, 985

Grade 8

- The first disciples worshiped together, followed Jesus' teachings, and cared for one another.
- Jesus offers eternal life to those who believe.
- Through Jesus we are forgiven and made whole again.
- Conversion is an ongoing process, nurtured by the Holy Spirit.
- The Catholic Church is made up of Eastern Catholics and Roman Catholics, united by a common creed, the sacraments, and the leadership of the pope.
- Christ desires that we work and pray toward the unity of all baptized Christians.

Mark 10:46–52; Luke 7:36–50, 19:1–10; John 15:1–10, 17:20–26; Romans 8:10   CCC: 1948; 1490, 2018–2020, 2025, 2027; 810, 816–819, 838, 1208, 1318, 1320

Grade 7

- Jesus sent his disciples into the world and asks us to work together to spread his message.
- The Holy Spirit uses many different ways to teach us how to pray.
- Jesus is the head of the Church, the Mystical Body of Christ.
- We are all united with one another as part of Christ's Body to help build God's kingdom.
- The Church is both a sign and instrument of the communion between God and his people.
- A personal relationship with God, nourished by prayer, helps us bring his love and truth to others.

Acts 9:1–5; Matthew 6:9–13, 18:12–20; John 1:43–51, 8:12   CCC: 935, 940, 2644, 2693; 779, 805–807; 45, 183, 620, 780, 2591, 2744

Grade 8

- The bishops are direct successors of the Apostles, and the pope is the direct successor of Peter.
- Guided by the Holy Spirit, the Church continues to teach the truth of Christ.
- The Church is universal, reaching out to the whole world and welcoming all people.
- Missionaries bring the Good News to people who have not yet come to know and believe.
- The pope and bishops belong to the Church's hierarchy, and guide the priests, deacons, religious communities, and the lay faithful.
- The laity bring the truth of God's kingdom to the world in which they live and work.

Matthew 13:31–33, 16:13–19; John 4:13–42; Acts 1:8–9, 2:1–4, 6:1–7   CCC: 869, 935, 936, 1593–1596, 2050, 2051; 849, 851, 854, 868; 937–945, 1591

Grade 7

- God made us with a free will, an intellect, and a soul, all of which help us choose to do good.
- Morally good actions require that their object, intention, and circumstance be good.
- A well-formed conscience will guide us to do what is right and good.
- All people possess the human dignity that comes from being made in God's image.
- We are to honor and protect the human dignity of all people from conception to death.
- Theological and cardinal virtues guide us in our choices and actions.

Matthew 5:38–48; 6:2–4, 7:12; Psalm 139:14–16; Philippians 4:8,13   CCC: 1711, 1713, 1757–1761, 1796, 1798, 1871–1876; 2319–2326; 1833–1841, 2393–2395

Grade 8

- We are called to put God first in our lives, to trust and hope in him.
- God's name is holy, and his name deserves respect and reverence.
- The Holy Family stands as a model for our own families.
- In the family, we grow in our understanding of right and wrong, and learn what's truly important.
- The common good focuses on the needs of the community and people as a whole.
- The Church works to insure that public and political authorities act with truth, justice, freedom, and solidarity for all people.

Matthew 5:33–35, 37, 22:34–40; Psalm 8:1; Luke 2:41–52; John 15:12   CCC: 2134–2140, 2161–2163; 2251, 2252; 1920–1926, 1943, 1944, 1947, 2327–2329, 2458

Grade 7

- Christ makes the Father known to us and makes it possible for us to share in his life.
- Baptism is a celebration of new life in Christ and incorporation into the Church.
- Confirmation seals us with the Gift of the Holy Spirit to live out our journey of faith.
- In the Eucharist we are fed with the Body and Blood of Christ and strengthened for mission.
- In Reconciliation we receive God's forgiveness and return to life with him and the Church.
- The Anointing of the Sick provides the seriously ill and suffering God's grace for strength, courage, and hope.

John 14:1–10; Galatians 3:26–28; Matthew 9:35–38; James 5:14–15   CCC: 1115, 1131; 1275, 1278–1282, 1316–1320, 1408, 1412–1416; 1486, 1490–1497, 1529

Grade 8

- Sunday observance includes participation in Mass, rest, and attention to living a holy life.
- Matrimony strengthens a couple to live out their promises and model the love Christ has for all.
- Through Holy Orders, men are ordained to service in the name of Jesus for the Church.
- Living by the virtues of modesty and chastity strengthens our lives, teaches us faithfulness, and honors human dignity.
- The liturgical year connects our lives more closely to the Paschal mystery of Jesus.
- The Eucharist is at the very heart of what it means to be Catholic.

Ephesians 6:21; John 1:1–11; Ecclesiastes 3:1–8   CCC: 2021–2023, 2190–2195; 1592, 1597, 1600–1664, 2396, 2397, 2400, 2530, 2533; 1193–1195, 1407

Grade 7

- We discern our vocation with the help of family, the Church, and prayer.
- The Church asks us to share our time, talent, and treasure.
- God's kingdom is present but not yet complete.
- As Jesus' followers we are called to end injustice for the sake of God's kingdom.
- Christian hope is based on trusting in God and that we will be united with him forever.
- Jesus will come at the end of time to judge the living and the dead, and the kingdom will be complete.

Luke 2:41–52, 4:14–22, 10:2; Matthew 13:31–32, 25:31–46; John 11:1–44   CCC: 941–944, 1666, 2253, 2694; 550, 2552–2556, 2800; 658, 682,1051,1054–1060

Grade 8

- Sacramentals are holy objects, prayers, and practices that help us respond to God's grace.
- Religious art, especially icons, helps us glorify God and honor the saints.
- The Church is a communion of saints uniting believers in heaven, in purgatory, and on earth.
- The Church honors Mary as the greatest of saints with many feast days and devotions.
- The Church declares some people canonized saints for their lives of heroic virtue and holiness.
- Throughout her history, the Church has strived to live Jesus' message of love, hope, and faith.

Acts 2:42–47; Exodus 20:2–5; Luke 1:26–45; 1 Peter 4:16   CCC: 960, 962, 1053, 1677, 1679, 2141; 973, 974, 1195; 851, 852

PEOPLE OF FAITH

Grade K

Holy Simeon
Moses
Saint Catherine of Siena
Saint John the Baptist
Saint Philip the Apostle
Saint Pier Giorgio Frassati
Saint Thérèse of Lisieux

Grade 1

Blessed Mother Teresa of the Child Jesus
Blessed Pedro Calungsod
Blessed Pope John XXIII
Frederick William Faber
Mary, Mother of God
Michelangelo
Saint Albert the Great
Saint Angela Merici
Saint Dominic
Saint Emily de Vialar
Saint Frances Cabrini
Saint Giuseppina Bakhita
Saint Louise de Marillac
Saint Moses the Black
Saint Nicholas
Saint Patrick
Saint Pedro de San Jose Betancur
Saint Terese of Jesus of the Andes
Saint Thomas of Villanova
Venerable Father Solanus Casey
Zecharaih, Elizabeth, and John

Grade 2

All Saints
Bishop James Augustine Healy
Blessed Julian of Norwich
Blessed Marguerite Bays
Blessed Mariano de Jesus
Blessed Pope John Paul II
Blessed Teresa of Calcutta
David
Mary, Mother of God
Saint Anthony Claret
Saint Brigid of Kildare
Saint John Berchmans
Saint Juan Diego
Saint Luke
Saint Paul
Saint Peter
Saint Pius X, Pope
Saint Tarsicius
Saint Teresa Margaret Redi
Saint Victor, Pope
Venerable Pierre Toussaint

Grade 3

Blessed Bartholomew Osypiuk
Blessed Joseph Vaz
Blessed Luigi & Blessed Maria
Jean Donovan
Pierre Teilhard de Chardin
Saint Clement of Rome
Saint Dismas
Saint Elizabeth of Hungary
Saint Francis of Assisi

Saint Genevieve
Saint Gregory the Great
Saint Isaac Jogues
Saint John of Matha
Saint Margaret of Scotland
Saint Mary Ann of Quito
Saint Mary Magdalene
Saint Peter Canisius
Saint Pio (Padre Pio)
Saints Perpetua and Felicity
Sister Thea Bowman
Thomas Merton

Grade 4

Aaron and Miriam
Blessed Frederic Ozanam
Blessed Kateri Tekakwitha
Catherine de Hueck Doherty
Cesar Chavez
Korean Saints and Martyrs
Mary, Mother of God
Naomi and Ruth
Saint Bede
Saint Charles Lwanga
Saint Jane Frances de Chantal
Saint Joan of Arc
Saint John of God
Saint Katharine Drexel
Saint Margaret Mary Alacoque
Saint Martin de Porres
Saint Mary Magdalen Postel
Saint Maximilian Kolbe
Saint Teresa Benedicta
Saints Anne and Joachim
Venerable Matt Talbot

Grade 5

Blessed M. V. Rosal Vasquez
Dorothy Day
Michael the Archangel
Queenship of Mary
Saint Athanasius
Saint Augustine
Saint Benedict
Saint Catherine of Siena
Saint Cecilia
Saint Clare of Assisi
Saint Cyril of Jerusalem
Saint Francis Xavier
Saint Hildegarde of Bingen
Saint Jerome
Saint John Vianney
Saint Marguerite Bourgeoys
Saint Paul Miki
Saint Robert Ballarmine
Saint Stephen, martyred
Saint Thomas Aquinas
Saint Thomas More

Grade 6

Blessed Dorothy C. Orozco
Blessed Fra Angelico
Blessed Peter To Rot
Father John Carroll
Saint Birgitta of Sweden

Saint Charles Borromeo
Saint Elizabeth Ann Seton
Saint Faustina Kowalska
Saint Hilda of Whitby
Saint Ignatius of Loyola
Saint John Baptist de la Salle
Saint John Neumann
Saint John the Baptist
Saint John the Evangelist
Saint Matthias
Saint Monica
Saint Rose Philippine Duchesne
Saint Teresa Benedicta
Saint Teresa of Avila
Venerable Catherine McAuley
Women Martyrs of El Salvador

Grade 7

Archbishop Oscar Romero
Blessed Aloysius Stepinac
Blessed Carlos Manuel Cecilio Rodriguez Santiago
Blessed Kateri Tekakwitha
Blessed Theodore Guerin
Pope Leo XIII
Saint Catherine of Genoa
Saint Frances of Rome
Saint John Bosco
Saint Joseph
Saint Lorenzo Ruiz
Saint Ludmilla
Saint Madeleine Sophie Barat
Saint Margaret Ward
Saint Martin de Porres
Saint Mary MacKillop
Saint Matthew
Saint Peter Claver
Saint Rafqa
Saints Maria Zhao-Guo, Mary Zhao, Rosa Zhao
Venerable Pierre Toussaint

Grade 8

Blessed Cyprian Michael Iwene Tansi
Blessed Damien De Veuster
Blessed Edmund Ignatius Rice
Blessed Elizabeth Catez
Blessed Maria Anna Barbara Cope
Blessed Miguel Pro
Blessed Victoria Rasoamanarivo
Father Eusebius Kino
Mechthild von Magdeburg
Pere (Father) Jacques Marquette
Saint Benedict the Black
Saint Josefina Bakhita
Saint Marcella
Saint Maria del Transito de Jesus Sacramentado
Saint Peter Damien
Saint Prisca and Saint Aquila
Saint Thomas
Saints Perpetua and Felicity
Venerable Louis Martin and Zelie Guerin
Venerable Mariam Thresia Chiramel Mankidiyan
Venerable Samuel Mazzuchelli

Create an environment for prayer within our classroom. This space can serve as a center to help students understand the beauty, depth, and sublimity of prayer.

Make the Celebrate step in *Call to Faith* an integral part of each lesson.

Have students memorize certain prayers so that they can pray them spontaneously.

Use a Bible or the Lectionary when proclaiming Scripture during prayer.

Lectionary Link—this feature, found on the Celebrate page of each chapter, helps you connect the Sunday readings to life through a process called "Break Open the Word." The readings for each week are found on the website.

Liturgy Link—this feature, found on the Celebrate page of each chapter, gives practical tips for engaging students in the closing prayer celebration.

Visit **www.osvcurriculum.com** for a selection of *Call to Faith* musical CDs designed for each grade level.

Also available at **www.osvcurriculum.com**:
And With Your Spirit by acclaimed Catholic songwriter and performer John Burland includes 14 songs with lyrics based on the revised Roman Missal to enrich your lessons with students.

Prayer and Worship

Catechesis always leads into prayer. Through prayer, Christians develop a close relationship with Jesus Christ, with God the Father, and with the Holy Spirit. In prayer, believers allow the Lord to touch their hearts, to lead them with his teachings, and to unite them with fellow Christians.

Thus, prayer is essential for anyone growing in faith. It is an important mission of catechesis to help students grow in their appreciation of prayer and to model a life of prayer for them.

Break Open the Word

1. **Prepare minds and hearts to listen to God's word.**
   a. **Light a candle.**
   b. **Move the group to a special environment for prayer.**
   c. **Invite students to quiet their thoughts.**
   d. **Ask students to listen to what God is saying in this reading.**
2. **Proclaim the Gospel.**
3. **Allow for a moment of silent reflection.**
4. **Read the sharing question.**
5. **Share responses to the question.**

4th GRADE

Nine- and Ten-year olds

Suggestions

- Help students understand the spirit as well as the letter of the law when it comes to rules and games.
- Emotionally, fourth graders may experience changes from elation to sadness within a very short period of time. Assure them that these mood swings are normal at this age.
- Because the peer group is enormously important to fourth graders, provide a variety of small group experiences for them.
- Teasing and other forms of negative peer pressure should be addressed firmly.
- Encourage positive peer pressure of group projects and team efforts.

Know The CHILD

The fourth grader is at the midpoint of the traditional elementary school-age years. These students are emerging and beginning to interact in the world around them. They are beginning to seek independence, and they have a high activity level. They want to do things and to participate in groups. For some children, this period may not be smooth. There will be days when they may behave in ways that make them seem older or younger than their years. Be patient with them as they experiment with new ways of talking or behaving.

As with students of any age, prolonged bouts of sadness or anger in a fourth grader may indicate emotional problems, reaction to a difficult home situation, or frustration resulting from learning disabilities. Follow school or parish policies for offering help to troubled students.

At fourth grade, students have begun to internalize and express a moral code shaped by their families, school, Church, and the wider culture. Fourth graders are very concerned about fairness and rights. This may limit their understanding of the larger meaning of justice. They may be very concerned about rules and regulations, and can often be overly scrupulous in judging themselves and others.

Whether you are an experienced catechist or a beginner, it is always important to keep in mind the emotional and developmental progress of your students. Doing so will give you perspective on your work with them.

The way of teaching that we learn from the Gospels is called, in the *General Directory for Catechesis,* the "pedagogy of Jesus." This method allows gradual learning about Christ and the Church through age-appropriate words and activities.

Catholic Social Teachings

Seven Principles of CATHOLIC SOCIAL TEACHING

- Care for God's Creation
- Life and Dignity of the Human Person
- Rights and Responsibilities of the Human Person
- The Dignity of Work and the Rights of Workers
- Solidarity of the Human Family
- Call to Family, Community, and Participation
- Option for the Poor and Vulnerable

For the past 115 years or so, Catholic social teaching has grown to occupy an increasingly important place in catechesis and in Catholic life. Recently, Church leaders have urged all those in the ministry of catechesis to include the social teachings of the Church in all aspects and at all grade levels of religious instruction and faith formation.

Call to Faith steps up to this challenge by providing a curriculum for Catholic Social Teachings. It is the first of its kind in an elementary religion series. Following the recommendations of a task force convened by the U.S. Catholic Bishops in 1995, *Call to Faith* provides "Faith in Action," a comprehensive, age-appropriate lesson at the end of each unit that correlates to the text. Following this *Call to Faith* curriculum, learners of every age will be deeply motivated by the Catholic social teaching and ready to live it in their own lives.

"Faith in Action" sessions follow a three step process:

- **Discover** This step describes the Catholic social teaching being presented in the unit and engages students in understanding it.

- **Connect** This step gives interesting examples and the witness of people and groups who are living out the teaching.

- **Serve** This step encourages students to make choices about how they can practice the principle.

Educational research proves that there are different ways in which people learn. The names of these different ways of learning, or intelligences, follow.

Verbal/Linguistic learning occurs best through reading, writing, telling stories, and discussing ideas.

Musical learning occurs best through singing, listening to music, and remembering melodies.

Mathematical/Logical learning occurs best through solving problems, analyzing, and applying logic.

Visual/Spatial learning occurs best through visualizing, looking at pictures, drawing, and creating.

Bodily/Kinesthetic learning occurs best through physically moving, processing knowledge through bodily sensations, dancing, and acting.

Interpersonal learning occurs best through interviewing people, sharing about one's feelings, and cooperating with others on tasks.

Intrapersonal learning occurs best through working alone, and reflecting.

Naturalist learning occurs best through exploring nature and living things.

Dr. Howard Gardner, of Harvard University, revolutionized education with his theory of multiple intelligence. He theorized that there was not only one kind of intelligence. Rather, there were different ways in which people learned. Applying this theory to faith formation shows that there are also many different ways in which people come to know God.

The most common and recognizable form of intelligence is **verbal/linguistic**. People who learn in this way prefer parables, story telling, creative writing when learning new faith concepts. Those with **musical** intelligence learn best through listening to different kinds of music, making up songs, or singing throughout the lesson.

Those with **logical/mathematical** intelligence enjoy studying the origins of different religions, using clues to identify Biblical characters, or examining the true cost of poverty.

Learners with **visual/spatial** intelligence put faith concepts into concrete terms through painting or photography or unique inventions. The learners eager to act out a story or to dance a prayer are those with **bodily/kinesthetic** intelligence, who feel comfortable using their bodies to take in information.

Those with **interpersonal** intelligence thrive on community and cooperation, and those with **intrapersonal** intelligence know themselves well and enjoy journaling and reflection.

Those with **naturalist** intelligence use God's creation to learn.

Using Gardner's theory in the faith formation classroom is an opportunity to reach all students, regardless of their learning styles.

Reaching
ALL LEARNERS

A student's intelligence is not the only factor in how he or she will learn. Learning is also affected by family situations, learning disorders, and mental or physical impairments. The lessons and teaching methods in *Call to Faith* have been carefully crafted in order to meet the needs of all learners.

A special feature in your Teacher Edition, called "Reaching All Learners," will provide you with tips, suggestions, and proven ways to include students with different learning styles and abilities in your lesson. Some of the suggestions will help you make provisions for physical and mental challenges your children may face, while other suggestions will help you respond to the diverse ways children learn and experience the world. By varying your teaching strategies, you can help students enhance the range of their learning capabilities.

To accommodate various exceptionalities, consider these general modifications in your classroom management:

- move the child closer to the board or teacher
- allow the child to be a mentor/tutor or to have a mentor/tutor
- designate readers prior to class reading
- provide large print or projected print
- allow the child to use a tape recorder or note-taker
- give oral tests and assessments, and give oral feedback
- allow the child to use a chalkboard, laptop, or an alternative to paper and pencil
- give positive reinforcement for desired behavior and replacement skills for inappropriate behavior
- be swift and consistent with discipline
- have classroom rules displayed, and discuss them frequently
- maintain a routine, and practice daily procedures
- provide multimedia and alternate classroom environments
- give oral directions as well as print directions and explain thoroughly; question students to assess their understanding

The effects of academic deficiencies, learning disabilities, distressed home environments, and poor health can hinder learning. If a child struggles with learning tasks, or shows signs of emotional strain, consider the possible causes and these exceptionalities:

- Large motor or fine motor skill issues can affect movements from walking to handwriting.
- Hearing, speech, visual, and processing issues can obstruct the reception of information as well as alter the ability to follow procedures.
- Emotional issues—like anxiety, withdrawal, and terror—are commonly disguised by outward behaviors like attention seeking, memory loss, and aggression.
- Cognitive issues can result in reading difficulties, loss of impulse control, and distractibility.

"People learn and grow in many different ways"

The Vocation to Teach

Sustaining the vocation to teach as Jesus did takes time and rarely happens without some struggle. At the beginning of each chapter in this Teacher Edition, you will find short essays designed to help you sustain your spirit. These essays will assist you in the ongoing process of assessing the spiritual dimensions of your catechetical commitment, reviewing the expectations that put your vocational commitment at risk, and examining proactive ways of adapting to those challenges.

Perhaps the essence of the grandparent's message was this: The task of sustaining your call is about representing the faith, deeply and authentically, to those you teach.

 Visit www.osvcurriculum.com for more Sustaining Your Spirit Resources

Sustaining Your Spirit

Some years ago, a new catechist was struggling to meet the requirements and expectations of effective religious education. Challenged by striving for creative activities and perfectly facilitated classroom discussions, the new catechist felt her commitment beginning to fade.

One day a grandparent arrived early to pick up a student. Instead of waiting in the parking lot, this woman lingered just outside the open door of the classroom, listening to the closing prayer.

Shortly after dismissal, she appeared in front of the catechist and, without a word of introduction, nodded toward the classroom window. The catechist could see students waiting for their rides—the younger children running, playing, and laughing, and the older ones standing in tight circles sharing accounts of the day's events.

It was the landscape of the young—fully alive. The grandparent looked directly at the catechist and said with feeling and certainty: "You may be the only Bible that they ever *really* read."

Your students may not remember all of the material and experiences that you offer them, but they will remember the way that your life and your presence reveals your faith. Your dedication to the commitments and challenges of this ministry will help shape others' lives.

Planning the Year

Consider the Basics

- How many times a week will I teach religion?
- What is the time frame for each lesson?
- How many sessions are scheduled for the year?
- What impact will other parish and school activities (retreats, liturgies, assemblies) have on my session schedule?

Celebrating the Seasonal Lessons

- Eight lessons are tied to the seasons and feasts of the liturgical year.
- The teaching year may be planned to determine where each lesson will fit best.
- Lessons are flexible and can be adapted for either 20- or 60-minute sessions.
- Lessons may be taught individually or may accompany a chapter that discusses the relevant season.
- The Family Faith page is a reproducible master and includes a background on the season, a family prayer, and a family activity.

Using the Catholic Source Book

- The Source Book is an age-appropriate resource for young learners.
- It has five sections: Scripture, Creed, Liturgy, Morality, and Prayer.
- Optional activities appear in designated boxes in the Teacher Edition of the Catholic Source Book.

Covering the Chapters

- *Call to Faith* contains seven units and twenty-one chapters.
- Each chapter is divided into five sessions of approximately 30–40 minutes each.
- Each chapter wrap-up provides a review of material and suggestions for families.
- Activity Masters are fully integrated into the chapter theme and can be used before, during, or after the catechetical sessions.
- Review features provide a quick assessment of what children have learned and offer an immediate application of each lesson.
- Unit reviews and tests measure children's progress in the acquisition of religious knowledge, beliefs, and practices; they also promote children's development of a faith vocabulary.

Benefiting from Faith in Action

- *Call to Faith* contains seven Faith in Action sessions, one at the end of each unit.
- Each of these sessions corresponds to one of the Catholic Social Teaching themes.
- These sessions may be used in a flexible time frame—in 20-minute sessions over three days, or as one 60-minute session.

Call to Faith COMPONENTS

Student Editions (Grades K–8) help children deepen their faith through compelling stories, activities, prayers, and seasonal celebrations. Family Faith pages help families participate in their children's faith formation. (Available for parish, school, and bilingual programs)

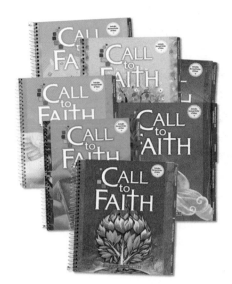

Teacher Editions (Grades K–8) provide all the tools for success—easy-to-use planners, Catechism and GDC connections, a simple three-step catechetical process, a wealth of resources and optional activities, plus activity and assessment reproducibles. (Available for parish, school, and bilingual programs)

Faith at Home: Nurturing Households of Faith features practical suggestions, tips for sharing and celebrating faith at home, and more—all in an engaging magazine.

Call to Faith Music CDs (Grades K–8) offer a repertoire of liturgical music to accompany every chapter and seasonal celebration. Each set includes 30 songs on two CDs.

People of Faith Collection (Grades K–6) includes 133 vibrantly illustrated cards—each with a brief biography and prayer. These cards are excellent tools for encouraging children to learn from examples set by people of faith.

Lectionary Links: Breaking Open the Word visually displays the Sunday lectionary readings along with compelling faith-sharing questions for different ages in an interactive format. Lectionary Links are available for Years A, B, and C.

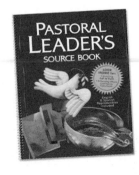

Pastoral Leader's Source Book provides practical resources including professional development articles, implementation models, resources for parish adults, and parent and catechist orientation sessions—plus a separate section for implementing whole community catechesis. Included is a CD-ROM with PowerPoint® presentations that provide tools for training and formation sessions.

Reflect n' Connect Conversation Starter for Intergenerational Gatherings, an inflatable beach ball designed for years of use, offers an active way for connecting people of all ages.

Call to Faith COMPONENTS

Technology Tools for Your Ministry: No Mousing Around!, by Tim Welch, features wit, wisdom, and above all clarity about the technology tools now available to parish ministers. This is a great introduction to the world of technology and a challenging invitation to use every means available today to tell the Story of Jesus Christ, and tell it well.

Move! Pray! Celebrate! Music CD and DVD, by John Burland, feature songs of faith that assist in the celebration of Catholic identity with in school and parish communities Includes specific Scripture and Catechism references for each song plus a new Mass Setting.

God Loves Me: Calling Children to Faith Through Song (Grades K–6), by John Burland, features a variety of contemporary songs for children of all ages that align with the **Call to Faith** catechetical themes.

Big AL LIVE DVDs (Grades K–6) are excellent for beginning a parish meeting, for parent programs of any kind, for intergenerational faith gatherings, or for children to watch by themselves. Each DVD presents ten different Gospel values. The brief and engaging presentations include a short Scripture reading, a reflection from Fr Joe Kempf, a discussion with Big Al, and a prayer.

CALL to FAITH e connect

your online source for lifelong catechesis

www.CalltoFaitheConnect.com

Call to Faith eConnect features a state-of-the-art network that enhances and expands *Call to Faith*. Innovative web tools include multimedia catechetical support, moderated forums, year-round planning tools, online professional development, educational games, podcasts, communication tools…even music and videos for school, parish, and home! Visit *www.CalltoFaitheConnect.com* to try it now.

Grade 4 Contents

iii

© Our Sunday Visitor Curriculum Division

UNIT 1
REVELATION........................ 40

1 God's Plan...................... 41
■ God loves and cares for all creation and has a plan for the world.
■ Everything God wants you to know about him is contained in Scripture and in the Tradition of the Church.
SCRIPTURE
Jonah and the Big Fish
The Book of Jonah

2 God Is Faithful 49
■ God's covenant with Abraham reveals that God is always faithful to his people.
■ Sin is present in the world because of human choice.
SCRIPTURE
In the Garden
Genesis 3
God Calls Abram
Genesis 12, 15, 17, 21

3 The Ten Commandments... 57
■ God gave you the Ten Commandments to help you be faithful to him and his covenant.
■ The commandments tell you ways to love God and others.
SCRIPTURE
Joseph and His Brothers
Genesis 37, 42, 44, 45
The Exodus from Egypt
Exodus 2, 14, 15
The Journey Continues
Exodus 17–20

Unit 1 Review 65

© Our Sunday Visitor Curriculum Division

UNIT 2
TRINITY............................ 66

4 In God's Image.............. 67
■ Every person is worthy of respect because he or she is created in God's image.
■ Each person has a soul that will live forever.
SCRIPTURE
Made in God's Image
Genesis 1:27

5 Created for One Another.... 75
■ God created people for one another, and all must work for the common good. Such love of neighbor reflects the love of the Holy Trinity.
■ No one can believe alone, just as no one can live alone.
SCRIPTURE
The Communal Life
Acts 2:42–45

6 Making Good Choices 83
■ God has given you free will so that you can make good choices.
■ Your conscience is the "inner voice" that helps you choose what is good.
SCRIPTURE
The Good Samaritan
Luke 10:30–37

Unit 2 Review 91

© Our Sunday Visitor Curriculum Division

UNIT 3
JESUS CHRIST.......................... 92

7 You Are Blessed!.............93
■ The Beatitudes are eight teachings that describe the reign of God that Jesus announced when he lived on earth.
■ The Beatitudes show you how to live and act as a follower of Jesus.
SCRIPTURE
The Sermon on the Mount
Matthew 5:1–10

8 The Great Commandment.............. 101
■ The Great Commandment is to love God with all your heart, strength, and mind, and to love your neighbor as yourself.
■ The Great Commandment sums up all the teachings of the Ten Commandments.
SCRIPTURE
The Rich Young Man
Matthew 19:16–22

9 Honoring God 109
■ The first three commandments teach you to honor God above all else, respect his name, and worship him on Sunday.
■ These commandments tell you believe in, trust, and love God.
SCRIPTURE
The Golden Calf
Exodus 32:1–20

Unit 3 Review 117

iv

v

vi

vii

Catholic Source Book

Faith in Action: Catholic Social Teaching

viii

Welcome to Call to Faith!

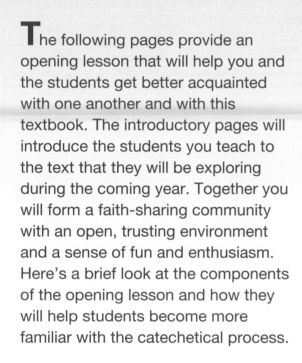

The following pages provide an opening lesson that will help you and the students get better acquainted with one another and with this textbook. The introductory pages will introduce the students you teach to the text that they will be exploring during the coming year. Together you will form a faith-sharing community with an open, trusting environment and a sense of fun and enthusiasm. Here's a brief look at the components of the opening lesson and how they will help students become more familiar with the catechetical process.

About You

This page, along with the Activity Master that appears on page 5A, will serve as an "ice-breaker" to get your group talking, sharing, interacting, and having fun together.

About Your Faith

The activities and suggestions on this page will help you assess where students are on their faith journeys. Students are called to share what they already know about the Catholic faith, the Bible, and Church Tradition—topics they will build on as they grow in faith with your help and the guidance of the entire Church community.

About Your Book

Both you and the students will get a "sneak preview" of the textbook and become familiar with the features and symbols that will guide you through the lessons, stories, activities, and celebrations included in every chapter.

A Call to Faith

During this prayer celebration, you and the students will bond as a community of faith through ritual, Scripture, discussion, prayer, and song.

May **you** and the **students** find **holiness, joy,** and **many blessings** during your year of **discovery** and **faith!**

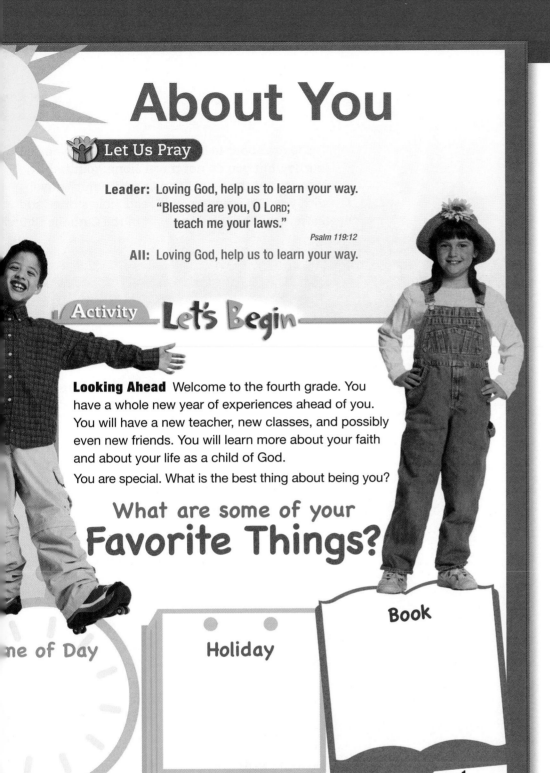

About You

Let Us Pray

Leader: Loving God, help us to learn your way.
"Blessed are you, O LORD;
teach me your laws."

Psalm 119:12

All: Loving God, help us to learn your way.

Activity — Let's Begin

Looking Ahead Welcome to the fourth grade. You have a whole new year of experiences ahead of you. You will have a new teacher, new classes, and possibly even new friends. You will learn more about your faith and about your life as a child of God.

You are special. What is the best thing about being you?

What are some of your Favorite Things?

Time of Day

Holiday

Book

1

About You

Objective: To look forward to the year ahead

Let Us Pray

Have students move to your classroom prayer space. In the space, have a crucifix and a Bible opened to the psalm verse. Read aloud the psalm verse, and have students repeat it after you.

Activity

- Read aloud the text under Looking Ahead. Tell students that this year together is a new beginning for you, too, and that you are looking forward to getting to know them.

- Have a volunteer read aloud the question in the next paragraph. Allow time for students to share responses.

- Direct students' attention to the questions about their favorite things. Have students write their responses in the spaces provided.

- Point out both the variety of responses you receive and any responses chosen by more than one student.

★ REACHING ALL LEARNERS

Diversity You can begin exploring the diversity of students in your class through their responses to the activity questions.

- Ask what students enjoy most about their favorite holidays. Their descriptions of the sights, sounds, and activities they enjoy may be a clue as to how individual students learn best—through pictures, sounds, words, or bodily movement.

About Your Faith

Objective: To explore knowledge of the Catholic faith and how this book will be used

About Your Faith

Invite volunteers to tell about trips they have taken. Ask what preparations they made and who went with them. Responses will vary.

• Read aloud the paragraph.

• Ask students how studying religion is like a journey in faith. Possible responses: You go a little farther every year; classmates are like traveling companions.

Activity

• Draw a large cross on chart paper.

• Read aloud the Reflect statement, and allow time for students to think.

• Arrange students in pairs to discuss what they know about the Catholic faith.

• Distribute pieces of colored paper, cut into interesting shapes. Have each student write a fact about the Catholic faith on one of the shapes.

• Invite students to come forward and attach their paper shapes to the cross shape.

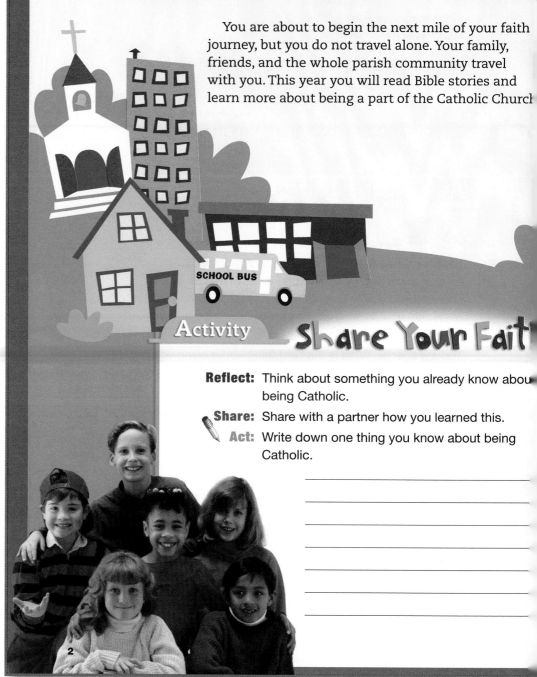

About Your Faith

You are about to begin the next mile of your faith journey, but you do not travel alone. Your family, friends, and the whole parish community travel with you. This year you will read Bible stories and learn more about being a part of the Catholic Church.

Activity Share Your Faith

Reflect: Think about something you already know about being Catholic.

Share: Share with a partner how you learned this.

Act: Write down one thing you know about being Catholic.

_____

_____

_____

_____

_____

_____

_____

2

QUICK TIP

Assess Prior Learning The activity above gives you an opportunity to learn how far students have already come on the journey of faith.

• Walk among students as they discuss the Catholic faith. Listen for any misunderstandings that you may need to correct.

• You may wish to save the chart paper with the cross shape and students' responses. After several weeks invite students to add more facts to the chart.

About Your Book

Your book will help you to learn more about your
faith, important people of faith, and ways Catholics
celebrate faith.

Activity Connect Your Faith

Go On A Scavenger Hunt As you read your book, you
will find lots of different things. To get to know your book,
look for the features listed below. Write down where you
find each of them.

 SCRIPTURE   Page _____

BIOGRAPHY   Page _____

 Words of Faith   Page _____

Faith Fact   Page _____

People of Faith   Page _____

Let Us Pray   Page _____

Focus   Page _____

About Your Book

Summarize the text.

• Tell students that the textbook is
like a map or guidebook that will
help them as they continue the
journey of faith.

Activity

• Explain the concept of a scavenger
hunt because some students may
not have participated in one.

• You may wish to arrange students in
pairs for this activity, with one
strong reader and one less proficient
reader in each pair.

• Read aloud the directions. Tell
students to write the number of the
page on which they find each
feature.

• Invite different student partners to
tell where they found each of the
seven features. Note that not every
pair will have the same responses
because each feature can be found
on many pages.

OPTIONAL ACTIVITY

Journey of Faith Use the metaphor of a journey of
faith to extend the scavenger hunt activity.

• Place seven textbooks around the room, each open
to a page showing one of the listed features.

• Arrange students in pairs ("travel buddies" or
"search teams"), and have them search the room
until each pair finds all seven textbooks.

Multiple Intelligence: Bodily/Kinesthetic

CATECHIST BACKGROUND

Textbook Features

• Biographies help children relate the content
to their lives.

• Words of Faith define important vocabulary.

• Faith Facts are quick ways to
arouse interest.

• People of Faith stories are about saints.

• Focus questions give a context for
information.

A Call to Faith

Objective: To respond to the call to be followers of Jesus

 Let Us Pray

Tell students that in this celebration, they will learn how Jesus calls people to be his followers.

Prepare

Choose one student to be the reader. You will serve as the prayer leader.

• Display a cross or crucifix in the prayer space.

• Have students write petitions asking for guidance on their journey of faith.

Gather

Have students move to the prayer space and sit comfortably in a circle.

Listen to God's Word

• Follow the order of prayer on pages 4–5.

A Call to Faith

Gather

Pray the Sign of the Cross together.

Leader: Blessed be God.

All: **Blessed be God forever.**

Leader: Let us pray.
Bow your heads as the leader prays.

All: **Amen.**

Listen to God's Word

Reader: A reading from the Holy Gospel according to Matthew.
Read Matthew 9:9–13.
The Gospel of the Lord.

All: **Praise to you, Lord Jesus Christ.**

Dialog

Why do you think Jesus went and ate with Matthew after he called him to be a disciple?

How can you answer Jesus' call to follow him?

Prayer of the Faithful

Leader: Lord, the first disciples answered your call. They believed in you and followed you. We believe in you, too. Please hear our prayers.
Respond to each prayer with these words.

All: **Lord, hear our prayer.**

4

 SCRIPTURE BACKGROUND

The Call of Matthew   This scripture passage shows Jesus reaching out and doing the unexpected.

• Matthew was a tax collector. Most faithful Jews would have regarded him as a sinner who cheated others.

• Jesus shares food and hospitality with Matthew and other sinners, who are considered unclean.

• Jesus uses this occasion to describe his mission: saving sinners.

 LECTIONARY LINK

Break Open the Word   Read last week's Sunday Gospel. Invite children to think about what the reading means to them as they try to follow Christ's example. For questions related to the weekly Gospel reading, visit our website at **www.osvcurriculum.com.**

GO online **Visit www.osvcurriculum.com for weekly Scripture readings and seasonal resources.**

Answer the Call

Leader: Matthew responded to Jesus' call to follow him. He welcomed Jesus into his life and his home. You can welcome Jesus into your life, too. *Come forward as your name is called. Bow to the cross and say aloud "I will follow you, Jesus."*

You are all followers of Jesus. Welcome one another with a sign of his peace.

Go Forth!

Leader: Let us go forth to welcome Christ into our lives.

All: **Thanks be to God.**

Sing together.

We are called to act with justice,
we are called to love tenderly,
we are called to serve one another;
to walk humbly with God!

"We Are Called" © 1988, 2004, GIA Publications, Inc.

5

- Read the first Dialogue question aloud. Allow time for students to think before you call on them. Say that sharing a meal is a way of showing welcome and friendship.
- Then read aloud the second question. Affirm students for their responses.
- Invite students to read their petitions during the Prayer of the Faithful.

Answer the Call

- Invite each student to come forward, bow to the cross, and say, "I will follow you, Jesus." The student should then return to the circle.
- Have students share a hug or a handshake as a sign of peace.

Go Forth!

- End the celebration with enthusiasm and joy.
- Have students sing the song once while they are still in the prayer space.
- You may wish to have students sing the song again as they leave the prayer space and return to the classroom area.

LITURGY LINK

The Victorious Cross In the Roman Empire, crucifixion was the means of capital punishment.

- Through the death and Resurrection of Jesus, the cross is now a symbol of victory and life.
- Bowing to the cross is a gesture of profound respect. It honors the role of the cross in God's plan of salvation.

Who's Who

Who's Who is a reference book about important people—a collection of their biographies, or facts about their lives. To God, all people are important. In God's Who's Who book, every person in the world would be listed.

Use this space to plan your listing in God's Who's Who book. Draw a picture of yourself, and complete the sentences to tell why you are special.

My name is _____.

My family includes _____.

My favorite activity is _____.

My favorite song is _____.

My favorite food is _____.

My favorite school subject is _____.

One thing that I can do really well is _____.

My interests and hobbies include _____.

Some day I hope that I will _____.

I am special because _____.

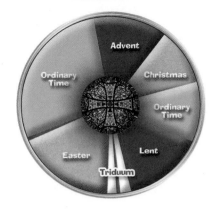

Seasonal Lessons

By means of the yearly cycle the Church celebrates the whole mystery of Christ, from his incarnation until the day of Pentecost and the expectation of his coming again.

General Norms for the Liturgical Year and the Calendar, 17

Liturgical Environment

Since these celebrations are meant to have a different tone and flavor than the other lessons the environment you set for them is important. Factors to include in setting the environment are:

- Color
- Silence
- Music
- Symbols

The heart of these sessions is the celebration. Take time to determine whether your prayer space is appropriate for the ritual or is there something else, such as, moving furniture, adding plants or flowers, or moving to another place that would create a more reflective prayer-filled environment. Use the appropriate liturgical colors for seasons and feasts:

- Green for Ordinary Time
- White or gold for Christmas and Easter
- Purple for Advent and Lent
- White for Feasts of Mary
- Red for Pentecost

The use of primary symbols, water, oil, the cross, the Scriptures, and candles is very important. Display them prominently and reverently in your prayer space.

The Role of Music

Besides the music from the *Call to Faith* CDs suggested in your teacher edition, use of meditative music at the beginning of a service or during a meditation time will also enhance a prayerful atmosphere for the children. Do not be afraid of silence. It is good for students to have time to reflect.

The Church Year

Within the flow of what most people experience as a calendar year, from January first to December thirty-first, there is another year—the liturgical or church year. This year, which is not dependent on the civil calendar begins on the first Sunday of Advent or the fourth Sunday before Christmas, and ends on the feast of Christ the King, the last Sunday of Ordinary Time. For Christians, as it unfolds each year, the liturgical year is a time of grace and favor because it celebrates and remembers the person of Jesus Christ and the paschal mystery of his life, death and Resurrection. Easter, the feast of Jesus' Resurrection is the most important and principal feast of the church year. Another significant feast is Christmas—the celebration of the birth of Jesus. These feasts determine the flow of the church year. Each of them is preceded by a season of preparation: Advent for Christmas and Lent for Easter. Each feast is followed by a number of weeks of celebration called the Christmas season and the Easter season. There are also thirty-three to thirty-four Sundays of the Church year called Ordinary Time. Ordinary Time celebrates the events and teachings of Jesus' public life. During the year, as the Church celebrates the mysteries of Christ it also honors Mary who is closely linked to the saving actions of her son, and the saints who are faithful examples of how to live the Christian life.

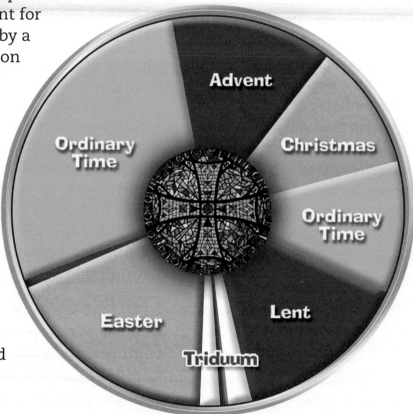

In these eight sessions you will find a celebration for each of the liturgical seasons of the church year including the Triduum and a celebration for Mary and one of the saints. Use your class calendar to plan ahead for each of these lessons to coincide with the season or feast during Ordinary Time.

Liturgical Catechesis

These celebrations follow a process of liturgical catechesis which includes forming students in the language, rituals, structure, and order of the liturgy. The process of liturgical catechesis contained in each session includes:

- A reflection about the context of the feast being celebrated.
- A ritual celebration built around a text taken from the rites or Lectionary. Within the celebration there is always participation in some ritual action.
- An opportunity for reflection and action that flow from the celebration.

The Scriptures

The Scripture readings in these sessions are meant to be proclaimed and probed with the students. Give them ample time to respond to the dialogue questions. The purpose of the dialogue is to find out what they heard in the proclamation of the word and to explore their thoughts. Always ask open-ended questions and refrain from trying to control the dialogue.

The Students

Elementary grade students like to be involved in ritual prayer. Involve them in preparing the environment, writing additional prayers, or preparing alternate questions for the scripture dialogue. Vary the roles of leader and reader so everyone gets a chance. Unlike younger children they need to have stories attached to symbols and signs. Meet this need by sharing scripture or life stories which relate to the symbol or ritual in the celebration. For example, read some of the scripture stories about water such as the crossing of the Red Sea or walking on the water, before a celebration using water in the ritual. Or, explore students' experiences of being cared for, before a celebration which involves signing or laying on of hands. Have volunteers research the origins of the ritual actions or symbols that are being used in the celebration and have them share their report before or after the celebration.

The Church's Seasons

Different things happen at different times during the year. During fall, school starts and the leaves change color. In winter trees are bare and the days are short. When spring comes the flowers bloom, the days get longer, and people want to spend time outside. Summer brings warmer days, school break, and long hours of fun.

The Church has seasons, too. The seasons of the Church year recall important events in the lives of Jesus, Mary, and the saints. In every season the Church prays together to remember all the gifts that come from God the Father and his Son, Jesus.

The Church prays using different words and actions. Here are some of them.

Words and Actions

The Bible is honored by bowing and sitting before it in silence.

The Cross is honored by kneeling in front of it or kissing it.

The sign of Christ's peace is offered with a handshake.

The Sign of the Cross is marked on foreheads, hearts, and lips.

Holy water is used as a reminder of Baptism.

Your class will use these words and actions to celebrate the different seasons.

6

The Church Year

Advent

Christmas

Ordinary Time

Lent

Triduum

Easter

Ordinary Time

Mary, Our Mother

Apart from those seasons having their own distinctive character, thirty-three or thirty-four weeks remain in the yearly cycle that do not celebrate a specific aspect of the mystery of Christ

General Norms for the Liturgical Year and the Calendar, 43

Catechist Formation

The period of Ordinary Time is devoted to the mystery of Christ in all of its aspects. This liturgical season is called Ordinary Time because the weeks are numbered in order, not because the season is "ordinary" in the usual sense of that word.

Through the celebration of the saints, the Church comes in contact with important aspects of the mystery of Christ. Most prominent among these celebrations are the many feasts in honor of the Virgin Mary. The Feast of Our Lady of Sorrows, celebrated on September 15, is one such remembrance. This feast is one of the few in the Church's calendar which includes a sequence, or poem. The *Stabat Mater*, often sung during the Stations of the Cross, begins by recalling how Mary stood at the foot of the cross (*John 19:23–27*).

Although Mary rarely speaks in the Gospels, her presence and sorrowful acceptance of Jesus' mission give strong testimony to the way in which life can emerge from suffering and death. When the disciples could not understand why Jesus had to suffer and die, Mary remained as a model of acceptance and faith. She came to share fully in the fruits of that suffering: Christ's Resurrection and his promise of new life for all.

Reflect **How does faith help you in times of suffering, distress, or crisis?**

Environment

Materials:

Bible or lectionary
White tablecloth
Crucifix
Call to Faith **Grade 4**
  Music CD
Icon of Our Lady of Sorrows (optional)

- Cover the prayer table with the white cloth, and place the crucifix, Bible, and icon of Our Lady of Sorrows on the table.

- Place the table in a central location so that it becomes a focal point of the celebration.

Ordinary Time

The Church honors Mary, the Mother of God, in every season of the year. During Ordinary Time, following the feast of the Holy Cross, the Church celebrates the Feast of Our Lady of Sorrows on September 15. This feast emerged during the Middle Ages, and it affirms the suffering that Mary endured as the Mother of God. As the first disciple of her Son, Mary participated profoundly in the redemptive work of Jesus.

Since the fourteenth century, Catholics have named seven events as the seven sorrows of the Blessed Virgin. These include: the prophecy of Simeon, the flight into Egypt, the loss of the child Jesus in the temple, meeting Jesus on Calvary, the crucifixion and death of Jesus, Jesus taken down from the cross, and Jesus laid in the tomb.

Every family has endured suffering. Mary can be a wonderful model of fortitude, especially as a family faces difficult times. Make Mary an example in your home.

Family Celebration

Many people have a deep devotion to Mary, the Mother of Sorrows. Praying seven Hail Marys in honor of the seven sorrows of Our Lady on a daily basis is a prayer tradition of our Church. During the month of September, perhaps your family could pray the Hail Mary at dinner or bedtime.

> **Hail Mary**
> Hail Mary, full of grace, the Lord is with you. Blessed are you among women, and blessed is the fruit of your womb, Jesus. Holy Mary, Mother of God, pray for us sinners, now and at the hour of our death. Amen.

Family Activity

Through his actions Christ taught his followers that compassion is far more powerful than pain and suffering. As a family, you can relieve the suffering of others. Here are two ideas.

- As a family, plan a day to visit to a lonely relative, neighbor, or friend. Bring this person flowers, or have your children make him or her a special picture. Perhaps this person could use some extra help around the house, such as emptying trashcans, watering plants, or raking leaves.

- Take a trip to your parish food pantry or to a local charity. Ask for a list of needs, and then take your family shopping. Children learn by example; if you are generous in sharing, you will teach your child to be compassionate.

Sorrowful Mother

- Help students focus by asking them to close their eyes and think of a sad time in their lives or in the lives of their families.
- Exercising discretion and tact, offer an example of a sad time from your own life, or ask a volunteer to do so.
- Ask students whether they think the Holy Family had sad times, too.
- Summarize the first paragraph.

Mary, Our Model of Faith

- Have volunteers read paragraphs two and three aloud.
- Discuss the sorrows that Mary had to face. Liken them to some of the sorrows that students face. For example, Mary watched as Jesus faced rejection. Mary accepted her grief as Christians are called to do.
- Ask students how Mary can be a model during personal times of sadness.
- ❷ **Who are some other role models in your life?** Affirm students who respond, especially those who name people of faith.

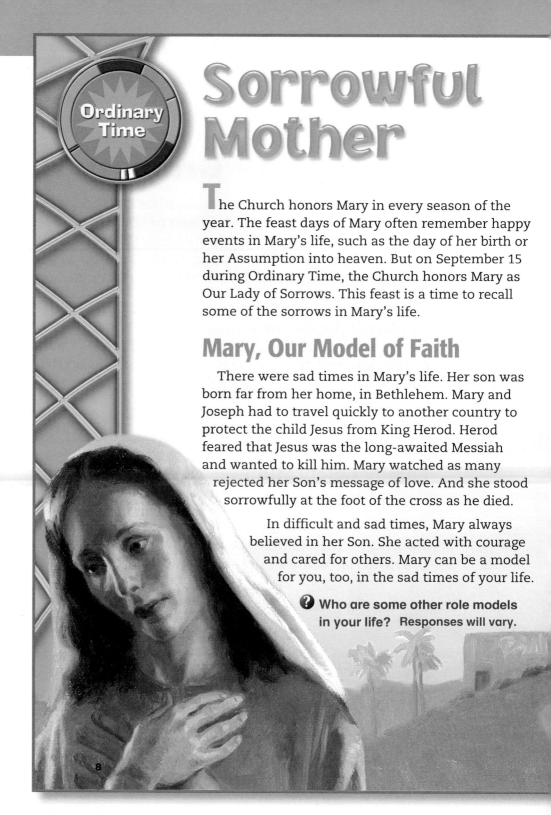

Ordinary Time

Sorrowful Mother

The Church honors Mary in every season of the year. The feast days of Mary often remember happy events in Mary's life, such as the day of her birth or her Assumption into heaven. But on September 15 during Ordinary Time, the Church honors Mary as Our Lady of Sorrows. This feast is a time to recall some of the sorrows in Mary's life.

Mary, Our Model of Faith

There were sad times in Mary's life. Her son was born far from her home, in Bethlehem. Mary and Joseph had to travel quickly to another country to protect the child Jesus from King Herod. Herod feared that Jesus was the long-awaited Messiah and wanted to kill him. Mary watched as many rejected her Son's message of love. And she stood sorrowfully at the foot of the cross as he died.

In difficult and sad times, Mary always believed in her Son. She acted with courage and cared for others. Mary can be a model for you, too, in the sad times of your life.

❷ **Who are some other role models in your life?** Responses will vary.

SEASONAL RESOURCES

Book You may find the following resource helpful.

- *The Way of Compassion: Into the Heart of the Seven Sorrows of Mary.* Richard C. Antall (Our Sunday Visitor). This is a modern reflection on and explanation of the seven sorrows of Mary.

CULTURAL CONNECTION

Virgen de Dolores In Mexico, the Feast of Our Lady of Sorrows is associated with Mexican Independence Day, which is celebrated on September 16.

- The call that began the war for independence— the *Grito de Dolores*—occurred in Dolores, a town named for the Virgin of Sorrows.
- *Grito* signifies both the "shout" for freedom and the Virgin's sorrow over the sufferings of the Mexican people.

Celebrate Mary

Gather

Pray the Sign of the Cross together.

Leader: Blessed be God.

All: **Blessed be God forever.**

Sing together.

Take, O take me as I am;
summon out what I shall be;
Set your seal upon my heart
and live in me.

"Take, O Take Me As I Am" © 1994, Iona Community,
GIA Publications, Inc., agent

Leader: Let us pray together for God's mercy.

Lord Jesus, you forgive us and rescue us from
the pain of sin.
Lord, have mercy.

All: **Lord, have mercy.**

Leader: Christ Jesus, you have given us Mary as
a model of courage and patience.
Christ, have mercy.

All: **Christ, have mercy.**

Leader: Lord Jesus, as we remember Mary's sorrows,
we express sorrow for our failure to love.
Lord, have mercy.

All: **Lord, have mercy.**

Leader: Let us pray.

Bow your heads as the leader prays.

All: **Amen.**

9

Celebrate Mary

Gather

- Use the *Call to Faith* Grade 4 CD, track 1. Practice the gathering song once before beginning the celebration.
- Use a moment of silence to call students to worship.
- As you lead students in prayer, lift your hand as a gesture for the students to begin the response. Use the same gesture to begin the hymn.
- Follow the call and response prayer.
- Leader's prayer: **God, our Father, as your Son was raised on the cross Mary, his mother, stood beside him. May we be united with his suffering and share in his Resurrection.**

PRAYER

Lord, Have Mercy One purpose of the *Kyrie*, or the *Lord, Have Mercy,* is to help unify the worshipping community.

- This prayer is about asking for personal forgiveness and about reflecting on who we are and who we are called to become.
- The *Kyrie* emphasizes praising God's mercy for those times when we have not acted as the Body of Christ in the world.

LECTIONARY LINK

Simeon's Prophecy The reading for the students' celebration is in the lectionary under the Feast of the Presentation of the Lord on February 2 (*Luke 2:22–35*).

- In this Gospel, Simeon's hopes are fulfilled when he sees the child Jesus. Simeon predicted Mary's sorrow, which would result from her son's role in the world.
- Even Mary, so loved by God, was to endure suffering.

Listen to God's Word

- Proclaim the reading.
- Pause a moment for silent reflection.
- Allow time for students to reflect silently on the dialogue questions. Ask volunteers to share their responses.

Meditation

- Have students close their eyes and quiet their minds for meditation.
- Say the following, pausing between each sentence: **When you are hurt or suffering, imagine a kind person with an arm around you, saying, "I know how you feel." Your hurt may not go away completely, but that gentle touch and soft voice may make your suffering easier. Mary is Jesus' Mother and she is your mother, too.**
- Leader's prayer: **Jesus, help us remember that we can always turn to you and your Blessed Mother.**

Go Forth!

Pray the prayer and response.
- Sing together the song.

Listen to God's Word

Reader: A reading from the holy Gospel according to Luke.

Read Luke 2:22–35.
The Gospel of the Lord.

All: **Praise to you, Lord Jesus Christ.**

Dialogue

Why did Simeon's message cause Mary sorrow?

If you had been in the Temple, what question would you have asked Simeon?

Meditation

Sit in silence before the cross as the leader leads you in a meditation on Our Lady of Sorrows.

Leader: Let us pray . . .

All: **Amen.**

Go Forth!

Leader: Let us go forth in Mary's spirit of faith, hope, and love for her Son.

All: **Thanks be to God.**

Sing together.

Take, O take me as I am;
summon out what I shall be;
set your seal upon my heart
    and live in me.

"Take, O Take Me As I Am" © 1994, Iona Community,
GIA Publications, Inc.

10

RITUAL

Imagination and Faith   Guided meditation joins together the faculty of imagination with the gift of faith.

- Imagining scenes from the bible is a traditional way of personalizing the meaning of the scriptures.
- Throughout the centuries, the faith of many saints was deepened through the use of meditation.

LITURGY LINK

Liturgical Colors   Although the Feast of Our Lady of Sorrows occurs in Ordinary Time, the liturgical color for its celebration is white—the color for all Marian feasts.

- Because this feast follows the Feast of the Triumph of the Holy Cross, the color red is sometimes worn to represent the great sorrow Mary endured at the foot of the cross.

Compassion

Mary watched as her Son suffered and died at the hands of those who did not understand him. Sorrow is still felt today whenever someone sees a loved one hurting. But from your sorrow can grow greater caring and compassion for the suffering of the whole world. Compassion for others is more powerful than pain. That is the message of the gospel.

❓ When have you felt sorrow when someone you loved was hurting? Responses will vary.

ACTIVITY
The Sorrowful Mysteries

The Sorrowful Mysteries name five events in Jesus' Passion. Each mystery can also teach you a virtue that will make you a stronger Christian. On separate paper, make a drawing of one of the Sorrowful Mysteries, or show a way that you can learn and live its virtue. Pray a decade of the Rosary on Tuesday or Friday of this week and reflect on the mystery you chose:

- The Agony in the Garden (repentance)
- The Scourging at the Pillar (purity)
- The Crowning with Thorns (courage)
- Carrying the Cross (patience)
- The Crucifixion (self-denial)

Compassion

- Ask a volunteer to read aloud the first paragraph on page 11.
- Introduce and explain the word *compassion*, which comes from a Latin word meaning "to suffer with."

❓ When have you felt sorrow when someone you love was hurting? Have students reflect and then write a paragraph in response to the question. Ask for volunteers to share their writing.

Activity

- Give each student a sheet of paper.
- Have students draw one of the Sorrowful Mysteries or one way they can live its virtue.
- Encourage students to pray one decade of the Sorrowful Mysteries of the Rosary each day this week.

OPTIONAL ACTIVITY

The Rosary The activity for this feast asks each student to draw a picture.

- Ask students to share their drawings.
- Ask what virtue students can learn from the Sorrowful Mysteries and how they might live it.
- Close by reciting the fifth Sorrowful Mystery of the Rosary, the crucifixion.

Mutiple Intelligence: Intrapersonal

 LOVE AND SERVE

Compassion in Action The gospel message is one of compassion. As a class, adopt a needy parish family.

- Ask students to donate canned food, new clothing, or toys. Invite parent volunteers to help deliver these goods to the family.
- Stay in touch with the family and consider helping them on Thanksgiving and Christmas.

Advent

Prepare for Jesus

"Advent has a twofold character: as a season to prepare for Christmas when Christ's first coming to us is remembered; as a season when that remembrance directs the mind and heart to await Christ's Second Coming at the end of time. Advent is thus a period for devout and joyful expectation."

General Norms for the Liturgical Year and the Calendar, 39

Catechist Formation

The four-week season of Advent marks the beginning of the liturgical year of the Church. Until December 16, the focus of the season is an anticipation of the second coming of Christ. Then, from December 17 through December 24, liturgies prepare the faithful to celebrate Christ's birth on Christmas.

John the Baptist is a prominent figure during Advent. He invited people to be baptized in water as they acknowledged their sins. John emphasized that accepting this baptism meant a change of heart as well as a change of behavior. At the same time, he made it clear that his mission was to prepare the way for someone greater than himself. The one who would follow John would baptize not only with water but also with the Holy Spirit and with fire (*Matthew 3:11*).

The expectation of this "greater" person, Jesus Christ, is the crowning characteristic of the season of Advent. As the preaching of John the Baptist prepared for the coming of Christ, the Church also prepares for Jesus by answering the call to a change of heart.

Reflect **In what ways do you prepare for the coming of Christ into your life?**

Environment

Materials:

Table
Purple cloth
Advent wreath
Matches
Call to Faith Grade 4
  Music CD

- Place students' desks in a circle.
- Put the prayer table in the center of the circle.
- Decorate the prayer table with the cloth and wreath.

Advent

Anticipation is often joyful, as when a family awaits the arrival of a new baby. Mary and Joseph felt this sense of expectation with the coming of Jesus. The Jewish people too, had been waiting for centuries for the coming of the Messiah.

Each year, in the four weeks before Christmas, the Church celebrates Advent, which prepares for Christ's coming and begins the liturgical year. During this season, the assembly relives the anticipation of the Messiah. Purple, the color of the season and a sign of penance, reminds the People of God to prepare.

During Advent, the faithful ready their hearts for when he will come again. Building tolerance for your family members through forgiveness is a good way to begin.

Family Celebration

God calls each person to be a sign of Christ's presence in the world. With prayerful and open hearts we can respond to God's call. Praying the Lord's Prayer slowly and thinking about each phrase is a good way to start the process of changing one's heart. Before or after dinner, light a candle on your Advent wreath, and pray together the prayer that Jesus taught us. Then exchange a sign of peace.

> *Our Father, who art in heaven, hallowed by thy name. Thy kingdom come, thy will be done, on earth as it is in heaven. Give us this day our daily bread, and forgive us our trespasses, as we forgive those who trespass against us. And lead us not into temptation, but deliver us from evil. Amen.*

Family Activity

It is important to mark the season of Advent as a family. Here are some things you can do as a family during the weeks before Christmas to keep the focus on preparing for the coming of Christ.

- Take time out for a discussion about how you would prepare if you knew that a special guest was coming to your house for Christmas. Emphasize such things as, making room, cleaning up and getting ready for the guest. Then, discuss what family members can do during the season of Advent to spiritually prepare for the coming of Jesus. What thoughts or actions need to be cleaned up?

- Write the name of each family member on a small piece of paper. Fold these papers and place them in a bowl. At mealtime, ask each family member to pick a name. For the next week, secretly do something extra for the person whose name you picked, such as putting away toys, taking on a chore, or treating the person kindly. At the end of the week, reveal the name you selected. If you choose your own name, be extra nice to everyone!

Prepare for Jesus

- Quiet students with a moment of silence.
- Drape a purple cloth over the front of the prayer center.
- Explain to students that purple is the Church's color for Advent. Tell them that purple means both *penance* and *preparation*.
- Ask students what Catholics prepare for during Advent.
- Have a volunteer read the opening paragraph.

Change Your Heart

- Ask students to share any family Advent traditions.
- Ask volunteers to read aloud these two paragraphs.
- ❷ **How can you prepare for Jesus' coming?** Organize the class in small groups to discuss the question. Tell the groups to focus on how they need to change to prepare for Christ's coming at Christmas.

Advent

Prepare for Jesus

The Church celebrates the Season of Advent for the four weeks before Christmas. Advent is a time of waiting and preparing for Jesus' second coming. Advent is a time to look into your heart and see how you can be a better follower of Jesus. The Advent seasonal color of purple stands for penance.

Change Your Heart

The weeks before Christmas are often a time for making wish lists, decorating the tree, or shopping for presents. However, the Church takes time to do more. Catholics prepare for Christmas by reflecting on the gift of the Incarnation. God sent his only Son to be the Savior of all people.

Taking time for daily prayer before the Advent wreath with your family gives you time to reflect on Jesus' love. Small acts of sacrifice and penance can help you to turn your heart toward Jesus and to show greater love for others.

❷ **How can you prepare for Jesus' coming?**
Responses will vary.

12

 SEASONAL RESOURCES

Book You may find the following resource helpful.

- *Advent 2003, The Joyful Promise of Advent: Daily Gospel Meditations and Prayers.* Rev. Joseph D. Creedon (Twenty-Third Publications). The author presents ways to grow spiritually during the Advent season.

 CULTURAL CONNECTION

Advent Prayer Traditionally, Polish families consider Advent to be one of the most important liturgical seasons.

- Special church services called "Roraty" (from the first words of a Latin hymn, *Rorate coeli*) are celebrated daily.
- The service begins in darkness and the Church is gradually lit. The service is meant to show alertness for Christ's coming.

Celebrate Advent

Gather

Sing together the refrain.

Come, O Lord, change our hearts!
Emmanuel, God is with us.

"Come, O Lord" © 1997, GIA Publications, Inc.

Pray the Sign of the Cross together.

Leader: Our help is in the name of the Lord.

All: **Who made heaven and earth.**

Leader: Let us pray.

Bow your heads as the leader prays.

All: **Amen.**

I confess to almighty God
and to you, my brothers and sisters,
that I have greatly sinned,
in my thoughts and in my words,
in what I have done
and in what I have failed to do,

Gently strike your chest with a closed fist.

through my fault, through my fault,
through my most grievous fault;

Continue:

therefore I ask blessed Mary ever-Virgin,
all the Angels and Saints,
and you, my brothers and sisters,
to pray for me to the Lord our God.

Leader: May almighty God have mercy on us, forgive us
our sins, and bring us to everlasting life.

All: **Amen.**

13

Celebrate Advent

Gather

- Call students to worship with the single ring of a bell.
- Invite students to join you in singing the hymn. Use the *Call to Faith* Grade 4 Music CD to rehearse the suggested song.
- Begin the prayer by leading students in the Sign of the Cross.
- Lead the opening prayer.
- Leader's Prayer: **God, our Father, open our hearts to change. Show us how to become more like your Son, Jesus.**
- Pray the Penitential Act. Remind students to bow as indicated.

PRAYER

Penitential Act The Penitential Act provides a moment of silent recollection to help people focus on the reading.

- It is not a moment to ask God to forgive personal sins.
- It is a time to ask God to forgive our communal failure to live as a sign of Christ's presence in the world.

LECTIONARY LINK

Change of Heart The reading for the students' celebration is from the second Sunday of Advent, cycle B.

- This Gospel reveals that a change of heart is required in order to live in God's kingdom.
- The Gospel according to Mark uses the term *metanoia*, or conversion, to describe this change of heart.

Listen to God's Word

- Invite a volunteer to proclaim the Gospel as students stand.
- Invite students to sit and discuss the Dialogue questions.

Raise Hands in Prayer

- After lighting one of the Advent candles, ask students to reflect silently on ways they can "prepare the way of the Lord" in their hearts.
- After a few minutes, signal students to stand. Ask students to raise their hands and join you in the prayer.
- Exchange a sign of peace.

Go Forth!

- Pause for a moment of silence, and then lead the closing acclamation.
- Using a hand gesture, encourage students to respond clearly and enthusiastically.

Listen to God's Word

Reader: A reading from the Holy Gospel according to Mark.

Read Mark 1:1–8.
The Gospel of the Lord.

All: **Praise to you, Lord Jesus Christ.**

Dialogue

How did John tell the people to prepare for the coming of the Messiah?

What does it mean to repent?

Raise Hands in Prayer

Sit before the wreath in silence and reflect on ways you will try to change your heart.

Leader: Lord, we want your Spirit to change our hearts and prepare for your coming. Be with us as we pray.

Stand, raise your hands, and pray the Lord's Prayer.

Leader: Let us offer one another a greeting of peace as a sign of our desire to change our hearts.

All exchange a sign of peace.

Go Forth!

Leader: Let us go forth to prepare the way of the Lord.

All: **Thanks be to God.**

RITUAL

Unity The Lord's Prayer and the sign of peace are expressions of reconciliation and unity, not just a prayer and a gesture of friendship.

- As we pray for forgiveness, we vow to forgive others.
- When we offer a sign of peace, we offer a symbol of reconciliation.

LITURGY LINK

Liturgical Colors Violet (or purple) is the seasonal color of Advent. Reserved for royalty in ancient times, today it is a symbol of preparation for Christ the King.

- The Advent wreath, from Germanic tradition, was lit during winter as a symbol of hope for the coming of spring.
- Christians use this symbol for hope in Christ, the everlasting light.

The Path of Love

John told the people who were waiting for the Messiah that they would have to change. He said, "Prepare the way of the Lord, make straight his paths" (*Mark 1:3*).

❷ **What changes can you make that will straighten your path and bring you closer to Jesus?** Responses will vary.

(ACTIVITY)
Show Your Love

Make a coupon book of loving actions you can do for members of your family. You might include things like reading a book to a younger sibling, washing the dog without complaining, cleaning up your room, or taking someone's turn doing the dishes. Give one person in your family a coupon each day this week.

15

The Path of Love

- Direct students to sit. Ask a volunteer to read the first paragraph on page 15.

❷ **What changes can you make that will straighten your path and bring you closer to Jesus?** Ask pairs of students to share with each other what changes they could make to bring them closer to Jesus.

- Invite volunteers to share their ideas with the class.

- Provide students with paper and scissors, and then read the activity instructions.

- If time permits, give students an opportunity to make at least one coupon for each family member.

- If no time remains, assign the activity as homework. After a week, ask each student how his or her family reacted to this activity.

OPTIONAL ACTIVITY

Prepare the Way   Have each student use a separate sheet of paper to draw a pathway with a symbol of Jesus at the end of the path.

- Have students create road signs along the path that indicate ways in which they will prepare for the coming of Christ.

- For example, A "Stop" sign could say: Help Mom clean a mess my little brother made.

Multiple Intelligence: Visual/Spatial

LOVE AND SERVE

Respect   Advent is a time to prepare the way for the kingdom of God. Help students see that God can reign in their lives through their actions.

- When someone treats others with respect and dignity, that person shows Christ's presence in the world. If a student befriends someone who has been marginalized, that student is Christ for others.

Christmas

God's Greatest Gift

Next to the yearly celebration of the paschal mystery, the Church holds most sacred the memorial of Christ's birth and early manifestations.

General Norms for the Liturgical Year and the Calendar, 32

Catechist Formation

The Christmas season extends from the vigil of Christmas to the Sunday after the Feast of Epiphany. The birth of Christ is called the Incarnation (meaning "in the flesh").

The Feast of Epiphany commemorates the three magi who traveled from afar to bring homage to the child whose star they had seen. The gifts that the kings offered testify to the greatness they recognized in the child Jesus. Because these visitors were not Jewish, the story also reveals that the gift of God's only Son is given to all humankind.

God's gift of Christ to the world is an event that continues every day. Each time the Church gathers for Mass, a procession with gifts of bread and wine ends at the altar. Through the power of the Holy Spirit, God gives himself to humans by transforming these gifts into the Body and Blood of Christ.

Reflect   **In what ways do you bring the gift of God's only Son to other people?**

Environment

Materials:

Manger scene, including statuettes of the three kings
Light or candle
White cloth
***Call to Faith* Grade 4 CD**

- Place the white cloth on the table.
- Place the crèche on the table, and set the kings to one side.
- Clear enough room to allow students to process around the prayer space.

Family Faith

Christmas

Amid all the gift giving, the meaning of Christmas may get lost. The Feast of Epiphany helps shift the focus from material gifts to the gift that is Jesus. The Church celebrates the Christmas season until the Feast of the Baptism of Jesus in January. Epiphany, the twelfth day of Christmas, is the day that Christ revealed himself to the whole world.

Epiphany means "showing forth." The visit of the magi on Epiphany is a symbol and a prophecy that all shall worship Christ. In Scripture and in the music of liturgy, the assembly recognizes Jesus as the Most High. The gifts of the magi become the gifts of the assembly to Christ, as the People of God reverence and worship the Lord.

As a family, you can celebrate Epiphany in your home in many ways. Start by remembering that the season of Christmas doesn't end on Christmas Day.

Family Celebration

Don't put away that manger scene just yet! Epiphany celebrates the arrival of the magi or the three kings. Light a candle or lamp. As a family, place the three kings near the crèche. Sing a round of "We Three Kings" as your prayer before bedtime this evening. Ask your child to lead you.

> We three kings of Orient are, Bearing gifts we traverse afar
>
> Field and fountain, Moor and mountain, Following yonder star.
>
> O star of wonder, star of night, Star with royal beauty bright,
>   Westward leading still proceeding,
>
> Guide us to thy perfect Light.
>
> "We Three Kings of Orient Are" © 2001, GIA Publications, Inc.

Family Activity

One way to celebrate the Feast of Epiphany is by marking the home's doorway with the initials of the magi: Caspar, Melchior, and Balthazar. Obtain a piece of chalk and gather your family around the front door of your home. Pray, "Lord, bless this doorway and all who enter here. Help us to be generous and welcoming to those who cross this threshold." Then, use the chalk to mark the doorway with the initials of the magi. This tradition reminds family members to bring Christ to all whom they encounter.

Your family can give gifts to god from the heart as the magi did. Here is one idea.

- Reflect on your gifts as a family and the needs in your community. Make a commitment to get involved in some kind of service program in your area.

God's Greatest Gift

- Give students a few minutes to quiet themselves.
- Ask students whether they can name the magi who came to visit the baby Jesus.
- List the guesses on the board.
- Tell students that the Bible never names the magi, but Tradition calls them Caspar, Balthazar, and Melchior. Their story is important because they represent all the people of the world that Jesus came to save.
- Summarize the first three paragraphs.

Precious Gifts

- Have volunteers read aloud the fourth paragraph.
- Discuss the meaning of *Epiphany*.
- Talk about the gifts of gold, frankincense, and myrrh. Make sure that students comprehend the symbolism of each gift.
- ❓ **What gifts of reverence and worship can you offer Jesus?** Encourage students to keep a list of the group's responses and try to act on them during the coming week.

God's Greatest Gift

The Church's Season of Christmas begins with the Mass of Christmas Eve on December 24 and continues for almost three weeks. The feast of Epiphany comes in the middle of the Christmas season. The season ends in January with the feast of the Baptism of the Lord, the Sunday after Epiphany.

The word *Epiphany* means "showing forth." On Epiphany the Church remembers the visit of the three Magi, often called wise men, to the infant Jesus.

The Magi came from distant lands, followed a bright star to find the infant Jesus, honored him, and gave glory to God. Epiphany celebrates the belief that Jesus came to earth to save everyone.

Precious Gifts

To honor the Savior and show him reverence, the Magi brought him gifts of gold, frankincense, and myrrh. The gift of gold, a precious metal, showed that they thought of Jesus as worthy of the highest honor. Frankincense, an incense with a pleasing smell, represented the holiness of Jesus. Myrrh is a symbol of preserving and saving. This gift was a sign that Jesus would die for the salvation of all people.

❓ **What gifts of reverence and worship can you offer Jesus?** Responses will vary.

16

 SEASONAL RESOURCES

Book You may find the following resource helpful:
- *Stations of the Nativity.* Lawrence Boadt (Paulist Press). This book of stations is a reflection on fourteen events that surround the birth of Jesus, from the Annunciation to the visit of the magi.

 CULTURAL CONNECTION

Water and the Epiphany In the Greek Orthodox tradition, the blessing of water is the high point of the Feast of Epiphany.

- The celebrant incenses the water and makes the Sign of the Cross in it three times. A wooden cross is also immersed three times in the water.

Celebrate Christmas

Gather

Pray the Sign of the Cross together.

Leader: Blessed be the name of the Lord.

All: **Now and forever.**

Sing together the refrain.

O star of wonder, star of night,
Star with royal beauty bright,
Westward leading, still proceeding,
Guide us to thy perfect Light.

"We Three Kings of Orient Are" Traditional

Leader: Let us pray.

Bow your heads as the leader prays.

All: **Amen.**

Listen to God's Word

Reader: A reading from the Holy Gospel according to Matthew.

Read Matthew 2:9–11.
The Gospel of the Lord.

All: **Praise to you, Lord Jesus Christ.**

17

Celebrate Christmas

Gather

- Practice the hymn before beginning the celebration. Use *Call to Faith* Grade 4 CD, track 3.
- Use a moment of silence to call students to worship, and then pray aloud with them the opening verse and response.
- Sing the hymn together.
- Leader's Prayer: **God, our Father, you revealed your Son, Jesus, to the world by the guidance of a star. Lead us to heaven by the light of faith.**

Listen to God's Word

- Invite a student to serve as reader.
- Have students remain standing for the Gospel.

 PRAYER

The Sign of the Cross The Sign of the Cross, made on the forehead, breast, and shoulders, was common in private devotion by the fifth century.

- In the West, the gesture is made by extending the thumb and first two fingers; these three represent the Trinity.

- The last two fingers are closed against the palm; these symbolize the humanity and divinity of Jesus.

LECTIONARY LINK

Epiphany The Gospel for the students' celebration is located in the lectionary under the Feast of Epiphany.

- The Gospel according to Matthew emphasizes that Jesus' message is consistent with Judaism. Yet, throughout this Gospel, the Jewish leaders misunderstand Jesus.

- The magi, though foreigners and gentiles, can see the Christ Child for who he is: the King of the Jews.

- Encourage students to reflect on and discuss the dialogue questions.

Procession of Gifts

- Ask each student to write on a slip of paper a Christmas promise that states a way he or she will honor Jesus.
- Walk with students in a procession around the room, singing the refrain of "We Three Kings."
- Lead students to the crèche, and help them place the statues and their Christmas promises.

Go Forth!

- After the procession is completed, have students stand in a circle.
- Pray the prayer of dismissal.
- Conclude with the hymn.

Dialogue

Why did the Magi honor the child Jesus?

How do you honor Jesus today?

Procession of Gifts

Leader: May all kings bow before him,
all nations serve him.

Psalm 72:11

All: **Every nation will adore you.**

Sing as you walk in procession, carrying the statues of the three kings. Place the statues and your Christmas promises in the crèche.

Go Forth!

Leader: Let us go forth to bring the Christmas gifts of peace, love, and joy to all we meet.

All: **Thanks be to God.**

Sing together the refrain.

O star of wonder, star of night,
Star with royal beauty bright,
Westward leading, still proceeding,
Guide us to thy perfect Light.

"We Three Kings of Orient Are" Traditional

RITUAL

Movement and Prayer Remind students to walk in single file or in pairs for the classroom procession.

- A liturgical procession is a significant movement of persons. It is accompanied by a hymn or psalm.
- The combination of movement and music into a rhythmic pattern encourages a prayerful spirit.

LITURGY LINK

Liturgical Symbols White is the liturgical color that dominates vestments and adorns the crèche during the Christmas season.

- White is the symbol of Baptism and the new life of Christ.
- The symbol of the magi and the gifts used during the students' celebration are reminders that the best gift one can bring to the infant King is the gift of oneself.

Gifts from Jesus

The star led the Magi to Jesus. They worshipped Jesus, the light of the world, bringing him gifts for a king. The gifts given to Jesus, he gives to you. By becoming one of us, Jesus brought all people the opportunity to be saved (myrrh), to be holy (frankincense), and to be honored (gold).

❷ **In what ways have you seen Jesus' gifts of salvation, holiness, and dignity at work in the world?**
Responses will vary.

(ACTIVITY)

Make a Group Mural

Make a group mural titled "Gifts for All." Draw a way that you will bring the message of Jesus to others in the weeks ahead.

19

Gifts from Jesus

- Give students a moment to reflect on the celebration.
- Invite a volunteer to read aloud this paragraph.
- ❷ **In what ways have you seen Jesus' gift of salvation, holiness and dignity at work in the world?** Ask students to share their thoughts on the question. You may wish to give an example to start the discussion.

Activity

- Have students work individually on their drawings, or assign the drawing activity as homework.
- Help students combine their drawings into a mural with scissors and glue. Display the completed project in the classroom.
- As an alternative, provide a large sheet of poster board or butcher paper, and have students work together to design and draw the mural.

OPTIONAL ACTIVITY

Give Gifts Brainstorm with students some ways that they can bring the gifts of frankincense (holiness), myrrh (salvation), and gold (honor) to others in the classroom.

- Encourage students to bring these gifts to one another in the coming weeks.
- Ask students to record the things they have done. Discuss their results.

Multiple Intelligence: Interpersonal

LOVE AND SERVE

Honor Others Help students understand the gift of honor by showing respect for those who may be marginalized by society.

- Encourage students to help their families recognize those who are hungry and homeless.
- Saying "Hello" or offering food can make a difference in the lives of suffering people.

Called to Leadership

Rather, especially on . . . Sundays, they [the weeks of Ordinary Time] are devoted to the mystery of Christ in all its aspects.

General Norms for the Liturgical Year and the Calendar, 43

Catechist Formation

Thirty-three or thirty-four weeks in the Church's liturgical calendar are called Ordinary Time. During this season, Church members hear about and reflect upon Christ's life and ministry, particularly through the Sunday Gospels. The liturgical color for Ordinary Time is green.

Ordinary Time includes celebration of many important people of faith who have been declared saints. The Conversion of Paul, celebrated on January 25, recalls Paul's unique encounter with Christ. It was a life-changing event. Paul's recovery of his sight moved him to recognize Christ as the Savior and to turn away from persecuting Christ's followers. After his conversion, Paul became one of the strongest witnesses to faith in Christ. Through his preaching and writing, he spread the good news to many areas of the world.

The focus of Paul's preaching was to help others realize Christ in their lives. Recalling Paul's conversion demonstrates that personal contact with Christ helps people turn away from evil and become witnesses to the faith.

Reflect **What changes have come about in your life because of your contact with Christ?**

Environment

Materials:

Bible or Lectionary
Cross (not a crucifix)
Image of Saint Paul
Candle or lamp
Green cloth
***Call to Faith* Grade 4**
   Music CD

- Create a worship space with enough room for students to come up for a blessing.

- Cover the prayer table with the green cloth.

- Arrange the cross, the image of Saint Paul and the candle on the table.

Ordinary Time

During Ordinary Time the Church celebrates the feast days of many saints. The conversion of Saint Paul is celebrated on January 25.

Paul was a zealous Jew, born around the time of Jesus. After Jesus' death, he saw the conversion of Jews to Christianity as a threat to his traditions and faith. He began to persecute those who followed Christ, arresting them. Then, on the road to Damascus, the blinding light of the risen Christ stopped Paul in his tracks. Jesus asked Paul to answer for his actions. Paul had a change of heart because he met the risen Christ, and became a central figure in the growth of the early Church.

Not everyone has a conversion experience as dramatic as Paul's was. Changes usually take place gradually. There are daily opportunities to become better Christians, starting within one's own family. As a parent, you can lead your children by being open to the experience of having a change of heart.

Family Celebration

On this feast we are reminded that God calls everyone to conversion. Gather your family members. Select a leader. Have each member of the family stand and approach the leader. Use the following blessing.

> **Leader:** [Name], God calls you by name to go forth in the spirit of Saint Paul to give witness to the good news of Jesus, [while making the sign of the cross of the person's forehead, say the following:] in the name of the Father, and of the Son, and of the Holy Spirit.
>
> **Family Member:** Amen!

When all members of the family have been blessed, have the youngest member of the family switch roles with the leader, pray the prayer of blessing, and sign the leader's forehead.

Family Activity

After his conversion, Saint Paul spread the good news. He knew his weaknesses, and he prayed for the strength he needed to share the message of Jesus. Like Paul, God's people are also called to spread the message of Jesus.

At your next mealtime, recognize your strengths. For example, perhaps one child is outgoing and another shares well. Tell each family member in turn about a strength you recognize in him or her. Family members will then do the same. Afterwards, discuss how these qualities will help your family share Jesus' message.

Called to Leadership

- Summarize the paragraph. Discuss the meaning of *conversion*, which is a change of heart.
- Ask students to name events that can cause significant change in a person's life—for example, an accident, a death, marriage or a new baby.
- Then, talk about daily conversions, ordinary experiences such as apologizing or learning from an error, that can change a person gradually.
- Summarize the first paragraph.

A Change of Heart

- Ask volunteers to read aloud the next three paragraphs.
- Ask students how Paul was changed. He became a follower of Jesus.
- Make sure that students recognize that Paul's conversion enabled him to spread Jesus' message.
- ❓ **What are some ways your parish preaches the good news?** Encourage responses.

Ordinary Time

Called to Leadership

The Church celebrates the feasts of many saints during Ordinary Time. The feast of the conversion of Saint Paul highlights an important event in his life and in the life of the Church. The Church celebrates Saint Paul's conversion on January 25.

A Change of Heart

Paul was born a Jew in Jesus' time. His Jewish name was Saul. Paul was a faithful Jew, and he worried as he watched the growth in numbers of Jesus' followers after Jesus' death. He saw these disciples as a threat to his traditional Jewish beliefs. Paul began bringing them to the authorities in order to arrest them.

Everything changed when Paul met Jesus on the road to Damascus. He was traveling there to punish some Christians. Instead he experienced the Risen Christ in a vision. Jesus said to him, "Saul, Saul, why are you persecuting me?" (Acts 22:7). After that Paul changed his ways.

Paul became a central figure in the growth of the early Church. Because he met the Risen Christ as the Apostles did, he is called an Apostle, too. His missionary journeys, his many letters, and the power of his preaching helped Christianity to spread far and wide in the world.

❓ **What are some ways your parish preaches the good news?** Responses will vary.

20

SEASONAL RESOURCES

Book You may find the following resource helpful.

- *Fifty-Seven Saints.* Anne Eileen Heffernan, FSP (Daughters of St. Paul). This book includes a chapter that describes the life of Saint Paul.

CULTURAL CONNECTION

A Holy Kiss Paul directed Christians to "greet one another with a holy kiss" (*Romans 16:16*). Eastern Rite Catholics greet each other during Mass with a reverent embrace.

- The greeters bow their heads to the right, then to the front, and then to the left of the recipients, saying, "Christ is revealed among us."
- Recipients reply, "Blessed is the revelation of Christ."

The Suffering Servant

- Show students a picture of a heart, a stop sign, and a cross.

- Ask students what each shape means, and write their responses on the board or on chart paper.

- Discuss how symbols (for example, the heart and cross) have many meanings, but a sign (for example, the stop sign) has only one.

- Have a moment of silence. Then summarize the first paragraph.

The Cross

- Have volunteers read aloud the three paragraphs.

- Discuss the Way of the Cross. Focus on the sacrifices that Jesus made and the burdens he carried along the journey to Calvary while knowing he was going to die.

- Reflect again on the symbol of the cross. Discuss how a symbol of death became a symbol of new life.

- ❓ **Where do you see crosses?** Tell students to pay special attention during the coming week and notice any crosses they see around them.

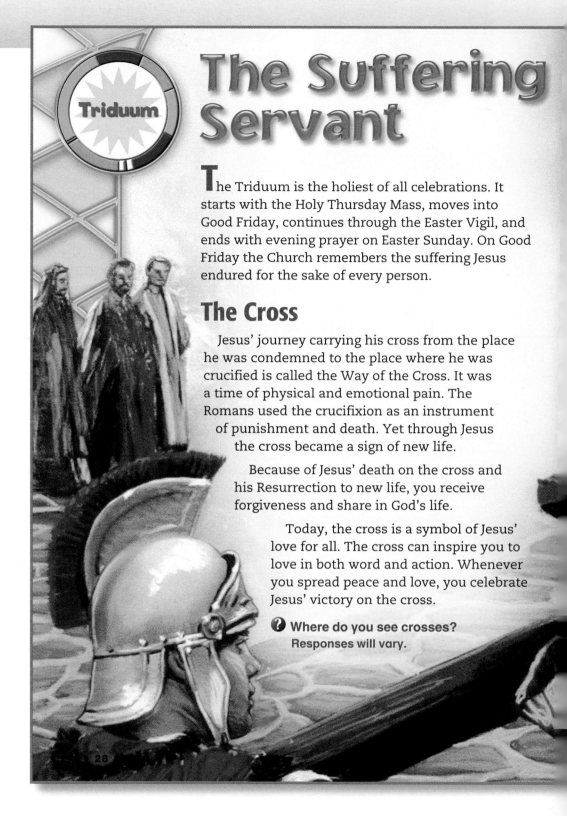

The Suffering Servant

Triduum

The Triduum is the holiest of all celebrations. It starts with the Holy Thursday Mass, moves into Good Friday, continues through the Easter Vigil, and ends with evening prayer on Easter Sunday. On Good Friday the Church remembers the suffering Jesus endured for the sake of every person.

The Cross

Jesus' journey carrying his cross from the place he was condemned to the place where he was crucified is called the Way of the Cross. It was a time of physical and emotional pain. The Romans used the crucifixion as an instrument of punishment and death. Yet through Jesus the cross became a sign of new life.

Because of Jesus' death on the cross and his Resurrection to new life, you receive forgiveness and share in God's life.

Today, the cross is a symbol of Jesus' love for all. The cross can inspire you to love in both word and action. Whenever you spread peace and love, you celebrate Jesus' victory on the cross.

❓ **Where do you see crosses?**
Responses will vary.

28

 SEASONAL RESOURCES

Book You may find the following resource helpful.

- *Lent: The Sunday Readings: Stories and Reflections.* Megan McKenna (Orbis). This book is a collection of stories and meditations on the meaning of the readings of Lent, including the Triduum.

 CULTURAL CONNECTION

Triduum Bread One Mexican-American tradition is to eat *pan dulce* (sweet bread), or *pan de semita* (Jewish bread) during Holy Week.

- Many Jews settled in Southern Texas and Mexico. Eating *pan de semita* during Holy Week recalls the Jewish practice of eating unleavened bread during Passover.

The Triduum

The Church celebrates the Triduum, the holiest three days of the Church year, during Holy Week. The Triduum begins with the Mass of the Lord's Supper on Holy Thursday evening and ends with evening prayer on Easter Sunday. Holy Thursday marks Jesus' last meal with his apostles and his washing of the apostles' feet. On Good Friday the Church remembers the suffering and death that Jesus endured for the sake of all. At the Holy Saturday Vigil, the Church witnesses both the fear and darkness that followed Jesus' death and the light and joy of the Resurrection. On this night the Church initiates new members through the Sacraments of Baptism, Confirmation, and the Eucharist.

Jesus suffered and died on the cross to free humans from the power of sin and death. The cross is a symbol of Jesus' great love for his people. Whenever you spread the peace and love of Christ, you celebrate Christ's victory on the cross. The cross can inspire your family to spread God's love, beginning within the walls of your own home.

Family Celebration

During Holy Week, you might place a crucifix or cross on the dinner table. Before the main meal on Good friday, lead your family in prayer. Then have each family kiss or reverently touch the cross. End with the Lord's Prayer.

> **Leader:** As Easter draws near, we gather as a family to celebrate God's saving love. As a sign of gratitude for your great sacrifice, we honor this cross.
>
> *Sing or say together:*
>
> We proclaim your Death, O Lord, and profess your Resurrection until you come again.

Family Activity

During the Triduum your family can make sacrifices to help bring the hope of salvation to those in need. Eat a light dinner at home one evening, and give the money you save to a needy family, or, instead of going to the movies, visit a convalescent hospital or an elderly family member in need of cheer. Be sure to make the decision as a family.

The Suffering Servant

Therefore the Easter Triduum of the passion and resurrection of Christ is the culmination of the entire liturgical year.

General Norms for the Liturgical Year and the Calendar, 18

Catechist Formation

The Easter Triduum begins with the Mass of the Lord's Supper on the evening of Holy Thursday and ends with evening prayer on Easter Sunday. The high point of the Triduum is the Easter Vigil. In this celebration, which always occurs during the night before Easter Sunday, the Church awaits the Resurrection and celebrates the Sacraments of Initiation with those who have been preparing as catechumens.

The Good Friday liturgy recalls the Passion and death of Christ. The Liturgy of the Word proclaims the story of Jesus' suffering and death. Then those gathered intercede for the Church and for the world. The second part of the liturgy offers Christians an opportunity to venerate the cross. Finally, the Church shares the Bread and Wine that were consecrated on Holy Thursday.

Without the eyes of faith, the cross would signify only death and destruction. Christians venerate the cross because they have come to see that Christ's willing sacrifice has transformed an instrument of death into a vehicle of unending life. From that cross Jesus handed himself over to the Father and poured out his Spirit on our behalf. Therefore, the proper attitude to have on Good Friday is gratitude.

Reflect **What are the images and thoughts that come to mind when you reflect on the cross of Christ?**

Environment

Materials:

Red cloth
Cross or crucifix
***Call to Faith* Grade 4 CD**

- Place the prayer table in the center of the worship space.

- Cover the table with a red tablecloth, and place the cross in the center.

- Use as little light as possible for this celebration.

- Dim the room lights, and do not light a candle.

Growing Spiritually

Your body is growing every day. Growing in spirit is equally important. Just as you feed your body, so must your soul be fed. The spiritual discipline of prayer strengthens you so that you can avoid sin and prepare for the joy of Easter.

❷ What habits of prayer do you already have?

❷ What is your plan for strengthening your life of prayer during this Lent?
Responses will vary.

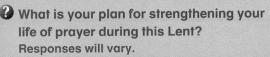

ACTIVITY

On Good Soil

On a separate piece of paper, draw a tree and its roots. Beneath the roots of the tree, list six ways you could try to deepen your life of prayer during Lent. Try one way during each of the six weeks of Lent.

27

Growing Spiritually

- Water the rosebush or other plant that you displayed to the group.
- Read aloud the first paragraph on page 27.
- ❷ **What habits of prayer do you already have? What is your plan for strengthening your life of prayer during this Lent?** Remind students of practices such as silent prayer, spontaneous prayer, memorized prayers, and meditation.

Activity

- Give students a few minutes to complete this activity, or assign it for homework.
- Encourage students to display their lists at home as reminders. After Easter, invite volunteers to share how well their suggestions worked.

OPTIONAL ACTIVITY

Growth in Christ Provide each student a pot, a seed, and soil. Have students plant their seeds and place the pots near a light source.

- Help students care for their seedlings during Lent.
- Remind students that as their plants are growing. so is their relationship with Christ.

Multiple Intelligence: Naturalist

LOVE AND SERVE

Lenten Service Catholic reformer Dorothy Day once said that even the poor deserve something beautiful.

- As a class, choose an area that is in need of sprucing up (in need of resurrection).
- Plant flowers, clean up garbage, or help any residents who could use assistance.

- If students have trouble with the second question, tell them to think of "good fruit" as "good deeds."

Kneel in Silence

- Ask students to kneel and pray silently for God's help in bearing good fruit during Lent.
- Leader's intercessions:

  Lord God, may our celebration of Lent turn our lives to god and the life that comes from believing in his Son, Jesus.

  Lord God, be with us as we pray together, and when we pray alone.

  Lord God, may our lives be lived in fruitful service to you and our neighbors.

- Lead the prayers and the responses.

Go Forth

- Lead students in the closing prayer.
- Invite students to respond with a resounding "Thanks be to God!"

Dialogue

Why does Jesus say that it is better to pray in secret?

How can prayer help you to yield "good fruit"?

Kneel in Silence

Quietly ask God to strengthen you to turn toward his love and to be faithful to the gospel.

Prayer of the Faithful

Leader: God does not desire our death but rather that we should turn from our sins and have life. Let us pray that we may sin no more and so bear good fruit.

Respond to each prayer with these words.

All: **Lord, hear our prayer.**

Go Forth!

Leader: Lord, may our Lenten prayer strengthen us so that we may bear good fruit and be good news.

All: **Thanks be to God.**

RITUAL

Silence   Prayer is often thought of as speaking with God. Silence is also important in prayer, however.

- Silence helps the person praying focus attention on God.
- Listening is a vital part of any conversation. Silence during prayer is an opportunity to listen for the voice of God.

LITURGY LINK

Liturgical Colors   The color purple is used during the season of Lent in the spirit of repentance.

- The stark environment of the church at Lent reminds God's people of their sinfulness and brokenness. It is a reminder that without Christ's death and resurrection, God's people could not be saved.

Celebrate Lent

Gather

Sing together.

O Lord, hear my prayer,
   O Lord, hear my prayer:
when I call answer me.
O Lord, hear my prayer,
   O Lord, hear my prayer,
Come and listen to me.

"O Lord, Hear My Prayer" © 1982, Les Presses de Taizé,
GIA Publications, Inc., agent

Pray the Sign of the Cross together.

Leader: Oh Lord, open my lips.

All: **That my mouth shall proclaim your praise.**

Leader: Let us pray.

Raise your hands as the leader prays.

All: **Amen.**

Listen to God's Word

Reader: A reading from the Holy Gospel according to Matthew.

Read Matthew 6:5–8.
The Gospel of the Lord.

All: **Praise to you, Lord Jesus Christ.**

25

Celebrate Lent

Gather

- Practice the hymn before beginning the service. Use *Call to Faith* Grade 4 CD.
- Call students to worship with a tap of a drum or soft music.
- Lead students through the Introductory Rite.
- Invite students to raise their hands in the *orans* posture as you pray.
- Leader's prayer: **God, our Father, during the Season of Lent, grant us the grace to turn away from sin and be faithful to the gospel.**

Listen to God's Word

- Have students stand as you proclaim the Gospel.
- Then have students sit in a circle for discussion.

PRAYER

The Body and Prayer   The *orans* position is suggested for the opening prayer of the celebration. Simply stand with hands open and palms facing upwards.

- This posture suggests praise, pleading, and vulnerability.
- It is often used by the assembly during the liturgy of the Eucharist.

LECTIONARY LINK

Vine and Branches   The reading for the celebration is found in the lectionary for the fifth and sixth Sundays of Easter, respectively, in cycle B.

- Vines and branches are multi-layered symbols. In the Scriptures, Israel, divine Wisdom, and the Son of Man are depicted as vines. Jesus' followers are the branches.

An Unselfish Spirit

- Bring in a plant that needs pruning; a miniature rosebush, for example.
- Ask students which branches need pruning and why.
- Discuss how pruning will help this plant grow.

Spiritual Discipline

- Ask volunteers to read aloud the text on page 24.
- Explain to students the meaning of fasting and almsgiving.
- Ask students what "spiritual growth" means. Possible response: a better relationship with God
- Point out that fasting and almsgiving are forms of sacrifice. Discuss how sacrifice helps a person grow and change.
- ❷ **What are some things you can prune away to grow as a follower of Jesus?** Students' responses may include bad habits, distractions during prayer, or unloving thoughts and actions.

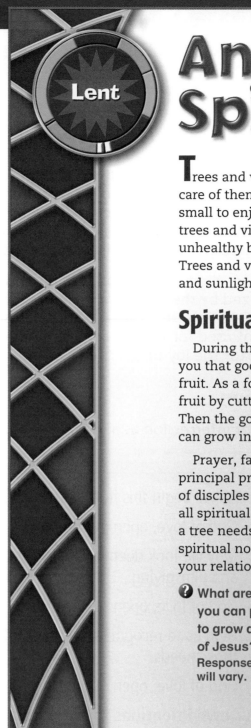

Lent

An Unselfish Spirit

Trees and vines can grow wild when no one takes care of them. They produce sour fruit or fruit too small to enjoy. That is why it is important to prune trees and vines. *Pruning* means cutting off dead and unhealthy branches so that the best fruit can grow. Trees and vines also require plenty of soil, water, and sunlight.

Spiritual Discipline

During the Season of Lent, the Church reminds you that good pruning is needed to produce good fruit. As a follower of Jesus, you can produce good fruit by cutting away bad habits and selfishness. Then the good fruit of love, sharing, and forgiveness can grow in you.

Prayer, fasting, and almsgiving are the three principal practices of Lent. These are the practices of disciples of Jesus. Prayer is the foundation for all spiritual discipline. It is like the soil a tree needs to grow. It gives you spiritual nourishment and deepens your relationship with God.

❷ **What are some things you can prune away to grow as a follower of Jesus?** Responses will vary.

24

SEASONAL RESOURCES

Video   You may find the following resource helpful.

- *The Angel's Lenten Season* (14 min). Twenty-Third Publications. The angel helps students understand the heart of the Lenten message: to become like Jesus.

CULTURAL CONNECTION

Penitential Acts   Mexican Catholics are traditionally very devoted to Lent.

- Most Mexican Catholics give up eating meat entirely during Lent.
- During Holy Week, Catholics in some villages re-enact Jesus' way of the cross. Many participate by walking on their knees.

Lent

By the time people have reached adulthood, most have had a life-altering experience, such as a new job, a marriage, or the birth of children. These responsibilities require people to change bad habits, to sacrifice, and to learn selflessness. Lent, which means *spring,* is also a time to change old ways in preparation for Easter. Prayer, fasting, and almsgiving are the three traditional "pillars" of Lent that help families grow in Christ.

The Church celebrates the forty days of Lent beginning with Ash Wednesday. Repentance, symbolized by the signing with ashes, is the spirit in which Lent begins. This repentant spirit is reflected in the color purple used for church vestments and in the stark environment used for liturgy. Lent reminds us of both our constant need for God and our hunger for the joy of the risen Christ.

Family Celebration

Pray these prayers of intercession as a mealtime or bedtime prayer.

> **Leader:** As we begin this holy season of Lent, be with us. We pray . . .
>
> **All:** God of love, open our hearts.
>
> **Leader:** May we look deeply at our lives, through prayer, fasting, and almsgiving.
>
> **All:** God of love, open our hearts.
>
> **Leader:** Help us to recognize the needs of others and respond to those needs.
>
> **All:** God of love, open our hearts.
>
> **Add your own intentions for your family.**

Family Activity

Pretzels can symbolize the importance of prayer and fasting during the season of Lent. Pretzels are made out of flour, water and salt and they are shaped in the form of arms crossed in prayer. As a family, bake pretzels for Lent. Before you put them in the oven, pray the following:

"Lord, we pray that these pretzels remind us that through prayer, fasting, and almsgiving we grow in Christ. Amen."

Pretzel Recipe

Fill large mixing bowl with $1\frac{1}{2}$ cups warm water and dissolve 1-tablespoon of yeast into the water. Add 1-teaspoon salt and 1 teaspoon sugar. blend in 4 cups of flour. Knead dough until smooth. Roll small balls of dough into ropes and fold into a pretzel shape. Place on lightly greased cookie sheet. Bake at 425 degrees for 12–15 minutes. Makes approx. one dozen pretzels.

Lent

An Unselfish Spirit

For the Lenten liturgy disposes both catechumens and the faithful to celebrate the paschal mystery: catechumens, through the several stages of Christian initiation; the faithful, through reminders of their own baptism and through penitential practices.

General Norms for the Liturgical Year and the Calendar, 27

Catechist Formation

The season of Lent begins with Ash Wednesday and lasts for forty days until the Easter Triduum. Lent is a period of purification and enlightenment, and a time of penance. Through prayers and penitential practices, members of the Church acknowledge their complete dependence on the mercy and compassion of God.

In *John 12:24*, Jesus observes that unless a grain of wheat dies, it cannot bear fruit. Jesus was referring to his own death, but also to the life of discipleship. Dying to self is an important Christian practice, and Lent provides Christians an opportunity to make it a deeper part of their lives. Ashes symbolize the call to die to self; prayer, fasting, and almsgiving aid in the process.

Christians recognize that Jesus' suffering and death brought about reconciliation between God and humans. The faithful witness to this reconciliation by their willingness to participate in a life of sacrifice.

Reflect **What are the ways that dying to self brings life to you or to others?**

Environment

Materials:

Purple cloth
Willow branches
Broken pots
Cross (not a crucifix)
Container of water
***Call to Faith* Grade 4 CD**

• Drape the purple cloth on the table, and decorate it with a few of the branches, the broken pots, and the cross.

The Help of the Holy Spirit

Saint Paul knew his weakness, and prayed that the Holy Spirit would give him the gifts he needed to share the message of Jesus with others. You are called to do the same. Sometimes it will be easy, and sometimes it may be very difficult. But the Holy Spirit is always with you.

❷ In what ways can you lead others to know the good news of Jesus?
Responses will vary.

(ACTIVITY)

Words of Faith

Saint Paul's letters to the Christian communities he started encouraged them to increase their faith in Jesus and to live the gospel. Design a note card and write a message to another Christian. Remind him or her of the good news of Jesus.

23

The Help of the Holy Spirit

- Read aloud the paragraph at the top of page 23.
- ❷ In what ways can you lead others to know the good news of Jesus?
  Discuss the question with the class. List their responses on the board or on chart paper.
- Remind students of the saying that actions often speak louder than words.

Activity

- Invite a volunteer to read aloud the directions for the activity.
- Distribute art materials and have students design their note cards.
- Have each student write a note that encourages its recipient to live his or her faith.

OPTIONAL ACTIVITY

Student Letters   Pauline letters included the following: sender, addressee, greeting, thanksgiving, body, and final greeting. (See *Colossians 1:1–5, 15–18.*)

- Direct each student to write a letter to another student using the Pauline form.
- The letters content should tell something the student has learned about Saint Paul.

Multiple Intelligence: Verbal/Linguistic

LOVE AND SERVE

Christian Service   Encourage students to look for ways to bring Christ's message to others through service.

- Some ways to serve others include these: Stand up for students who are being teased; give money to someone who forgot his or her lunch; help someone carry books.

Signing of the Senses

- Tell students that they will now participate in a ritual of blessing that will strengthen them to change their hearts and follow Christ.

- Have each student come forward to be signed. Repeat the blessing for each student.

- When all students have been signed, continue with the leader's prayer.

Go Forth!

- Conclude with the closing blessing and response.

Signing of the Senses

Step forward one by one as the leader signs your eyes, lips, and hands with the cross of salvation. After each person is signed, say the following.

All: **Christ will be your strength! Learn to know and follow him!**

GIA Publications

After the signing of the senses, bow your head as the leader prays.

Leader: Lord Jesus, we place ourselves entirely under the sign of your cross, in the name of the Father, and of the Son, and of the Holy Spirit.

All: **Amen.**

Go Forth!

Leader: Let us go forth in the spirit of Saint Paul to bring the message of Jesus to all.

All: **Thanks be to God.**

22

RITUAL

The Senses and Faith The signing of the senses is often reserved for catechumens or those preparing for the Sacraments of Initiation.

- The senses enable people to experience the outside world and to interact with it.

- Making the sign of the cross over each of the senses is a prayer that consecrates the whole person to God.

LITURGY LINK

Environment The liturgical color for the feast of the Conversion of Saint Paul is green, since this feast occurs in Ordinary Time.

- The light used in this celebration symbolizes the blinding light of Christ.

- Saint Paul experienced blindness, which symbolized that before his conversion he could not see the truth of the faith.

Celebrate Paul

Gather

Pray the Sign of the Cross together.

Leader: Our help is in the name of the Lord.

All: **Who made heaven and earth.**

 Sing together the refrain.

All grownups, all children,
all mothers, all fathers
Are sisters and brothers in the fam'ly of God.

"All Grownups, All Children" © 1997, GIA Publications, Inc.

Leader: Let us pray.

Bow your heads as the leader prays.

All: **Amen.**

Listen to God's Word

Reader: A reading from the Acts of the Apostles.

Read Acts 9:19b–22.
The word of the Lord.

All: **Thanks be to God.**

Dialogue

How did Paul change as a result of meeting the Risen Christ?

What gifts did Saint Paul bring to the Church?

21

Celebrate Paul

Gather

- Call students to worship by dimming the lights. Light a candle or lamp.
- Lead students in the greeting and response, and then in singing the hymn. Use the *Call to Faith* Grade 4 CD, track 4.
- Leader's prayer: **Father of all, give us the strength to change our hearts and to follow your Son, Jesus. May we help bring his good news to the world.**

Listen to God's Word

- Have students sit, and then proclaim the reading. Pause for a moment of silence.
- Invite students to reflect on and discuss the dialogue questions.
- Point out that Paul's change of heart showed in how he acted toward others.
- Remind students that all people can change their hearts to be better followers of Jesus and that all people can use their gifts to help the Church spread Jesus' message.

 PRAYER

Prayer Posture Expressing inward sentiment through an outward action helps gives expression to faith. During the Introductory Rite, students are asked to bow their heads.

- Bowing one's head during prayer is an ancient symbol of reverence for God and indicates acceptance of God's will.

 LECTIONARY LINK

Paul's Conversion The reading for the celebration, the second of three accounts of Paul's conversion, is used in the lectionary for this feast.

- An Apostle is one who witnessed the Risen Christ. Paul, through his conversion, witnessed the risen Christ and gave witness to Christ before all.

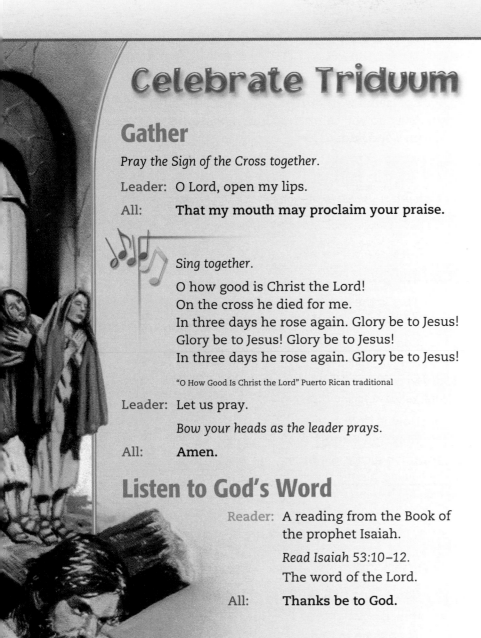

Celebrate Triduum

Gather

Pray the Sign of the Cross together.

Leader: O Lord, open my lips.

All: **That my mouth may proclaim your praise.**

Sing together.

O how good is Christ the Lord!
On the cross he died for me.
In three days he rose again. Glory be to Jesus!
Glory be to Jesus! Glory be to Jesus!
In three days he rose again. Glory be to Jesus!

"O How Good Is Christ the Lord" Puerto Rican traditional

Leader: Let us pray.

Bow your heads as the leader prays.

All: **Amen.**

Listen to God's Word

Reader: A reading from the Book of the prophet Isaiah.

Read Isaiah 53:10–12.
The word of the Lord.

All: **Thanks be to God.**

Celebrate Triduum

Gather

- Practice the hymn before beginning the celebration.
- Tell students that they will have the opportunity to venerate, or show respect for, the cross.
- Call students to worship with a moment of silence.
- Lead students in prayer and song using the *Call to Faith* Grade 4 CD, track 6.
- Leader's prayer: **Gracious Father, we thank you for the gift of your Son, Jesus. May we always remember the life-giving sacrifice he made for us all.**

Listen to God's Word

- Ask students to gather around the cross in the center of the worship space. Have them remain standing for the reading.

PRAYER

Christian Unity The Introductory Rites are symbols of God's work in his people.

- The Introductory Rites anticipate the fulfillment of God's kingdom, when there shall be no injustice or divisions.
- As the members of the assembly gather, they become one in Christ. It is no different in student celebrations.

LECTIONARY LINK

Suffering Service The reading for this lesson is found in the lectionary during the celebration of Good Friday.

- The reading unfolds a spirituality of suffering in which pain is redemptive.
- Jesus, the suffering servant, is the fulfillment of the Scripture. He accepted suffering for all people and redeems them through the cross.

- Make sure that students understand the connection between Isaiah's words and Christ's sacrifice.
- Pray the prayers.
- Invite students to kneel in silent prayer after each prayer is prayed. Have them stand again for the next prayer.

Jesus, thank you for loving us, even to the point of the cross. Help us to love others, even when it becomes difficult to do.

Lord Jesus, give us true vision to see those who are suffering around us and to comfort them.

Father, help us to celebrate the Triduum this year with grateful hearts for what Jesus did for us on the cross.

Honor the Cross

- Demonstrate how students are to reverence the cross and then invite them to come forward individually.
- When all have reverenced the cross, pause for silent reflection.

Go Forth!

- Give the parting blessing.
- Instruct students to return in silence to their places.

Dialogue

The Book of Isaiah was written long before the birth of Jesus. Why do you think the Church reads this passage on Good Friday?

Prayer of the Faithful

After each prayer, kneel for a moment in silent prayer, then stand as the leader prays.

Honor the Cross

Leader: This is the wood of the cross, on which hung the Savior of the world.

All: **Come. Let us worship.**

Stand and say the following acclamation three times, bowing deeply first to the left, then to the right, then to the center, always facing the cross.

All: **Holy is God!**
          Holy and Strong!

Step forward in silence, one by one, and reverence the cross by bowing, kissing the cross, or offering some other sign of reverence.

Go Forth!

Leader: Confessing that Jesus is Lord to the glory of God, go forth in the peace of Christ.

All: **Thanks be to God.**

Depart in silence.

RITUAL

Venerate the Cross   The practice of unveiling and venerating the Cross on Good Friday began in the Church of Jerusalem.

- Three times during the liturgy, while the cross is unveiled, the choir sings "Behold the Wood of the Cross" and the assembly responds with "Come let us adore."

LITURGY LINK

Liturgical Colors   Black was once used as the liturgical color for Good Friday. Black symbolized the absence of light and the attitude of mourning.

- Today, red vestments are usually worn on Good Friday. Red symbolizes suffering and the blood of Jesus.

New Life

The passage from the Book of Isaiah was written long before Jesus was born. Isaiah told the people that someday one of God's servants would suffer for the sins of many. Jesus suffered and died to free all people from sin and to bring them back to God's friendship. That is why the Church calls Jesus the Suffering Servant.

❷ **What are some ways you can imitate the love of Jesus in word and action?** Responses will vary.

(ACTIVITY)

A Flower Cross

Make flower petals out of art paper or colored tissue. Write on the flower petals some act of kindness or sacrifice that you will do during the Triduum. Glue the flowers onto a cardboard cross. Let your flower-cross be a reminder of your faith that the way of the cross leads to life.

31

New Life

- Have students continue sitting silently for a few moments following the liturgy.
- Ask a volunteer to read aloud the first paragraph on page 31.
- ❷ **What are some ways you can imitate the love of Jesus in word and action?** Praise students for practical suggestions and encourage them to try a different suggestion every day for a week.

Activity

- Read the directions aloud, and distribute art paper or colored tissue.
- Give students a few minutes to write acts of kindness or sacrifices on their flower petals.
- Direct students to glue their petals on a cardboard cross that you will display for the duration of the Easter season.

OPTIONAL ACTIVITY

Bulletin Board As a class, make a Triduum themed bulletin board.

- Have each student write and illustrate a thank you card to Jesus in gratitude for the new life made possible by his suffering and death.
- Display the cards on the bulletin board.

Multiple Intelligence: Visual/Spatial

💟 LOVE AND SERVE

Sacrificial Love Jesus showed us the joy that comes when we sacrifice for others. Students can share this joy.

- Have students create Easter cards and distribute them at a convalescent center or retirement community during Holy Week.
- Encourage students to sacrifice their time to make extra cards.

Easter

Light of the World

The fifty days from Easter Sunday to Pentecost are celebrated in joyful exultation as one feast day, or better as one "great Sunday."

General Norms for the Liturgical Year and the Calendar, 22

Catechist Formation

For those who have been baptized, the Easter season is known as the period of *mystagogy* (interpretation of mystery). It is a time for the newly baptized to reflect on their experience of the sacraments and on their participation in the life of the Church.

During each Mass of the Easter season, the Paschal candle burns brightly in a central place in the sanctuary. The words of the Easter Proclamation, or *Exsultet,* which was sung during the Easter Vigil, convey the significance of this candle. This is the light that pierces through the darkness of sin and evil. This is the light that shines forth like the dawn of Christ's Resurrection. This light is Christ himself.

Whenever Christians are baptized, the Paschal candle is also lit. The newly baptized receive baptismal candles that are lit from the Paschal candle. Those who are baptized thus become children of the light in Christ. The Church prays that this light of Christ will be preserved by faith and burn brightly all the days of these new Christians' lives.

Reflect **How does the light of Christ help you see your life in a new or different way?**

Easter

Imagine the joy that the followers of Christ felt when they learned that Jesus was alive! On Easter morning, the faithful rejoice, just as the first followers of Christ did. They celebrate as the People of God, who have received the precious gift of salvation.

The celebration of the Easter season includes the fifty days following the Triduum. The liturgies reflect the joy of salvation. The Alleluia is sung often. The Gospels proclaim the Easter event and celebrate what God did in Jesus. In the sprinkling rite, all renew their baptismal commitments. The Church celebrates as an Easter people.

The new life of spring breaks through the death of winter. Jesus' Resurrection is a sign of new life, too; it is God's triumph over death. Jesus turned the darkness of sin into the light of love. Your family, fueled by the joy of the Resurrection, can reflect Christ's light in their everyday actions.

Family Celebration

The Alleluia is a prayer of praise and thanksgiving. Celebrate with joy in the Resurrection at your evening meal. Encourage your child to lead you. Turn off all lights, and then light a candle to symbolize the light of Christ.

> **Leader:** Jesus, we praise you for your Easter victory over the darkness of sin and death.
>
> **All:** Alleluia!
>
> **Leader:** Increase our joy during these fifty days of Easter, and transform us by the light of your Resurrection.
>
> **All:** Alleluia!

Family Activity

Light is a symbol of Christ. Create an Easter candle for your home. Obtain a large white candle, about three to four inches in diameter. Use construction paper, markers, and other materials to create symbols of the Resurrection, such as a cross made of flowers, and symbols of light or baptismal water. Use pushpins or needles to attach these symbols to the candle. Each evening during Easter, light the candle as a part of mealtime or bedtime prayers. Let it be a symbol of Christ's triumph over death and sin in your home.

Light of the World

- Turn off the lights, and then light a candle or a single lamp.
- After a moment of silence, ask students to describe the light. What effect does it have on the room?
- Write students' responses on the board or on chart paper.
- Ask students to name some of the things that light can do. Possible responses: brighten, warm, show the way, help plants grow
- Have volunteers read aloud the first two paragraphs.

Light in the Darkness

- Read aloud the third and fourth paragraphs.
- Invite students to name the signs of joy that can be seen and heard during the Easter season. the Alleluia, flowers and plants, white cloth
- ❷ **What are some ways Jesus is light for you?** Responses may include that Jesus brings happiness, shows the way, or drives out darkness.

Easter

Light of the World

On Easter the Church celebrates Jesus' Resurrection. When Jesus was raised from the dead on the third day, he conquered the power of sin and death. The Church celebrates Easter for fifty days from Easter Sunday to Pentecost.

The Easter season is one of joy and gladness. Alleluias are sung once again. Flowers and plants fill the churches, signs of the new life Christ brings. Choirs sing Glory to God! and the altar is draped in white cloth. All are signs of the light that Jesus brings into the world.

Light in the Darkness

In the northern hemisphere, Easter comes at a time when the darkness of winter has given way to spring. Leaves appear on trees and flowers blossom. Spring is a season of new life.

Jesus' Resurrection is a sign of the new life that bursts forth in the bright light of the sun. Jesus triumphed over the selfishness that leads people away from God. He turned the darkness of sin into the light of love. That is why Jesus is called the Light of the World.

❷ **What are some ways Jesus is light for you?** Responses will vary.

32

 SEASONAL RESOURCES

Book You may find the following resource helpful.

- *Journey into Joy: Stations of the Resurrection.* Andrew Walker (Paulist Press). This is a book of reflections on some of the best-known religious art that portrays the events surrounding the Resurrection.

CULTURAL CONNECTION

An Easter Meeting The Filipino culture has an Easter celebration called *salubong*.

- At dawn on Easter, two processions—one led by the icon of the Risen Christ and the other led by an image of the Sorrowful Mother—journey on church grounds from opposite directions.
- The processions converge. Applause and music announce the happy meeting of Mary and her son.

Celebrate Easter

Gather

Pray the Sign of the Cross together.

Leader: Light and peace in Jesus Christ our Lord. Alleluia.

All: **Thanks be to God, alleluia.**

Reader: Christ is our light in the darkness!

All: **Alleluia, alleluia, alleluia.**

Reader: Christ shows us the path of love and light!

All: **Alleluia, alleluia, alleluia.**

Reader: Christ is the Way, the Truth, and the Life!

All: **Alleluia, alleluia, alleluia.**

Leader: Let us pray.

Bow your heads as the leader prays.

All: **Amen, Alleluia.**

Listen to God's Word

Reader: A reading from the Holy Gospel according to Matthew.

Read Matthew 28:1–10.
The Gospel of the Lord.

All: **Praise to you, Lord Jesus Christ.**

Dialogue

What was your first thought as you heard this gospel?

What did Jesus tell the women?

33

Celebrate Easter

Gather

- Practice the song "Easter Alleluia" before beginning the liturgy.
- Call students to worship with a moment of silence.
- Lead students through the parts of the Introductory Rite.
- Leader's prayer: **God, our Father, Jesus rose victorious over the darkness of sin. May we live in the light of Easter each day of our lives.**

Listen to God's Word

- Have students stand as you proclaim the Gospel.
- Ask students to imagine walking down the street and meeting a friend who has just died. Help students understand the feelings that the women in the Gospel must have had.
- Invite students to reflect on and discuss the dialogue questions.
- Point out that Jesus calls all of his followers to spread the good news.

PRAYER

Praise God! The word *alleluia* comes from the Hebrew verb *hallel,* "to praise," and from *Yah,* a shortened form of "Yahweh." Therefore, *alleluia* means "Praise Yahweh!"

- The Alleluia is a prayer of community rejoicing in the greatness of God.
- The body can aid in creating a spirit of prayer and praise. Invite students to sing the Alleluia with arms raised.

LECTIONARY LINK

Fear and Belief The Gospel used for the students' celebration is taken from the Gospel for the Easter Vigil, cycle A.

- The women found an empty tomb. They did not yet understand what Jesus had taught about his death.
- The good news that greeted the women was frightening and confusing, yet they went forth to share the news.

Blessing with Holy Water

- Model bowing before the Paschal candle and making the Sign of the Cross with holy water.
- Guide students one by one through the ritual action.
- Lead students in song. Use the *Call to Faith* Grade 4 CD, track 7.
- Leader's prayer: **Jesus, Light of the World, continue to help and guide us throughout our lives. May we always give you praise and honor for the gifts of light and new life.**

Go Forth!

- Lead the Go Forth! Prayer.
- Elicit a joyful "Alleluia" from the students with a hand gesture.

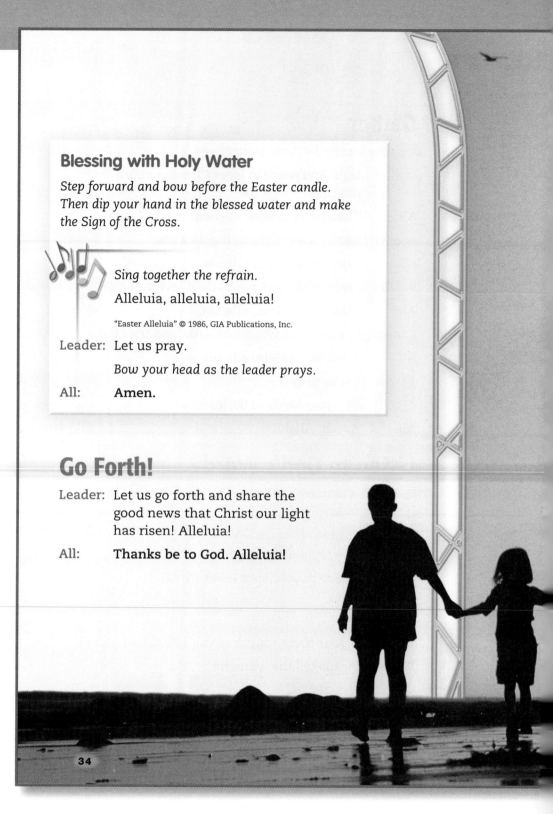

Blessing with Holy Water

Step forward and bow before the Easter candle. Then dip your hand in the blessed water and make the Sign of the Cross.

Sing together the refrain.

Alleluia, alleluia, alleluia!

"Easter Alleluia" © 1986, GIA Publications, Inc.

Leader: Let us pray.

Bow your head as the leader prays.

All: **Amen.**

Go Forth!

Leader: Let us go forth and share the good news that Christ our light has risen! Alleluia!

All: **Thanks be to God. Alleluia!**

34

RITUAL

Holy Water   The significance of holy water is directly linked to the water of Baptism.

- The use of holy water in rituals such as the Sign of the Cross or a sprinkling rite is meant to recall Baptism.
- During the Easter Season, the assembly renews baptismal vows and is sprinkled with holy water.

LITURGY LINK

Easter Symbols   White is a symbol of light, of rejoicing, and of the Resurrection. It is the color used during the Easter season. Water is also a symbol of the Resurrection and of new life.

- In the waters of Baptism, one dies to sin and is resurrected into a new life in Christ. Therefore, water is an appropriate and significant Easter symbol.

Let Your Light Shine

Did you ever notice that outside on a dark night, away from the lights of the city, the stars seem brighter? In a similar way, the light of Christ brightens the darkness of the world. In the midst of sadness and violence, Christ's light shines even more brightly. In the midst of loneliness or rejection, the light of Christ's love is there to warm the heart that is hurting.

What are some things you can do to help others to know the light of Christ's love?
Responses will vary.

ACTIVITY

The Light of the World

On poster board, make a Christ candle. Decorate your candle with symbols of Jesus as the Light of the World. Draw seven rays of light radiating from the candle flame. On the rays write things you and your family can do each week during the Easter season to bring Christ's light into your neighborhood and community. Share your ideas with your family.

35

Let Your Light Shine

- Read aloud the paragraph on page 35.

- Recall with students the discussion of light they had before the celebration. Remind them that Jesus is Light in the darkness of sin, confusion, and death.

❷ What are some things you can do to help others to know the light of Christ's love? Discuss concrete ways in which students can bring the light of Christ to others.

Activity

- Read aloud the directions for the activity.
- Assign this project for homework.
- Have students bring in their posters to share with the class. Ask each student to share at least one thing that his or her family has done or will do to bring Christ's light to the world.

OPTIONAL ACTIVITY

Take Action   Draw an Easter candle with a large flame on chart paper. Cut small flame shapes from red and yellow paper.

- Invite students to write on the small flames ways they have shared the light of Christ. Have students glue these to the large flame on the poster.
- Try to fill the large flame by the end of the Easter season.

Multiple Intelligence: Visual/Spatial

 ## LOVE AND SERVE

Justice and Light   Justice begins on the playground. Challenge students to be light for others who face rejection or who are the objects of teasing.

- For example, a child who is pushed around or ignored needs a good friend.
- Fourth graders can be peacemakers who befriend those who are alienated.

Pentecost

The Power of the Holy Spirit

The weekdays after the Ascension until the Saturday before Pentecost inclusive are a preparation for the coming of the Holy Spirit.

General Norms for the Liturgical Year and the Calendar, 26

Environment

Materials:

Red tablecloth
Symbol of the Holy Spirit
Bible
Cross, candle, and bowl
    of water
Call to Faith Grade 4 CD

- Before class, encourage students to bring food and clothing as gifts to be offered in the celebration.

- Cover the prayer table with the red cloth, and place the cross, candle, symbol, and bowl of water on it.

- Open the Bible, and place it on the table.

- Leave room around the table for students' gifts.

Catechist Formation

Although Pentecost marks the end of the Easter Season, for the Church it signals a new beginning in carrying out the mission of Christ in the world. At Pentecost we celebrate the outpouring of the Holy Spirit that takes root in the hearts of believers. The readings for Pentecost recall how the first disciples were transformed from fearful self-doubters to courageous missionaries.

The *Lectionary of the Roman Missal* includes a sequence, or poem, for the Feast of Pentecost. Entitled *Veni, Sancte Spiritus* (Come, Holy Spirit), this ancient hymn recalls ways in which the Church has experienced the gift of the Holy Spirit. Among these are the Holy Spirit as "father of the poor," "the soul's most welcome guest," and "most blessed light divine."

The Holy Spirit empowers the faithful. The power given, however, is not earthly or political power. The New Testament shows how he empowered members of the early Christian community to serve others and to carry the good news of Christ to the ends of the earth.

Reflect   **In what unique ways has God blessed you with the power of the Holy Spirit?**

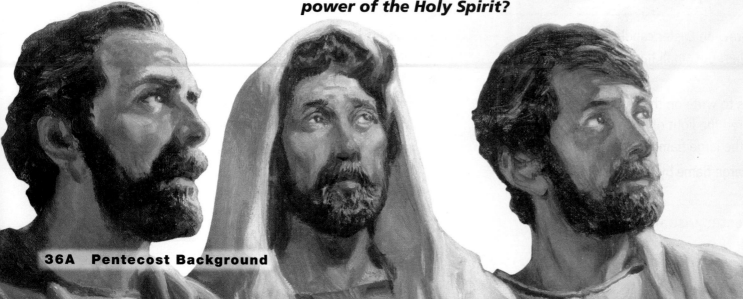

Pentecost

Feeling abandoned and afraid, the Apostles had locked themselves in a hidden room when suddenly the Spirit of Christ appeared and breathed new life into them. The Apostles were inflamed with new courage and sent forth to continue Christ's saving work. Catholics celebrate this day as the birthday of the Church, or Pentecost, on the seventh Sunday after Easter.

The liturgical color for this celebration is red, which symbolizes the fire of Pentecost and the power of the Holy Spirit. In scripture readings, music, and gestures, the Church celebrates God's empowering actions through the gifts of the Holy Spirit. Pentecost Sunday is an uplifting celebration of God's ongoing work in the world.

Through the gifts of the Holy Spirit, Catholics are given wisdom and strength to carry out the Church's mission. Sent forth from the celebration of Pentecost, your family can participate in the work of the Spirit.

Family Celebration

Celebrate Pentecost at home. Say this prayer before your family Pentecost meal.

> **Leader:** Come, Holy Spirit, fill the hearts of your faithful.
>
> **All:** And kindle in them the fire of your love.
>
> **Leader:** Send forth your Spirit and they shall be created.
>
> **All:** And you will renew the face of the earth.
>
> *Let us pray*
>
> **Leader:** Lord, by the light of the Holy Spirit you have taught the hearts of your faithful. In the same Spirit help us to relish what is right and always rejoice in your consolation. We ask this through Christ our Lord.
>
> **All:** Amen.

Family Activity

Pentecost is called the birthday of the Church because the Apostles were empowered by the Holy Spirit to go forth and spread the good news. One way that your family can celebrate the birthday of the Church is to bake a birthday cake. Decorate the cake with seven candles to represent the seven gifts of the Holy Spirit. Light the candles and sing Happy Birthday to the Church. While eating the cake, discuss how your family can go forth and spread the good news.

The Power of the Holy Spirit

- Point out the liturgical color for the feast of Pentecost in the prayer center.

- Ask students to explain what red symbolizes, and record their answers on the board or on chart paper.

- Ask a volunteer to read aloud the first paragraph.

Pentecost Today

- Have two volunteers read aloud the second and third paragraph.

- Remind students that the beginning of the Church is also known as the birthday of the Church.

- Invite students to share memories of birthday parties they have attended. Point out the aspects of the parties that feature gathering as a group, celebrating, and sharing joy.

❷ **How is the Holy Spirit active in the world today?** Help students understand that the Holy Spirit is active in Church celebrations and when Christians share the love of Jesus.

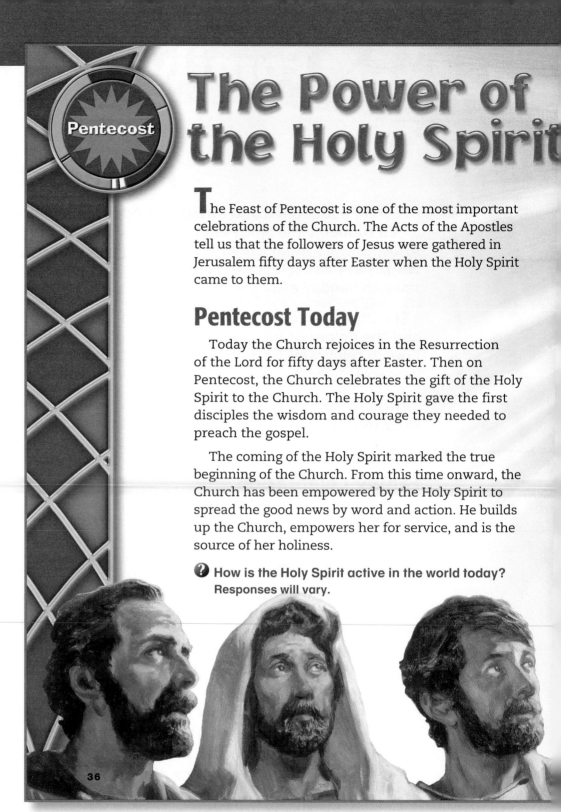

Pentecost

The Power of the Holy Spirit

The Feast of Pentecost is one of the most important celebrations of the Church. The Acts of the Apostles tell us that the followers of Jesus were gathered in Jerusalem fifty days after Easter when the Holy Spirit came to them.

Pentecost Today

Today the Church rejoices in the Resurrection of the Lord for fifty days after Easter. Then on Pentecost, the Church celebrates the gift of the Holy Spirit to the Church. The Holy Spirit gave the first disciples the wisdom and courage they needed to preach the gospel.

The coming of the Holy Spirit marked the true beginning of the Church. From this time onward, the Church has been empowered by the Holy Spirit to spread the good news by word and action. He builds up the Church, empowers her for service, and is the source of her holiness.

❷ **How is the Holy Spirit active in the world today?**
Responses will vary.

36

 SEASONAL RESOURCES

Book   You may find this resource helpful.

- *Spirit With Us: Faith Stories for Young Children.* Judith Dunlap and Mary Cummins Wlodarski (St. Anthony Messenger Press). This is a collection of stories that help children understand how the Spirit has been present in the Church over time.

 CULTURAL CONNECTION

Symbols of Fire   Many Italian Catholics have a custom of scattering rose petals from the ceiling of the church to recall the miracle of the tongues of fire that descended upon the Apostles on Pentecost.

- In Sicily, Pentecost is called *Pascha rosatum*.
- The name comes from the red vestments worn on the Solemnity of Pentecost.

Celebrate Pentecost

Gather

Pray the Sign of the Cross together.

Leader: Light and peace in Jesus Christ our Lord, alleluia.

All: **Thanks be to God, alleluia.**

Sing together.

If you believe and I believe,
And we together pray,
The Holy Spirit must come down
And set God's people free,
And set God's people free,
And set God's people free;
The Holy Spirit must come down
And set God's people free.

"If You Believe and I Believe" © 1991, GIA Publications, Inc.

Leader: Let us pray.

Bow your heads as the leader prays.

All: **Amen.**

Listen to God's Word

Reader: A reading from the Acts of the Apostles.

Read Acts 2:1–11.
The Word of the Lord.

All: **Thanks be to God.**

37

Celebrate Pentecost

Gather

- Call students to worship with a moment of silence.
- Invite students to prayer and await their response.
- Lead students in song using the *Call to Faith* Grade 4 CD, track 8.
- Leader's prayer: **God our Father, you have given us new birth in Baptism. Strengthen us with your Holy Spirit, and fill us with your light.**

Listen to God's Word

- Have students stand as you proclaim the scripture verses.
- Pause briefly for reflection.

 PRAYER

Music and Song The voice is the primary instrument in liturgical worship. Music, too, expresses emotions and communicates a message.

- Music allows worshipers a window into the sacred.
- Though not indispensable to liturgy, music enhances one's participation in worship.

 LECTIONARY LINK

Fire and Spirit The reading for the students' celebration is the first reading for Pentecost Sunday in all three cycles.

- God appeared as fire when he made the covenant with Moses and the people.
- In *Acts 2:1–11,* the Spirit—as fire—empowers the Apostles to announce the new covenant.

- Invite students to reflect on and discuss the dialogue questions.
- Re-read parts of the scripture reading, if necessary, to help students uncover the three things that happened.

Offering of Gifts

- Lead students in procession and song as they bring their gifts to the prayer table.
- After all students have placed their gifts, lead the prayers.

Go Forth!

- Lead the concluding prayer. Show through your voice the importance of going forth in love and service, to glorify the Lord.
- After students respond, have them return to their seats.

Dialogue

What are three things that happened to the disciples because of the coming of the Holy Spirit?

How can the Holy Spirit strengthen you?

Offering of Gifts

Sing together, "If You Believe and I Believe." As you sing, come forward in procession and place gifts for the poor at the base of the prayer table.

Prayer of the Faithful

Leader: Let us pray for the Church and the world, that all will be open to the power of the Holy Spirit.

Respond to each prayer with these words.

All: **Send us your Spirit, O Lord.**

Go Forth!

Leader: May God bless us and give us the gifts of the Holy Spirit forever. And let us go forth in love and service to all God's people, alleluia.

All: **Thanks be to God, alleluia!**

38

RITUAL

Symbolic Movement Processions have been used throughout Church history to symbolize that the Christian life is a communal journey toward God.

- The symbolic movement of a procession recalls the Exodus and the call of all Christians to journey together in the footsteps of Christ.

LITURGY LINK

Liturgical Colors The liturgical color for the celebration of Pentecost is red, symbolizing the fire of the Holy Spirit.

- The dove, fire, and wind are also symbols of the Holy Spirit.
- A drum or a trumpet is sometimes used to represent the driving wind the Apostles experienced with the coming of the Holy Spirit.

Gifts of the Holy Spirit

Many stories in the Acts of the Apostles tell how the Holy Spirit guided the followers of Jesus to spread the Good News of Jesus. The disciples told all who would listen about the life of Jesus and his commandment of love. But they lived the way of Jesus as well. You are called to do the same today.

At Baptism you received the gifts of the Holy Spirit—wisdom, understanding, right judgment, courage, knowledge, reverence, and fear of the Lord. In Confirmation you will be strengthened with these gifts.

❷ When has the Holy Spirit helped you to use one of these gifts? Responses will vary.

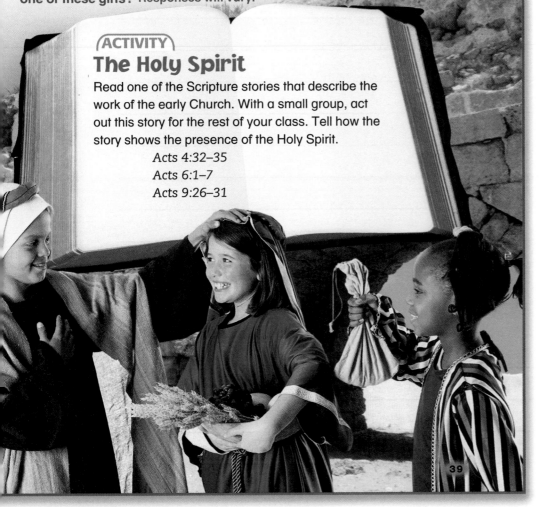

(ACTIVITY)
The Holy Spirit

Read one of the Scripture stories that describe the work of the early Church. With a small group, act out this story for the rest of your class. Tell how the story shows the presence of the Holy Spirit.

Acts 4:32–35

Acts 6:1–7

Acts 9:26–31

39

Gifts of the Holy Spirit

- Invite volunteers to read aloud the first two paragraphs on page 39.

❷ When has the Holy Spirit helped you to use one of these gifts? You may need to give an example from your own life to start the discussion.

Activity

- Organize students in three groups, and assign each group one of the readings.
- Read aloud the directions, and then give a Bible to each group.
- As a class, discuss each group's answers.

OPTIONAL ACTIVITY

Birthday Party   Pentecost is the birthday of the Church. Celebrate with a birthday cake.

- Bring in a cake with white frosting. Read aloud *Acts 2:1–11*.
- Place twelve candles on the cake for the tongues of fire. Add seven pieces of red fruit or candy for the gifts of the Spirit.

Multiple Intelligence: Visual/Spatial

LOVE AND SERVE

Spiritual Gifts   Students may need the Gifts of the Holy Spirit when they hear derogatory remarks about other cultures and customs.

- Students use knowledge to recognize that racist jokes or belittling remarks are hurtful.
- Urge them to use the gift of courage to confront those who discriminate.

Catechist's Notes

_____

_____

_____

_____

_____

_____

_____

_____

_____

_____

_____

_____

_____

_____

_____

_____

_____

_____

Unit 1
Revelation

In this unit you will...

learn that God communicates a loving plan for all of creation. We learn of this in Scripture and Tradition. God stays true and faithful to his promises. Through his covenants, God keeps telling and showing people that he will be faithful, even though we sin. He helps us understand how to be faithful to him. Through the Ten Commandments, God revealed how he wants all of his children to live.

 **Chapter 1**
 **Chapter 2**
 **Chapter 3**

 What do you think you will learn in this unit about God's covenant?

40

© Our Sunday Visitor Curriculum Division

UNIT 1 OPENER

Preview Unit Theme

Tell students that Unit 1 is about Revelation.

- Read aloud the text on page 40 of the student edition. Tell students they will learn more about these things in the next three chapters.

- Ask students what they think God's plan for creation is.

- Invite volunteers to share what they know of the Ten Commandments.

Overview

Faith Focus

- God's care of the world and plan for all creation is providence. (CCC 302–308)
- You learn about God in Scripture and the Tradition of the Church. (CCC 80–83)

Catechism Connection

The *Catechism* explains that God fully reveals his plan in his Son, Jesus Christ. *(CCC 50)*

NDC Link

The *Directory* states that God revealed himself to us fully by sending his own Son. It is the task of catechesis to proclaim the person and message of Jesus to every person and to all nations. (See *NDC*, 16A–B.)

Resources

BOOK
*In His Light.** Anderson, William. Our Sunday Visitor Curriculum Division. "In Search of God." Explicates sections of the *Catechism* regarding God and creation.

DVD/VHS
*Inspired: Stories and Songs Inspired by the Scriptures.** Our Sunday Visitor Curriculum Division. "Creation" (8:56 min.). A poetic rendition of the creation story.

*Available at www.osvcurriculum.com

 Catechist Resources
For interactive lesson planner, chapter resources, and activities
www.osvcurriculum.com

 How varied are your works, Lord!
In wisdom you have wrought them all;
the earth is full of your creatures.

Psalm 104:24

God's Plan for You

Around you are many signs of the presence of God. From the simplicity of a single cell to the vastness of the cosmos, you have much to marvel at and much that shows you the graciousness of our Creator. Who else but a loving God would begin and sustain such intricate patterns of life?

Creation is the means by which your reason and experience help you understand God's plan for you. But God helps you even more. He reveals himself through Scripture and Tradition as well. In Scripture you see that humanity's history has been filled with times of salvation and grace. In Tradition you see how people are chosen to celebrate, teach, and serve as God's own family. Just as God named all creation "good," you are continually called in your time to be a co-worker in that same plan for goodness, justice, and peace.

Providence

As you experience the gift of creation, you learn that God brought everything into being and that he continues to care deeply for all created things. He provides what is needed for all of creation to grow toward perfection. This is an essential teaching. It affirms that God is neither detached nor distant, but with you always. His loving care for all creation is called *providence*. One response is to care for others as he cares for you.

Reflect   *When have you been most aware of the providence of God in your life?*

God's Plan for Creation

Do you remember the old spiritual, "He's Got the Whole World in His Hands"? At the heart of this song are the beliefs that everything is created by God and that everything has meaning and purpose.

From a fourth grader's point of view, the world can be confusing. It is reassuring to most students to be ushered into the trust that "God has you and me, brother [sister], in his hands." Trusting in God's loving plan gives students a compass to help them find their way to hope; this trust assures them that they have identity as children of God. Most students will welcome this message.

- Invite students to look at creation from God's loving perspective.

- Take time to identify good in the world, such as efforts to recycle instead of wasting resources.

- Fourth graders are ready to encounter new stories from the Old Testament. They are becoming sophisticated enough in their thinking to understand that the story of Jonah is a story of God's providence and love.

Learning

- I can understand what stories from the Bible really mean if you help me. Let me act them out or retell them myself.

- I can work well in a group or with a partner. Be sure to give me clear directions.

- I like to create things. Give me activities that let me draw and write.

Listening to the Call of Vocation

The word *vocation* comes from the root word *vocare*, which means "to call." Where do you think the call of vocation comes from?

- The call of vocation comes from God. You may try to discern your vocation by praying or submitting your will to the will of God.

- You may also look inward, analyzing your talents and interests to find out what comes naturally for you.

Research indicates that the way you view a vocation directly affects your ability to discern and sustain it.

Reflect **In which direction do you usually turn to hear the call?**

Catechist's Prayer

Loving God, you created the whole world and all life. Help me use my gifts to honor life and touch the world with your love and mercy. Amen.

Weekly Planner

Objectives	Lesson Process	Materials

1 Invite

10 minutes

Page 41
Objective:
To learn the concept of God's plan

🙏 **Let Us Pray:** Psalm 32:8
- Pray the psalm verse.
- Explore the patterns in a kaleidoscope.
- Write poems about the beauty of a kaleidoscope.

☐ Kaleidoscope (if possible)
☐ Paper
☐ Pencils or pens

2 Explore

40 minutes

Pages 42–43
Objective:
To understand the meaning of creation

- Read the creation poem.
- Identify and pantomime action words in the poem.
  Activity Complete the Share Your Faith Activity.

☐ Board or chart paper
☐ Blank postcards
☐ Markers
☐ Local telephone directory

Pages 44–45
Objective:
To recognize that God has a plan for humans

✝ **Scripture:** Book of Jonah
- Begin vocabulary packets.
- Proclaim and discuss the story of Jonah.
  Activity Complete the Connect Your Faith Activity.
Words of Faith providence, Scripture, revelation

☐ Index cards

3 Celebrate

10 minutes

Page 46
Objective:
To pray to God for his guidance in our lives

🙏 **Let Us Pray:** Psalm 121
- Organize class in groups.
- Gather students for prayer.
- Celebrate a Psalm of Hope.

🎵 **Hymn:** "Psalm 121"

Activity Complete the Bible Time Line Activity, page 222 and 223

☐ Hymnals
☐ Music CD

Wrap Up

Review and Apply

Page 47
- Review the chapter concepts.
- Complete the Live Your Faith Activity.

Family Faith

Page 48
- Introduce the page, and assign it as a family activity.
- Read about Mary, Mother of God.

ACRE Connection, Domain 1—Our Loving Creator

Home Connection

GO online www.osvcurriculum.com
Family Faith activities, feasts and seasonal resources, saint features, and much more

CALL to FAITH
e connect

- Online planning tools include chapter background and planner, activity master, customizable test, and more.
- Enhancement activities for each step of the catechetical process, including alternative prayer experiences and blessings.
- Games, activities, interactive review, alternative assessment, and more for children

www.calltofaitheconnect.com

Chapter 1 God's Plan

Let Us Pray

Leader: Creator God, we thank you for your guidance.
"I will instruct you and show you the way
you should walk,
give you counsel and watch over you."

Psalm 32:8

All: Creator God, we thank you for your guidance. Amen.

Activity Let's Begin

Kaleidoscope Have you ever looked through a kaleidoscope? As you turn the tube, small bits of colored glass or plastic at the far end are reflected in two mirrors. As you turn the kaleidoscope, the colored bits arrange themselves into thousands of beautiful patterns.

• Write a haiku—a type of poem—about the beauty of the kaleidoscope patterns on this page.
Responses will vary.

41

1 Invite

Objective: To learn the concept of God's plan

Let Us Pray

Tell students to move to your classroom prayer space. In the space, have a crucifix and a Bible opened to the psalm. With students, pray the psalm verse aloud three times, very slowly. Ask what the verse means to them.

Activity

• Ask a volunteer to read the text aloud.

• Have students describe what a kaleidoscope does.

• If possible, show students a real kaleidoscope and discuss how it compares with their descriptions.

• Guide the group through the poetry writing activity. As a class, write a haiku to serve as an example.

• Tell students that their group is like a kaleidoscope, with each person contributing a different piece to a beautiful pattern.

OPTIONAL ACTIVITY

Water Colors Colorful designs will enhance the haiku.

• Distribute paper towels and watercolors.

• Have each student mix a color and gently dab it onto the towel. The color will spread and fade. Continue with other colors.

• Students can glue their poems to the towels.

Multiple Intelligence: Visual/Spatial

CULTURAL AWARENESS

Haiku The haiku is the shortest form of Japanese poetry. Its modern form dates to the 1890s.

• A haiku has 17 syllables, usually set as three units of five, seven, and five syllables.

• Descriptive words tell a story about or create a picture. Most haiku are about nature. For example:

Glories of color
Paint the autumn sky with fire.
Leaves tumble and die.

Objective: To understand the meaning of creation

 Focus

What did God say about all that he had made? List students' responses on the board or on chart paper.

God's Creation

Read the paragraph aloud. Ask students to tell what they know about creation from Bible stories.

The Creation

Tell students that James Weldon Johnson uses many images to tell the creation story as a poem.

- Tell students to close their eyes and picture the images as you read the poem aloud.

- Then have students read the poem silently and identify the action words (*smiled, reached, gathered, flung, hurled,* and so on).

- Read the poem aloud again, and invite students to pantomime the action.

Explore

God's Creation

 Focus What did God say about all that he had made?

The world is something like a kaleidoscope. Its complex patterns and movements give clues to God's amazing plan for creation. In this poem the poet imagines a powerful God who walks and talks like a man. Read to learn how the poet thinks God feels about creation.

A POEM

The Creation

. . . And far as the eye of God could see
Darkness covered everything.
Blacker than a hundred midnights
Down in a cypress swamp.

Then God smiled,
And the light broke,
And the darkness rolled up on one side,
And the light stood shining on the other,
And God said: "That's good!"

Then God reached out and took the light
in his hands,
And God rolled the light around in his hands
Until he made the sun;
And he set that sun a-blazing in the heavens.
And the light that was left from making the sun
God gathered it up in a shining ball
And flung it against the darkness,
Spangling the night with the moon and stars.
Then down between
The darkness and the light
He hurled the world;
And God said: "That's good!"

42

CATECHIST BACKGROUND

Author James Weldon Johnson (1871–1938) was a teacher, poet, songwriter, and civil rights activist. He honored the voice of black oral tradition in his poetry.

- "The Creation" describes the power and beauty of creation and the tenderness of God's relationship with humanity.

- This poem is featured in the video *God's Trombones* (Vision Video, 1996).

JUSTICE AND PEACE

Care for the Earth In *Mother and Teacher*, Pope John XXIII recommended three stages for putting principles into practice: "observe, judge, act." (236)

- Have students remove litter from the parish grounds.

- Explain that keeping the earth clean is part of care for creation.

Catholic Social Teaching: Care for Creation

Then God made the seven seas and all the forests and
plants and animals and even rainbows. But God decided to
make even more.

Then God sat down—
On the side of a hill where he could think;
By a deep, wide river he sat down;
With his head in his hands,
God thought and thought,
Till he thought: I'll make me a man!

Up from the bed of the river
God scooped the clay;
And by the bank of the river
He kneeled him down;
And there the great God Almighty
Who lit the sun and fixed it in the sky,
Who flung the stars to the most far corner of the night,
Who rounded the earth in the middle of his hand;
This great God,
Like a mammy bending over her baby,
Kneeled down in the dust
Toiling over a lump of clay
Till he shaped it in his own image;

Then into it he blew the breath of life,
And man became a living soul.

From the poem by James Weldon Johnson

 What did you learn about God from this poem?
Responses will vary.

Activity Share Your Faith

Reflect: In what ways does the world show God's love
and care for his creation?

Share: With a partner, name some of these ways.

Act: Make a scenic postcard design of one part of
the world that shows God's love and care.

43

Activity

- Distribute blank postcards and markers to complete the scenic postcard activity.
- Ask students who they think would enjoy receiving a postcard from their group. Have them think of people who might appreciate a friendly greeting. (You might mention a local children's hospital or parish members who are elderly.)
- Have students write their greetings on the backs of their postcards.
- Provide students with a local telephone directory. Assist in locating addresses.
- Be sure to mail the postcards.

Quick Review

God's creation is good. His love and creativity, and generosity can be seen in all of creation.

REACHING ALL LEARNERS

Gifted Children Students who finish all of their work ahead of time may need enhancements to keep them occupied and to extend their learning.

- Ask students to create additional postcards for friends and family members.
- Extend the activity by having each of these students keep a journal of other creative ways of representing God's love and care for creation.

 My Journal

Objective: To recognize that God has a plan for humans

 **Focus**

Where does God reveal his plan for you? **List students' responses on the board or on chart paper.**

God's Plan

Read aloud the paragraph.

- Have each student create his or her own packet of vocabulary cards. Distribute index cards, and have students write the word *providence* on the front of the card and its definition on the back of the card.

Jonah and the Big Fish

Proclaim the scripture story.

- Ask volunteers to retell the story.
- Discuss the questions.

Explore

Faith Fact

The ancient town of Nineveh is located near the Tigris River in present-day Iraq.

God's Plan

 **Focus** Where does God reveal his plan for you?

God has a loving plan for creation. As God's plan unfolds, he keeps everyone and everything in his loving care. This is called **providence**. In this Bible story from the Old Testament, you will learn about Jonah, a man who tried to avoid God's plan for him.

✝ **SCRIPTURE** Book of Jor

Jonah and the Big Fish

God told Jonah to tell the people of Nineveh, "The Lord has seen your sins. Change your sinful ways, or you are doomed!" Jonah got on a ship and sailed away to hide from the Lord.

God made a storm come up, and the ship was about to be broken to pieces. The sailors ran and found Jonah sleeping. "Pray to your God, that he may save us!" they cried. Jonah thought that God was punishing him, so he asked the sailors to throw him into the sea. As soon as they did, the sea became calm.

The Lord sent a giant fish that swallowed Jonah. Inside the fish, Jonah had some time to think, and he decided to follow the Lord. Three days later the fish spit him onto dry land. God was merciful to Jonah and also to the people of Nineveh, who listened to Jonah and changed their ways.

Based on the Book of Jona

❓ **Why do you think Jonah tried to run from God?**
He was afraid and didn't want the job.
❓ **Have you ever avoided doing something that you knew you should do? What happened?**
Responses will vary.

44

💡 **QUICK TIP**

Vocabulary Packets Have students continue building their vocabulary packets to use in matching games throughout the year.

- End each lesson with a quick review.
- Frequent practice will help students articulate their faith.

✝ **SCRIPTURE BACKGROUND**

Jonah Initially, students may respond to the story of Jonah as an exciting adventure tale. Fourth graders, however, are old enough to begin considering the deeper meaning of the story.

- The important lessons for students are that Jonah was a part of God's plan and that God showed love and mercy to the people of Nineveh.

- Both of these points are good examples of God's providence in action.

Following God's Plan

The story of Jonah is in the Old Testament of the Bible. The Bible, also called **Scripture**, is God's word written in human words. There are many more stories in the Old Testament that can show you how others have followed God's plan. Then, in the New Testament, you can see God's Son, Jesus, answering his Father's call perfectly. Through Jesus you can learn how you are to respond to God's plan for you. The Holy Spirit, whom Jesus sent to the Church, will help you.

God's Revelation

God has made himself known gradually throughout history by words and deeds and the experience of people. The truth that God has told the world about himself is called **revelation**. Revelation is found in Scripture and in the Tradition of the Church.

What did Jonah do to figure out how to fit into God's plan for him? He took time to think and decided to follow the Lord.

What do you think is God's plan for you? Responses will vary.

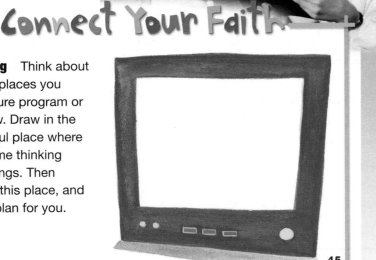

Activity

Connect Your Faith

Your Best Thinking Think about quiet and beautiful places you have seen on a nature program or on another TV show. Draw in the TV screen a peaceful place where you could spend time thinking about important things. Then imagine yourself in this place, and think about God's plan for you.

45

Following God's Plan

Read the paragraph aloud to introduce the concept of God's plan.

God's Revelation

Have students read the paragraph silently.

- Discuss the word *revelation*. Ask students to tell some of the things they know about God, and list these on the board or on chart paper.
- Invite volunteers to respond to the questions in the text.

Activity

- Read the directions aloud.
- Invite volunteers to tell where they go to think about important things.
- Encourage students to use both words and pictures in their drawings.

◎ Quick Review

God's loving plan for everyone is called *providence*. God reveals himself through Scripture and the Tradition of the Church.

OPTIONAL ACTIVITY

Models Invite students to make models of the quiet thinking places they have described.

- Provide shoe boxes, cardboard, clay, or other materials for students to use in creating three-dimensional models.

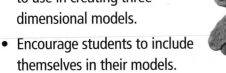

- Encourage students to include themselves in their models.

Multiple Intelligence: Visual/Spatial

Celebrate

Objective: To pray to God for his guidance in our lives

 Let Us Pray

Tell students that they will pray a psalm that asks for God's help.

Psalm of Hope

Prepare

Choose a leader for the prayer service. Organize the class in groups to read the parts marked *Group 1* and *Group 2*.

 Use the *Call to Faith 4* CD, track 1, to rehearse the suggested song.

Gather

Have students gather in the prayer space with their books.

Pray

• Follow the order of prayer as it appears on page 46.

• Leader's concluding prayer: **Lord, we thank you for the care and guidance that you have shown us. May we always turn to you for help in following your plan.**

Psalm of Hope

 **Let Us Pray**

Gather and begin with the Sign of the Cross.

Sing together the refrain.

Guiding me, guarding me, the Lord is by my side; guiding me, guarding me, the Lord upholds my life.

"Psalm 121" © 1988, GIA Publications, Inc.

Leader:	Loving God, hear us today as we pray.
Group 1:	I raise my eyes toward the mountains. From where will my help come? My help comes from the LORD, the maker of heaven and earth.
All:	*Sing refrain.*
Group 2:	God will not allow your foot to slip. Truly, the guardian of Israel never slumbers nor sleeps.
All:	*Sing refrain.* **The LORD will guard you from all evil. The LORD will guard your coming and going both now and forever.** *Sing refrain.*

Based on *Psalm 121*

Leader:	Let us pray. *Bow your heads as the leader prays.*
All:	**Amen.**

46

 LITURGY LINK

Petition and Prayer of the Faithful Encourage students to pray by allowing them to voice their concerns and needs in the context of prayer. These are prayers of petition.

• Prayers for others are intercessions.

• Prayers after the Creed at the Sunday liturgy are called the Prayer of the Faithful. This title changed from "General Intercessions" when we began to implement the English translation of the Third Edition of the Roman Missal in November 2011.

 LECTIONARY LINK

Break Open the Word Read last week's Sunday Gospel. Invite students to think about what the reading means to them as they try to follow Christ's example. For questions related to the weekly Gospel reading, visit our website at **www.osvcurriculum.com**

 GO online **Visit www.osvcurriculum.com for weekly Scripture readings and seasonal resources.**

Review and Apply

A **Check Understanding** Circle True if a statement is true, and circle False if a statement is false. Correct any false statements.

1. God's plan for people is revealed gradually.

   (True)   False _____

2. Revelation is found only in creation.

   True   (False)_____**It is found in Scripture and the**_____
   Tradition of the Church.

3. God's plan for creation has been destroyed.

   True   (False) **God's plan for creation continues today.**

4. Providence is God's loving care for all of creation.

   (True)   False _____

5. Jesus always followed God his Father's plan for him.

   (True)   False _____

B **Make Connections** Write a brief response. What are some ways that you can learn more about God's plan for you?

Responses will vary.

_____

_____

Activity — Live Your Faith

Make a Plan Use this calendar to list one way you will look for God and his guidance each day next week.

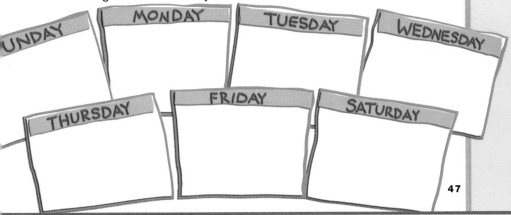

47

Review and Apply

Use the Quick Review statements from the catechist Explore pages to review the lesson concepts.

A **Check Understanding** Ask students to identify the statements that are true. Then discuss the corrections they made to the false statements.

B **Make Connections** Ask each student to write his or her response. Have students discuss their responses. Encourage students to record other responses in a notebook.

Activity

- Assist students in creating a time line for the week. Help them decide how to label the time line with the ways that they will look for God's guidance in the next week.

- You may wish to suggest examples such as these: I will read the Bible. I will ask my parents to pray with me.

OPTIONAL ACTIVITY

Activity Master 1: Caring for Creation Distribute copies of the activity found on catechist page 48A.

- Tell students to use what they have learned in this chapter for the activity.

- As an alternative, you may wish to send this activity home with students.

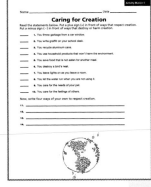

▲ **Activity Master 1**

Family Faith

Remind students to discuss the Family Faith page at home. Encourage them to read the passage from 2 Samuel.

Activity

- Pass a kaleidoscope around the room to show students how it works.
- Demonstrate the craft so that students can explain it at home.

People of Faith

Tell students about Mary, Mother of God.

- Additional days on which Catholics honor Mary include January 1 (Mother of God), May 31 (the Visitation), August 15 (the Assumption), December 8 (the Immaculate Conception), and December 12 (Our Lady of Guadalupe).
- You may wish to have students start a People of Faith album. Have students cut and paste the People of Faith feature into booklets in class or at home.

 Visit **www.osvcurriculum.com** for weekly scripture readings and seasonal resources.

UNIT 1: CHAPTER 1

Family Faith

Catholics Believe

- God loves and cares for all creation and has a plan for the world.
- Everything God wants you to know about him is contained in Scripture and in the Tradition of the Church.

✝ SCRIPTURE

Read *2 Samuel 7:12–17* to learn about God's providence for the people of Israel.

GO online www.osvcurriculum.com
For weekly scripture readings and seasonal resources

Activity
Live Your Faith

Make a Kaleidoscope Talk with your family about what you have learned about God's providence. Then make a kaleidoscope pattern. Cut some colored paper into shapes like the pieces of colored glass in a kaleidoscope. Give two pieces of paper to each family member. Ask each person to draw or glue pictures on the pieces that show God's loving care at work in creation. Glue the pieces to a large piece of paper to make a beautiful kaleidoscope pattern.

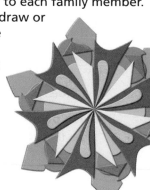

▲ **Mary, Mother of God**

People of Faith

Mary cooperated with God's plan. Because she did, Jesus was able to reveal fully his Father's plan for creation. Mary's "yes" to the Angel Gabriel's announcement opened the way for the Son of God's birth through the power of the Holy Spirit. Mary opened her heart to listen for the voice of God. She was a woman of prayer and stillness, always saying "yes" to God. Mary is the model of holiness for the whole Church. January 1 is the feast of Mary, the Mother of God.

🙌 Family Prayer

Mary, Mother of God and mother of all, help us say "yes" to God always. Show us the way of love. Amen.

In Unit 1 your child is learning about REVELATION.

48 **CCC** *See Catechism of the Catholic Church 80–83, 302–308 for further reading on chapter content.*

❓ HOW DID I DO?

My session was

☐ *one of the best ever!* ☐ *pretty good.* ☐ *in need of improvement.*

In what discussions and activities were students most interested?

_____

What activity did I most enjoy teaching?

_____

In what area do I need to improve?

_____

Name _____ Date _____

Caring for Creation

Read the statements below. Put a plus sign (+) in front of ways that respect creation. Put a minus sign (−) in front of ways that destroy or harm creation.

_____ **1.** You throw garbage from a car window.

_____ **2.** You write graffiti on your school desk.

_____ **3.** You recycle aluminum cans.

_____ **4.** You use household products that won't harm the environment.

_____ **5.** You save food that is not eaten for another meal.

_____ **6.** You destroy a bird's nest.

_____ **7.** You leave lights on as you leave a room.

_____ **8.** You let the water run when you are not using it.

_____ **9.** You care for the needs of your pet.

_____ **10.** You care for the feelings of others.

Now, write four ways of your own to respect creation.

11. _____

12. _____

13. _____

14. _____

Answers can be found in the back of the Catechist Manual.

God Is Faithful
CATECHIST FORMATION

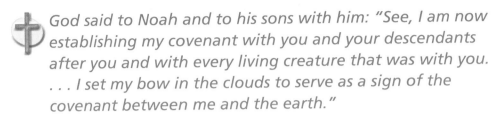

Faith Focus

- God made a covenant with Abraham and has always remained faithful to that covenant. (CCC 59–61)
- Sin exists in the world because humans have chosen to turn away from God. (CCC 385–389)

Catechism Connection

The *Catechism* points out that Jesus Christ is the "new Adam" who redeems the world from its enslavement to sin. (CCC 504)

NDC Link

It is the call of all who are baptized to proclaim and demonstrate the Christian faith to all to help bring about a change in minds and hearts and lead others to a conversion to Christ. (See *NDC*, 17A.)

Resources

📖 BOOKS
*The Humongous Book of Bible Skits.** Group Publishing. "Ruth." Recounts the story of Ruth and Naomi in child-friendly fashion.

Go and Do Likewise: Catholic Social Teaching in Action. Crosthwaite, Mia. Twenty-Third Publications. "What Is Social Justice?" Provides information and reflections on social justice issues.

*Available at www.osvcurriculum.com

 Catechist Resources
For interactive lesson planner, chapter resources, and activities
www.osvcurriculum.com

✝ *God said to Noah and to his sons with him: "See, I am now establishing my covenant with you and your descendants after you and with every living creature that was with you. . . . I set my bow in the clouds to serve as a sign of the covenant between me and the earth."*

Genesis 9:8–10, 13

Original Sin and God's Faithfulness

The disobedience of Adam and Eve in the Genesis story shows that from the beginning of creation, humans have chosen to turn away from God. The choice of the first humans resulted in original sin, a condition in which all people share; but it also resulted in God's promise to send a redeemer. Today, even though you know the ways in which you have turned away from God, you also know that he is always faithful and always calls you back to himself.

Covenant

The covenant that God made with Noah and with Abraham and Sarah established a permanent and durable connection between God and his people. This covenant continues through each succeeding generation of the Jewish people.

God's faithfulness reached its ultimate fulfillment with the institution of the New Covenant in Jesus Christ. His death, Resurrection, and Ascension forged the sacred relationship between God and his people into one that promises eternal life and happiness. As a result of your Baptism, you too participate in this covenant relationship with God. He, who will never abandon you, continually calls you deeper into relationship with him.

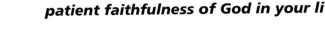

Reflect **When have you experienced the patient faithfulness of God in your life?**

God's Faithfulness

The word *covenant* may be new to fourth graders, but *promise* is a very familiar concept. At this age, students have had experiences of making and keeping (or breaking) promises and of having promises made to them. Most find the making and keeping of promises an important personal transaction—an almost sacred one. You can extend that sense of the sacred to students' relationship with God.

- Fourth graders value faithfulness in friends and family. To help them understand the value of being true to others, use examples from their experience, such as supporting a friend who is being teased.

- Fourth graders are developing a moral code. Encourage them to reflect on scripture stories to help guide their choices and faithfully respond to God.

- Explain to students that Abraham, Sarah, Noah, Ruth, and Naomi are role models of faithful friendship and covenant living.

Loyalty

- I understand that it is important to be a loyal friend. Tell me stories about kids who are loyal to one another.

- I learn how to work with others from teamwork. Maybe our group should work on team activities.

- I am learning how important it is to keep promises. Always keep yours to me.

The Vocation To Teach

The vocation to teach develops differently for each person. Teaching as a vocation has a unique flavor to it. You cannot change its flavor or its taste. Just as root beer and orange soda each taste a certain way, so does the vocation to teach. Some people claim they always knew they would teach. Others never imagined they would be involved in education.

- This vocation comes with the conviction that you can succeed despite economic, domestic, or institutional deficits.

- It also comes with moments of doubt about your effectiveness.

Reflect **Which of these two flavors do you taste more frequently in your catechetical vocation?**

Catechist's Prayer

Dear God, thank you for calling me to be a part of a community of faith. With your grace I can work with others to bring about a better world. Amen.

Weekly Planner

Objectives	Lesson Process	Materials

1 Invite

10 minutes

Page 49
Objective:
To understand the concept of faithfulness

🙏 **Let Us Pray:** Psalm 145:13
• Pray the psalm verse.
• Focus on the theme.
• Read and discuss the poem.

---

2 Explore

40 minutes

Pages 50–51
Objective:
To discuss God's faithfulness and original sin and its effects

✝ **Scripture:** Genesis 3
• Proclaim the scripture story.
• Lead a discussion of the scripture story, and reflect on the story in small groups.
Activity Complete the Share Your Faith Activity.
Words of Faith original sin

☐ Board or chart paper
☐ Pencils or pens
☐ Newspaper clippings
☐ Large poster board
☐ Index cards

Pages 52–53
Objective:
To understand the meaning of *covenant*

✝ **Scripture:** Genesis 12:1–8, 15:1–5, 17:5–9, 15; 21:1–3
• Proclaim the scripture story of Abram.
• Develop vocabulary words.
Activity Complete the Connect Your Faith Activity.
Words of Faith covenant , faithful

☐ Highlighters of varied colors
☐ Colored pencils or markers
☐ Copies of Activity Master 2 on page 56A

---

3 Celebrate

10 minutes

Page 54
Objective:
To ask for God's mercy when we have been unfaithful

🙏 **Let Us Pray**
• Gather as a community.
• Practice the responses.
• Celebrate a Prayer for Mercy.
🔥 **Hymn:** "General Intercessions"

Activity Complete the Old Testament Passages Activity, page 224 and 225

☐ Hymnals
☐ Music CD
☐ Incense and a bowl (optional)
☐ Bible

Wrap Up

Review and Apply

Page 55
• Review the chapter concepts.
• Complete the Live Your Faith Activity.

Family Faith

Page 56
• Introduce the page, and assign it as a family activity.
• Read about Naomi and Ruth.

ACRE Connection, Domain 1—God's Covenant with the Jews

Home Connection

GO online www.osvcurriculum.com
Family Faith activities, feasts and seasonal resources, saint features, and much more

CALL to FAITH
e connect

• Online planning tools include chapter background and planner, activity master, customizable test, and more.
• Enhancement activities for each step of the catechetical process, including alternative prayer experiences and blessings.
• Games, activities, interactive review, alternative assessment, and more for children

www.calltofaitheconnect.com

God Is Faithful

Let Us Pray

Leader: We place our trust in your faithfulness, O God.

"The Lord is trustworthy in every word,
and faithful in every work."

Psalm 145:13

All: We place our trust in your faithfulness, O God. Amen.

 **Activity** *Let's Begin*

A Very Bad Day

My day was going smooth as silk,
'Til the cat leapt up and spilled my milk.
As I was mopping up the floor,
My mom was calling from the door.
"Hurry up! We'll all be late!"
I grabbed the toast left on my plate.
Just as we reached the end of the block,
I noticed I had no left sock.
I got to school five minutes late,
I guess my toast will have to wait.
As I raced inside the classroom door,
My homework lay on the living room floor!

• What do you do when you have a
  bad day? **Responses will vary.**

49

1 Invite

Objective: To understand the concept of faithfulness

Let Us Pray

Explain that meditative prayer is quietly thinking about God's word. Invite students to go to the prayer space. Play quiet music, and ask students to close their eyes. Pray the psalm verse aloud slowly.

Activity

• **Ask** a volunteer to read aloud A Very Bad Day.

• Ask volunteers to share their experiences of having a bad day.

• Tell students that faithfulness is an important quality when things go wrong. Explain that even when they have a very bad day, God remains faithful in loving them.

• Direct students to answer the question that follows the poem. Then have them share their responses.

OPTIONAL ACTIVITY

Faithfulness Consider scenarios that describe behavior that is or is not faithful.

• Make two cards for each student. Label one card "faithful" and the other card "not faithful."

• Distribute the cards, and have students hold one up as you describe each scenario.

• Remind the group that God is always faithful.

Multiple Intelligence: Interpersonal

QUICK TIP

Extend the Poem Invite each student to write or illustrate a new line for the poem A Very Bad Day. Display or share students' creative work.

Objective: To discuss God's faithfulness and original sin and its effects

 Focus

How does God show his faithfulness? List students' responses on the board or on chart paper.

Humans Choose Sin

Tell students that the Bible begins with the Book of Genesis. This book introduces the first humans in the second creation story.

- Ask students what they know about the first humans.

In the Garden

Proclaim the scripture story.

- Stress that both Adam and Eve are responsible for their actions.
- Discuss the question.
- Organize students in groups of three. Ask each group to think of three ways that life would have been different for the first humans if they had not disobeyed God. Responses will vary.
- Ask group members to list three things that may tempt them. Then discuss how they respond to the temptations.

Explore

Humans Choose Sin

 Focus   How does God show his faithfulness?

For the first humans, known as Adam and Eve in the Old Testament creation story, there was a time when every day was a good day. But one day Satan, who was God's enemy, came to Eve in the form of a snake and tempted her. We learn from the Book of Genesis what Adam and Eve did.

✠ SCRIPTURE   Genesi

In the Garden

In the Garden of Eden was one special tree that God told Adam and Eve not to touch. But Satan convinced Eve that if she and Adam ate the fruit of that tree, they could be more like God. Adam and Eve did as Satan said; but after they sinned, they felt ashamed. They learned how it felt to do something wrong.

Everything got harder for Adam and Eve. God sent them away from the garden. They had to work to find food and shelter. From then on, jealousy, sadness, and fighting were in the world.

Based on Genesis 3

❓ **Why do you think the first people chose to disobey God?** Possible response: because they wanted to be more like God

50

✠ SCRIPTURE BACKGROUND

Creation   The creation stories convey important religious truths rather than historical events.

- The story of Adam and Eve shows how sin affects relationships with God.
- Biblical accounts emphasize that it was humans' choice, not God's, that changed humanity's initial relationship with God.

onsequences

Humans were created to share God's life and to be appy with God forever. By disobeying God, the first eople broke their friendship with God. This sin of the rst humans is called **Original Sin** because since that hoice was made, sin has been present throughout the orld. Original Sin affects every human. Ignorance, the clination to sin, suffering, and death all came into the orld as a result of Original Sin.

Even though God sent Adam and ve away from the garden, he did ot abandon them. God remained ithful. In return he wanted all umans to be free and faithful to im, so that they could be happy rever.

The Book of Genesis then tells nother famous story, the story of oah. The point of Noah's story is hat even when people continued to n and to disobey God, God was ithful.

Words of Faith

Original Sin is the choice of the first people to disobey God.

Activity · Share Your Faith

Reflect: Think of some stories in the news that are examples of the effects of Original Sin in the world today.

Share: In a small group, talk about ways that people can act as God wants them to act in these situations.

Act: Write two examples here.

_____

_____

Responses will vary.

_____

51

Consequences

Read aloud the text.

- Tell students the story of Noah.
- Discuss with students how God was faithful to Noah.
- Have each student make a vocabulary card for the term *original sin*.

Activity

- Distribute newspaper clippings on various topics.
- Have students work in small groups to choose articles that provide examples of the effects of original sin in the world. Then have the groups complete the activity. Display the articles on poster board.

 Quick Review

God is always faithful, even when humans disobey. God wants humans to be free to make choices and to experience faith and true happiness.

REACHING ALL LEARNERS

Use Literature   Many children learn best through stories. Recognizing faithful love in stories can help students develop appreciation for this grace.

- Tell or read stories from familiar literature or current videos that illustrate faithfulness in relationships.
- Some examples are *Charlotte's Web* and *The Velveteen Rabbit*.

OPTIONAL ACTIVITY

Noah   Spend time reviewing the story of Noah.

- Emphasize that the flood was a consequence of human sin and that the rainbow was a symbol of God's faithful promise.
- Ask students to write a song about Noah to the tune of a popular song.

Multiple Intelligence: Musical

Objective: To understand the meaning of *covenant*

 **Focus**

**What did God promise to Abram?
List students' responses on the board or on chart paper.**

God's Plan Revealed

Tell students that they are now going to explore the story of Abram. Remind them that God is faithful and that people can respond in faithfulness to God.

God Calls Abram

Distribute highlighters of different colors. Ask the group to read silently.

• Ask students to highlight the words of Abram with one color and the words of God in another color.

• Discuss the question in the text.

• Tell students that Abram built altars of thanksgiving to maintain his relationship with God through trying times.

• Have students form groups of three. Ask each group how they could grow closer to God in difficult times.
Responses will vary.

Explore

God's Plan Revealed

 Focus   What did God promise to Abram?

After a long time, God called a man named Abram to help humans remain faithful. God revealed his plan to Abram in a new way.

✝ SCRIPTURE   Genesis 12:1–8; 15:1–5; 17:5–9, 15; 21:

God Calls Abram

Abram lived long, long ago in an ancient city called Haran. God told Abram to leave his country and much of his family and go to a new land called Canaan. God told Abram, "I will bless you and make your descendants into a great nation." Abram obeyed God. He took his wife Sarai, his brother's son Lot, and all their possessions on the long journey to the new land.

Abram and his family were never alone on their difficult journey. They knew that God was always with them. Every time Abram reached a stop on the journey, he built an altar of thanksgiving to the Lord.

Many years later, after Abram had settled in the land of Canaan, the Lord spoke again to him, saying, "Don't be afraid! I will protect and reward you."

Abram replied, "Lord, you have given me everything I could ask for, except children."

The Lord told Abram, "Look at the sky and count the stars. That is how many descendants you will have."

 What is something you have been asked to do that was very hard? Responses will vary.

52

✝ SCRIPTURE BACKGROUND

Abraham and Sarah   In the time of Abraham and Sarah, about four thousand years ago, polytheism, or the worship of many gods, was common.

• Abraham and Sarah's faith led them not only to a new land but also to a new understanding of God.

• The story of Abraham and Sarah continues to inspire Christians with what it means to believe in and trust the one true God.

God's Covenant with Abraham

God appeared to Abram again. God made a **covenant** with Abram and his descendants for all time. God told Abram that the land of Canaan would belong to Abram and his descendants forever. He said that Abram would be the father of many nations and that these people would be God's people. As a sign of the covenant, God changed the names of Abram and his wife Sarai to Abraham and Sarah. Soon after that, even though Sarah was old, she had a son, whom the couple named Isaac.

Based on *Genesis* 12:1–8, 15:1–5, 17:5–9, 15; 21:1–3

❓ **How did Abraham and Sarah follow God's will?** Possible responses: They were patient, they trusted God, they didn't give up.

Abraham and Sarah never turned away from God. Like Abraham and Sarah, you are **faithful** to God every time you obey his laws and make loving choices.

Common Ancestors

Abraham is considered an ancestor in faith of Christianity, Judaism, and Islam. These religions see their origins in Abraham's free response to God's revelation that he was the one God they should believe in and follow.

Words of Faith

A **covenant** is a sacred promise or agreement between God and humans.

To be **faithful** is to be steadfast and loyal in your commitment to God, just as he is faithful to you.

Activity — Connect Your Faith

Show Faith Write your first name in colorful letters. Around your name, write words that tell how you show that you are faithful to God.

53

God's Covenant with Abraham

Introduce the words *covenant* and *faithful*. Add them to their vocabulary packets.

- Proclaim the scripture story. Emphasize that God made and kept promises to Abraham and Sarah.
- Discuss the question with students.

Common Ancestors

Tell students that Abraham and Sarah's story is important to people of many faiths. Have them read this paragraph to learn why.

Activity

- Have partners brainstorm words that show faithfulness.

◎ Quick Review

God promised Abram that his descendants would be God's people forever.

OPTIONAL ACTIVITY

Activity Master 2: Being Faithful Distribute copies of the activity found on catechist page 56A.

- Students should use what they have learned in this chapter to complete the activity.
- As an alternative, you may wish to send this activity home with students.

▲ Activity Master 2

💡 QUICK TIP

Religions Students often hear how major world religions differ. Tell them about commonalities as well.

- The text mentions Abraham as a common ancestor in faith.
- Other commonalities include monotheism, prayer, prophets, and communal public worship.

Objective: To ask for God's mercy when we have been unfaithful

 Let Us Pray

Tell students that they will pray for God's mercy, or forgiveness.

Prayer for Mercy

Prepare

Light a small amount of incense in a bowl, if possible.

- You will act as leader for this prayer.

 Use the *Call to Faith 4* CD, track 2, to rehearse the suggested song.

Gather

Gather in the prayer space.

Pray

- Follow the order of prayer on page 54.
- An optional Bible reading is *Galatians 3:6–9.*
- Leader's concluding prayer: **God our Father, we know that your faithful love is always available. Help us grow in faithfulness.**

Celebrate

Prayer for Mercy

 Let Us Pray

Gather and begin with the Sign of the Cross.

 *Sing together the refrain.*

God ever-faithful,
God ever-merciful,
God of your people,
hear our prayer.

"General Intercessions" © 1990, GIA Publications, Inc.

Leader:	For times we have failed, we pray,
All:	*Sing refrain.*
Reader 1:	For people in the world who have been hurt by our neglect, we pray,
All:	*Sing refrain.*
Reader 2:	For times when we were unfaithful to God's covenant of love, we pray,
All:	*Sing refrain.*
Leader:	Let us pray. *Bow your heads as the leader prays.*
All:	**Amen.**

54

 LITURGY LINK

Incense Incense is symbolic in several ways.

- In its burning, it represents the fervor, sincerity, and sacrificial love of the one praying.
- Its fragrance shows honor.
- The rising smoke symbolizes the hope that the prayers will be acceptable to God.

 LECTIONARY LINK

Break Open the Word Read last week's Sunday Gospel. Invite students to think about what the reading means to them as they try to follow Christ's example. For questions related to the weekly Gospel reading, visit our website at **www.osvcurriculum.com.**

 GO online Visit www.osvcurriculum.com for weekly Scripture readings and seasonal resources.

A **Work with Words**   Fill in the blanks, using terms from the Word Bank.

WORD BANK

faithful
sin
Exodus
covenant
hope
names
friendship

1. By disobeying God, the first people broke their _____friendship_____ with him.

2. One consequence of the disobedience of Adam and Eve is the inclination to _____sin_____.

3. God always remains _____faithful_____ to his people.

4. God made a _____covenant_____ with Abraham and his descendants.

5. As a sign of the covenant, God changed the _____names_____ of Abram and Sarai.

B **Check Understanding**   Write one thing you have learned about God from each of the following stories.

In the Garden _____Responses will vary._____

God Calls Abram _____

Activity — Live Your Faith

Your Commitment   On a separate sheet of paper, create a sign that expresses your commitment to being faithful to God's love for you. You can connect your sign with those of other group members to create a covenant banner.

55

Review and Apply

Use the focus questions from the catechist Explore pages to review the lesson concepts.

A **Work with Words** Read aloud the directions. Tell students to fill in the answers from the Word Bank.

B **Check Understanding**   Ask each student to write his or her responses to the items. Have students discuss their responses.

Activity

• Distribute sheets of paper and markers or other art materials.

• Read aloud the directions, and invite students to complete the activity.

✠ **JUSTICE AND PEACE**

A Human Response   The human response to God's covenant of love should be faith.

• Christians follow God's call by respecting the value and dignity of all human life.

Catholic Social Teaching: Life and Dignity

Family Faith

Remind students to discuss the Family Faith page at home. Encourage students to read the passages from Genesis.

- Display a travel brochure or a sample brochure that you have made.
- Read aloud the directions.

People of Faith

Tell students about Naomi and Ruth.

- Explain that during the time in which Naomi lived, widowed and childless women were unprotected and in need of help. Point out that Ruth was loyal to Naomi because of the compassion and affection that she felt for her mother-in-law.
- Remind students to add Naomi and Ruth to their People of Faith albums. Encourage them to pray the Family Prayer at home with their families.

 Visit **www.osvcurriculum.com** for weekly scripture readings and seasonal resources.

UNIT 1: CHAPTER 2
Family Faith

◉ Catholics Believe

- God's covenant with Abraham reveals that God is always faithful to his people.
- Sin is present in the world because of human choice.

✝ SCRIPTURE

Read *Genesis 13*, *Genesis 21:1–8*, or *Genesis 25:7–11* to find other stories about Abraham and Sarah.

GO online www.osvcurriculum.com
For weekly scripture readings and seasonal resources

Activity
Live Your Faith

Travel Brochure Share with your family one thing that you learned in class. Then imagine that you could visit the places where Abraham and Sarah traveled. As a family, make pages for a travel brochure that tells about their experiences. Think of the stories in this chapter. Look in a Bible to find a map of Abraham's journey. Bring your brochure to share with the group.

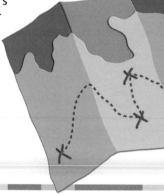

People of Faith

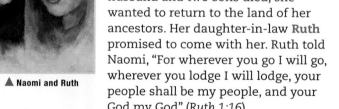
▲ Naomi and Ruth

Naomi was an Israelite who, because of a great famine, left her home to live among people of another land. While living in this land, she remained faithful to the God of Israel. When her husband and two sons died, she wanted to return to the land of her ancestors. Her daughter-in-law **Ruth** promised to come with her. Ruth told Naomi, "For wherever you go I will go, wherever you lodge I will lodge, your people shall be my people, and your God my God" (*Ruth 1:16*).

In Unit 1 your child is learning about REVELATION.

56 **CCC** *See Catechism of the Catholic Church 59–61, 385–389 for further reading on chapter content.*

🙌 Family Prayer

Loving God, please help us remain faithful to our covenant relationship with you, as Ruth and Naomi did. Amen.

❓ HOW DID I DO?

My session was

☐ *one of the best ever!* ☐ *pretty good.* ☐ *in need of improvement.*

In what discussions and activities were students most interested?

_____

What activity did I most enjoy teaching?

_____

In what area do I need to improve?

_____

Name _____ Date _____

Being Faithful

Read each statement. If the sentence tells of faithfulness, color the letter that has the sentence number beneath it. The colored letters will reveal a hidden message.

1. Eve chooses to disobey God.

2. God continues to love the first humans.

3. Abram offers thanksgiving to the Lord.

4. God promises Abram the land of Canaan.

5. God promises Abraham and Sarah many descendants.

6. You make fun of someone.

7. God continues to forgive humans.

8. You remember to pray.

9. You spread a rumor about another person.

10. God creates a beautiful world.

11. You go out of your way to help others.

12. You disobey your parents.

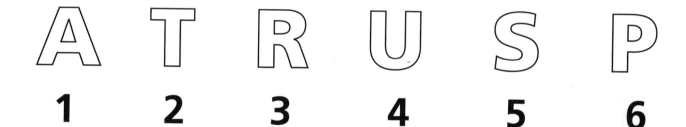

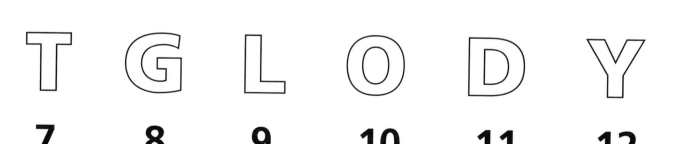

Answers can be found in the back of the Catechist Manual.

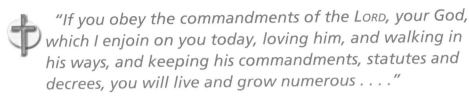

Faith Focus

- The Ten Commandments present ways to show love for God and for one another. (CCC 2055)
- The Ten Commandments are also guides to being faithful to God's covenant. (CCC 2060–2061)

Catechism Connection

The *Catechism* reminds us that Jesus came to fulfill the Old Law. Only the Son of God could perfectly fulfill it. (CCC 577–580)

NDC Link

According to the *Directory*, the Ten Commandments and the Beatitudes are key points of reference for use in the task of moral formation. (See *NDC*, 44.)

Resources

BOOK
Moses: When Harriet Tubman Led Her People to Freedom. Weatherford, Carole Boston. Jump At The Sun. Focuses on Tubman's religious inspiration for freeing slaves.

DVD/VHS
In the Footprints of God: Moses (90 min.). Oblate Media. Retraces Moses' journeys and tells about his life of leadership.

 Catechist Resources
For interactive lesson planner, chapter resources, and activities
www.osvcurriculum.com

✝ *"If you obey the commandments of the LORD, your God, which I enjoin on you today, loving him, and walking in his ways, and keeping his commandments, statutes and decrees, you will live and grow numerous . . . ."*

Deuteronomy 30:16

The Ten Commandments

Moses presented the struggling Israelites with the simple wisdom of God's will for them in the Ten Commandments. For the Israelites, the keeping of the commandments made the difference between life in a new land and death in the desert.

Today the simplicity of the Ten Commandments speaks to you clearly. If you respect the lives and property of others, you live in peace. If you honor your body and promote human dignity, you open yourself to love and respect. If you honor and thank your God, you gain inner harmony, wisdom, and grace. Sin can enslave you and restrict your access to these good things. Faithfulness to the Ten Commandments—through incorporation into the Paschal Mystery through the Sacraments—releases you from the bondage of sin.

Old Law to New Law

Throughout their history, the Israelites were sustained by the covenant they made with the one true God. They tried to be faithful to his commandments. Jesus, however, perfectly fulfilled and built upon the Law of Moses. Their Mosaic Law led directly to the new law of Jesus—to the Great Commandment of love.

Reflect **When and how have you experienced the freedom of living one of the commandments?**

The Commandments

The Ten Commandments help people develop responsible ways to treat one another and learn to love God. Most fourth graders have developed respect for authority and rules, and they understand that rules protect people for the betterment of everyone.

- Point out that love for God, ourselves, and others is at the heart of the Ten Commandments. Invite students to give examples of ways to live the commandments in their daily lives.

- Help students expand their moral thinking by pointing out that Joseph's act of forgiveness pleased God and brought happiness and freedom to Joseph and his family.

- Encourage students to memorize the Ten Commandments. Make sure that students understand the meaning of each commandment and how it can be applied to their lives.

The Old Testament

- I like to hear about Bible heroes like Joseph and Moses. Tell me these stories in a variety of ways.

- I may be good at memorizing. Let me try to memorize the Ten Commandments.

- Help me understand why rules are important. Let me help you make the rules for our group.

Blessed Assurance

Catechesis can be risky. You place yourself before students, parents, and administrators. Some of us become timid and fearful about embracing the possibilities that arise from teaching. Teachers who place themselves in front of students faithfully and with confidence have much to gain.

Many have discovered that this kind of quiet confidence comes from their past. Their confidence came from some person or group that assured them that they were trustworthy and capable.

Now and then, you may need to revisit that person or group to renew your confidence. This will help you recapture and reclaim that blessed assurance.

Reflect   **Who comes to mind as one that gave you such a blessed assurance about yourself?**

 Catechist's Prayer

Lord of love, free my heart from prejudice and lack of concern. Help me teach your law of love and compassion through my words and actions. Amen.

Weekly Planner

Objectives	Lesson Process	Materials

1 Invite

10 minutes

Page 57
Objective:
To understand the importance of doing God's will

🌷 **Let Us Pray:** Psalm 40:9

- Pray the psalm verse.
- Read The Golden Eggs.
- Discuss the lesson that the story teaches.

☐ Board or chart paper

---

2 Explore

40 minutes

Pages 58–59
Objective:
To learn how God led his people to freedom

✝ **Scripture:** Genesis 37:1–4, 42:6–8, 44:1–12, 45:4–5
Exodus 2:1–10, 14:10–31, 15:19–21

- Proclaim the scripture stories.
- **Activity** Complete the Share Your Faith Activity.

☐ Pencils or pens
☐ Paper

Pages 60–61
Objective:
To learn the Ten Commandments and explain the meaning of each one

✝ **Scripture:** Exodus 17–20

- Proclaim the scripture story.
- Explain the meaning of the Ten Commandments.
- **Activity** Complete the Connect Your Faith Activity.

Words of Faith Ten Commandments

☐ Index cards
☐ Copies of Activity Master 3 on page 64A

---

3 Celebrate

10 minutes

Page 62
Objective:
To give thanks and praise to the Lord

🌷 **Let Us Pray:** Psalm 126

- Practice the song refrain.
- Select readers.
- Celebrate a Psalm of Celebration.

🎵 **Hymn:** "Sing Our God Together"

- **Activity** Complete the Ten Commandments Activity, page 234 and 235

☐ Hymnals
☐ Music CD
☐ Bible

Wrap Up

Review and Apply

Page 63
- Review the chapter concepts.
- Complete the Live Your Faith Activity.

Family Faith

Page 64
- Introduce the page, and assign it as a family activity.
- Read about Aaron and Miriam.

ACRE Connection, Domain 5—The Ten Commandments

Home Connection

GO online www.osvcurriculum.com
Family Faith activities, feasts and seasonal resources, saint features, and much more

CALL to FAITH
e connect

- Online planning tools include chapter background and planner, activity master, customizable test, and more.
- Enhancement activities for each step of the catechetical process, including alternative prayer experiences and blessings.
- Games, activities, interactive review, alternative assessment, and more for children.

www.calltofaitheconnect.com

Chapter 3 The Ten Commandments

Let Us Pray

Leader: Loving Father, help us hear your voice and know your will.

"To do your will is my delight;
my God, your law is in my heart!"

Psalm 40:9

All: Loving Father, help us hear your voice and know your will. Amen.

Activity — Let's Begin

The Golden Eggs There once lived a farmer and his wife who were very poor. One day, a beautiful goose strutted across their path. The woman sighed, "What a beautiful bird!"

The goose followed the couple home. The next morning, they found that the bird had laid a golden egg. Each day the goose laid yet another golden egg. Soon the couple became rich.

But the farmer grew impatient for more gold. "I will kill the goose and slice her open," he thought, "and I'll have all her eggs at once." So he cut open the goose, but inside there were no more golden eggs. And now he had no goose!

• What does this story teach you? Share your response with the group.
Possible response: Greed doesn't pay.

57

---

1 Invite

Objective: To understand the importance of doing God's will

Let Us Pray

Ask students to gather in the prayer space. Pray aloud the psalm verse, and then ask students to conclude the prayer. Ask a volunteer to explain the meaning of the psalm verse.

Activity

• Ask a volunteer to read aloud The Golden Eggs.

• Ask another student to retell the story in his or her own words.

• Discuss the question that follows the story.

• Ask whether the farmer was doing God's will when he killed the goose. Why or why not? No; his only reason for killing the goose was greed.

• Copy the Graphic Organizer from the Quick Tip box onto the board or chart paper. Use it to help students understand the relationship between actions and consequences. Encourage students to add their own examples.

OPTIONAL ACTIVITY

Folktales Many cultures use folktales to teach life lessons. Jesus taught life lessons through parables.

• Invite students to share folktales from the cultures of their heritage.

• Compare stories and parables in Scripture to folktales that carry similar messages.

Multiple Intelligence: Verbal/Linguistic

QUICK TIP

Graphic Organizer

Cause		Effect
Farmer kills goose.	→	No goose, no golden eggs
	→	

Objective: To learn how God led his people to freedom

 **Focus**

Who helped lead God's people to freedom? List students' responses on the board or on chart paper.

Journey to Freedom

Read aloud the introduction to the scripture story. Point out that sometimes our actions keep us from being truly free.

Joseph and His Brothers

Proclaim the scripture story. Tell students to listen carefully as you read and to think about a time when they acted as Joseph did.

- Ask students to summarize the story of Joseph. Possible response: Joseph was sold into slavery. He won a place of honor with Pharaoh. He forgave his brothers.

- Ask the question at the bottom of the page. Affirm the responses of those who share.

Explore

Journey to Freedom

 Focus Who helped lead God's people to freedom?

In the story of "The Golden Eggs," the husband was a slave to greed. Here are two Bible stories about how God led his people from slavery to freedom.

SCRIPTURE Genesis 37:1–4, 42:6–8, 44:1–12, 45:4

Joseph and His Brothers

Jacob, one of Abraham's descendants, had twelve sons. Jacob's older sons hated their younger brother Joseph because he was their father's favorite.

One day Joseph's brothers threw him into a dry well. Then they sold him as a slave in Egypt. They told their father that wild animals had killed Joseph. Now more of their father's goods would belong to them.

Over the years, Joseph's power to tell the meaning of dreams won him a place of honor with Pharaoh, the leader of Egypt. During a famine, Joseph's brothers came to the court to beg for grain. The brothers did not recognize Joseph, but Joseph knew them.

To test them, Joseph had servants fill the brothers' sacks with grain and put a silver cup into the sack of his brother Benjamin. Later he had his servants follow them and discover the silver cup in the sack. Joseph then told the brothers that Benjamin was to be his slave.

Benjamin's brother Judah pleaded for him, saying that their father would be brokenhearted if Benjamin did not return. At this news, Joseph wept and told the men that he was their brother. He forgave them.

Based on *Genesis 37:1–4, 42:6–8, 44:1–12, 45:4–*

 When have you forgiven someone as Joseph did?
Responses will vary.

58

REACHING ALL LEARNERS

Role-Play Some students with language difficulties may prefer to role-play the story of Joseph instead of giving an oral summary.

- Organize students in small groups, and have them practice performing the scene in which Joseph tests his brothers and then forgives them.

- Invite small groups to perform the scene for the whole group.

From Slavery to Freedom

When Joseph's brothers sold him as a slave, they caused problems for themselves as well. It was only when Joseph forgave his brothers that his family knew real freedom and happiness again.

The Exodus from Egypt

Many years later God's people, the Israelites, were slaves in Egypt. Their male children were being killed, so one Israelite mother hid her baby boy in a basket near the Nile River. When Pharaoh's daughter found the baby, she kept him and named him Moses. She raised him at court as her son.

When Moses grew older, God called him to be a leader of his people. God asked Moses to tell Pharaoh to stop hurting the Israelites, but Pharaoh did not listen.

Finally, Moses was able to lead the Israelites out of Egypt. At the Red Sea, Moses raised his staff and the waters parted for the Israelites to pass through.

Based on Exodus 2:1–10, 14:10–31, 15:19–21

Do you think it was hard for Moses to leave Pharaoh's court? Why or why not?
Possible responses: Yes, because he had grown up there. No, because he would be with his own people.

Activity   Share Your Faith

Reflect: When have you been jealous of someone else because of his or her gifts or belongings?

Share: Tell a partner why you were jealous of this person and how you handled the situation.

 Act: Imagine that you are writing a musical, and use a familiar tune to help you write a song that explains the situation.

59

From Slavery to Freedom

Emphasize how the choices of Joseph's brothers affected Joseph and his family.

- Discuss how forgiveness helped both Joseph and his brothers.

The Exodus from Egypt

Have students read the scripture passage silently.

- Discuss with students why Moses led the Israelites out of Egypt.
- Discuss the questions in the text.
- Invite students to share some words or phrases that describe Moses.

Activity

- Ask students to think about the question and to share their responses with a partner.
- Brainstorm with students a list of songs, and help them match their words to the tune.
- Ask volunteers to share their songs.

Quick Review

Joseph and Moses helped show the way to freedom. God wants his people to live in freedom.

SCRIPTURE BACKGROUND

The Exodus Review with students that when Moses and the Israelites were crossing the desert, through Moses God parted the Red Sea so that the Israelites could escape from the Egyptians. Tell students that this shows that when you put your trust in God, he will provide for you. He may not provide for you in the way you expect, but you need to trust in his care.

QUICK TIP

Film Students may enjoy seeing scenes based on the Bible stories on these pages. You may be able to rent the film *Prince of Egypt* online or through your local library.

Objective: To learn the Ten Commandments and explain the meaning of each one

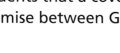 **Focus**

How do the Ten Commandments help you be free? List students' responses on the board or on chart paper.

A Guide from God

Tell students that they will learn that the Ten Commandments showed the Israelites how to live.

The Journey Continues

Talk with the class about what things guide them through life.

- Proclaim the Scripture. Ask students to imagine how difficult the journey must have been.

- Have students make a vocabulary card for *Ten Commandments*.

- Discuss the question in the text. Affirm students who respond.

Living God's Covenant

Read the paragraph aloud. Tell students that a covenant is a special promise between God and his people.

A Guide from God

 Focus How do the Ten Commandments help you be free?

The Israelites were free from slavery, but they still needed God's help.

✝ S C R I P T U R E   Exodus 17—

The Journey Continues

Words of Faith

The **Ten Commandments** are the summary of laws that God gave Moses on Mount Sinai. They tell what is necessary in order to love God and others.

After the Israelites crossed the Red Sea, they wandered in the desert for years. They forgot that God had saved them from slavery in Egypt. Moses struggled to keep order among God's people and to find food and water for them. He complained to God about his hard job, and God helped him.

In the desert, God called Moses up to Mount Sinai. After God showed his power with thunder and lightning, he gave Moses the **Ten Commandments** to show the people how they were to live.

Based on Exodus 17—20

❓ **Why do you think the Ten Commandments are important?**
Responses will vary.

Living God's Covenant

Just as the Ten Commandments helped the Israelites live their covenant relationship with God, the commandments are also a guide for you. They tell you the minimum that is required to love God and others. The first three commandments show you how to be faithful to God. The last seven show you how to treat other people with love. The chart on the next page names the Ten Commandments and explains what each one means for you.

60

✝ **S C R I P T U R E   B A C K G R O U N D**

The Ten Commandments The commandments were meant to be rules that put God first and also protected the community. The agreement between God and the community gave people guidance in their relationships with God and with one another.

OPTIONAL ACTIVITY

Children's Literature Students may enjoy reading or listening to *A Mountain of Blintzes* by Barbara Diamond Goldin (Harcourt, Inc.). It tells the story of a family preparing for *Shavuot,* the Jewish holiday celebrating the day that Moses received the Ten Commandments.

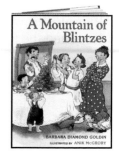

Multiple Intelligence: Verbal/Linguistic

The Ten Commandments

The commandment	What the commandment means
1. I am the Lord your God. You shall not have strange gods before me.	• Place your faith in God alone. • Worship, praise, and thank the Creator. • Believe in, trust, and love God.
2. You shall not take the name of the Lord your God in vain.	• Speak God's name with reverence. • Don't curse. • Never call on God to witness to a lie.
3. Remember to keep holy the Lord's day.	• Gather to worship at the Eucharist. • Rest and avoid unnecessary work on Sunday.
4. Honor your father and your mother.	• Respect and obey your parents, guardians, and others who have proper authority.
5. You shall not kill.	• Respect and protect the lives of others and your own life.
6. You shall not commit adultery.	• Be faithful and loyal to friends and family. • Respect God's gift of sexuality.
7. You shall not steal.	• Respect the things that belong to others. • Share what you have with those in need.
8. You shall not bear false witness against your neighbor.	• Be honest and truthful. • Do not brag about yourself. • Do not say untruthful or negative things about others.
9. You shall not covet your neighbor's wife.	• Practice modesty in thoughts, words, dress, and actions.
10. You shall not covet your neighbor's goods.	• Rejoice in others' good fortune. • Do not be jealous of others' possessions. • Do not be greedy.

Activity

Connect Your Faith

Commandments and You This week you made a number of decisions. Write down one decision you made, and tell which commandment you followed when you made that decision.

Responses will vary.

_____

_____

61

The Ten Commandments

Organize students in small groups, and assign one or two commandments to each group.

• Allow five minutes for each group to discuss examples of ways that they could apply the commandments to their everyday lives.

• Ask one student from each group to share the group's examples with the class.

• Write on the board the words *God* and *Others*. Ask volunteers to tell which commandments honor God (1–3) and which tell how to treat others. (4–10) Record students' responses under the appropriate headings.

Activity

• Read the directions aloud. Tell students that thinking carefully about each commandment will help them respond. Invite students to share their decisions.

Quick Review

The Ten Commandments are God's laws for living happily in freedom.

3 Celebrate

Objective: To give thanks and praise to the Lord

 Let Us Pray

Tell students that they will sing and pray the way the Israelites did when they escaped from Egypt.

Psalm of Celebration

Prepare

Choose four readers. You will be the leader.

 Use the *Call to Faith 4* CD, track 3, to rehearse the suggested song.

Gather

Invite students to gather in the prayer space with their books.

Pray

- Follow the order of prayer on page 62.
- An optional reading is *Isaiah 43:1–4.*
- Leader's concluding prayer: **Thank you, God, for giving us your holy words. Help us follow your commandments faithfully.**

Celebrate

Psalm of Celebration

 Let Us Pray

Gather and begin with the Sign of the Cross.

Sing together the refrain.

Sing, O people, sing our God together, raise your voices: sing alleluia!

"Sing Our God Together" © 1993, GIA Publications, Inc.

Leader:	The Lord gives us the commandments as a way of living. Let us praise God for the gift of salvation.
Reader 1:	Then was our mouth filled with laughter, on our lips there were songs.
All:	*Sing refrain.*
Reader 2:	What marvels the LORD worked for us! Indeed we were glad.
All:	*Sing refrain.*
Reader 3:	Those who are sowing in tears will sing when they reap.
All:	*Sing refrain.*
Reader 4:	They go out, they go out, full of tears; they come back, they come back, full of song.
All:	*Sing refrain.*
Leader:	Let us pray. *Bow your heads as the leader prays.*
All:	**Amen.**

Based on *Psalm 126*

62

 LITURGY LINK

Songs   Songs are an integral part of the liturgy. They invite everyone to participate in prayer and praise.

- Include familiar liturgical songs in your prayer experiences.

- Encourage students to sing in loud, clear voices to show their love for God.

 LECTIONARY LINK

Break Open the Word   Read last week's Sunday Gospel. Invite students to think about what the reading means to them as they try to follow Christ's example. For questions related to the weekly Gospel reading, visit our website at **www.osvcurriculum.com.**

 Visit www.osvcurriculum.com for weekly Scripture readings and seasonal resources.

A Work with Words
Match each description in Column 1 with the correct term in Column 2.

Column 1

<u>d</u> **1.** forgave his brothers

<u>e</u> **2.** Israelites' place of slavery

<u>b</u> **3.** leader of Egypt

<u>a</u> **4.** led Israelites to freedom

<u>c</u> **5.** some of God's laws

Column 2

a. Moses

b. Pharaoh

c. Ten Commandments

d. Joseph

e. Egypt

B Check Understanding
Write these commandments. Tell a partner one way to keep each commandment.

3rd: Remember to keep holy the Lord's day.

4th: Honor your father and your mother.

5th: You shall not kill.

7th: You shall not steal.

Activity Live Your Faith

Commandment Bookmark Design a bookmark with a saying on each side. On the front, write a way to keep one of the first three commandments. On the back, write a way to keep one of the last seven commandments. Decorate your bookmark.

Rest on Sunday

Be honest and Truthful

63

Review and Apply
Use the focus questions from the catechist Explore pages to review the lesson concepts.

A Work with Words
Read aloud the directions, and have students complete the matching exercise. Discuss their responses.

B Check Understanding
Read aloud the directions. Remind students that they may refer to page 61 of the text. Allow time for partners to share.

Activity

- Provide materials for the bookmark activity.
- If time is short, you may want to have students complete the project at home.
- Encourage students to use the bookmarks in their textbooks.

 JUSTICE AND PEACE

Get-Well Cards In *Everyday Christianity*, the U.S. Catholic bishops state that children learn by actions.

- Obtain your parish's list of people who are sick.
- Have students make get-well cards using construction paper, markers, and other materials.

Get Well

Catholic Social Teaching: Life and Dignity

Family Faith

Remind students to discuss the Family Faith page at home. Encourage students to read the passage from the Gospel according to Matthew.

> Activity

- Review with students that a *covenant* is a special promise between God and humans.
- Read aloud the activity directions, and make sure that students understand how to do the activity.

People of Faith

Tell students about Aaron and Miriam.

- Aaron was the spokesperson for his brother Moses to the Pharaoh. Miriam, the sister of Moses, led the ritual dance and song of gratitude with her tambourine. You will find her song in *Exodus 15:20–21*.
- Remind students to add Aaron and Miriam to their People of Faith albums. Encourage them to pray the prayer at home with their families.

 Visit **www.osvcurriculum.com** for weekly scripture readings and seasonal resources.

CHAPTER 3
Family Faith

⊙ Catholics Believe

- God gave you the Ten Commandments to help you be faithful to him and his covenant.
- The commandments tell you ways to love God and others.

✝ SCRIPTURE

Read *Matthew 5:43–48* to learn about the importance of loving both friends and enemies.

GO online www.osvcurriculum.com
For weekly scripture readings and seasonal resources

Activity
Live Your Faith

Covenants With your family, discuss what you learned about living God's covenant. Then write a family covenant. Begin by writing ways that you will show love and respect for one another. Then, write a promise to love God and others. Sign your names to the covenant, and display it where all can see it.

People of Faith

Aaron was the older brother of Moses. He assisted his brother in the Exodus from Egypt and during the years in the desert. Aaron was a high priest, responsible for the worship and sacrifice that would keep the Israelites on the path God had set for them. **Miriam** was the sister of Aaron and Moses. She is called a prophet—a person who speaks the truth to the people about God. She led the women in song and dance after the escape from Egypt.

▲ **Aaron and Miriam**
c. 1800 B.C.

🌱 Family Prayer

God our Father, help us see and follow your guidance, as Aaron and Miriam did. Give us patience on our faith journey. Amen.

In Unit 1 your child is learning about REVELATION.

64 **CCC** See Catechism of the Catholic Church 2055, 2060–2061 for further reading on chapter content.

❓ HOW DID I DO?

My session was

☐ *one of the best ever!* ☐ *pretty good.* ☐ *in need of improvement.*

In what discussions and activities were students most interested?

_____

What activity did I most enjoy teaching?

_____

In what area do I need to improve?

_____

Name _____ Date _____

The Ten Commandments

Unscramble the words to complete the Ten Commandments.

1. I am the Lord your God. You shall not have **(egasrtn)** _____
   (dsog) _____ before me.

2. You shall not **(etka)** _____ the name of the Lord your God in
   (aniv) _____.

3. **(memReerb)** _____ to keep **(ylho)** _____ the Lord's day.

4. Honor your **(fteahr)** _____ and your **(tomhre)** _____.

5. You **(llhsa)** _____ not **(ikll)** _____.

6. You shall not **(mocmit)** _____ **(adtrulye)** _____.

7. You **(halls)** _____ not **(lstae)** _____.

8. You shall not bear **(flsae)** _____ **(tiwnses)** _____ against
   your neighbor.

9. You shall not **(vocet)** _____ your neighbor's **(weif)** _____.

10. You shall not **(cotve)** _____ your neighbor's **(gdoos)** _____.

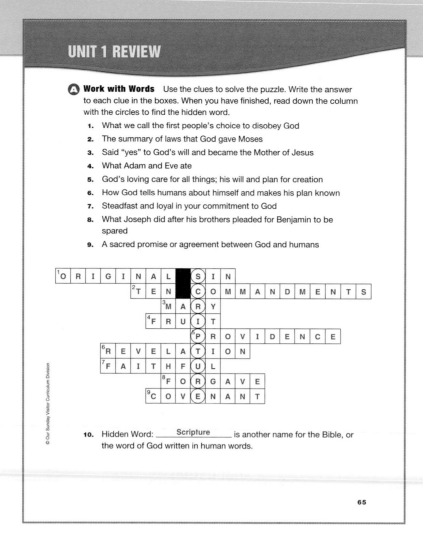

Ⓐ Work with Words Use the clues to solve the puzzle. Write the answer to each clue in the boxes. When you have finished, read down the column with the circles to find the hidden word.

1. What we call the first people's choice to disobey God
2. The summary of laws that God gave Moses
3. Said "yes" to God's will and became the Mother of Jesus
4. What Adam and Eve ate
5. God's loving care for all things; his will and plan for creation
6. How God tells humans about himself and makes his plan known
7. Steadfast and loyal in your commitment to God
8. What Joseph did after his brothers pleaded for Benjamin to be spared
9. A sacred promise or agreement between God and humans

1. ORIGINAL SIN
2. TEN COMMANDMENTS
3. MARY
4. FRUIT
5. PROVIDENCE
6. REVELATION
7. FAITHFUL
8. FORGAVE
9. COVENANT

© Our Sunday Visitor Curriculum Division

10. Hidden Word: _____Scripture_____ is another name for the Bible, or the word of God written in human words.

Unit Review

The Unit Review is designed to prepare students for the Unit Assessment. This page focuses on vocabulary words and the main concepts presented in the chapters.

Each review contains various sections that will appeal to the many different learning styles of your students. There are puzzles to engage students' attention, as well as true-false, multiple-choice, short-answer, and fill-in-the-blank exercises.

Direct students to complete the review, and check their responses. Determine areas in which students still need practice, and review those sections of the unit.

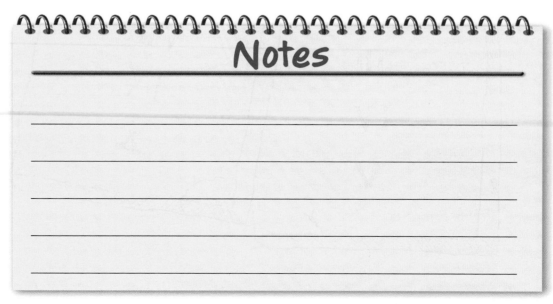

Notes

Name _____ Date _____

God's Covenant

(A) Work with Words   Match each description in Column 1 with the correct term in Column 2.

Column 1

_____ **1.** God's loving care

_____ **2.** one who tried to avoid God's plan

_____ **3.** the truth God has shown the world

_____ **4.** the word of God in human words

_____ **5.** one whose descendants are as numerous as the stars

_____ **6.** being steadfast and loyal in commitments to God

_____ **7.** the first humans' choice to disobey God

_____ **8.** a sacred promise or agreement joining God and people

Column 2

a. Jonah

b. revelation

c. Abraham

d. covenant

e. providence

f. Scripture

g. faithful

h. original sin

(B) Check Understanding   Circle the letter that best completes the sentence or answers the question.

9. To live in a loving relationship with God and each other, the people of Israel followed the

    a. laws of Egypt.
    b. Ten Commandments.
    c. civil laws.
    d. laws of nature.

10. Which of the following did NOT come about as a result of sin?

    a. jealousy
    b. sadness
    c. fighting
    d. boredom

11. With her husband, Sarah is an ancestor to all of these faiths except

    a. Christianity.
    b. Islam.
    c. Judaism.
    d. Hinduism.

ASSESSMENT

Answers can be found in the back of the Catechist Manual.

Unit 1 Assessment   65A

Name _____ Date _____

12. Which person was sold as a slave by his brothers?

    a. Abraham

    b. Jacob

    c. Joseph

    d. Aaron

13. Which leader of the chosen people parted the Red Sea?

    a. Moses

    b. Miriam

    c. Noah

    d. Nineveh

14. The first three commandments show people how to

    a. pray.

    b. be faithful to God.

    c. care for creation.

    d. work for love and justice.

15. God asked Abram and Sarai to journey to

    a. Egypt.

    b. Canaan.

    c. Eden.

    d. Jerusalem.

Ⓒ Make Connections Use the five terms below to write a one-paragraph answer.

    plan   time   faith   sin   save

16–20. In this unit, you read scripture stories about creation and Adam and Eve, Jonah and the big fish, Abraham, Joseph, and Moses. Summarize one of these stories, and tell what it teaches you about God.

_____

_____

_____

_____

_____

_____

_____

ASSESSMENT

Answers can be found in the back of the Catechist Manual.

Unit 2
Trinity

In this unit you will...

learn that you are made in God's image and likeness and are to live and love in community. Showing love to others is a way we reflect the love of the Holy Trinity. Sin is the failure to do so. You will learn that Persons of the Trinity help you to do good and avoid evil. You do this by using your free will and following your conscience.

Chapter 4   Chapter 5   Chapter 6

 What do you think you will learn in this unit about faithful people?

66

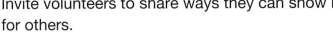

UNIT 2 OPENER

Preview Unit Theme

Tell students that Unit 2 is about the Trinity.

- Read aloud the text on page 66 of the student edition. Tell students they will learn more about these things in the next three chapters.

- Ask students what they think it means to be made in God's image.

- Invite volunteers to share ways they can show love for others.

In God's Image

CATECHIST FORMATION

✝ *"For 'In him we live and move and have our being,' as even some of your poets have said, 'For we too are his offspring.'"*

Acts 17:28

The Human Soul

Humans have a spiritual dimension that is no less real than the physical one. This spiritual dimension of humans is called the soul. Humans, however, are not divided creatures, one part body and another part soul. The soul completes a human and makes each person a whole being.

Humans are made in God's image. All humans are bound as brothers and sisters, regardless of individual differences. Being created in God's image is humanity's most profound common trait. Body and soul share in the dignity of the image of God. The soul is the gift of life breathed into humans by the Creator. The soul is immortal and will transcend even the death of the physical body.

Dignity and Respect

Human dignity comes first from the fact that all people are creations of God. Therefore, humans are products of love, wisdom, and goodness beyond understanding. Respect for life at all stages is the only appropriate response to such divine generosity. Human life is sacred because all humans are offspring of the sacred. There can be no greater dignity than this.

Reflect *In what ways does your life show honor to God and respect for others?*

Respect

The virtue of respect is something that is better modeled than lectured about. You have an excellent opportunity, in this chapter, to encourage students to grow in their respect for themselves and for others.

The word *respect* means "a second look"—moving beyond one's preconceived notions and stereotypes to find the image of God in all people. Here are some ways that you can help students practice respect.

- Ban teasing, name-calling, gossip, and insults from all group interchange, even when the intent is "humorous." Names *do* hurt.

- Show respect for differences by encouraging students to participate in whatever way they feel comfortable. Some are talkers. Others are listeners, writers, artists, or dancers.

- Have students role-play common situations of unfairness or injustice that they encounter at school or in the neighborhood. Invite the group to suggest respectful solutions.

- Incorporate prayers, songs, crafts, and snacks from diverse ethnic and cultural traditions into your time together to help students learn respect for differences.

Dignity

- I am concerned about fairness. Encourage me to speak up when I see others treated unfairly.

- I am curious about other lands and cultures. Give me opportunities to learn about all kinds of people.

- Sometimes I want to be like everyone else. Help me appreciate my unique gifts.

Engagement with Others

Blessed assurance in yourself is important. It is also important to experience significant and constructive engagement with others. Doing so enables you to

- see firsthand the goodness of others.
- recognize that sometimes a task is best addressed by a team.
- replenish your level of empathy.
- see that you can still benefit from different styles and approaches.

Engagement with others sustains your spirit by pulling you past your own limitations and by restoring your faith in yourself and others.

	Lone Ranger				Engaged with others
Reflect **Rate yourself**	1	2	3	4	5

Catechist's Prayer

God and Father of all, help me and my students remember that we are created in your image. Guide us to see your Son, Jesus, in every person we meet. Fill us with your Holy Spirit as we learn to break down the sinful walls of injustice. Amen.

Weekly Planner

Objectives	Lesson Process	Materials

1 Invite

10 minutes

Page 67
Objective:
To recognize that everyone is created in the image of God

🙏 **Let Us Pray:** Psalm 104:30

- Pray the psalm verse.
- Read the poem.
- Discuss what is special about each student.

---

2 Explore

40 minutes

Pages 68–69
Objective:
To appreciate the dignity of human life

✝ **Scripture:** Genesis 1:27

- Read and discuss the Rosa Parks story.
- Proclaim the scripture story.
- **Activity** Complete the Share Your Faith Activity.

Words of Faith dignity, soul

Materials:
- ☐ Board or chart paper
- ☐ Copies of Activity Master 4 on page 74A
- ☐ Pencils or pens

Pages 70–71
Objective:
To discover how a failure to love leads to sin

- Discuss sin as a failure to love.
- Examine the differences between mortal and venial sin.
- Introduce the concept of social sin.
- **Activity** Complete the Connect Your Faith Activity.

Words of Faith sin, social sin

---

3 Celebrate

10 minutes

Page 72
Objective:
To pray for the dignity of all people

🙏 **Let Us Pray**

- Rehearse the responses.
- Gather as a community.
- Celebrate a Prayer for Dignity and Respect.
- **Hymn:** "Behold, I Make All Things New"

- **Activity** Complete the Act of Love Activity, page 248 and 249

Materials:
- ☐ Hymnals
- ☐ Music CD
- ☐ Bible

Wrap Up

Review and Apply

Page 73
- Review the chapter concepts.
- Complete the Live Your Faith Activity.

Family Faith

Page 74
- Introduce the page, and assign it as a family activity.
- Read about Saint Edith Stein.

ACRE Connection, Domain 5—Dignity of the Human Person

Home Connection

GO online www.osvcurriculum.com
Family Faith activities, feasts and seasonal resources, saint features, and much more

CALL to FAITH e connect

- Online planning tools include chapter background and planner, activity master, customizable test, and more.
- Enhancement activities for each step of the catechetical process, including alternative prayer experiences and blessings.
- Games, activities, interactive review, alternative assessment, and more for children

www.calltofaitheconnect.com

Chapter 4 In God's Image

Objective: To recognize that everyone is created in the image of God

🙌 Let Us Pray

Leader: God, we give you praise and thanks for all creation.
"When you send forth your breath, they are created,
and you renew the face of the earth."
Psalm 104:30

All: God, we give you praise and thanks for all creation. Amen.

🙌 Let Us Pray

Ask students to move to the classroom prayer space. In the space, have a crucifix and a Bible opened to the psalm. Tell students to sit quietly for a moment. Ask them to be attentive to their own breathing. Remind them that breath is a sign of life and a symbol of the Holy Spirit. Pray aloud the psalm verse.

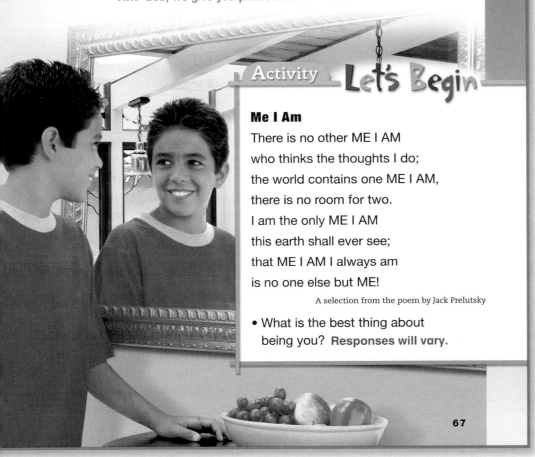

Activity · Let's Begin

Me I Am

There is no other ME I AM
who thinks the thoughts I do;
the world contains one ME I AM,
there is no room for two.
I am the only ME I AM
this earth shall ever see;
that ME I AM I always am
is no one else but ME!

A selection from the poem by Jack Prelutsky

• What is the best thing about being you? **Responses will vary.**

67

Activity

• Slowly read "Me I Am."

• Next, do a choral reading of the poem. Ask students to join in each time they see the words "Me I Am."

• Finally, ask each student to think of a response to the question that follows the poem. Allow time for sharing.

• Tell students that their responses are what make them different and special. Then tell them that they are also special because they are made in the image of God. In the next part of the lesson, they will learn what this means.

Make Thumbprint Portraits Extend the poem by having students show their individuality.

• Tell students that each person's fingerprints are unique.

• Have each student make a thumbprint on a poster board and personalize it.

Multiple Intelligence: Visual/Spatial

✦ CATECHIST BACKGROUND

Poet Jack Prelutsky was born in New York in 1940. Although his poetry appeals to children, Prelutsky says that he didn't like poetry as a child and became interested in it only later in life. Now he spends much of his time sharing his poetry with young admirers in schools and libraries.

Objective: To appreciate the dignity of human life

 **Focus**

What does it mean to be created in the image of God? List students' responses on the board or on chart paper.

An Image of Love

Introduce the biography of Rosa Parks by summarizing the first paragraph. Ask students if they know who Rosa Parks is. Encourage responses.

Rosa Parks

Read aloud the biography of Rosa Parks. Ask students to think about how they might feel if they were treated as Rosa was.

- Emphasize that because all humans are created in God's image, everyone has dignity and is worthy of respect. The Rosa Parks story is an example of this truth.

- Invite discussion of the question in the text. Begin by sharing examples from your own experience.

Explore

Faith Fact

James Augustine Healy was the first African American Catholic bishop in the United States. He was named bishop of Portland, Maine, in 1875.

68

An Image of Love

 Focus What does it mean to be created in the image of God?

God has given you life. He has created you and all people to reflect his own image of love. God's image can shine in you and in every person you meet. The story of Rosa Parks teaches us that all people should be treated equally.

A BIOGRAPHY

Rosa Parks

On the evening of December 1, 1955, Rosa Parks boarded a public bus in Montgomery, Alabama, and took a seat in the *white section*. The bus filled quickly, and soon there were no more seats. The driver noticed that Rosa, a black woman, was not sitting in the *colored section*. He asked Rosa to move to the back of the bus, but she refused. She did not argue. She simply did not move.

Before the 1960s, African Americans were unjustly treated because of their skin color. They were separated from the rest of society in many ways. Long after that day on the bus, Rosa Parks wrote, "Our mistreatment was just not right, and I was tired of it. I kept thinking about my mother and my grandparents, and how strong they were. I knew there was a possibility of being mistreated, but an opportunity was being given to me to do what I had asked of others."

 When have you observed that someone was being treated in a certain way simply because of the color of his or her skin? Responses will vary.

★ **REACHING ALL LEARNERS**

Visual Learners Some students are visual learners. They need to see words and pictures.

- Use a picture or a prop when telling a story.
- Write key words on the board or on chart paper.
- Point out the illustrations and photos in the text as you tell the story.

Created with Dignity

Rosa Parks was a true hero of the struggle for human rights in the United States. Yet she began by doing one simple thing on a day when she was tired. Rosa expressed the very basic Christian belief that all people have **dignity** because they are created in God's image.

SCRIPTURE

God created man in his image;
in the divine image he created him;
male and female he created them.

Genesis 1:27

God made you with a human body, and you have a **soul** that will live forever. God gave you the ability to think, to love, and to make choices. You can make choices for human dignity every day.

Activity

Share Your Faith

Reflect: Think of a time when you or someone you know showed respect or treated someone with dignity.

Share: Tell a partner what happened.

Act: List some ways you can protect the dignity of others.
Possible responses: Be polite, include others, and don't bully or tease.

69

Created with Dignity

Read aloud the first paragraph. Then have a strong reader proclaim the scripture passage.

- Tell students that this passage comes from the story of creation. Explain that people have dignity because they are created in the image of God.

- Ask students to silently read the last paragraph. Call on volunteers to summarize the abilities that God gave humans that enable them to make choices for human dignity.

Activity

- Assign partners, and have students share a time when they treated someone with dignity or respect. Then have partners work together to list ways of treating others with dignity.

Quick Review

All people are created in God's image and are equal in dignity. It is important to treat all people with respect.

✝ SCRIPTURE BACKGROUND

Soul Humans are the only creatures created in God's likeness because they are the only ones who have immortal souls. The human body shares in the dignity of this image of God.

- Because humans have both body and soul, their creation unites the world of matter and spirit.

- God created people with the capacity to share in his divine nature. This is the source of human dignity and worth.

OPTIONAL ACTIVITY

Activity Master 4: Human Dignity in Scripture Distribute the activity on catechist page 74A.

- Help students locate the scripture passages.

- As an alternative, you may wish to send this activity home with students.

▲ Activity Master 4

Objective: To discover how a failure to love leads to sin

 **Focus**

What is sin? List students' responses on the board or on chart paper.

Made to Love

Ask a volunteer to read aloud the first paragraph to introduce the topic of sin. Ask students what happens when they act in a loving way.

Failure to Love

Draw students' attention to the heading and the highlighted word.

- Tell them that "failure to love" is one definition of *sin*. Have them silently read the first paragraph.
- Read aloud the first sentence of the next paragraph. Have students continue reading silently.
- Copy the graphic organizer onto the board or chart paper. Work with students to name differences between mortal and venial sins.
- Ask which kind of sin fourth graders are more likely to commit. venial sin

---

Explore

Made to Love

Focus What is sin?

God created you to be united to him and to all people. Every time you act in a loving way, you deepen your connection to God and to the members of the Church, the Body of Christ. When you choose to treat someone badly, you hurt this person and the whole community of faith. You choose not to show love and respect.

Failure to Love

Sin is always a failure to love. A sinful thought, word, or act also hurts your friendship with God. Sin affects you, too, and keeps you from becoming the person God wants you to be.

There are two kinds of personal sin—mortal and venial. Serious sins, such as murder, are called mortal sins. They destroy the friendship a person has with God and with others. In order for a sin to be mortal, the act must be seriously wrong, you must know that it is seriously wrong, and you must freely choose to do it anyway.

Venial sins are less serious sins. They are things that you do, such as disobeying, cheating, and lying, or bad habits that you develop, such as being lazy or dishonest. Sometimes sin is a failure to act. This is a sin of omission. An example of this would be to remain silent when someone tells a joke that makes fun of another person or group. Venial sin hurts your friendship with God and others, but it does not destroy it.

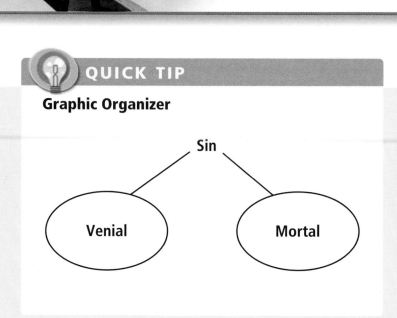

70

QUICK TIP

Graphic Organizer

Sin

Venial   Mortal

Love and Respect

Social sin refers to the results of sin that can build up over time in a community or nation. One example of social sin is not allowing someone of a certain race or group to buy a house in a certain neighborhood. Rosa Parks acted against inequality and social sin. She defended her own dignity and the dignity of others.

All people are equal. Every person has dignity and is worthy of respect because he or she is made in God's image. Because he is the Son of God, Jesus is the perfect image of God. You are called to become more like Jesus and to reflect the love and care that he shows all people.

Words of Faith

Sin is a deliberate thought, word, deed, or omission contrary to the law of God.

Social sin is a sinful social structure or institution that builds up over time so that it affects the whole society.

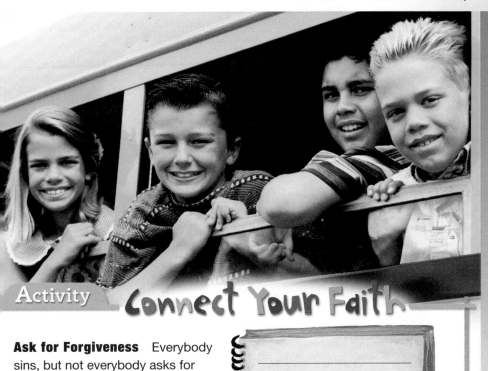

Activity

Connect Your Faith

Ask for Forgiveness Everybody sins, but not everybody asks for God's forgiveness. Write a personal prayer, asking God's forgiveness for some of your past actions.

71

Love and Respect

Conclude this section of the lesson by asking students to read these paragraphs silently.

- **Ask students to recall how Rosa Parks made a difference.** By refusing to move to the back of the bus, she defended her dignity and the dignity of others.

- Remind students that every person is worthy of respect because he or she is made in God's image.

Activity

- Have a volunteer read aloud the directions.
- Then give students time to think and write.
- Allow students' prayers to remain personal by not asking them to share aloud.

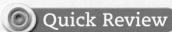 **Quick Review**

Sin is a failure to love. It hurts you, others, and your relationship with God. Social sin is sin that builds up so that it affects a whole society.

OPTIONAL ACTIVITY

Write a Group Prayer Have students write a group prayer instead of individual ones.

- When students write a prayer, use it in a celebration.
- Print the words on the board or on chart paper.
- Have students create gestures.

Our Prayer

Merciful God, Forgive us when we sin.

Multiple Intelligence: Interpersonal

JUSTICE AND PEACE

Explain Racism Explain that practices such as requiring African Americans to sit at the back of the bus and refusing to consider people of color for certain jobs are examples of racism.

- The U.S. Conference of Catholic Bishops, in *Brothers and Sisters to Us*, called racism "a sin that divides the human family."
- The faithful are urged to speak out against racism.

Catholic Social Teaching: Life and Dignity

3 Celebrate

Objective: To pray for the dignity of all people

 Let Us Pray

Tell students that they will pray for the dignity of human life.

Prayer for Dignity and Respect

Prepare

Choose a leader for the prayer.

• Practice the response with students.

 Use the *Call to Faith 4* CD, track 4, to rehearse the suggested song.

Gather

Invite students to gather in the prayer space.

Pray

• Follow the order of prayer on page 72.

• Optional reading: *Matthew 4:8–11.*

Celebrate

Prayer for Dignity and Respect

 Let Us Pray

Gather and begin with the Sign of the Cross.

 Sing together.

Behold, behold, I make all things new, beginning with you and starting from today.
Behold, behold, I make all things new, my promise is true, for I am Christ the way.

"Behold, I Make All Things New" © 1994, The Iona Community, GIA Publications, Inc., agent

Reader:	God of life,
All:	**We pray for the dignity of life.**
Reader:	God of creation,
All:	**We pray for the dignity of life.**
Reader:	God, the source of all life,
All:	**We pray for the dignity of life.**
Reader:	God, the protector of all humanity,
All:	**We pray for the dignity of life.**
Leader:	God, we give you praise and thanks for all creation.
All:	**Amen.**

72

 LITURGY LINK

Choose a Reader   Make sure that each student acts as prayer leader or reader sometime during the year. Be aware of what the leader or reader is required to do in each prayer service. In this celebration, the reader reads short phrases rather than a long passage. You may wish to select a student who is not a confident reader.

LECTIONARY LINK

Break Open the Word   Read last week's Sunday Gospel. Invite students to think about what the reading means to them as they try to follow Christ's example. For questions related to the weekly Gospel reading, visit our website at **www.osvcurriculum.com**.

 Visit www.osvcurriculum.com for weekly Scripture readings and seasonal resources.

Review and Apply

A **Check Understanding** Mark each statement True or False. Correct each false statement. **Corrections will vary.**

1. A bully can never reflect God's image.
   _____False_____ **Everyone reflects God's image.**

2. God is with everyone at all times in all places.
   _____True_____

3. You commit a mortal sin when you cheat on a spelling test. _____False_____ **You commit a venial sin.**

4. Rosa Parks was a victim of social sin. _____True_____

5. Each person is unique, created by God. _____True_____

B **Make Connections** Why are all people worthy of respect?
Responses will vary.
_____
_____
_____

Activity — Live Your Faith

Show Respect Like Rosa Parks, some people or groups of people do not get the respect they deserve. What advice would you give to a person who is treating someone else with little or no respect?

Possible response: Remember that all people are made in God's image.
_____
_____

73

Review and Apply

Use the focus questions from the catechist Explore pages to review the lesson concepts.

A **Check Understanding** Have students identify each of the five statements as true or false. Ask volunteers to share how they changed the false statements to make them true.

B **Make Connections** Invite volunteers to share their responses to the question.

Activity

• Ask students to work in groups to brainstorm possible advice.

• After the students have completed the activity, ask for volunteers to share their responses.

OPTIONAL ACTIVITY

Human Life Collage Supply old magazines, and ask students to find pictures that show humans treating one another with dignity and respect.

• Glue these pictures to poster board.

• Use markers to add words or ideas that encourage others to respect all persons.

Multiple Intelligence: Visual/Spatial

Family Faith

Remind students to discuss the Family Faith page at home. Encourage students to read the passage from Leviticus.

Activity

- Demonstrate the craft, or show students a sample you have made.

People of Faith

Tell students about Teresa Benedicta of the Cross (given name: Edith Stein).

- Edith Stein respected the Jewish faith of her family until her conversion to Catholicism. She made this conversion decision after reading the autobiography of Saint Teresa of Ávila. When Edith Stein became a Carmelite nun, she chose the name Sister Teresa Benedicta of the Cross. She reminds people of the importance of forgiveness.

- Remind students to add Saint Teresa to their People of Faith albums. Encourage them to pray the prayer at home with their families.

 Visit **www.osvcurriculum.com** for weekly scripture readings and seasonal resources.

UNIT 2: CHAPTER 4
Family Faith

Catholics Believe

- Every person is worthy of respect because he or she is created in God's image.
- Each person has a soul that will live forever.

✝ SCRIPTURE

Read *Leviticus 19:1–18, 31–37* to learn other ways in which you can respect others and yourself and treat each person with dignity.

 GO online www.osvcurriculum.com
For weekly scripture readings and seasonal resources

Activity
Live Your Faith

Inside and Outside When we respect our own dignity and that of others, we give honor to God, who has created us in his image. Gather some paper bags and magazines. Find pictures that show how you think others see you. Glue the pictures on the outside of a bag. Then find and place pictures inside the bag that show what God sees in you. Invite each person to share the contents of the bag if he or she wishes.

People of Faith

Saint Teresa Benedicta was a teacher, a convert, and a Carmelite nun. Born Edith Stein, she lived during the first part of the twentieth century and took the name Teresa Benedicta. Her life was dedicated to teaching, especially the teaching of young girls and women. During the Nazi persecution of Jews, Edith was arrested and executed at Auschwitz. She is a model of the importance of forgiveness and reconciliation during a time of great violence. Saint Teresa's feast day is August 9.

▲ **Saint Teresa Benedicta 1891–1942**

🙌 Family Prayer

Saint Teresa, may your life be a model. Pray for us that we might learn to forgive, even our enemies. Amen.

74 *In Unit 2 your child is learning about the TRINITY.* **CCC** See Catechism of the Catholic Church 355–357, 362–366 for further reading on chapter content.

❓ HOW DID I DO?

My session was

☐ *one of the best ever!*   ☐ *pretty good.*   ☐ *in need of improvement.*

In what discussions and activities were students most interested?

_____

What activity did I most enjoy teaching?

_____

In what area do I need to improve?

_____

Name _____ Date _____

Human Dignity in Scripture

Every person is created in God's image and is worthy of respect. Jesus respected the dignity of everyone he met, especially the outcasts of society.

Read the verses listed below, and complete the chart.

Scripture	Whom did Jesus treat with dignity?	How did Jesus show that he respected the person?
1. *Matthew 8:1–4*	a man with leprosy	Jesus touched and healed him.
2. *Mark 2:13–17*	tax collectors and sinners	Jesus ate with them and spent time with them.
3. *Luke 7:36–50*	a sinful woman	Jesus allowed the woman to kiss and anoint his feet; he forgave her.
4. *Luke 19:1–10*	Zacchaeus	Jesus stayed at his house
5. *John 4:4–42*	a Samaritan woman	Jesus spoke with her and promised her "living water."

Answers can be found in the back of the Catechist Manual.

Chapter 4 Activity Master 74A

Overview

Faith Focus

- **God created people to live and work and worship in communities.** *(CCC 1905–1906)*
- **Demonstrating love for one's neighbor is a way of reflecting the love of the Holy Trinity.** *(CCC 1878)*

Catechism Connection

The *Catechism* states that the morality of human acts depends on the object, the intention, and the circumstances of an action. *(CCC 1757)*

NDC Link

Catechesis helps build up the Body of Christ. When you teach, you are leading others in the Christian community on behalf of both the local church and the community of all believers. (See *NDC*, 19C.)

Resources

BOOKS
Catholic Bible Stories for Children. Ball, Ann with Will, Julianne M. Our Sunday Visitor. Stories of witness, worship, and tradition build on faith formation.

What Is Right and Wrong and How Do We Know? Huebsch, Bill. [Growing Faith Project series] Twenty-Third Publications. Summarizes teachings on morality and conscience.

*Available at www.osvcurriculum.com

 Catechist Resources
For interactive lesson planner, chapter resources, and activities
www.osvcurriculum.com

 The commandments, "You shall not commit adultery; you shall not kill; you shall not steal; you shall not covet," and whatever other commandment there may be, are summed up in this saying, [namely] "You shall love your neighbor as yourself."

Romans 13:9

Christian Morality

Morality begins with relationships—your conscious choice to live with God and with others in peace and with compassion. The more you choose good, alone or with others, the better your relationships with God and others will be. Choosing what is morally good goes along with learning to live in accordance with God's laws. God's laws are your practical guides to morality.

Your loving God always supports you in living by his laws. Your relationships with those in your community—in your parish, for example—help you by surrounding you with other believers. Your relationships with God and others help you form a correct conscience and develop life-affirming habits.

The Common Good

All communities, from your immediate family to entire nations, survive and thrive only when there is recognition of the common good, the needs of the group and all its members. Working for the common good is not simply enlightened self-interest; it is an authentic Christian practice. As a Catholic, you are called by the grace of your Baptism to respect all persons, promote the well-being of everyone, and work for justice and peace. Promoting the common good is central to the mission of Christ.

Reflect **How have you promoted the common good?**

Christian Community

Fourth graders are entering a stage of faith that is characterized by wanting to belong. Help students better understand the Christian community by putting it in the context of what students know from belonging to teams or clubs.

- Recall stories from Scripture, including those of the early Church. Point out how Catholics today are united with earlier Christians in consistent values of respect, service, and sharing.

- Remind students of factors that make teams or groups more likely to succeed: Members must work together; everyone must develop his or her skills.

- Clarify the gospel values that promote the common good by citing real-life examples— anyone from Mother Teresa to a leader in your own parish.

Community

- I like to solve problems. Let me brainstorm solutions that benefit the group.

- I can help build community. Show me ways to be supportive of others.

- I want to know more about other people. Help me understand how people of all cultures make our community special and unique.

Multiple Belonging

People who are comfortable belonging to groups of people possess a wealth of resources. Sustaining the spirit to teach is easier for those who have been raised in one core group of people but have now learned how to move smoothly within another group. The second group may have a different economic or educational level, value system, or ethnicity.

Living within just one core group can lead to a narrow sense of what is important, a poor sense of what is needed, and limited ways of coping with tough times. Belonging to multiple groups can help sustain your spirit by broadening your ability to handle difficulties, communicate, and appreciate what others cherish.

Reflect **How has belonging to multiple groups helped you sustain the spirit to teach?**

Catechist's Prayer

Loving God, thank you for the community of faith that supports me as I teach these students. May it support them as they work for the common good. Amen.

Weekly Planner

	Objectives	Lesson Process	Materials
1 Invite · 10 minutes	**Page 75** **Objective:** To understand that God created humans to live in loving relationships	**Let Us Pray:** Psalm 24:1 • Pray the psalm verse. • Read the poem. • Discuss the question.	
2 Explore · 40 minutes	**Pages 76–77** **Objective:** To define the connection between love of neighbor and love of God	• Read the story aloud, and have students present it as a readers' theater. • Discuss the question. • Explore the concept of the common good. **Activity** Complete the Share Your Faith Activity. **Words of Faith** community	☐ Board or chart paper ☐ Pens or pencils ☐ Index cards ☐ Paper, crayons, scissors, and glue
	Pages 78–79 **Objective:** To explain what it means to live a moral life	**Scripture:** Acts 2:42–45 • Read about and discuss the lives of early Christians. • Discuss how the Church helps people lead moral lives. **Activity** Complete the Connect Your Faith Activity. **Words of Faith** morality, parish	☐ Small container ☐ Copies of Activity Master 5 on page 82A
3 Celebrate · 10 minutes	**Page 80** **Objective:** To pray as a community of faith	**Let Us Pray** • Rehearse the responses. • Process to the prayer space. • Celebrate a Prayer for Community. **Hymn:** "Love One Another" **Activity** Complete the Virtues Activity, page 238 and 239	☐ Hymnals ☐ Music CD

Wrap Up

Review and Apply

Page 81
• Review the chapter concepts.
• Complete the Live Your Faith Activity.

Family Faith

Page 82
• Introduce the page, and assign it as a family activity.
• Read about Saint John of God.

ACRE Connection, Domain 5—Christian Morality

Home Connection

GO online www.osvcurriculum.com
Family Faith activities, feasts and seasonal resources, saint features, and much more

CALL to FAITH e connect

• Online planning tools include chapter background and planner, activity master, customizable test, and more.
• Enhancement activities for each step of the catechetical process, including alternative prayer experiences and blessings.
• Games, activities, interactive review, alternative assessment, and more for children.

www.calltofaitheconnect.com

 **Let Us Pray**

Leader: We thank you, O Creator, for all the gifts we share.
"The earth is the LORD's and all it holds,
the world and those who live there."

Psalm 24:1

All: We thank you, O Creator, for all the gifts we share. Amen.

Activity Let's Begin

The Chain of Life

The human race is a kind of chain
That binds the world as one.
We share the earth below our feet
And live beneath the sun.
Bodies, faces, voices, hands—
We each are given these.
All humans share the gift of life
And share a hope for peace.

• Who are three links in your chain
of life? **Responses will vary.**

75

Objective: To understand that God created humans to live in loving relationships

 **Let Us Pray**

Have students gather in the prayer space, and pray the psalm verse by asking a student to read it very slowly. Invite volunteers to give examples of gifts that God has given to humans.

Activity

• Ask for eight volunteers. Have each of them read aloud one line of the poem.

• Discuss the question that follows the poem. Invite students to share some ways that all humans are connected. Encourage students to refer to the poem to help them.

OPTIONAL ACTIVITY

The Circle of Life Have students perform Internet or library research on the concept of the "circle of life." Point students toward books or websites with examples of life cycles of animals, plants, and environments. Lead discussions on the varieties of life on Earth and the relationships among different life forms.

Multiple Intelligence: Visual/Spatial

Objective: To define the connection between love of neighbor and love of God

 Focus

What does love of neighbor have to do with love of God? List students' responses on the board or on chart paper.

Created to Love

Ask a student to read aloud the introduction to the lesson. Tell students to listen to find out how two brothers show love for one another.

Holy Ground

Remind students of the meaning of the word *holy*. dedicated to God, sharing in God's divine nature

- Read aloud Holy Ground. Then have students present the story as a readers' theater. Ask volunteers to read the parts of the narrator, Solomon, and the two men.

- Discuss with students why the two brothers are a good example of love of neighbor.

- Ask the question that follows the story.

76

Created to Love

 Focus   What does love of neighbor have to do with love of God?

From the time of the first humans, people have formed groups. God's plan is for people to live together in love. This story shows how God wants people to live.

A STORY

HOLY GROUND

One night King Solomon noticed a man carrying sacks of wheat from one barn to another. "He must be a thief," Solomon thought. Soon a different man appeared, carrying sacks of wheat back to the original barn!

The next day Solomon called each man before him separately. To the first he said, "Why do you steal from your neighbor in the middle of the night?"

"I do not steal," the man said. "My neighbor is also my brother. He has a wife and children to feed, but he won't take any extra money from me. So every night I secretly carry wheat from my barn to his."

Solomon asked the second man the same question. The man answered, "I have a big family to help me, but my brother has to pay for help, and so he needs more wheat. He won't take it from me, so at night I secretly give the wheat to him."

Solomon said, "The holiest ground in Israel is here, where brothers love each other this much. I shall build a temple here."

From a Jewish teaching story

 Why would a place where people share be a good spot for a temple?
Possible response: because the people who share are following God's plan

---

CULTURAL AWARENESS

Jewish Teaching Stories   Teaching stories have always been a way of remembering and instructing.

- Jewish spiritual leaders, called rabbis, express profound truths through stories.
- These teaching stories present moral lessons through vivid characters, memorable dialogue, and meaningful metaphors.
- Jesus followed this tradition by using parables.

QUICK TIP

Gestures   Use simple gestures to pantomime the story for students who are acquiring English. You may want to use gestures with action words such as *carry, steal, take, give,* and *build* to help students better understand the story.

Community of Love

The two brothers in the story tried to provide for each other's needs. Solomon called their land holy because he knew that God is present whenever people show their love for one another. The brothers had formed a **community** of love.

❓ **What are some other practical ways that members of a community show their love for one another?**
Responses will vary.

The Common Good

You learned in the last chapter that God made all people in his image. You are more clearly an image of God when you reflect the love of the Holy Trinity to others.

People who live in true communities work for the common good by

- respecting the dignity of each person and acknowledging each person's right to freedom and self-expression, as long as others are not hurt.
- making sure that every person has a way to get the things that are necessary for life, such as food, shelter, and clothing.
- providing peace, security, and order in the community.

Words of Faith

A **community** is a group of people who hold certain beliefs, hopes, and goals in common.

Activity — Share Your Faith

Reflect: How do people in your neighborhood work for the common good?

Share: Tell the class about one of these activities.

Act: Draw something that represents this activity. Add your drawing to those of others in the class to make a collage.

77

Community of Love

Have students silently read this paragraph. Then discuss the lesson of the story.

- Define the word *community*, and have students make a vocabulary card for it.
- Spend time on the discussion question. Possible responses: by taking meals to people who are sick, by raising money for local causes

The Common Good

Ask volunteers to read aloud the three ways that people work for the common good.

- Discuss ways that fourth graders can work for the common good.

Activity

- Give an example of people working for the common good in your community. Then have students complete the activity.
- Display the collage.

◎ Quick Review

Christians form communities that reflect the love of the Holy Trinity and work for the common good.

OPTIONAL ACTIVITY

Illustrate Laws God has laws that help people live together. So do communities.

- Discuss laws and the common good. For example, speed limits help keep the streets safe.
- Ask students to name a community law and to illustrate how that law helps people.

Multiple Intelligence: Mathematical/Logical

Explore

Objective: To explain what it means to live a moral life

Focus

What does it mean to live a moral life? List students' responses on the board or on chart paper.

Christian Living

Introduce the Scripture by reading aloud the first two paragraphs.

• Tell students that a community tries to achieve a balance between rights and responsibilities.

The Communal Life

Proclaim the Scripture.

• Discuss with students how the early Christians formed a community.
  by breaking bread, praying, sharing

• Allow time to brainstorm possible responses to the question.

Christian Living

Focus What does it mean to live a moral life?

Faith Fact

According to legend, third-century twin doctors Cosmas and Damian were nicknamed "moneyless ones" because they treated anyone who was sick for free!

Each person has individual rights that are balanced with a responsibility to respect and protect the rights of others. No one has unlimited freedom or an unlimited right to the earth's goods. When everyone's rights are in balance, the kingdom of God is close at hand.

You can see a good example of this in the story of the early Christians. From this passage we learn how they lived in the years just after the Resurrection and Ascension of Jesus.

SCRIPTURE

Acts 2:42–45

The Communal Life

They devoted themselves to the teaching of the apostles and to the communal life, to the breaking of the bread and to the prayers. Awe came upon everyone, and many wonders and signs were done through the apostles. All who believed were together and had all things in common; they would sell their property and possessions and divide them among all according to each one's need.

Acts 2:42–45

St. Lawrence Giving the Treasure of the Church to the Poor by Bernardo Strozzi

❓ What examples can you give of people today who live as early Christians did?
Possible response: people who live in monasteries or convents

78

SCRIPTURE BACKGROUND

The Acts of the Apostles The Acts of the Apostles are sometimes referred to as "the acts of the Holy Spirit" because this book recognizes the guidance of the Holy Spirit in the development of community life. The Acts provide important information about life in the earliest Christian communities, such as their sharing of goods, their celebration of the Eucharist, and their early attempts at organization.

JUSTICE AND PEACE

Think Globally Blessed Pope John Paul II, in *The Hundredth Year*, emphasized the world's interconnectedness.

• Point out that despite our differences, we are one human family.
• Discuss how people's actions affect their neighbors.

Catholic Social Teaching: Solidarity

Love One Another

The early Christians formed a community based on a common faith in Jesus Christ and his message. Their faith and love are an example for you today. Faith is your "yes" to all that God has revealed. God created all men and women equal and in his image. So respect for the rights and needs of others is part of faith.

Just as you cannot live in isolation from others, so you cannot believe alone. You believe as part of a larger community of faith. As a Christian believer, you are called to live a good moral life.

Moral Living

The Christian moral life is a way of living in right relationship with God, yourself, and others. Christian **morality** includes following the Ten Commandments, the teachings of Jesus, and the teachings of the Church. It also includes following the good and just laws that work for the common good.

Christian families and your **parish** community are places where you can learn to live the Christian moral life.

Words of Faith

Morality means living in right relationship with God, yourself, and others. It is putting your beliefs into action.

A **parish** is a Catholic community with shared spiritual beliefs and worship.

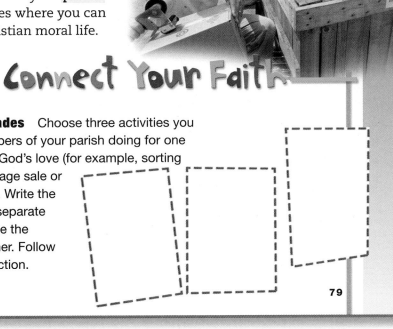

Activity

Connect Your Faith

Service Charades Choose three activities you have noticed members of your parish doing for one another that show God's love (for example, sorting clothes for a rummage sale or ushering for Mass). Write the activities on three separate slips of paper. Place the papers in a container. Follow your teacher's direction.

79

Love One Another

Read this section aloud. Point out that the early Christians took Jesus' example as their model and that Christians today do the same.

Moral Living

Ask students to read this section to identify what helps a Christian lead a moral life.

• Have students make vocabulary cards for the Words of Faith.

Activity

• Have students write each activity on a separate slip of paper. Collect all the slips in a container.

• Have students take turns choosing a slip of paper and acting out the activity on it while other students try to guess the activity being pantomimed.

• Discuss how each activity shows God's love.

Quick Review

Christian morality helps people live as a community of faith. People in communities have both rights and responsibilities.

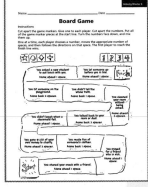

Let Us Pray

Objective: To pray as a community of faith

Tell students that they will pray for the good of the community.

Prayer for Community

Prepare

Choose three readers, and rehearse the refrain. You will be the leader.

 Use the *Call to Faith 4* CD, track 5, to rehearse the suggested song.

Gather

Process to your prayer space.

Pray

- Follow the order of prayer on page 80.
- Optional reading: *1 John 4:7–12.*
- Leader's concluding prayer: **Dear God, bless our community. Help us work for the good of everyone.**

Celebrate

Prayer for Community

 Let Us Pray

Gather and begin with the Sign of the Cross.

 *Sing together the refrain.*

Love one another. Love one another,
    as I have loved you.
Care for each other. Care for each other,
    as I care for you.

"Love One Another" © 2000, GIA Publications, Inc.

Reader 1: In this chain of life, we pray for our community.
All: **May we always respect one another.**
    Sing refrain.
Reader 2: In the chain of this parish community, we pray for greater peace, security, and order.
All: **May we always respect one another.**
    Sing refrain.
Reader 3: In the chain of our community gathered here, we pray for a right relationship with God, others, and ourselves.
All: **May we always respect one another.**
    Sing refrain.
Leader: Let us pray.
    Bow your heads as the leader prays.
All: **Amen.**

80

 LITURGY LINK

The Orans Position   You may wish to have students pray the Prayer for Community in the orans position of prayer, an ancient Jewish and early Christian position of readiness.

- Tell students to raise their arms extended out to the sides, elbows bent, with their palms open upward.
- When the prayer is finished, have students lower their arms.

 LECTIONARY LINK

Break Open the Word   Read last week's Sunday Gospel. Invite students to think about what the reading means to them as they try to follow Christ's example. For questions related to the weekly Gospel reading, visit our website at **www.osvcurriculum.com.**

 Visit www.osvcurriculum.com for weekly Scripture readings and seasonal resources.

Review and Apply

Ⓐ Work with Words Solve the crossword puzzle.

Across

3. We show respect for everyone's rights when we work for the _____.

5. When we show this to others, we follow God's way and live a moral life.

Down

1. A group of people with similar beliefs, working together toward a common goal

2. Living in right relationship with God, self, and others

4. Members of a community _____ on one another.

Crossword puzzle answers:
- 1 Down: COMMUNITY
- 2 Down: MORALITY
- 3 Across: COMMONGOOD
- 4 Down: DEPEND
- 5 Across: LOVE

Ⓑ Make Connections Why does your faith in God need to be expressed with others? **Responses will vary.**

Review and Apply

Ⓐ Work with Words Have students complete the crossword puzzle.

Ⓑ Make Connections Ask students to write their responses to the question. Invite volunteers to share their responses.

Activity

- Read aloud the activity.
- Assign groups to create a play for each of the suggested locations.
- Allow time for groups to work together and practice before presenting their play.

Activity Live Your Faith

🖊 **Moral Choices** With a small group, create a one-act play in which the main character makes a moral choice for others in school, on the playground, or at home. Outside of class, write the script and make copies for each character. Think of simple props and costumes. Practice your play, and perform it for your class next week.

81

★ REACHING ALL LEARNERS

Accessible Plays Make sure that each student has a role in his or her group's play.

- Consider having the students create pantomimes if the group includes students who have hearing or speech difficulties.

- A student who has limited mobility may enjoy taking the part of a narrator.

Family Faith

Remind students to discuss the Family Faith page at home. Encourage students to read the Third Letter of John.

Activity

• Tell students that the Scripture they are to discuss with their families begins with the passage on page 78.

• Invite students to report on the results of their family discussions.

People of Faith

Tell students about Saint John of God.

• John lived in Portugal and Spain. When he was 55, he became ill after saving a man from drowning. As he lay dying, John's only concern was for the people he served. When the archbishop of Granada promised to care for them, John died peacefully.

• Remind students to add Saint John of God to their People of Faith albums. Encourage them to pray the prayer at home with their families.

 Visit **www.osvcurriculum.com** for weekly scripture readings and seasonal resources.

UNIT 2: CHAPTER 5

Family Faith

Catholics Believe

■ God created people for one another, and all must work for the common good. Such love of neighbor reflects the love of the Holy Trinity.

■ No one can believe alone, just as no one can live alone.

SCRIPTURE

Read the Third Letter of John for advice about how a Christian community should receive strangers.

 www.osvcurriculum.com For weekly scripture readings and seasonal resources

Activity
Live Your Faith

Christian Actions Read the passage about the communal life from *Acts 2:42–47*. Talk with your family about ways you could share with others as the early Christians did. List your ideas, and choose just one. After doing the action, talk about the experience. Discuss how each family member contributed to the good of others.

▲ Saint John of God
1495–1550

People of Faith

Once a soldier and a bookseller, **John of God** gave his life to providing for those who were poor, homeless, or sick in body or mind. He set himself to doing things to help those in need, such as providing them with food and renting a house to give them shelter. This was the beginning of the order of the Brothers of Saint John of God. Saint John's love and care for those in need continues today. The brothers provide hospitality and care for those who are poor. Saint John's feast day is March 8.

In Unit 2 your child is learning about the TRINITY.

82 **CCC** *See Catechism of the Catholic Church 1905–1912 for further reading on chapter content.*

Family Prayer

Saint John, pray for us that we may find the wisdom to see people in need, even when the needs are not obvious. Guide us to be generous in giving gifts, time, and possessions for the good of others. Amen.

? HOW DID I DO?

My session was

☐ *one of the best ever!* ☐ *pretty good.* ☐ *in need of improvement.*

In what discussions and activities were students most interested?

_____

What activity did I most enjoy teaching?

_____

In what area do I need to improve?

_____

Name _____ Date _____

Board Game

Instructions

Cut apart the game markers. Give one to each player. Cut apart the numbers. Put all of the game marker pieces at the start line. Turn the numbers face down, and mix them up.

One at a time, each player chooses a number, moves the appropriate number of spaces, and then follows the directions on that space. The first player to reach the finish line wins.

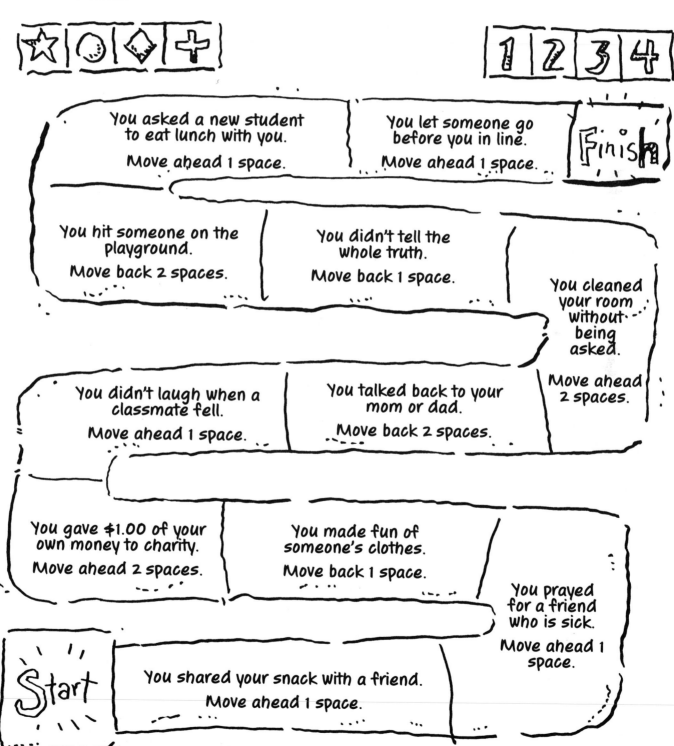

You asked a new student to eat lunch with you.

Move ahead 1 space.

You let someone go before you in line.

Move ahead 1 space.

Finish

You hit someone on the playground.

Move back 2 spaces.

You didn't tell the whole truth.

Move back 1 space.

You cleaned your room without being asked.

Move ahead 2 spaces.

You didn't laugh when a classmate fell.

Move ahead 1 space.

You talked back to your mom or dad.

Move back 2 spaces.

You gave $1.00 of your own money to charity.

Move ahead 2 spaces.

You made fun of someone's clothes.

Move back 1 space.

You prayed for a friend who is sick.

Move ahead 1 space.

Start

You shared your snack with a friend.

Move ahead 1 space.

Making Good Choices

CATECHIST FORMATION

Faith Focus

- **God created humans to have free will.** (CCC 1704)
- **Conscience helps us do good and avoid evil. It is an inner sense of what is right and wrong.** (CCC 1706–1786)

Catechism Connection

The *Catechism* emphasizes the role of the Holy Spirit in using free will and developing conscience. (CCC 1704–1706)

NDC Link

The *Directory* shows that the process of catechesis is carried out not only by the catechist handing on the teachings of Christ, but by the model or example he or she provides by living a Christian life. (See *NDC*, 29E.)

Resources

BOOK
A New Look at Grace. Huebsch, Bill. Twenty-Third Publications. Reveals the grace-filled heart of Jesus by using stories and poem-like forms.

DVD/VHS
Encounters with the Commandments (18 min.). Oblate Media. Investigates the meaning and importance of the Ten Commandments.

GO online Catechist Resources
For interactive lesson planner, chapter resources, and activities
www.osvcurriculum.com

✝ *For you were called for freedom, brothers. But do not use this freedom as an opportunity for the flesh; rather, serve one another through love.*

Galatians 5:13–14

Free Will

God wants humans to come freely to his love. Free will gives you the power to make choices and to act upon them. This is both the right and the responsibility of Catholics trying to be disciples of Jesus. Humans don't always choose good. Sometimes they choose to sin. If you cannot freely decide how to act, you cannot truly choose good.

You mature spiritually and morally as you exercise your free will. You learn from your good choices as well as from your mistakes. Free will makes you accountable. God asks you to be part of his plan and then lets you choose your response.

Conscience

Within every human is a conscience that moves him or her to make good choices and avoid bad choices. Scripture and Tradition feed and inform your growing conscience as you navigate through the various choices in your life. The Holy Spirit is always ready to assist you. Your informed conscience brings you closer to God and the Christian community.

Reflect **What people or events have been most important in forming your conscience?**

Moral Development

Fourth graders are just entering the stage of moral development that allows them to discern right from wrong independently of adults. They are learning to make responsible choices as they learn to distinguish between conflicting desires. They are also beginning to see that the intentions behind behavior are significant. How can you help fourth graders learn to use the gift of free will and to choose wisely?

- Help your students pray to learn what God desires their choices to be.

- Encourage students to consider the Ten Commandments, the teachings of Jesus, and the Tradition of the Church as they evaluate choices.

- Help students explore the reasons for their actions.

- Give students opportunities to consider better or best choices, not simply right or wrong choices.

Participation

- I like to role-play. Give me chances to enact modern-day scenes and Bible stories.

- I need practice in making choices. Let me help decide on class rules and procedures.

- Let me do simple classroom chores. They help me become a more responsible person.

Marginality

Many who sustain a life committed to the good of others can describe times in which they were ignored or marginalized. You may also feel marginalized as a catechist. You may find that others push you to the margins because of your values, your convictions, your educational level, your financial status, or even your geographic roots.

Marginality, that lonesome place of exclusion and insignificance within a school or parish program, does not have to hamper your ability to sustain the spirit to teach. Resilient people have used occasional experiences of marginalization to reexamine and reaffirm their core values.

Reflect **When have you been marginalized, and has it helped or hindered your ability to sustain the spirit to teach?**

Catechist's Prayer

God of Wisdom, open the minds and hearts of students in my class to use the gifts of free will and conscience to make good choices. Guide them to recognize your voice. Amen.

Weekly Planner

	Objectives	Lesson Process	Materials
1 Invite	**10 minutes** **Page 83** **Objective:** To think about making choices	🙏 **Let Us Pray:** Psalm 119:66 • Pray the psalm verse. • Discuss the idea that people are free to make choices. • Explore how to make choices.	
2 Explore	**40 minutes** **Pages 84–85** **Objective:** To learn about the use and consequences of free will	• Read or tell the story. • Discuss the idea that all choices have consequences. **Activity** Complete the Share Your Faith Activity. **Words of Faith** free will	☐ Board or chart paper
	Pages 86–87 **Objective:** To identify the meaning of conscience and the path to conscience formation	✝ **Scripture:** Luke 10:30–37 • Proclaim the scripture story. • Identify the ways in which conscience is formed. **Activity** Complete the Connect Your Faith Activity. **Words of Faith** conscience	☐ Pencils or pens ☐ Copies of Activity Master 6 on page 90A
3 Celebrate	**10 minutes** **Page 88** **Objective:** To meditate on God's will	🙏 **Let Us Pray:** 1 Kings 19:9–14 • Explain meditation. • Prepare students for meditation. • Celebrate a Prayer of Reflection. 🎵 **Hymn:** "My Soul in Stillness Waits" **Activity** Complete the Conscience Activity, page 234 and 235	☐ Hymnals ☐ Music CD ☐ Bible

Wrap Up

Review and Apply

Page 89
• Review the chapter concepts.
• Complete the Live Your Faith Activity.

Family Faith

Page 90
• Introduce the page, and assign it as a family activity.
• Read about Saint Charles Lwanga.

ACRE Connection, Domain 5—Conscience

Home Connection

GO online www.osvcurriculum.com
Family Faith activities, feasts and seasonal resources, saint features, and much more

• Online planning tools include chapter background and planner, activity master, customizable test, and more.

• Enhancement activities for each step of the catechetical process, including alternative prayer experiences and blessings.

• Games, activities, interactive review, alternative assessment, and more for children.

www.calltofaitheconnect.com

Chapter 6 Making Good Choices

Let Us Pray

Leader: God, give me the wisdom to make good choices.

"Teach me wisdom and knowledge,
for in your commands I trust."
Psalm 119:66

All: God, give me the wisdom to make good choices. Amen.

Activity Let's Begin

Think About Choices When you were younger, your parents made most of your choices. Now that you are older, you are able to make more choices for yourself.

- What kinds of choices does your family let you make? **Responses will vary.**

- What is an important choice that you have made? **Responses will vary.**

83

Objective: To think about making choices

Let Us Pray

Have students move to the prayer space. Pray aloud the first sentence of the prayer. Then invite students to pray each line of the psalm aloud after you. Ask students to conclude the prayer.

Activity

- Ask a student to read aloud the opening sentences of Think About Choices.

- Have students read the questions and reflect on their responses.

- Invite students to share their responses.

OPTIONAL ACTIVITY

Role-play Organize the class into small groups. Invite the groups to

- List examples of good choices that members have made in the past week.

- Choose one decision to role-play.

- Show what happened as a result of that choice.

Multiple Intelligence: Bodily/Kinesthetic

QUICK TIP

Games with Rules Playing games can help students think about free will and responsibility.

- Have students discuss when they cannot make their own decisions.

- Ask students to imagine the confusion that would result if each player created his or her own rules.

Objective: To learn about the use and consequences of free will

 **Focus**

What is the proper use of free will? List students' responses on the board or on chart paper.

Choices and Consequences

Summarize the first paragraph. Discuss with students the fact that all choices have consequences.

Julia Decides

Read aloud the story. Then ask two volunteers to act out the story.

- Discuss the question that follows the story.

- Ask students to think about the consequences that might have occurred if another choice had been made in the story.

- Ask volunteers to share their ideas.

  Possible responses: Julia would not have won the award; Julia's coach and team might have been angry with her.

Choices and Consequences

Focus What is the proper use of free will?

You have the freedom to make choices, but all choices have consequences. In this story, Julia learns a lesson from a choice she makes.

A STORY

Julia Decides

"Come on, Julia!" said Monica. "I really want to see the new movie at the Crosstown Cinema. I thought you wanted to see it, too."

"I do want to see it," Julia replied. "Maybe we can see it next week. My coach just called an extra soccer practice for this afternoon. I have to go."

"Well, you can go to soccer practice if you want to," said Monica. "I am going to the movie."

After Monica left, Julia got ready for practice. "I can see that movie later with my sister Lila," she thought as she tied her shoes. "Right now I have to work on my goal tending. The team is counting on me."

When Julia finally saw the movie, she enjoyed it. However, not as much as she enjoyed winning the award for most improved player at the end of the season!

❓ What is something that happened because of Julia's choice? Possible response: She improved and won the award.

84

Children's Literature You may wish to read *The Crane Wife* by Odds Bodkin (Harcourt, 2002) as an alternative story.

- This Japanese tale is about a lonely sail maker who nurses an injured crane. The story parallels the themes of this lesson.

Multiple Intelligence: Verbal/Linguistic

Created with Free Will

Julia's story shows that all choices have consequences. You are responsible for your choices, too.

When God created you in his image, he gave you **free will**. With your free will, you make choices. Sometimes your choices are between right and wrong. Sometimes, as in Julia's case, they are between better and best. Whenever you make a good choice, you use God's gift of free will properly and you grow closer to God.

A Helping Hand

God gives you many gifts to help you make good choices. God's most important gift is grace, which is the power of his own life within you. You received grace in a special way in the Sacrament of Baptism. You grow in God's grace through the Sacraments, prayer, and good moral choices.

In addition to his grace, God gives you the Ten Commandments and the Church to help you. God is always helping you develop a more loving relationship with him.

Words of Faith

Free will is the God-given ability to choose between good and evil.

Activity

Share Your Faith

Reflect: Think of some times when your choices hurt your family or friends.

Share: In groups, discuss ways to make better choices.

Act: Imagine the next chapter in the story of Julia and Monica's friendship. Role-play what you think might happen.

85

Created with Free Will

Tell students to read these two paragraphs silently.

- Read aloud the last sentence of the section.
- Point out that growing closer to God is a consequence of a good choice.

A Helping Hand

Ask students to read aloud the text.

- Ask what gifts of God help humans do good and avoid wrong.
- List students' responses on the board.

Activity

- Invite students to think about some of their choices. Ask them to share their thoughts in small groups.
- Have students choose several situations and role-play them for the class.

 Quick Review

People are free to make choices, and they have help in making good decisions.

 CATECHIST BACKGROUND

Freedom Fourth graders' ideas about freedom usually revolve around freedom from rules or restrictions. You can deepen their understanding.

- Instead of *freedom from* something, emphasize *freedom to do* something—in this case, freedom to make good choices.
- Students should come to realize that freedom to make choices does not grant them freedom from responsibility for those choices.

★ **REACHING ALL LEARNERS**

Hearing Problems If there is a student with impaired hearing in your group, refer to the following guidelines.

- Speak slowly and distinctly.
- Give directions one step at a time.
- Provide both oral and written directions.
- Write the directions on the board or on chart paper.

Objective: To identify the meaning of conscience and the path to conscience formation

 Focus

What is a strong conscience? List students' responses on the board or on chart paper.

Choosing to Love

Read aloud and summarize the first paragraph.

The Good Samaritan

Have a proficient reader proclaim aloud the scripture story.

- Point out that the Jewish listeners would expect the priest and the Jewish leader to help others. However, the Samaritans were enemies of the Jews and would not be expected to help.

- Discuss the questions in the text.

Explore

Choosing to Love

 Focus What is a strong conscience?

Good choices help you grow as a moral person. They build good habits and strengthen your relationship with God and others. Jesus calls us to act in ways that show love, even toward people whom we do not know. One day Jesus told this story to a scholar of the law.

✝ SCRIPTURE   Luke 10:30–3*

The Good Samaritan

Jesus said, "A Jewish traveler going from Jerusalem to Jericho was attacked by robbers who beat, robbed, and left him on the side of the road.

"A priest saw the injured traveler and moved to the other side of the road. Later a Jewish leader came to the same place, and when he saw the traveler, he too moved to the other side of the road. Finally, a Samaritan came to the place where the traveler lay dying. Unlike the others, the Samaritan stopped. He treated and bandaged the traveler's wounds. He carried him on his own animal to an inn, where he cared for him. The next day, when the Samaritan was leaving, he gave the innkeeper money and told him, 'Take care of this man. If you spend more than what I have given you, I will repay you when I return.'"

Based on Luke 10:30–37

❓ **What was difficult about the choice the Samaritan made?** Responses will vary.

❓ **When is it difficult for you to make good choices?** Responses will vary.

86

 JUSTICE AND PEACE

Interdependence Catholics are called to work for justice and peace with "sisters and brothers all over the world."

- The U.S. Conference of Catholic Bishops calls this "a key test of a parish's 'Catholicity.'" *(Communities of Salt and Light)*

Catholic Social Teaching: Solidarity

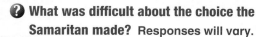 **SCRIPTURE BACKGROUND**

Samaritans The Jews and the Samaritans of Jesus' time had religious differences. Members of the two groups refused to speak to one another. Jesus' use of a Samaritan as the hero of his story is remarkable.

- Jesus' inclusion of the Samaritan as a merciful neighbor clearly indicates that the Samaritan is one of God's people.

God's Gift of Conscience

Good choices strengthen your relationship with God and others. Sin weakens or destroys that relationship. Sin is always a failure to love God and others. When you use your free will to sin, you always become less free.

You probably know when you have done something wrong, even if no one has seen you. The "inner voice" that tells you so is your **conscience**. Conscience is your free will and your reason working together. They direct you to choose what is good and avoid what is wrong.

You have the seeds of a strong conscience within you. It is your job to strengthen, or form, your own conscience. You cannot do this alone.

Words of Faith

Conscience is the gift from God that helps you know the difference between right and wrong and helps you choose what is right.

FORMING YOUR CONSCIENCE

The Holy Spirit	⟷	*Strengthens you to make good choices*
Prayer and study	⟷	*Help you think things through*
Scripture and Church teaching	⟷	*Guide your decisions*
Parents, teachers, and wise people	⟷	*Give you good advice*

Activity — Connect Your Faith

Dear Pam,

I'm invited to sleep over at my friend's house on Friday night. She has a video for us to watch. My parents already told me this video is not for children. I'm a little worried, but my friend said, "Don't be such a baby. They will never know." What should I do?

Confused

"Dear Pam" Imagine that you write an advice column in a newspaper. What advice would you give to help the letter-writer use God's gift of conscience?

_____

_____

_____

_____

_____

_____

87

God's Gift of Conscience

Have students read the first two paragraphs silently.

- Discuss the meaning of the word *conscience*.
- Invite volunteers to talk about times when they have listened to their consciences.
- Have four volunteers each read one line under Forming Your Conscience.
- Discuss who might give students good advice.

Activity

- Encourage the group to brainstorm advice for "Confused."
- Have students write what their advice would be.

⊚ Quick Review

A well-developed conscience helps you avoid sin and reminds you that everyone is a neighbor to be loved and respected.

OPTIONAL ACTIVITY

Activity Master 6: Word Puzzle
Distribute copies of the activity found on catechist page 90A.

- Tell students that when they solve the puzzle, they will find some good advice.
- As an alternative, you may wish to send this activity home with students.

▲ Activity Master 6

3 Celebrate

Objective: To meditate on God's will

 Let Us Pray

Tell students that they will pray to hear God's voice.

Prayer of Reflection

Prepare

Tell students that meditation is a form of prayer that will help them focus on and think about God.

• Today you will be both the leader and the reader.

♪ Use the *Call to Faith 4* CD, track 6, to rehearse the suggested song.

Gather

Make sure that students are seated comfortably in the prayer space.

Pray

• Follow the order of prayer on page 88.

• For an alternative meditation, see pages 53–57 of *Guided Meditations for Children* (Jane Reehorst, BVM, Our Sunday Visitor Curriculum Division).

Celebrate

Prayer of Reflection

 Let Us Pray

Gather and begin with the Sign of the Cross.

Leader: In prayer, you listen for God's voice to guide you. Close your eyes and think about a time when you were afraid and didn't know what to do. Listen to this story about a man named Elijah, who heard God's voice in a very surprising way when he was afraid.

Reader: *Read 1 Kings 19:9–14.*

Leader: Sit quietly and notice whether you can hear God whispering to you inside your heart. What is God saying to you? What do you want to say to God?

Leader: God of the whispering sound, help us be still and listen for your voice to guide us.

All: Amen.

 Sing together.

For you, O Lord, my soul in stillness waits, truly my hope is in you.

"My Soul in Stillness Waits" © 1982, GIA Publications, Inc.

88

 LITURGY LINK

Silence   Silence is important in prayer. The Church community experiences silence in prayer after the Scripture is proclaimed at Mass.

• Include short periods of quiet within your prayer experiences.

• Respect for silence helps teach reverence.

 LECTIONARY LINK

Break Open the Word   Read last week's Sunday Gospel. Invite students to think about what the reading means to them as they try to follow Christ's example. For questions related to the weekly Gospel reading, visit our website at **www.osvcurriculum.com**.

GO online Visit www.osvcurriculum.com for weekly Scripture readings and seasonal resources.

Review and Apply

A **Work with Words** Complete each sentence with the correct word from the Word Bank.

WORD BANK

moral
free will
conscience
God
others
consequences

1. When God created you in his image, he gave you ___**free will**___ to use in making good choices.

2. ___**Conscience**___ is the gift from God that helps you know the difference between right and wrong.

3. Good choices help you grow as a ___**moral**___ person.

4. Sin weakens or destroys your relationship with ___**God**___ and with ___**others**___.

5. Every choice you make has ___**consequences**___.

B **Make Connections** Mark the loving choices with a heart and the unloving choices with an X.

___X___ You do not finish your homework, and you lie about it.

___♥___ You send a card to a relative who is sick.

___♥___ You tell your parents when your younger brother or sister does something dangerous.

Activity — Live Your Faith

Make a Poster Steve's grandmother is watching him overnight. After she is asleep, Steve realizes that he could make a long distance call to his best friend who moved away. His grandmother would never know. What good advice would you give Steve?

• Work with a partner to design a poster.

• On the poster, write good rules for using the telephone.

Telephone Rules

89

Review and Apply

Use the focus questions from the catechist Explore pages to review the lesson concepts.

A **Work with Words** Have students fill in the blanks to complete each sentence.

B **Make Connections** Ask students to mark each statement with the appropriate symbol. Invite volunteers to share their answers.

Activity

• Have each student work with a partner for this activity.

• Make sure that students are clear on the steps involved: giving advice, designing a poster, and writing rules.

• Ask students to share their posters with the class.

OPTIONAL ACTIVITY

Examination of Conscience Have students work in small groups to write an examination of conscience.

• Collect the results.

• Compile them into a thorough list.

• Duplicate the list, and distribute copies to students.

Multiple Intelligence: Intrapersonal

Family Faith

Remind students to discuss the Family Faith page at home. Encourage students to read the passage from the Gospel of Matthew.

Activity

• Explain the activity by showing some examples of newspaper articles that demonstrate good and bad moral choices.

People of Faith

Tell children about Saint Charles Lwanga and his companions.

• Explain that there are more than six million Christians in Uganda, thanks in part to the bravery of Charles Lwanga and his friends.

• Remind students to add Saint Charles and his friends to their People of Faith albums. Encourage students to pray the prayer at home with their families.

 Visit **www.osvcurriculum.com** for weekly scripture readings and seasonal resources.

UNIT 2: CHAPTER 6
Family Faith

◎ Catholics Believe

■ God has given you free will so that you can make good choices.

■ Your conscience is the "inner voice" that helps you choose what is good.

✝ SCRIPTURE

Matthew 26:69–75 is about a choice Peter made the night before Jesus died. Read the story together, and talk about the lesson it teaches.

GO online www.osvcurriculum.com
For weekly scripture readings and seasonal resources

Activity
Live Your Faith

Read Together Read through the newspaper to find articles about people who have made good or bad moral choices. As a family, discuss how conscience guides people to make better moral decisions.

People of Faith

▲ Saint Charles Lwanga and his companions

Charles Lwanga was a young servant in the king's court in Uganda. The king hated Christians. He commanded his servants to join in immoral activities. Charles, the master of the court pages, and twenty-one other young Christians refused. They were killed in 1886 for following their consciences. They prayed while they were dying. Saint Charles Lwanga and his companions are known as the African Martyrs. Their feast day is June 3.

🙌 Family Prayer

Saint Charles, pray for us that we may follow our consciences, even when it is hard to do so. Help us learn from you the meaning of freedom. Amen.

In Unit 2 your child is learning about the TRINITY.
90 CCC *See Catechism of the Catholic Church 61, 69 for further reading on chapter content.*

❓ HOW DID I DO?

My session was

☐ *one of the best ever!* ☐ *pretty good.* ☐ *in need of improvement.*

In what discussions and activities were students most interested?

_____

What activity did I most enjoy teaching?

_____

In what area do I need to improve?

_____

Name _____ Date _____

Word Puzzle

Solve each clue, and write the answer on the lines provided. Then transfer the letters to the numbered spaces at the bottom of the page. You will discover a sentence that gives some good advice.

1. You can use the gift of free will to make _____ choices.
   ¯¯ ¯¯ ¯¯ ¯¯
   24 9 21 27

2. _____ weakens your relationship with God.
   ¯¯ ¯¯ ¯¯
   11 26 15

3. Prayer and _____ help you think things through.
   ¯¯ ¯¯ ¯¯ ¯¯ ¯¯
   11 3 25 27 4

4. Disobeying a _____ can have unfortunate consequences.
   ¯¯ ¯¯ ¯¯ ¯¯
   7 22 1 19

5. God will give you a second chance to make a _____ choice.
   ¯¯ ¯¯ ¯¯ ¯¯ ¯¯ ¯¯
   18 2 3 3 28 23

6. You can _____ on the Holy Spirit to help you.
   ¯¯ ¯¯ ¯¯ ¯¯
   7 17 1 20

7. Scripture and Church teaching can guide your _____.
   ¯¯ ¯¯ ¯¯ ¯¯ ¯¯ ¯¯ ¯¯ ¯¯ ¯¯
   27 2 12 13 11 26 5 10 11

8. Good choices help you grow _____ to God.
   ¯¯ ¯¯ ¯¯ ¯¯ ¯¯ ¯¯
   8 1 5 11 2 23

9. Conscience is like an _____ voice.
   ¯¯ ¯¯ ¯¯ ¯¯ ¯¯
   13 10 10 14 7

10. You can _____ your choices with your parents and teachers.
    ¯¯ ¯¯ ¯¯ ¯¯ ¯¯ ¯¯ ¯¯
    27 13 11 16 6 11 11

    ¯¯ ¯¯ ¯¯ ¯¯ ¯¯ ¯¯ ¯¯ ¯¯ ¯¯ ¯¯ ¯¯ ¯¯ ¯¯ ¯¯ ¯¯ ¯¯ ¯¯
    1 2 3   4 5 6 7   8 9 10 11 12 13 14 15 16 17

    ¯¯ ¯¯ ¯¯ ¯¯ ¯¯ ¯¯ ¯¯ ¯¯ ¯¯ ¯¯ ¯¯ .
    18 19 20 21 22 23   24 25 26 27 28

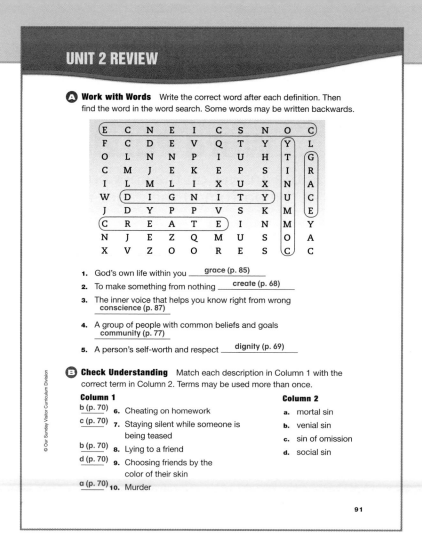

A **Work with Words** Write the correct word after each definition. Then find the word in the word search. Some words may be written backwards.

E	C	N	E	I	C	S	N	O	C
F	C	D	E	V	Q	T	Y	Y	L
O	L	N	N	P	I	U	H	T	G
C	M	J	E	K	E	P	S	I	R
I	L	M	L	I	X	U	X	N	A
W	D	I	G	N	I	T	Y	U	C
J	D	Y	P	P	V	S	K	M	E
C	R	E	A	T	E	I	N	M	Y
N	J	E	Z	Q	M	U	S	O	A
X	V	Z	O	O	R	E	S	C	C

1. God's own life within you _____ grace (p. 85)
2. To make something from nothing _____ create (p. 68)
3. The inner voice that helps you know right from wrong _____ conscience (p. 87)
4. A group of people with common beliefs and goals _____ community (p. 77)
5. A person's self-worth and respect _____ dignity (p. 69)

B **Check Understanding** Match each description in Column 1 with the correct term in Column 2. Terms may be used more than once.

Column 1

b (p. 70) **6.** Cheating on homework

c (p. 70) **7.** Staying silent while someone is being teased

b (p. 70) **8.** Lying to a friend

d (p. 70) **9.** Choosing friends by the color of their skin

a (p. 70) **10.** Murder

Column 2

a. mortal sin

b. venial sin

c. sin of omission

d. social sin

91

Unit Review

The Unit Review is designed to prepare students for the Unit Assessment. This page focuses on vocabulary words and the main concepts presented in the chapters.

Each review contains various sections that will appeal to the many different learning styles of your students. There are puzzles to engage students' attention, as well as true-false, multiple-choice, short-answer, and fill-in-the-blank exercises.

Direct students to complete the review, and check their responses. Determine areas in which students still need practice, and review those sections of the unit.

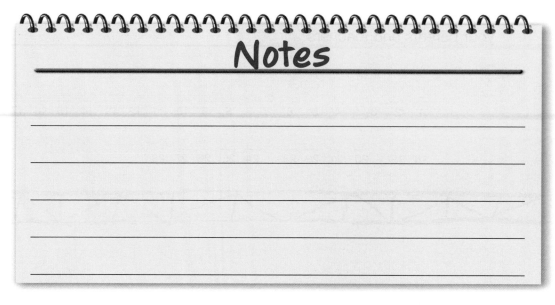

Notes

Name ______________________ Date ______________

A Faithful People

(A) Work with Words Match each description in Column 1 with the correct term in Column 2.

Column 1

_____ **1.** A group of people who share beliefs, activities, and goals

_____ **2.** Working for this helps a community become the best it can be.

_____ **3.** An act that is seriously wrong and chosen freely

_____ **4.** Saying "yes" to what God teaches

_____ **5.** Another term for dignity

_____ **6.** The spiritual part of a person

_____ **7.** All of these are made in God's image.

_____ **8.** Putting belief into action, living in right relationships

Column 2

a. common good
b. soul
c. community
d. morality
e. mortal sin
f. faith
g. humans
h. self-worth

(B) Check Understanding Circle the letter of the choice that best completes the sentence or answers the question.

9. One part of making a good moral decision, is thinking about ______________.

a. the consequences of my choices
b. what my friends would do
c. what I can gain from my decision
d. how to please my parents

10. Rosa Parks is most known for ______________.

a. becoming a saint
b. feeding the poor
c. writing poetry
d. working for human rights

11. Which is a sin of omission? ______________.

a. taking things from a store
b. talking in class during study time
c. lying about a friend
d. not helping someone in need

ASSESSMENT

Answers can be found in the back of the Catechist Manual.

Name ______________________________ Date ______________

12. Which of these is a social sin?

- **a.** murder
- **b.** hurting people of a certain race
- **c.** lying to avoid punishment
- **d.** being lazy

13. Christians grow in grace through all of the following except

- **a.** the sacraments.
- **b.** thoughtful choices.
- **c.** prayer.
- **d.** being selfish.

14. Which is not a venial sin?

- **a.** lying
- **b.** being lazy
- **c.** murder
- **d.** cheating

15. Jesus' story of the Good Samaritan teaches people

- **a.** how to pray.
- **b.** the Ten Commandments.
- **c.** to help others.
- **d.** to forgive.

(C) Make Connections Write a response to each question or statement.

16. How does respecting the dignity of others keep the commandments and honor God?

____

____

17. What is one thing you can do to reflect the love of Christ?

____

____

18. Why are all people worthy of respect?

____

____

19. Describe one way in which your class community might work for the common good.

____

____

20. Why is it important to live in community?

____

____

ASSESSMENT

 Answers can be found in the back of the Catechist Manual.

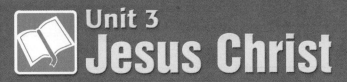

Unit 3
Jesus Christ

In this unit you will...

learn that Jesus wants people to be happy and to carry his message of the goodness of God's kingdom into the world. He shared that message in his teachings, most especially the Beatitudes. Jesus calls us to trust in the Father and to be a blessing to others by living the Great Commandment of love. Jesus teaches us to praise God with worship, by honoring his name, and by keeping Sunday holy.

 What do you think you will learn in this unit about life in Christ?

92

UNIT 3 OPENER

Preview Unit Theme

Tell students that Unit 3 is about Jesus Christ.

- Read aloud the text on page 92 of the student edition. Tell students they will learn more about these things in the next three chapters.

- Ask students how they think we carry Jesus' message of God's kingdom into the world.

- Invite volunteers to share examples of how they praise God.

Overview

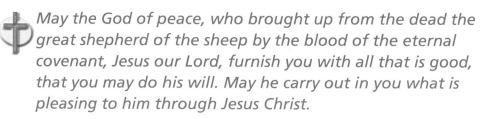

Faith Focus

■ In the Beatitudes, Jesus describes the reign of God that he brought to humans. *(CCC 1716, 1720)*

■ The Beatitudes teach Christians how to live as followers of Jesus. *(CCC 1723)*

Catechism Connection

The *Catechism* explains that the whole history of salvation is a blessing given to humans by God. *(CCC 1078–1079)*

NDC Link

The *Directory* states that although the Beatitudes are a point of reference for moral formation, catechesis must also include the practice of moral principles and their integration in everyday life. (See *NDC*, 42.)

Resources

📖 **BOOKS**

Saint Martin de Porres: Humble Healer. DeDomenico, Elizabeth Marie. Pauline Books. Demonstrates why this gentle healing saint has relevance today.

You Are My Friends: Gospel Reflections for Your Spiritual Journey. Stoutzenberger, Joseph. Twenty-Third Publications. "The Beatitudes." Reflects on the blessings and promises Jesus gave with the Beatitudes.

GO online **Catechist Resources**
For interactive lesson planner, chapter resources, and activities
www.osvcurriculum.com

 May the God of peace, who brought up from the dead the great shepherd of the sheep by the blood of the eternal covenant, Jesus our Lord, furnish you with all that is good, that you may do his will. May he carry out in you what is pleasing to him through Jesus Christ.

Hebrews 13:20–21

The Meaning of Blessing

God has been blessing the world from the beginning. After the Fall, God took a world that was headed toward death and turned it back toward life. He brought the Chosen People out of slavery, bestowed on them the gift of the Law, spoke through the prophets, and gave them his only Son, Jesus.

Because you are a baptized Christian, your actions, like those of Christ, can be a source of blessing for others. When you ask God's blessing on a meal or on another person, you acknowledge that it is God who gives all gifts and makes them holy. When you bring God's peace to another person, you are being a blessing for others.

The Beatitudes

Jesus taught the Beatitudes in the Sermon on the Mount. The Beatitudes reframe the blessings promised to the Israelites in the light of the Christian message. The Beatitudes reflect the way that Jesus lived his life. Jesus' actions brought to the world the peace, love, and justice that God desires. The Beatitudes tell us how to live in God's kingdom, now and always.

Reflect **What can you do today to be a blessing for others?**

The Beatitudes

Fourth graders have an ethical sense. They are governed by a strong sense of justice and do not like to see others mistreated. They are capable of empathy. They can grasp the goodness of Jesus' message in the Beatitudes.

- Help students visualize the setting in which Jesus taught, and invite them to describe what others may have said when they heard Jesus' words for the first time.

- The language of the Beatitudes may be challenging for students. Help students understand the Beatitudes by giving them examples of ways to live each one.

- Remind students that Jesus remained true to the message he carried from his Father and that he never stopped trying to help others understand it. Tell students that they can help others understand God's message through their words and actions.

Active Learning

- I like stories! Give me opportunities to use my imagination.

- I like working with others and listening to their ideas. Let us spend time doing group activities.

- I like to know what we're going to do in class today. Tell me what the plan is, and I'll be a better member of the group.

Habits of Mind

Blessed assurance and constructive engagement with others can help you develop good critical thinking habits. Solid thinking skills allow you to think beyond the obvious and to realize what contributes to difficult problems.

Those who sustain their spirit seek different views to enhance, but not compromise, their own. Others seek feedback from anyone familiar with their work, not just from friends. Practicing this kind of thinking—these habits of mind—allows you to harvest richer resources for sustaining your spirit.

Reflect *Circle the habit(s) of mind you would like to cultivate or improve:*

situational analysis   dialogue   seeking feedback

 Catechist's Prayer

God of peace, I thank you for the ways that your Spirit sustains me. Help me live the Beatitudes and teach students by my example. Amen.

Weekly Planner

Objectives	Lesson Process	Materials

1 Invite

10 minutes

Page 93
Objective:
To understand what it means to be blessed

Let Us Pray: Psalm 136:1
- Pray the psalm verse.
- Explore what it means to be blessed.
- Discuss responses to the question.

☐ Board or chart paper

2 Explore

40 minutes

Pages 94–95
Objective:
To explain what it means to be a blessing for others

- Read or tell the story of The Happy Prince.
- Direct small-group discussion of the story.
- **Activity** Complete the Share Your Faith Activity.

☐ Pencils or pens
☐ Copies of Activity Master 7 on page 100A

Pages 96–97
Objective:
To explain the meaning of the Beatitudes

Scripture: Matthew 5:1–10
- Proclaim the scripture story.
- Discuss the meaning of the Beatitudes.
- **Activity** Complete the Connect Your Faith Activity.

Words of Faith Beatitudes

☐ Paper
☐ Crayons or markers

3 Celebrate

10 minutes

Page 98
Objective:
To ask for God's blessing

Let Us Pray: Philippians 4:4–7
- Rehearse the music.
- Gather as a community.
- Celebrate a Prayer of Blessing.

Hymn: "For Your Gracious Blessing"

Activity Complete the Oral Tradition Activity, page 224 and 225

☐ Hymnals
☐ Music CD

Wrap Up

Review and Apply

Page 99
- Review chapter concepts.
- Complete the Live Your Faith Activity.

Family Faith

Page 100
- Introduce the page, and assign it as a family activity.
- Read about Saint Martin de Porres.

ACRE Connection, Domain 5—The Beatitudes

Home Connection

GO online www.osvcurriculum.com
Family Faith activities, feasts and seasonal resources, saint features, and much more

CALL to FAITH e connect

- Online planning tools include chapter background and planner, activity master, customizable test, and more.
- Enhancement activities for each step of the catechetical process, including alternative prayer experiences and blessings.
- Games, activities, interactive review, alternative assessment, and more for children.

www.calltofaitheconnect.com

Chapter 7 You Are Blessed!

 Let Us Pray

Leader: All glory to you, God!
"Praise the LORD, who is so good;
God's love endures forever."
Psalm 136:1

All: All glory to you, God! Amen.

Activity Let's Begin

Be Blessed You may have heard someone say, "We are so blessed!" Some people think of prizes, gifts, or lots of money as blessings. Others think of good health, the love of family, or the joy of good times with friends.

• What do you think it means to be blessed? **Responses will vary.**

93

Objective: To understand what it means to be blessed

 Let Us Pray

Ask students to move to your classroom prayer space. In the space, have a crucifix and a Bible opened to the psalm. Invite students to raise their hands in prayer. Pray the psalm verse together.

Activity

• Ask students what it means to say "We are so blessed." Ask for examples from the text and from the students' own experience.

• Record these responses on the board or on chart paper. Discuss any responses that are unclear.

• Ask what blessing is shown by the photograph. the blessing of sharing time with family members

• Tell students that everyone is blessed in countless ways. Share some of your own blessings with the group.

OPTIONAL ACTIVITY

Create a Blessing Prayer Students may be familiar with the word *bless* from mealtime blessings.

• Ask students to share their mealtime blessings.

• Encourage students to work together on a prayer and then sing it to a popular tune.

Multiple Intelligence: Musical

QUICK TIP

Talk About Blessings Some students may be experiencing difficult situations at home and find it hard to feel blessed.

• Say that even when someone is troubled, some blessings can be found.

• Ask volunteers to give examples of times when something good came from a bad situation.

• To ensure privacy, suggest that they give examples from TV programs or movies.

Objective: To explain what it means to be a blessing for others

 Focus

What does it mean to be a blessing for others? List students' responses on the board or on chart paper.

True Happiness

Tell students that happiness is one kind of blessing.

The Happy Prince

Gather the group in a story circle.

• Ask students to think about a time when they saw someone who was unhappy and to tell what they did about it.

• Tell them that in this fable, a prince and a tiny swallow learn both the joy and the price of being a blessing for others.

• Read the first part of the story aloud, pausing to discuss the question at the bottom of the page.

True Happiness

 Focus   What does it mean to be a blessing for others?

In this retelling of a famous story, happiness is spread by unlikely partners.

A STORY

THE HAPPY PRINCE

High above the city, on a tall column, stood the statue of the Happy Prince. He was gilded all over with thin leaves of gold; for eyes he had two bright sapphires, and a large red ruby glowed in his sword-hilt.

One evening, a tiny swallow that was flying south stopped to rest in the statue's shadow. She looked up and saw tears coming from the prince's eyes.

"Why are you weeping?" the swallow asked. "I thought you were the Happy Prince!"

"When I was alive," answered the statue, "anything sad was hidden from me. But now I look down and see all of the city's pain.

"Look! There is a poor seamstress working on a beautiful gown for the queen. Her little boy has a fever. He would like oranges, but she has only river water to give him. Will you take her the ruby from my sword?" The swallow hesitated but then agreed.

"Just this once!" she said.

 Why do you think the swallow agreed to stay and help the prince?
Possible response: She saw that people were in need.

94

CATECHIST BACKGROUND

Being a Blessing   Fourth graders may have difficulty understanding that it is sometimes necessary to make sacrifices to be a blessing.

• Discuss the sacrifices the prince in the story makes.

• Point out that the pleasures and possessions people have on earth last for a short time but the happiness they will experience in God's kingdom lasts forever.

THE PRICE OF HAPPINESS

Each day, the prince convinced the swallow to stay on. Together, they gave away all the riches the prince had, including his sapphire eyes and the leaves of gold covering his garments.

When winter came, the swallow soon died from the cold. City leaders melted down the statue to make something else from it. But when they did, its heart would not burn! The prince's heart and the dead swallow ended up side by side in a trash heap.

God looked down one day from heaven and said to an angel, "Bring me the two most precious things in the city." The angel brought him the prince's heart and the dead bird.

"You have chosen well," said God, "for in my kingdom of heaven this little bird shall sing forevermore, and the Happy Prince shall praise me."

Activity

Share Your Faith

Reflect: How does the Happy Prince know who needs help?

Share: By the end of the story, who is blessed? Discuss your response with a partner.

Act: Describe one way that you can be a blessing for others.

Possible responses: Help others; spread happiness.

95

The Price of Happiness

Continue reading to the end of the story.

- Have students scan the story for blessing words and actions of the prince and the swallow.

- Ask students what they think the heading, The Price of Happiness, means. Responses may include the fact that the swallow died and the statue was melted.

- Emphasize that the characters in the story brought happiness or blessings to others, even though they had to give up something themselves.

- Discuss with students how God rewards the prince and the swallow. He gives them eternal life in heaven.

Activity

- Organize students in pairs.
- Give students time to complete the activity, and invite them to share their ways of being a blessing for others.

◉ Quick Review

God calls each person to be a blessing for others. Spreading happiness is important but may require sacrifices.

⬟ REACHING ALL LEARNERS

Working in Groups Some students may need help working with a partner.

- Instead, have students count off to form larger groups.
- Choose a leader and a reporter for each group.
- Set definite time limits. For discussion groups, five minutes is probably sufficient.
- Ask for a report from each group so that everyone's work can be acknowledged.

OPTIONAL ACTIVITY

Activity Master 7: Being a Blessing Distribute copies of the activity found on catechist page 100A.

- Because each situation calls for two solutions, you may want to have students work in pairs.
- As an alternative, you may want to send this activity home with students.

▲ Activity Master 7

Objective: To explain the meaning of the Beatitudes

 Focus

What did Jesus teach about the true meaning of happiness? List students' responses on the board or on chart paper.

Jesus Brings God's Blessing

Tell students that God blesses those who care for others.

The Sermon on the Mount

Choose eight students to join you, and prepare each of them to read aloud one of the Beatitudes.

- Have these students join you in front of the group to proclaim the Scripture. You will read the two introductory lines.

- Ask volunteers to explain what they think each beatitude means. Record their responses. You may need to clarify words such as *meek, persecuted,* and *righteousness.*

Explore

Jesus Brings God's Blessing

 Focus   What did Jesus teach about the true meaning of happiness?

"The Happy Prince" tells who the writer believed would be blessed by God. In this Bible story, Jesus taught about who is blessed and how to be a blessing for others.

 SCRIPTURE   Matthew 5:1–10

The Sermon on the Mount

One day Jesus stood in the midst of his Apostles and a great crowd of followers. He taught them with these words:

"Blessed are the poor in spirit,
for theirs is the kingdom of heaven.

Blessed are they who mourn,
for they will be comforted.

Blessed are the meek,
for they will inherit the land.

Blessed are they who hunger and thirst
for righteousness,
for they will be satisfied.

Blessed are the merciful,
for they will be shown mercy.

Blessed are the clean of heart,
for they will see God.

Blessed are the peacemakers,
for they will be called children of God.

Blessed are they who are persecuted
for the sake of righteousness,
for theirs is the kingdom of heaven."

From *Matthew 5:1–10*

96

SCRIPTURE BACKGROUND

Beatitudes   Two Gospels contain the Beatitudes.

- In the Gospel according to Matthew, Jesus teaches on a mountainside. In the Gospel according to Luke, he teaches on a plain.

- In Matthew, Jesus is portrayed as the new Moses. In Luke, the focus is on Jesus' care for the poor.

The Beatitudes

The Church calls this teaching of Jesus the **Beatitudes**. The word *beatitude* means "blessing" or "happiness." The Beatitudes tell you how to be a blessing for others so that you, too, will be blessed by God. They are about the lasting happiness that God calls you to have. God desires all people to work for his kingdom and to share in eternal life with him.

Blessed are the poor in spirit . . .
Depend on God, not on material things.

Blessed are the meek . . .
Be gentle and humble with others.

Blessed are the merciful . . .
Forgive others and ask their forgiveness.

Blessed are the peacemakers . . .
Work to bring people together. Look for ways to solve problems peacefully.

Blessed are they who mourn . . .
Share other people's sorrows and joys.

Blessed are those who hunger and thirst for righteousness . . .
Help all people treat others justly, and help change unjust conditions.

Blessed are the clean of heart . . .
Be faithful to God and to God's ways.

Blessed are those who are persecuted for the sake of righteousness . . .
In difficult times, trust in God and stand up for what is right.

Activity

Connect Your Faith

A Blessing Scene On a separate sheet of paper, draw a picture of what you have done to live one of the Beatitudes.

97

The Beatitudes

Have students silently read the first paragraph and then underline the sentence that tells the purpose of the Beatitudes. The Beatitudes tell you how to be a blessing for others so that you, too, will be blessed by God.

- Compare students' ideas about what the Beatitudes mean with the chart on this page.
- On the board or on chart paper, draw the graphic organizer from the box below.
- Ask volunteers to describe everyday ways that they could live each beatitude. Write their ideas in the graphic organizer.

Activity

- Ask students to sketch one way that he or she has lived one of the Beatitudes.
- Ask volunteers to share their sketches.

 Quick Review

The Beatitudes teach how to be a blessing for others and find true happiness with God.

OPTIONAL ACTIVITY

Picture It Organize the students in small groups for a guessing game that expands on the Connect Your Faith activity.

- Assign each group a beatitude, and have them draw a scene which shows someone living that beatitude.
- Have groups take turns identifying the beatitude each group illustrated.

Multiple Intelligence: Visual/Spatial

QUICK TIP

Graphic Organizer

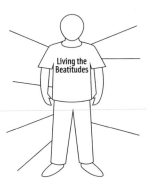

Objective: To ask for God's blessing

 **Let Us Pray**

Tell students that they will pray a prayer of petition, asking God for his blessing.

Prayer of Blessing

Prepare

Choose a leader and four readers for the prayer service.

 Use the *Call to Faith 4* CD, track 7, to rehearse the suggested song.

Gather

Invite students to gather in the prayer space with their books.

Pray

• Follow the order of prayer on page 98.

• You might include a reading of the Beatitudes.

Celebrate

Prayer of Blessing

 **Let Us Pray**

Gather and begin with the Sign of the Cross.

Leader:	Brothers and sisters, praise God, who is rich in mercy.
All:	**Blessed be God forever.**
Reader 1:	*Read Philippians 4:4–7.*
All:	**Blessed be God forever.**
Reader 2:	Loving God, you created all the people of the world, and you know each of us by name.
All:	**Blessed be God forever.**
Reader 3:	We thank you for our lives. Bless us with your love and friendship.
All:	**Blessed be God forever.**
Reader 4:	May we grow in wisdom, knowledge, and grace.
All:	**Blessed be God forever.**
Leader:	May we be blessed in the name of the Father, the Son, and the Holy Spirit.
All:	**Amen.**

 Sing together.

For your gracious blessing,
for your wondrous word,
for your loving kindness,
we give thanks, O God.

"For Your Gracious Blessing" Traditional

WE RECYCLE

98

 LITURGY LINK

Set the Mood Before you begin the celebration, ask students to sit quietly and remind themselves of God's presence.

• Ring a chime or bell to set the mood as you have students move to the prayer space.

• This sound will reinforce the fact that prayer time is different from other group activity times.

 LECTIONARY LINK

Break Open the Word Read last week's Sunday Gospel. Invite students to think about what the reading means to them as they try to follow Christ's example. For questions related to the weekly Gospel reading, visit our website at **www.osvcurriculum.com**.

 Visit www.osvcurriculum.com for weekly online Scripture readings and seasonal resources.

A **Work with Words** Complete the following paragraph with the correct words from the Word Bank.

Jesus gave us the ___Beatitudes___ to help us be a ___blessing___ for others. As we share our blessings with others, we help them find true ___happiness___. Through the ___eight___ Beatitudes, Jesus tells us about being blessed by God and finding true happiness. Some of the people who are blessed are those who are ___meek___, ___merciful___, ___poor___, and ___peacemakers___.

> **WORD BANK**
>
> blessing
> peacemakers
> poor
> happiness
> eight
> Beatitudes
> merciful
> meek

B **Make Connections** After studying this chapter, what other ways would you add to the definition of being blessed that you discussed on the Invite page?

___Responses will vary.___

Use the Quick Review statements from the catechist Explore pages to review the lesson concepts.

A **Work with Words** Have students complete the paragraph using the words in the Word Bank. Tell them to use each word only once. Have a volunteer read aloud the completed paragraph.

B **Make Connections** Ask students to write their responses to the question. Discuss their definitions.

Activity

- Allow time for students to brainstorm ideas for the activity. Suggest that students use a simple five-column graphic organizer, with one column for each of the five Ws, to organize their ideas.

- You may want to have students complete the activity at home and bring their articles to the next session.

Activity Live Your Faith

Beatitude News Use the five Ws—*Who, What, Where, When,* and *Why*—to write a newspaper article that shows people in your family or neighborhood living a Beatitude as they participate in an event.

My article will be titled: _____
___Responses will vary.___

_____

_____

99

 JUSTICE AND PEACE

Putting Others First Catholic teaching calls the faithful to put first the needs of those who are poor.

- One way to be a blessing is by providing those who are poor with access to basic necessities.

- Volunteering to give time or effort is also a way of sharing blessings.

Catholic Social Teaching: Option for the Poor

Family Faith

Remind students to discuss the Family Faith page at home. Encourage students to read the passage from the Gospel according to Luke.

Activity

- Explain the directions and show a sample chart that you have made.
- Tell students that any family member can add hearts to the chart.

People of Faith

Tell students about Saint Martin de Porres.

- As a child, Martin de Porres was considered very bright and exhibited a call to holiness at an early age. He used his healing skills to care for those who were poor and abandoned. He is the patron saint of public schools.
- Remind students to add Saint Martin de Porres to their People of Faith albums.

 Visit **www.osvcurriculum.com** for weekly scripture readings and seasonal resources.

UNIT 3: CHAPTER 7
Family Faith

Catholics Believe

- The Beatitudes are eight teachings that describe the reign of God that Jesus announced when he lived on earth.
- The Beatitudes show you how to live and act as a follower of Jesus.

SCRIPTURE

Read *Luke 6:20–26* to find out about the Beatitudes in the Gospel according to Luke.

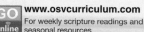 **www.osvcurriculum.com** For weekly scripture readings and seasonal resources

Activity
Live Your Faith

Blessing Chart Work at being a blessing. Make a chart titled "A Blessing for Others" to display in your home. Write each family member's name below the title. Each time you notice someone in the family living one of the Beatitudes, draw a heart next to his or her name. You can also write a word next to the name to tell the goodness that person showed.

People of Faith

▲ Saint Martin de Porres 1575–1639

Martin was born in Lima, Peru. His father was Spanish, and his mother was a freed black slave from Panama. Martin became a Dominican brother and spent his life doing simple good works for those in need. He went throughout the city, caring for those who were sick and poor. He was a blessing to all he met, even animals. Because he was meek and pure of heart, he saw that the simplest work gave honor to God if it served others.

Family Prayer

Saint Martin, help us do good for those in need. Give us strength to follow your example and live for others. Amen.

In Unit 3 your child is learning about JESUS CHRIST.

100 CCC *See Catechism of the Catholic Church 1716–1724 for further reading on chapter content.*

? HOW DID I DO?

My session was

☐ *one of the best ever!* ☐ *pretty good.* ☐ *in need of improvement.*

In what discussions and activities were students most interested?

_____

What activity did I most enjoy teaching?

_____

In what area do I need to improve?

_____

Name _____   Date _____

Being a Blessing

For each of the following situations, think of at least two ways that you could be a blessing for others.

Your mother has had a hard day at work and is tired. She is making dinner now, but the phone keeps ringing and your younger brother wants attention.

1. _____

2. _____

Mr. Hatsumi, who lives next door, has a broken leg. He has a hard time walking his dog and taking his trash to the curb. No one ever visits him.

1. _____

2. _____

Your best friend is sad and upset because his hamster died. He doesn't want to play or talk on the phone.

1. _____

2. _____

Your teacher introduces a new student, Bryn, to your class. Bryn doesn't know anyone to sit with at lunch and doesn't know where to catch the bus to go home.

1. _____

2. _____

Answers can be found in the back of the Catechist Manual.

The Great Commandment

CATECHIST FORMATION

✝ *[Jesus] said to him, "You shall love the Lord, your God, with all your heart, with all your soul, and with all your mind. This is the greatest and the first commandment. The second is like it: You shall love your neighbor as yourself."*

Matthew 22:37–39

Faith Focus

- The Great Commandment tells us to love God and to love our neighbor as ourselves. *(CCC 2055)*
- The Great Commandment is a summation of the Ten Commandments. *(CCC 2083, 2196)*

Catechism Connection

The *Catechism* reminds us that the works of mercy are also works of justice and are pleasing to God. *(CCC 2447)*

NDC Link

Catechesis on Christ's moral teachings and the Church's social teachings show us how to live our lives in accordance with Jesus' Gospel message of love. (See *NDC*, 43C.)

Resources

📖 **BOOK**
Still Preaching After All These Years: 40 More Seasonal Homilies. Bausch, William J. Twenty-Third Publications. Forty homilies that focus on the presence of Jesus in our lives and his call to discipleship.

💿 **DVD/VHS**
*Big Al Live! Vol. 2.** Our Sunday Visitor Curriculum Division. "Who Is Hungry Tonight?" (4:23 min.). Reinforces the need to provide food for everyone.
*Available at www.osvcurriculum.com

 Catechist Resources
For interactive lesson planner, chapter resources, and activities
www.osvcurriculum.com

Corporal Works of Mercy

Jesus says that the greatest commandment is the law of love for God and for neighbor. How do you love your neighbor? Wishing someone well or showing common courtesy is a good start, but it is not enough. You are called to show Christian charity to others by caring for their basic needs.

Compassionate service to others is shown through the Corporal, or physical, Works of Mercy. Christians have a responsibility to provide food, drink, shelter, and clothing to those in need; to be truly present and involved with those who are sick and imprisoned; and at the end of life, to bury the dead with dignity and prayer. These works are your ongoing mission. Doing them alone would be overwhelming. Fortunately, you are not alone! As part of a faith community, whether the parish or an outreach ministry, you can accomplish great works.

Preferential Love for the Poor

Wherever poverty exists, human misery exists, too. Poverty certainly means material deprivation, but it can also mean oppression, physical illness, or emotional and mental turmoil. Jesus always acted with compassion toward those who were suffering. The Church follows this example by working for justice, protection, and liberation, and by calling for preferential love for those who are poor.

Reflect   What kinds of poverty can you work to alleviate in your parish or community?

The Works of Mercy

The Great Commandment and the Corporal Works of Mercy are a way of life and a response to God's love. It is important that young people develop the virtue of charity, not out of pity for others, but in gratitude for all God has given them.

- Fourth graders want to be active and involved. One way to teach about charity is to give your students an opportunity to help others.

- Have your students make cards for a sick or bereaved parish member, or ask them to take up a small collection of canned goods for a local food pantry.

- Take a picture of the students in action, and then have them identify which Corporal Work of Mercy they have just practiced.

Helping Others

- I need concrete examples. Model for me how people practice the Works of Mercy.

- I have a real interest in helping people. Let's plan some service projects.

- I like stories about how Jesus helped people. Let me read them, hear them, act them out, and apply them to my life.

Vocational Seasons

In *The Courage to Teach,* Parker Palmer suggests that the teaching vocation consists of seasons. In some seasons we may be full of hope and new initiatives. At other times we may be "on low maintenance" and relaxed. Some people may be in a season of deep introspection even as others are experiencing a season of excitement or transitions.

The image of vocational seasons can be of great help in sustaining your spirit. If you are in a season that you don't enjoy, take consolation—the season will pass. Your catechetical vocation isn't over. On the other hand, if you are in a glorious vocational season, enjoy it to the full.

Reflect **Which vocational season are you in at this time: spring, summer, fall, or winter? Explain.**

 Catechist's Prayer

Loving God, open my eyes to the ways I can return your love by helping my neighbors. May my hands be ready to do the work of spreading your love. Amen.

Weekly Planner

	Objectives	Lesson Process	Materials
1 Invite — 10 minutes	**Page 101** **Objective:** To learn about showing God's love to others	🙏 **Let Us Pray:** Psalm 119:33 • Pray the psalm verse as a group. • Give examples of showing God's love. • Introduce God's law.	
2 Explore — 40 minutes	**Pages 102–103** **Objective:** To learn about the Great Commandment	✝ **Scripture:** Matthew 19:16–22, Matthew 22:37–40 • Proclaim the scripture story. • Compare the Ten Commandments with the Great Commandment. **Activity** Complete the Share Your Faith Activity. **Words of Faith Great Commandment**	☐ Board or chart paper ☐ Pencils or pens ☐ A list or poster of the Ten Commandments ☐ Magazines
	Pages 104–105 **Objective:** To learn how to live the Great Commandment and the Corporal Works of Mercy	• Present a readers' theater. • Identify ways of living the Corporal Works of Mercy. **Activity** Complete the Connect Your Faith Activity. **Words of Faith charity , Corporal Works of Mercy**	☐ A paper lantern and fan, or pictures of them, and a picture of a group of people ☐ Copies of Activity Master 8 on page 108A
3 Celebrate — 10 minutes	**Page 106** **Objective:** To ask God to help us live in charity and steadfast love for all	🙏 **Let Us Pray:** Corinthians 13:2–7 • Assign roles. • Gather for prayer. • Pray a Celebration of the Word. 🔥 **Hymn:** "Ubi Caritas/Live in Charity" **Activity** Complete the Corporal Works of Mercy Activity, page 236 and 237	☐ Hymnals ☐ Music CD ☐ Bible

Wrap Up

Review and Apply

Page 107
• Review the chapter concepts.
• Complete the Live Your Faith Activity.

 Family Faith

Page 108
• Introduce the page, and assign it as a family activity.
• Read about Saint Katharine Drexel.

ACRE Connection, Domain 5—Preferential Option for the Poor

Home Connection

GO online www.osvcurriculum.com
Family Faith activities, feasts and seasonal resources, saint features, and much more

• Online planning tools include chapter background and planner, activity master, customizable test, and more.
• Enhancement activities for each step of the catechetical process, including alternative prayer experiences and blessings.
• Games, activities, interactive review, alternative assessment, and more for children

www.calltofaitheconnect.com

Chapter 8 The Great Commandment

 **Let Us Pray**

Leader: Merciful God, help us know and do your will.

"Lord, teach me the way of your laws;
I shall observe them with care."

Psalm 119:33

All: Merciful God, help us know and do your will. Amen.

Activity Let's Begin

Signs of Love Elena keeps a photo album. Some of the pictures are of times and places in which she showed God's love to others. Other pictures show ways that other people showed God's love to her.

• If this were your album, what picture would you show of yourself? **Responses will vary.**

I was very sick today. Mom brought me food in bed.

My friends and I helped gather clothes for the needy.

GIRLS BOYS
CLOTHING DRIVE

101

Objective: To learn about showing God's love to others

 **Let Us Pray**

Have students gather in the prayer space. Play quiet, reflective music. Pray the psalm verse together. Ask students to think about how they will observe the laws of God. Follow with one minute of silence.

Activity

• Read aloud Signs of Love.

• Ask students which picture is of someone showing God's love to Elena and which is of Elena showing God's love to someone else. In the photo on the left, Elena's mother is showing God's love to Elena. In the photo on the right, Elena and her friend are showing God's love to others.

• Discuss the question in the text.

• Tell students that when people show God's love to others, they are following one of Jesus' teachings called the law of love. Explain that in this lesson, they will learn more about showing God's love to others.

OPTIONAL ACTIVITY

Photo Sharing Extend Elena's story, using real photos.

• Bring in photographs from your life that show people sharing God's love.

• Invite students to bring photographs next week.

• Display these photographs in the classroom.

Multiple Intelligence: Interpersonal

QUICK TIP

Be Sensitive Some students in your class may have been on the receiving end of food donations. Use language that treats their families respectfully.

• Avoid using phrases such as "the unfortunate," "the less fortunate," "the needy," or "the poor."

• Remind students that all families and all people need help at times, and that each person has dignity and worth.

Objective: To learn about the Great Commandment

 Focus

How is the Great Commandment like the Ten Commandments? List students' responses on the board or on chart paper.

Following Jesus

Introduce the scripture story by reading aloud the paragraph.

The Rich Young Man

Proclaim the scripture story. Ask students to listen for Jesus' advice to the rich young man.

• Read aloud the paragraph following the story to summarize the message.

• Have students read the story silently, substituting their own names every time the rich young man is mentioned in the story.

• Ask them to imagine how they would respond to Jesus' words.

• Spend some time on the discussion question.

Explore

Following Jesus

 Focus How is the Great Commandment like the Ten Commandments?

Elena and her family follow Jesus by sharing their love with others. Once, Jesus asked a young man to show his love for others in a very generous way.

✝ SCRIPTURE
Matthew 19:16–

The Rich Young Man

One day when Jesus was teaching, a young man asked "What must I do to live forever with God?"

Jesus answered, "Keep the commandments."

"Which commandments?" the young man asked. Jesus listed some of the Ten Commandments for him.

"I keep all those commandments!" the young man said happily. "What else do I need to do?"

"If you really wish to be perfect," Jesus said, "go and sell everything you have. Give the money to people who are poor. Then come and follow me."

The young man's smile faded, for he was very rich. He could not imagine giving everything away, so he went away sad.

Based on Matthew 19:16–22

Jesus asked the rich young man to make a very big sacrifice. He knew that the young man's love for his possessions could keep him from loving God completely. When Jesus tested the young man to see how important his possessions were, the young man could not part with them.

❓ **What possession would be the hardest for you to give away? Why?** Responses will vary

102

✝ SCRIPTURE BACKGROUND

Pharisees The Pharisees were known for their zealous observance of the Law. In addition to the Ten Commandments, there were hundreds of rules about worship, morality, and daily life.

• Some Pharisees tested Jesus to see whether he could be made to look irreligious.

• Instead, Jesus talked about observing the Law through living the Great Commandment.

The Great Commandment

Jesus taught that keeping the Ten Commandments includes more than checking off items on a list. Each commandment shows you a way to love God and love others with your whole heart and soul.

SCRIPTURE

"You shall love the Lord, your God, with all your heart, with all your soul, and with all your mind. This is the greatest and the first commandment. The second is like it: You shall love your neighbor as yourself. The whole law and the prophets depend on these two commandments."

Based on *Matthew 22:37–40*

Therefore, the **Great Commandment** sums up the Ten Commandments, the whole law, and what the prophets taught.

Words of Faith

The **Great Commandment** is the twofold command to love God above all and your neighbor as yourself.

Activity

Believe

Share Your Faith

Reflect: Look at an advertisement in a magazine. Does this ad support the teaching of Jesus?

Share: Share your response with a partner.

Act: As a group, write an ad that supports the teaching of Jesus.

103

The Great Commandment

Read the first paragraph aloud.

- Ask a volunteer to proclaim the Scripture slowly and reverently.
- Have students repeat aloud the two parts of the Great Commandment.
- Read aloud the paragraph following the Scripture.
- Display a copy of the Ten Commandments.
- Point out that the first half of the Great Commandment sums up the first three commandments, which are ways of loving and honoring God. The second half sums up the next seven, which name ways to treat others.

Activity

- Distribute magazines to the group, and have students complete the activity.
- Display students' ads in the classroom.

Quick Review

Jesus said to love God and to love your neighbor as yourself. The commandments tell you how to do this.

QUICK TIP

The Great Commandment   Since the Great Commandment is so important to Jesus' message, reinforce it whenever you can.

- Encourage students to memorize the Great Commandment.
- Students can make posters, bookmarks, or other reminders of the Great Commandment for home or classroom use.

OPTIONAL ACTIVITY

Buying Choices   The advertising industry often tries to tell consumers what to value most.

- Ask students to think of commercials that have persuaded them to buy or ask for games or toys.
- Ask whether those items were worth the money, and whether they still use the items.

Multiple Intelligence: Logical/Mathematical

Objective: To learn how to live the Great Commandment and the Corporal Works of Mercy

 Focus

How can you live the Great Commandment? List students' responses on the board or on chart paper.

Love in Action

Read aloud the introduction.

The Paper Dragon

Direct attention to the dragon illustration. Tell students that they will be reading a Chinese folktale.

- Display the following items or pictures of these items: a paper lantern, a folding fan, and a picture of a group of people.

- Assign the roles of Mi Fei, the dragon, and the narrator. Have the other students pantomime the action.

- When the lantern, fan, and painting are mentioned in the story, hold up the appropriate prop or picture.

104

Explore

Love in Action

 **Focus** How can you live the Great Commandment?

The command to love is not a weak or soft bit of advice, as this tale makes clear.

A FOLKTALE

The Paper Dragon

Long ago, a Chinese artist named Mi Fei was asked by his people to defend them against Sui Jen, a dragon. "Who dares to disturb me?" roared the dragon.

"I am Mi Fei," whispered the artist. "Spare our people."

The dragon's red eyes glowed. "Before I will do that, Mi Fei, you must perform three tasks. What is the most important thing your people have discovered?"

"I think it is paper," exclaimed Mi Fei.

"Ridiculous!" snorted the dragon. "Bring me fire, then, wrapped in paper, or I will destroy you!" After much thought, Mi Fei brought the dragon a paper lantern with a candle glowing inside.

Next, the dragon asked Mi Fei to bring the wind captured by paper. Mi Fei brought a paper fan.

The dragon gave Mi Fei his third task. "Bring me the strongest thing in the world, carried in paper." Mi Fei thought and thought. Then he painted all the loving people of his village. He returned, showed his painting, and said, "Love can move mountains; love brings light and life."

Suddenly, Sui Jen began to shrink. "Mi Fei," he said, "truly, the strongest thing in the world is love." When Mi Fei looked down, he found a small paper dragon.

❓ **What is the message of this story?** Responses will vary.

 CULTURAL AWARENESS

Dragons Dragons play a special role in Chinese culture.

- In China, the dragon symbolizes power, dignity, the emperor, and the Chinese people.

- Dragons in legend symbolize wisdom and generosity, but they are also temperamental.

- Dragons are featured in many cultural festivals and customs, such as the dragon dance and dragon boat races.

JUSTICE AND PEACE

Share with Others Jesus loved those who were poor, but he did not love poverty. Dealing with poverty is a moral imperative.

- Have a toy or book drive. Ask students to donate books or small toys that they do not use and offer them to a local homeless shelter, battered women's shelter, or hospital.

Catholic Social Teaching: Option for the Poor

Jesus Shows the Way

"The Paper Dragon" is only a folktale. However, it makes the very important point that the power of love can make a difference. God the Father sent his Son to show all people how to live in love as Mi Fei did. Jesus cared most for those who were poor, helpless, and suffering, and he calls all of his followers to do the same.

Acts of Charity

With the strength of the Holy Spirit, whom Jesus sent, you have the power to reach out to others in love, just as Jesus did. The Holy Spirit breathed **charity** into you at your baptism.

Jesus' Great Commandment tells you to love others as you love yourself. Christians see the needs of others and help meet those needs. The Church has named seven acts of kindness that you can do to meet the physical needs of others. They are called the **Corporal Works of Mercy**.

Words of Faith

Charity is the virtue of love. It directs people to love God above all things and their neighbor as themselves for the love of God.

The **Corporal Works of Mercy** are actions that meet the physical needs of others.

Activity — Connect Your Faith

Recognize Works of Mercy   Draw lines to match each Corporal Work of Mercy with an action. Then circle the actions that you have done.

Works of Mercy	Actions
Clothe the naked.	Volunteer to help serve a meal at a shelter.
Shelter the homeless.	Attend a funeral.
Feed the hungry.	Donate clothes to those in need.
Give drink to the thirsty.	Donate books to a prison.
Visit the imprisoned.	Visit a homebound relative.
Visit the sick.	Donate money to a homeless shelter.
Bury the dead.	Set up a free lemonade stand on a hot summer day.

105

Jesus Shows the Way

Have a volunteer read aloud the paragraph.

Acts of Charity

Introduce the word *charity*.

- Discuss the photograph with students.
- Have two students read aloud the text.
- Ask students to repeat the term *Corporal Works of Mercy*. Explain that *corporal* means "bodily" or "physical."
- Give examples of how practicing the Corporal Works of Mercy will help meet others' physical needs.

Activity

- Have students work in pairs to complete the activity.

Quick Review

The Corporal Works of Mercy are ways to show God's love to others, as the Great Commandment requires.

OPTIONAL ACTIVITY

Activity Master 8: Corporal Works of Mercy Mobile

Distribute copies of the activity found on catechist page 108A.

- Suggest that students look through magazines to find ideas for their symbols.
- As an alternative, you may wish to send this activity home with students.

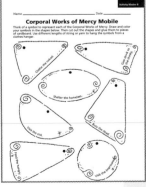

▲ Activity Master 8

Objective: To ask God to help us live in charity and steadfast love for all

 Let Us Pray

Tell students that this celebration will include prayers of petition.

Celebration of the Word

Prepare

Choose a leader and four readers.

 Use the *Call to Faith 4* CD, track 8, to rehearse the suggested song.

Gather

Ask students to gather in the prayer space.

Pray

- Follow the order of prayer on page 106.
- Optional reading: *Matthew 25:31–46*.
- Leader's concluding prayer: **God of love, we ask your help in living the Great Commandment. Teach us to show your love to others.**

Celebration of the Word

 Let Us Pray

Gather and begin with the Sign of the Cross.

Leader:	God of Mercy, we gather to remind ourselves of your love and mercy.
Reader 1:	A reading from the First Letter to the Corinthians. *Read 1 Corinthians 13:2–7.* The word of the Lord.
All:	**Thanks be to God.**
Reader 2:	Lord, give us the gift of patience.
All:	**We want to live in your love.**
Reader 3:	Lord, give us the gift of kindness.
All:	**We want to live in your love.**
Reader 4:	Lord, help us think of others.
All:	**We want to live in your love.**
Leader:	Let us pray. *Bow your heads as the leader prays.*
All:	**Amen.**

Sing together.

Ubi caritas et amor,
ubi caritas Deus ibi est.
Live in charity and steadfast love,
live in charity;
God will dwell with you.

"Ubi Caritas/Live in Charity" © 1979, Les Presses de Taizé, GIA Publications, Inc., agent

106

 **LITURGY LINK**

Latin The song "Ubi Caritas" ("Live in Charity") has Latin lyrics.

- Until the Second Vatican Council, Latin was the language used for worship in the Western Catholic Church.
- Share this historical background with the students, and note that Latin is still used occasionally at Mass.

 **LECTIONARY LINK**

Break Open the Word Read last week's Sunday Gospel. Invite students to think about what the reading means to them as they try to follow Christ's example. For questions related to the weekly Gospel reading, visit our website at **www.osvcurriculum.com**

 GO online Visit **www.osvcurriculum.com** for weekly Scripture readings and seasonal resources.

A **Check Understanding** Mark each statement True or False. Correct each false statement.

1. The Corporal Works of Mercy make it hard for you to grow as a Christian. _____False_____ They help you.

2. Only adults have the ability to care for and help others. _____False_____ Everyone can help.

3. The Great Commandment is a law of love. _____True_____

4. The Great Commandment can be restated in this way: "First love God; then love others as you love yourself." _____True_____

5. The virtue of charity helps you perform the Corporal Works of Mercy. _____True_____

B **Make Connections** Explain why this statement is true: When you live the Great Commandment, you are living the Ten Commandments. _____Responses will vary._____

Activity Live Your Faith

In Jesus' Footsteps Followers of Jesus try to walk in his footsteps day by day, continuing his works of love and kindness. On the path below, write one way in which you will try to show your love for God and others on each day next week.

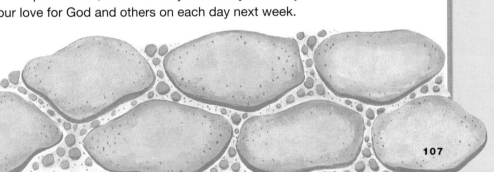

107

Review and Apply

Use the focus questions from the catechist Explore pages to review the lesson concepts.

A **Check Understanding** Have students complete the activity. Remind them to correct the false statements.

B **Make Connections** After students explain why the statement is true, call on volunteers to share their responses.

Activity

• Students may review Chapter 8 if they need help with the activity.

• When students have completed the activity, encourage them to share their ideas.

REACHING ALL LEARNERS

Sign Language Sign language is not just for students who are hearing-impaired.

• A simple true-false exercise will be more engaging if students can respond with signs instead of writing.

• Research simple sign language for appropriate words and phrases which can be used to enhance lessons or hymns.

Family Faith

Remind students to discuss the Family Faith page at home. Encourage students to read the passages from Isaiah and the Gospel according to Matthew.

Activity

• Read the directions aloud. Make sure that students understand what they are being asked to do.

People of Faith

Tell students about Saint Katharine Drexel.

• Tell students that Katharine Drexel watched her mother help families who needed rent money, and saw her father make donations to charity. Later, when she asked Pope Leo XIII to send more missionaries to Native Americans, he encouraged her to become a missionary.

• Remind students to add Saint Katharine Drexel to their People of Faith albums. Encourage them to pray the prayer at home with their families.

 Visit **www.osvcurriculum.com** for weekly scripture readings and seasonal resources.

UNIT 3: CHAPTER 8
Family Faith

Catholics Believe

■ The Great Commandment is to love God with all your heart, strength, and mind and to love your neighbor as yourself.

■ The Great Commandment sums up all of the teachings of the Ten Commandments.

✝ SCRIPTURE

Read *Isaiah 58:6–10* and *Matthew 25:34–40* to find the Corporal Works of Mercy in the Bible.

GO online www.osvcurriculum.com
For weekly scripture readings and seasonal resources

Activity
Live Your Faith

Acts of Love Design a greeting card, and make a special family food. Deliver both to someone who is sick, elderly, or a new parent or neighbor. Spend time visiting. On the way home, talk about the experience and how it felt to live the Great Commandment.

▲ Saint Katharine Drexel 1858–1955

People of Faith

Katharine Drexel devoted her money and her life to those who were poor. She did missionary work among African Americans and Native Americans. She founded the Sisters of the Blessed Sacrament to help educate members of these ethnic groups. Katharine also established many schools on Native American reservations and the first and only Catholic university for African Americans. Saint Katharine's feast day is March 3.

In Unit 3 your child is learning about JESUS CHRIST.

108 **CCC** *See Catechism of the Catholic Church 2055, 2083, 2196 for further reading on chapter content*

Family Prayer

Saint Katharine, pray for us that we may follow the way of Jesus. Help us live out the Corporal Works of Mercy in our daily lives. Amen.

? HOW DID I DO?

My session was

☐ *one of the best ever!* ☐ *pretty good.* ☐ *in need of improvement.*

In what discussions and activities were students most interested?

_____

What activity did I most enjoy teaching?

_____

In what area do I need to improve?

_____

Name _____ Date _____

Corporal Works of Mercy Mobile

Think of a symbol to represent each of the Corporal Works of Mercy. Draw and color your symbols in the shapes below. Then cut out the shapes and glue them to pieces of cardboard. Use different lengths of string or yarn to hang the symbols from a clothes hanger.

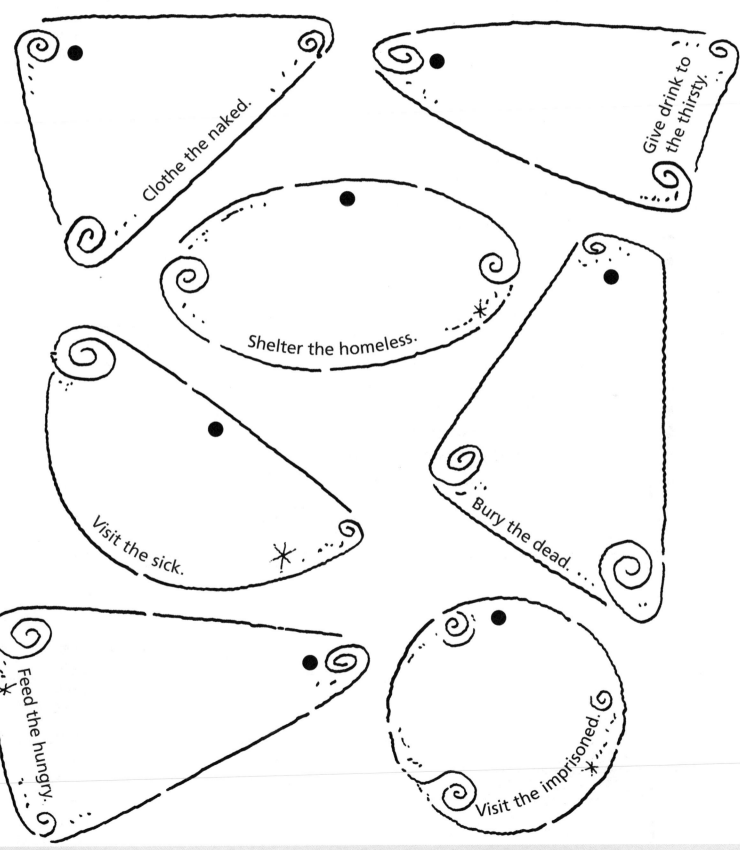

Overview

Faith Focus

- The Ten Commandments are the foundations of a moral life. *(CCC 2062)*
- The Ten Commandments lead the faithful to true freedom. *(CCC 2077)*

Catechism Connection

The *Catechism* reminds us that idolatry is treating anyone or anything other than God as divine. *(CCC 2113)*

NDC Link

The *Directory* states the importance of presenting catechesis on piety and popular devotions in such a way that their focus enriches Catholic doctrine and leads to sincere conversion and religious practice. (See *NDC*, 38C.)

Resources

BOOK
In the Beginning, There Were Stories: Thoughts about the Oral Tradition of the Bible. Bausch, William J. Twenty-Third Publications. Provides an ideal introduction to the oral tradition of the Bible.

DVD/VHS
Why Do We Go to Mass on Sundays? (13 min.). Oblate Media. Explains why the Church meets regularly to celebrate and share God's word and the Eucharist.

GO online Catechist Resources
For interactive lesson planner, chapter resources, and activities
www.osvcurriculum.com

✝ *Give to the LORD the glory due God's name. Bow down before the LORD's holy splendor!*

Psalm 29:2

No Other Gods

An entertainment phenomenon of the early twenty-first century was the TV talent contest known as *American Idol.* The show's format featured young singers vying against one another to be voted the most popular. Millions of viewers cast phone ballots to choose their "idol."

Talent is a gift from God, and no one is saying that shows like *American Idol* violate the first commandment. But fame, beauty, and wealth have certainly become idols to many Americans of all ages. The first three commandments, with their directive to put God first, speak as powerfully now as they did at the time when the Israelites danced before the golden calf.

Putting God First

The first three commandments lay out a surprisingly simple (although not always easy!) plan for avoiding the false gods that threaten to lead you astray. Get your priorities in order: God comes first. Be careful whom and what you honor (or dishonor) with your words. And put your time where your heart is, honoring God, family, and your own peace of mind with the Sabbath rest.

In a time when there is a golden calf on every corner, you can find real joy and certainty in living the first three commandments. When you put God first, everything else falls into place.

Reflect **What will you do to keep the Sabbath holy this week?**

Putting God First

Most fourth graders have been exposed to a wide range of influences. They are developing their values through a combination of lived experiences, increasing knowledge, and growing maturity. When students understand the respect due to God, they can begin to consider the respect due to those who are made in God's image: themselves and others.

- In practical terms, respecting God means putting him first in one's life. Ask fourth graders to consider what in life occupies their time and attention—sports, TV, friends, homework—and where God ranks on the list.

- Young people naturally feel awe and gratitude to God for the wondrous gifts of creation. Remind them that when they show respect for all of God's creatures, they show God the respect that is due him.

Respect for God

- I want to know more about God. Encourage me to talk about God.

- I can show respect for God. Help me learn the words for holy things and how to use the words properly.

- I like to use my talents. Give me opportunities to use them to praise God.

Living with Complexity

Most of us require clarity and consistency from the people around us. However, those who are comfortable with paradox, ambiguity, and complexity are better equipped to sustain the spirit to teach.

None of us should compromise our deepest principles of integrity. To do so would put our vocational spirit at risk. We can work at holding the contradictions in balance and living with the complexity of human imperfection. This will help us sustain the spirit to teach.

Reflect **How would you rate your ability to live with complexity and hold the contradictions in balance?**

Catechist's Prayer

Holy God, may my words show reverence for your name. May my actions show my love for you. May my students learn to honor you through their words and deeds. Amen.

Chapter 9

Weekly Planner

	Objectives	Lesson Process	Materials

1 Invite

10 minutes

Page 109
Objective:
To understand the importance of honoring accomplishments

🙌 **Let Us Pray:** Psalm 50:15
_____
• Pray the psalm.
• Read the story.
• Discuss what would belong in a family place of honor.

2 Explore

40 minutes

Pages 110–111
Objective:
To learn what the commandments say about honoring God

✝ **Scripture:** Exodus 32:1–20
_____
• Proclaim the scripture story.
• Discuss why God is due worship.
• Discuss sins against the first commandment.
  Activity Complete the Share Your Faith Activity.
Words of Faith worship , idolatry

Materials:
☐ Board or chart paper
☐ Pencils or pens
☐ Index cards

Pages 112–113
Objective:
To recognize ways of showing God honor and respect

• Read about how the third commandment teaches you to honor God.
• Discuss ways of keeping the Lord's day holy.
  Activity Complete the Connect Your Faith Activity.
Words of Faith blasphemy

☐ Copies of Activity Master 9 on page 116A

3 Celebrate

10 minutes

Page 114
Objective:
To sing to praise God, our Father

🙌 **Let Us Pray**
_____
• Rehearse the responses.
• Gather as a community.
• Celebrate a Prayer of Praise.
  🎵 **Hymn:** "Sing, Sing, Praise and Sing!"
_____
  Activity Complete the Lord's Prayer Activity, page 238 and 239

☐ Hymnals
☐ Music CD
☐ Bible

Wrap Up

Review and Apply

Page 115
• Review the chapter concepts.
• Complete the Live Your Faith Activity.

Family Faith

Page 116
• Introduce the page, and assign it as a family activity.
• Read about Saint Jane Frances de Chantal.

ACRE Connection, Domain 1—God the Father

Home Connection

 GO online www.osvcurriculum.com
Family Faith activities, feasts and seasonal resources, saint features, and much more

 **Call to Faith** e connect

• Online planning tools include chapter background and planner, activity master, customizable test, and more.
• Enhancement activities for each step of the catechetical process, including alternative prayer experiences and blessings.
• Games, activities, interactive review, alternative assessment, and more for children

www.calltofaitheconnect.com

Invite

Let Us Pray

Leader: We praise and honor your holy name, O Lord.

"Then call on me in time of distress;
I will rescue you, and you shall honor me."

Psalm 50:15

All: We praise and honor your holy name, O Lord. Amen.

Activity Let's Begin

A Place of Honor "What are you building?" Jeremy asked. "A spice rack?"

"No," said Vernique. "It's something for the whole family. It's a place of honor."

Jeremy was doubtful. "What does that mean? It just looks like a shelf."

"It's a place to put things that make us proud of our family," Vernique replied. "It's for Dad's bowling trophy and my science fair certificate—and Mom's picture that shows her shaking hands with the mayor."

"Can I put the pottery bowl I made there, too?"

"Sure," said Vernique.

• What would you put in a place of honor for your family?
Responses will vary.

109

---

1 Invite

Objective: To understand the importance of honoring accomplishments

Let Us Pray

Remind students that they can call on God for help at any time. Invite students to gather in the prayer space, and then pray the psalm verse together.

Activity

• Ask two students to read aloud the parts of Jeremy and Vernique.

• Ask students why the trophy, the certificate, the picture, and the bowl are going to be displayed in a place of honor. Possible response: The family is proud of them.

• Discuss the question in the text.

• Ask students what they might like to put in a place of honor for their class. Responses may include projects and drawings they have made, prayers they have written, and pictures of themselves.

• Ask students whether they can name a place for honoring God. Possible responses: at an altar, in a church, in their hearts

---

Wall of Honor Turn a bulletin board or wall into a place of honor for your group.

• Have each student draw something that he or she is proud of learning.

• Hang students' drawings in the place of honor.

Multiple Intelligence: Visual/Spatial

QUICK TIP

Prayer Space To keep your prayer space fresh and new, change the decorations from time to time.

• Arrangements of flowers, leaves, and shells reflect changes in nature.

• Religious artwork adds visual appeal.

• Candles, statues, and other decorations can be added.

Objective: To learn what the commandments say about honoring God

 **Focus**

What does it mean to praise and honor God? List students' responses on the board or on chart paper.

God's People Forget

Ask a volunteer to read this paragraph aloud.

• Remind students that people must honor and respect God because he created everyone and everything.

The Golden Calf

Proclaim the scripture story. Ask volunteers to pantomime the parts of Aaron, Moses, and the Hebrews while you read their words.

• Discuss the questions that follow the story.

• Ask students what the people should have done instead of making and worshiping the golden calf.
Possible response: They should have trusted in God and waited for Moses to return.

God's People Forget

 Focus What does it mean to praise and honor God?

Faith Fact
The ancient laws that God gave the Israelites through Moses are known as the Mosaic Law.

God created each person to be unique. God also created all humans to be alike in a most important way. He created everyone in his own image. Once, the Hebrew people forgot to show God the honor and respect that was due to the giver of such a gift.

✝ **SCRIPTURE** Exodus 32:1–

The Golden Calf

Moses was with God on Mount Sinai for forty days and forty nights. When the people became aware of Moses' delay, they gathered around Aaron and said to him, "Come, make us a god who will be our leader; as for the man Moses who brought us out of the land of Egypt, we do not know what has happened to him." Aaron collected all their gold and melted it down to be formed into a golden calf. Then Aaron built an altar before the calf and declared a feast. The people brought sacrifices and worshipped the calf, saying: "This is your God, O Israel, who brought you out of the land of Egypt."

God then told Moses to return to the people and tell them how angry he was. Moses returned to the camp and destroyed the calf, turning it to powder.

Based on *Exodus 32:1–20*

❓ **Why do you think the people made the golden calf?** They were afraid Moses wouldn't come back.
❓ **Why was Moses upset?** The people had disobeyed God.

110

✝ **SCRIPTURE BACKGROUND**

The Golden Calf The golden calf in *Exodus 32:1–20* has both a literal and a symbolic meaning.

• The calf is a graven image or idol, forbidden by the first commandment.

• The Hebrew people made this idol, emphasizing their doubt of God's faithfulness.

• The idol is gold, symbolizing the people's greed.

Honoring God

The sin of God's people occurred while Moses was receiving the stone tablets of the Ten Commandments from God. The first commandment says, "I am the Lord your God. You shall not have strange gods before me."

The first commandment requires you to honor and worship only God. **Worship** is the adoration and praise that is due to God. You worship God when you celebrate Mass with your parish community, when you pray, and when you live a life that puts God first. Worshipping an object or a person instead of God, as the people worshipped the golden calf, is called **idolatry**.

When you worship God, you show your belief in him as the source of creation and salvation. You show that you, and all creatures, rely on him for life. You show your trust and hope in him. This is why fortune-telling or thinking that we can control nature and know the things that God knows are against the first commandment.

What are some things that people sometimes place ahead of God? Possible responses: money, power, fame

Activity — Share Your Faith

Reflect: In what ways do you worship God?

Share: Share your responses with a partner.

Act: Choose the type of worship that means the most to you. Then write a few sentences explaining why this is your favorite way to worship.

Responses will vary.

_____

_____

_____

111

Honoring God

Ask students to read this section silently. Have them underline the words of the first commandment.

- Ask them what this commandment reminds people to do. keep God first in all they do

- Discuss the question about the things that people sometimes place ahead of God.

- Have students make vocabulary cards for *worship* and *idolatry* to add to their packets.

Activity

- Allow time for students to complete the activity. Ask volunteers to share their responses.

- Point out that doing the things they have listed is a good way for the students to honor God.

Quick Review

People worship God and owe him respect and honor because he created all life and offers all people salvation.

★ REACHING ALL LEARNERS

Paraphrase Many students may benefit from hearing the commandments restated in simpler language. For example, you may want to restate the first commandment as "Worship only God" to help students better understand it.

OPTIONAL ACTIVITY

Golden Calves Have students look through popular magazines for images that make wealth, beauty, and material things seem more important than anything.

- Cut simple calf shapes from gold paper, and have students decorate them with drawings or names of things people sometimes put before God.

Multiple Intelligence: Visual/Spatial

Objective: To recognize ways of showing God honor and respect

 **Focus**

What do the second and third commandments tell you to do? List students' responses on the board or on chart paper.

Respect for God

Ask a volunteer to read aloud the first paragraph. Tell students that to take a name "in vain" means to use it with disrespect.

- Have students read the next paragraph silently to learn how they are to use God's name.

- Review the meaning of *blasphemy*. Have students make vocabulary cards to add to their packets.

- Read aloud the third and fourth paragraphs, and discuss the questions.

Respect for God

 Focus What do the second and third commandments tell you to do?

The second commandment is connected to the first: "You shall not take the name of the Lord in vain." God's name is sacred, or holy, because God is sacred. When God called Moses to be the leader of his people, God revealed his name to Moses. God shared his name with his people because he loved and trusted them. In return God's people are to bless and praise God's holy name.

This commandment calls you to always use the name of God with reverence and respect. Respecting God's name is a sign of the respect God deserves. It is a sin against God's name to curse or to use God's name to swear to a lie. To seriously dishonor the name of God, Jesus Christ, Mary, or the saints in words or actions is called **blasphemy**.

You probably use God's name most often in prayer. Every time you make the Sign of the Cross, you call on the name of the Father, of the Son, and of the Holy Spirit. This is a reminder of your baptism. Calling on God's name strengthens you to live as a child of God and a follower of Christ.

The second commandment also reminds us that God calls each person by name. A person's name is a sign of that person's dignity. You are to use the names of others with respect.

❓ **What are some ways you use God's name?** Possible responses: I use God's name when I pray and at Mass.
❓ **How can you show others that you respect their names?** I can show respect for people's names by not using insulting nicknames.

112

Activity Master 9: Names of God Distribute copies of the activity found on catechist page 116A.

- Tell students to circle the names of God and answer the question.

- Consider sending this activity home.

▲ **Activity Master 9**

Keeping the Lord's Day

Following the first, second, and third commandments helps you love God and grow closer to him. The third commandment teaches you to honor God by celebrating Sunday, the greatest and most special day of the week for Christians. The third commandment is this: Remember to keep holy the Lord's day.

Sunday is the first day of the week. Jesus rose from the dead on the first day of the week. This is why Sunday is known as the Lord's day. Gathering on Sunday for the Eucharist has been the center of the Church's life since the time of the Apostles. This is because Sunday is the day of the Lord's Resurrection.

The Lord's Day

- Participate in the Sunday celebration of the Eucharist. This is the most important way to observe the third commandment.

- Rest and enjoy time with your family. Share a meal, read the Bible, or visit a relative you do not often see.

- Take part in parish activities, visit a retirement center, visit people in the community who are sick, or perform a work of service as a family.

- Respect the rights of others to rest and observe Sunday.

Words of Faith

Blasphemy is the sin of showing contempt for the name of God, Jesus Christ, Mary, or the saints in words or actions.

Activity — Connect Your Faith

Sunday Suggestions What are three other actions that you could take to remember the Lord's day?

Possible responses: pray, do volunteer work, invite a

friend to Mass

113

Keeping the Lord's Day

Ask students to share how their families honor the Lord's Day. Encourage response.

- Read aloud the first paragraph. Remind students that after God created the world, he rested.

- Have students read the next paragraph silently to learn why Sunday is a special day.

- Invite four students each to read aloud one of the ways to keep Sunday holy.

Activity

- Read aloud the directions and have students work on the activity.

- Encourage students to try one of the Sunday activities they have suggested.

Quick Review

The second commandment says to use God's name with respect. The third commandment says to honor God by keeping Sundays holy. Keeping these commandments is a way to grow closer to God.

✚ JUSTICE AND PEACE

The Right to Rest In his 1981 encyclical *On Human Work*, Blessed Pope John Paul II noted that workers have rights.

- the right to balance labor with rest
- the right to have a weekly day to rest, fulfill religious obligations, and spend time with family
- the right to a vacation

Catholic Social Teachings: Dignity of Work

Objective: To sing to praise God, our Father

 **Let Us Pray**

Tell students that today they will be using different names for God.

Prayer of Praise

Prepare

Select five readers, and practice the response with students.

 Use the *Call to Faith 4* CD, track 9, to rehearse the suggested song.

Gather

Process to the prayer space.

Pray

- Follow the order of prayer on page 114.
- For an optional scripture reading, use *Psalm 33:1–5* or *Psalm 34:1–4*.
- Leader's concluding prayer: **Holy God, may we remember to be thankful for all your blessings and give honor to your holy name.**

Celebrate

Prayer of Praise

 Let Us Pray

Gather and begin with the Sign of the Cross.

Sing together.

> Sing, sing, praise and sing! Honor God for ev'rything.
> Sing to God and let it ring. Sing and praise and sing!

"Sing, Sing, Praise and Sing!" © 2000, GIA Publications, Inc.

Leader:	Respond to each name of God by praying: We praise your name, O God.
Reader:	God, our Father,
All:	**We praise your name, O God.**
Reader:	All merciful and gracious God,
All:	**We praise your name, O God.**
Reader:	God, our Creator,
All:	**We praise your name, O God.**
Reader:	Compassionate God,
All:	**We praise your name, O God.**
Reader:	God, source of all life,
All:	**We praise your name, O God.**
Leader:	Let us pray. *Bow your heads as the leader prays.*
All:	**Amen.**

114

 LITURGY LINK

Glory to God   At Mass on most Sundays, the assembly sings or prays a hymn in praise of God—Father, Son, and Holy Spirit.

- Read this prayer with students. Have them point out the names of God mentioned.
- *And With Your Spirit* by John Burland (available at **www.osvcurriculum.com**) offers a version of "Glory to God" that includes lyrics from the revised Roman Missal.

 LECTIONARY LINK

Break Open the Word   Read last week's Sunday Gospel. Invite students to think about what the reading means to them as they try to follow Christ's example. For questions related to the weekly Gospel reading, visit our website at **www.osvcurriculum.com**

GO online Visit **www.osvcurriculum.com** for weekly Scripture readings and seasonal resources.

Review and Apply

A Check Understanding   Mark each statement True or False. Correct each false statement.

1. Worshipping things, or idols, is just as good as worshipping God. _____False_____   We must worship only God.

2. God created all humans in his own image. _____True_____

3. You can respect God and his works by not saying his name in an angry way. _____True_____

4. If you are truly holy in spirit, you do not need to worship at Sunday Mass. _____False_____   Catholics must worship at Sunday Mass.

5. Following the Ten Commandments helps you grow closer to God. _____True_____

B Make Connections   Write two ways to keep the first commandment.

Responses will vary.

_____

Write two ways to keep the second commandment.

Responses will vary.

_____

Activity Live Your Faith

Write a Story   Think about some events that occur within your family. Which ones bring people together? Write a short story that tells how one of these events strengthens your family's respect for God.

115

Review and Apply

Use the focus questions from the catechist Explore pages to review the lesson concepts.

A Check Understanding Have students decide whether each statement is true or false. Ask them to correct each false statement.

B Make Connections After students have completed the assignment, invite them to share their ways of keeping the commandments.

Activity

• Have students brainstorm some events that occur in their families. Remind them to choose the event that best strengthens their family's respect for God.

• Invite students to share their stories.

• You may wish to assign this writing activity as homework.

CATECHIST BACKGROUND

True or False   True-false exercises do not engage all students' thinking skills.

• Students get more from an exercise in which they are asked to correct false statements, as in the review above.

• Avoid asking questions that can be answered yes or no. Instead, ask "Why did . . . ," "How might you . . . ," or "What other actions . . . ?"

Family Faith

Remind students to discuss the Family Faith page at home. Encourage students to read the passage from Psalms.

> **Activity**

- Read aloud the directions.
- Invite volunteers to report on their family discussions next week.

People of Faith

Tell students about Saint Jane Frances de Chantal.

- The Order of the Visitation accepted some women who were old or sick, a practice that was not followed by other orders. In the United States her feast day was changed to August 18 to avoid conflict with that of Our Lady of Guadalupe on December 12.
- Remind students to add Saint Jane Frances de Chantal to their People of Faith albums.

 Visit **www.osvcurriculum.com** for weekly scripture readings and seasonal resources.

UNIT 3: CHAPTER 9
Family Faith

◎ Catholics Believe

- The first three commandments teach you to honor God above all else, respect his name, and worship him on Sunday.
- These commandments tell you to believe in, trust, and love God.

✝ SCRIPTURE

Read *Psalm 119:33–48* to discover the joy you can experience by following Christ's example and living by God's law.

GO online www.osvcurriculum.com
For weekly scripture readings and seasonal resources

Activity
Live Your Faith

Praise God When we perform actions that show our understanding of the first three commandments, we strengthen our love for God.

- Make a list of seven actions that you and your family can do this week to praise and honor God.
- Check off the actions as you and your family move through the week, but feel free to perform these actions more than once. No one can show too much love for God.

▲ Saint Jane Frances de Chantal
1572–1641

People of Faith

Jane Frances de Chantal was born into a noble family in France. She married and had seven children. When Jane became a widow, she devoted herself to the religious life. She met Francis de Sales in 1604 and grew spiritually under his guidance. Eventually, Jane founded the Order of the Visitation. These women cared for those in need. Saint Jane's feast day is December 12.

🙌 Family Prayer

Saint Jane, pray for us that we may be respectful of the dignity of others and of our own dignity. Amen.

In Unit 3 your child is learning about JESUS CHRIST.
116 **CCC** *See Catechism of the Catholic Church 2063–2065 for further reading on chapter content.*

❓ HOW DID I DO?

My session was

☐ *one of the best ever!* ☐ *pretty good.* ☐ *in need of improvement.*

In what discussions and activities were students most interested?

_____

What activity did I most enjoy teaching?

_____

In what area do I need to improve?

_____

Name _____ Date _____

Names of God

Read the names of God listed in the box. Then find and circle each name in the word search. The names run from left to right and from top to bottom.

CREATOR	FATHER	JESUS CHRIST	SON
LORD	SAVIOR		HOLY SPIRIT

```
A   J   Y   O   Z   U   E   P   T   M   E
J   E   S   U   S   C   H   R   I   S   T
Q   F   A   D   K   M   O   N   Q   D   S
B   W   V   N   L   I   L   G   H   C   Y
C   P   I   R   O   L   Y   D   S   Z   D
M   G   O   Q   R   H   S   O   N   B   L
T   S   R   N   D   R   P   E   D   K   J
K   R   X   G   U   V   I   Z   U   T   N
P   F   A   T   H   E   R   L   W   O   Q
W   B   N   E   D   O   I   B   X   A   B
G   Z   C   R   E   A   T   O   R   J   I
```

Write one way you will use God's name with respect this week.

_____

_____

Answers can be found in the back of the Catechist Manual.

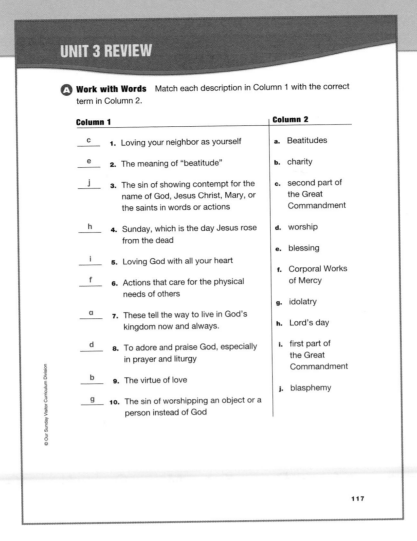

A **Work with Words**   Match each description in Column 1 with the correct term in Column 2.

Column 1	Column 2
__c__ 1. Loving your neighbor as yourself	a. Beatitudes
__e__ 2. The meaning of "beatitude"	b. charity
__j__ 3. The sin of showing contempt for the name of God, Jesus Christ, Mary, or the saints in words or actions	c. second part of the Great Commandment
__h__ 4. Sunday, which is the day Jesus rose from the dead	d. worship
__i__ 5. Loving God with all your heart	e. blessing
__f__ 6. Actions that care for the physical needs of others	f. Corporal Works of Mercy
__a__ 7. These tell the way to live in God's kingdom now and always.	g. idolatry
__d__ 8. To adore and praise God, especially in prayer and liturgy	h. Lord's day
__b__ 9. The virtue of love	i. first part of the Great Commandment
__g__ 10. The sin of worshipping an object or a person instead of God	j. blasphemy

© Our Sunday Visitor Curriculum Division

117

Unit Review

The Unit Review is designed to prepare students for the Unit Assessment. This page focuses on vocabulary words and the main concepts presented in the chapters.

Each review contains various sections that will appeal to the many different learning styles of your students. There are puzzles to engage students' attention, as well as true-false, multiple-choice, short-answer, and fill-in-the-blank exercises.

Direct students to complete the review, and check their responses. Determine areas in which students still need practice, and review those sections of the unit.

Notes

Name _____ Date _____

Life in Christ

(A) Work with Words   Match each description in Column 1 with the correct term in Column 2.

Column 1

_____ **1.** the law of love taught by Jesus

_____ **2.** seven acts of kindness

_____ **3.** how Christians show honor and respect to God

_____ **4.** using God's name disrespectfully

_____ **5.** another name for Sunday

_____ **6.** a blessing

_____ **7.** a prayer said for someone else

Column 2

a. Corporal Works of Mercy

b. blasphemy

c. intercession

d. Beatitude

e. Great Commandment

f. worship

g. Lord's Day

(B) Check Understanding   Circle the letter of the choice that best completes the sentence or answers the question.

8. Charity is the virtue of _____.

    a. trust
    b. forgiveness
    c. love
    d. happiness

9. According to Jesus' law of love, you must love others as _____.

    a. Jesus loves you
    b. your friends love you
    c. the Church loves you
    d. your teachers love you

10. Where did Moses receive the Ten Commandments?

    a. Mount Sinai
    b. Jerusalem
    c. Heaven
    d. Egypt

ASSESSMENT

Name _____ Date _____

11. I perform a Corporal Work of Mercy when I

    a. help wash the dishes.

    b. make good grades in school.

    c. give clothes to a charity.

    d. use water sparingly.

12. The golden calf was a problem because

    a. Aaron made it incorrectly.

    b. Moses' people worshiped it.

    c. it was made of everyone's riches.

    d. it didn't look like God.

Fill in each blank with the correct term from the Word Bank.

13. I asked Jesus what I needed to do to enter

heaven. _____

WORD BANK
first commandment
second commandment
third commandment
rich young man

14. "I am the Lord your God. You shall not have strange

gods before me." _____

15. "Remember to keep holy the Lord's

day." _____

16. "You shall not take the name of the Lord in vain." _____

C **Make Connections** Use the four terms below to write a one-paragraph response to the question.

    Great Commandment   charity

    kindness   works of mercy

17–20. How does Jesus want you to live?

_____

_____

_____

_____

_____

© Our Sunday Visitor Curriculum Division

ASSESSMENT

     Answers can be found in the back of the Catechist Manual.

Unit 4
The Church

In this unit you will...

learn that every person has a vocation to love and serve others. Mary and the saints are models and teachers of holiness for all of us. Jesus gave Church leaders the authority to explain Scripture and Tradition to the faithful. The Holy Spirit directs Church leaders in teaching and guiding the faithful.

Chapter 10

Chapter 11

Chapter 12

 What do you think you will learn in this unit about what the Church teaches?

118

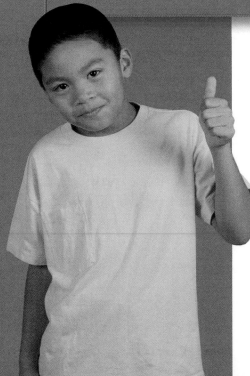

UNIT 4 OPENER

Preview Unit Theme

Tell students that Unit 4 is about the Church.

- Read aloud the text on page 118 of the student edition. Tell students they will learn more about these things in the next three chapters.

- Ask students why they think we need good leaders in the Church.

- Invite volunteers to share the names of saints and other teachers who model holiness.

Overview

Faith Focus

- **God calls every person to a vocation.** (CCC 941)
- **The reign of God is increased by people who live out their vocations.** (CCC 2046)

Catechism Connection

The *Catechism* notes that the Church is the place where Christians fulfill their vocations, along with all who are baptized. (CCC 2030)

NDC Link

The word of God nourishes and sustains evangelizers as well as those being evangelized so that each may grow and be led deeper into his or her own Christian life and faith. (See *NDC*, 17C.)

Resources

BOOKS
Hope through Heartsongs. Stepanek, Mattie. Hyperion. A collection of poems written by an extraordinary young man.

Special Stories for Disability Awareness: Stories and Activities for Teachers, Parents and Professionals. Leicester, Mal. Jessica Kingsley Publishers. Provides classroom activities that reinforce disability awareness.

 Catechist Resources
For interactive lesson planner, chapter resources, and activities
www.osvcurriculum.com

Called to Love
CATECHIST FORMATION

 When Samuel went to sleep in his place, the LORD came and revealed his presence, calling out as before, "Samuel, Samuel!" Samuel answered, "Speak, for your servant is listening."

1 Samuel 3:9–10

The Kingdom of God

There has never been a time when God was not in charge. From the first light of creation to this morning's sunrise, all humans have been under the loving dominion of God. His plan for humans has existed from the beginning. Humanity was created to live in peace, in justice, and in love.

By committing sin, humans strayed from God's plan. Jesus came to bring them back to a loving relationship with God and to fulfill God's reign. Jesus' death and Resurrection saved humans and restored them to their share in the kingdom. Humans still struggle and long for the completion that will come when Jesus returns. Humans wait in hope, cooperating with God in bringing about his reign. Christians' patience, faithfulness, and love show others that the reign of God is both possible and present—although incompletely—here and now.

Christian Vocations

God invites you to live a life of meaning and service. Single or married, ordained or layperson, you participate in making the world whole and holy. The wonder of this is that you are asked to live your vocation exactly where you are at the moment. Vocation is your attitude and your acceptance of God's presence in your words and actions. Using your gifts to benefit others is answering God's invitation with an open heart and willing hands.

Reflect *When have you felt that God was calling you?*

The Christian Vocation

God has a plan for everyone he created—a grand plan that will bring about the reign of God. Tell students that the reign of God will someday come in its fullness, when all people live peacefully in love and concern for one another.

- Invite to your sessions visitors who can tell about vocations in Church work, health care, politics, community service, and so on. Encourage students to ask these people questions about their vocations.

- Invite a priest, a deacon, a married couple, or a single person. Ask the visitors to share how their lives promote the reign of love, peace, and justice. This will help students better understand the concept of vocation and the life to which God calls them.

- Encourage students to research vocations that interest them.

Getting Involved

- I like to make a difference. Give me an opportunity to work on parish projects.

- I like to hear different points of view. Invite speakers or guests to some of our sessions.

- I enjoy group activities. Show me how to work peacefully with others.

Motivations

Many things probably motivated you to enter into the catechetical ministry. At the center of all ministry is a call from God to love and serve him and his Church. The love for Christ and others drives and motivates you to share the good news and work for the kingdom. Take time to think about what else motivated you to become a catechist. The process of naming and claiming the authentic motivations behind your commitment as a catechist can deepen your understanding of your role. Even motivations that may not seem ideal are important to examine.

Reflect **What motivations fuel your spirit to teach?**

Catechist's Prayer

Eternal God, may your loving plan reign in my heart. May my words bring peace to others and my actions show concern for their needs. Amen.

Weekly Planner

Objectives	Lesson Process	Materials
1 Invite — *10 minutes* — **Page 119** **Objective:** To recognize that everyone has an important purpose in life	**Let Us Pray:** Psalm 113:1 • Sing or pray the psalm. • Listen to the story. • Discuss ways to improve the world.	☐ Board or chart paper
2 Explore — *40 minutes* — **Pages 120–121** **Objective:** To learn the vocation of all Christians	**Scripture:** Jeremiah 1:5–8 • Proclaim the scripture story. • Describe the relationship between vocation and the kingdom of God. **Activity** Complete the Share Your Faith Activity. **Words of Faith** vocation , kingdom of God	☐ Pencils or pens ☐ Art materials
Pages 122–123 **Objective:** To learn ways that people can use their gifts to serve God	• Examine ways the laity serves God and the Church. • Discuss the relationship between vocation and finding one's heartsong. **Activity** Complete the Connect Your Faith Activity. **Words of Faith** laity	☐ Copies of Activity Master 10 on page 126A
3 Celebrate — *10 minutes* — **Page 124** **Objective:** To pray for peace	**Let Us Pray:** Colossians 1:2–5 • Gather as a community. • Write and pray heartsong prayers. • Celebrate a Meditation on Peace. **Hymn:** "Take, O Take Me As I Am" **Activity** Complete the Holy Trinity Activity, page 226 and 227	☐ Hymnals ☐ Music CD ☐ Bibles

Wrap Up

Review and Apply

Page 125
• Review the chapter concepts.
• Complete the Live Your Faith Activity.

Family Faith

Page 126
• Introduce the page, and assign it as a family activity.
• Read about Blessed Frederic Ozanam.

ACRE Connection, Domain 4—Kingdom of God

Home Connection

GO online www.osvcurriculum.com
Family Faith activities, feasts and seasonal resources, saint features, and much more

• Online planning tools include chapter background and planner, activity master, customizable test, and more.

• Enhancement activities for each step of the catechetical process, including alternative prayer experiences and blessings.

• Games, activities, interactive review, alternative assessment, and more for children.

www.calltofaitheconnect.com

Called to Love

Let Us Pray

Leader: God of love, we gladly serve and obey you.

"Praise, you servants of the LORD,
praise the name of the LORD."

Psalm 113:1

All: God of love, we gladly serve and obey you. Amen.

Activity — Let's Begin

Miss Rumphius In the story *Miss Rumphius,* a young girl named Alice Rumphius is challenged by her grandfather to make the world more beautiful. Many years later, the adult Alice discovers the lupine flower. She decides to make the fields and neighborhoods of her town more beautiful. Alice walks through the town and its fields, dropping lupine seed along her way. Now those empty lots and fields are carpets of blue every spring.

• What kinds of things would make the world around you a better place? How could you help? **Responses will vary.**

119

1 Invite

Objective: To recognize that everyone has an important purpose in life

Let Us Pray

Have students move to your classroom prayer space. In the space, have a crucifix and a Bible opened to the psalm. Ask students to create a melody to go with the psalm verse, or have them set the verse to a tune with which they are all familiar. Sing the verse as an opening prayer.

Activity

• Ask students whether they are familiar with the story. If someone in the class knows the story, ask that student to tell the group what happens in the story. Otherwise, read the story summary aloud.

• Have students discuss their responses to the question. Write their ideas on the board or on chart paper.

QUICK TIP

Musical Intelligence Many students' strongest learning style is through music. These students will remember the words of the psalm verses better if you set the words of the psalms to simple, familiar tunes or ask the students to do so. You may wish to provide students with simple percussion instruments.

Objective: To learn the vocation of all Christians

 **Focus**

What does it mean to have a vocation? List students' responses on the board or on chart paper.

God's Call

Discuss the meaning of the term *vocation*.

• Invite a volunteer to read aloud the paragraph that tells about Jeremiah.

The Call of Jeremiah

Proclaim the Scripture. Then have students read it aloud again, with two students reading the parts of God and Jeremiah.

• Ask students why God might have told Jeremiah not to say that he was too young. Responses may include that God would help him do the job.

• Discuss the questions that follow the Scripture.

God's Call

 Focus What does it mean to have a vocation?

Everyone has a **vocation**. A vocation is God's call to love and serve him and others. Sometimes God calls a person to a special role.

Once, long before Jesus was born, there was a young man who lived in the tiny kingdom of Judah, where the nation of Israel is today. His name was Jeremiah, which means "the Lord raises up." Jeremiah was called by God to speak the truth to his people in a time of great danger. They had lost their way and were being invaded by powerful nations. This is how Jeremiah remembered God calling him.

✝ SCRIPTURE Jeremiah 1:5–8

The Call of Jeremiah

"Before I formed you in the womb I knew you,
before you were born I dedicated you, a
prophet to the nations I appointed you.

Ah, LORD God! I said,
I know not how to speak; 'I am too young.'

But the LORD answered me,
Say not, I am too young. . . .
whatever I command you, you shall speak.
Have no fear before them,
because I am with you to deliver you."

From *Jeremiah 1:5–8*

 Have you ever felt that God wanted you to do something or to make a certain choice?

❷ How did you know? Responses will vary.

✝ SCRIPTURE BACKGROUND

Jeremiah The prophets called people back to faithfulness. Their message was ultimately one of hope, reminding people of God's faithfulness.

• Jeremiah prophesied during the destruction of Jerusalem.

• His prophecies included a covenant, written on the hearts of the people, and rebuilding Jerusalem.

The Kingdom of God

Not everyone hears God's call as clearly as Jeremiah did. Sometimes it takes many years of praying and listening to know your vocation. It will be yours alone because you are a unique child of God.

All vocations can be ways of making the **kingdom of God** more visible. God's reign is the world of love, peace, and justice that God intends. Jesus announced the reign of God and revealed it in his life and ministry. But the reign of God will not be here fully until the end of time. Every person must help God increase his reign.

What signs can you see of God's kingdom in the world now? Possible response: people who make peace and help others

Ways to Serve God

The Catholic Church recognizes three special ways in which people respond to God's call to serve: through the priesthood, through consecrated religious life, and through married life. Consecrated religious life is a state of life in which a person usually makes vows, or promises, of holiness.

Words of Faith

A **vocation** is God's call to love and serve him and others.

The **kingdom of God** is God's rule of peace, justice, and love that is here now but has not yet come in its fullness.

Activity — Share Your Faith

Reflect: Imagine that you are much older and that a film director is preparing a movie of your life.

Share: Work with a partner, and pretend that your partner is the film director. Suggest two scenes that he or she could shoot to show you helping increase God's reign.

Act: Choose one of the scenes you described, and draw it. After you have finished drawing, write a caption for the picture.

121

The Kingdom of God

Tell students that, like Jeremiah, each of them has a vocation, or a calling from God.

- Have students read these two paragraphs to learn the vocation of all Christians.
- Spend time on the discussion question. Encourage responses that relate to the Beatitudes.

Ways to Serve God

Ask a volunteer to read the paragraph aloud. Ask students to name people they know who serve God in these ways.

Activity

- Allow time for the drawing activity.
- Ask volunteers to share their work.

Quick Review

Everyone has a vocation—a call to help build the kingdom of God.

Explore

Objective: To learn ways that people can use their gifts to serve God

 **Focus**

How do Christians help God increase his reign? **List students' responses on the board or on chart paper.**

Serving the Church

Read aloud this section.

- Write the word *laity* on the board or on chart paper. Ask a volunteer to define the word.
- Tell students that it is through Baptism that God calls people to serve in special ways.

Many Gifts

Invite volunteers to read aloud each item from the list of roles.

- Encourage students to add to the list the names of other ministries and services in your parish.
- Discuss the questions. Point out that students can be altar servers, lectors, singers, or musicians.

Faith Fact

Since the Church began, the laity had important leadership roles, including teaching and missionary work.

Serving the Church

 **Focus** How do Christians help God increase his reign?

The Church recognizes that some people may choose to serve God by remaining single rather than choosing the priesthood, religious life, or married life. Single life is also a vocation. Both single and married people are part of the **laity**.

All who are baptized can choose to serve the Church and the parish community. Here are some of their special roles.

Many Gifts

- The pastor and pastoral associate lead and serve the parish community.
- The permanent deacon is ordained to assist the pastor, especially at Eucharist, marriages, and funerals, and to perform works of charity.
- The lector proclaims the word of God at the Liturgy of the Word.
- The Eucharistic minister of Holy Communion helps distribute Holy Communion at Mass and takes Holy Communion to those who are sick or housebound.
- Altar servers assist the priest at Mass by carrying the sacramentary, the sacred vessels, and the cross.
- Musicians lead the assembly in sung prayer.
- Catechists teach Scripture and the Catholic faith to members of the parish.

❓ **Who in your family has served in one of these special roles?**

❓ **What other roles are there? How could you share your gifts in one of these roles?** Responses will vary.

122

OPTIONAL ACTIVITY

Activity Master 10: People of God Distribute copies of the activity found on catechist page 126A.

- Tell students to think of the people in their parish who perform each role.
- As an alternative, you may wish to send this activity home with students.

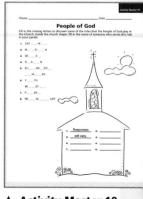

▲ **Activity Master 10**

sing Your Gifts

It can take many years to recognize your vocation in e. However, even while you are young you can use your fts from God to make a difference. Here is the story of boy who used his talent to bring a powerful message to e world.

BIOGRAPHY

Heartsongs

Mattie Stepanek was born with a rare form of uscular dystrophy. Although he used a wheelchair and eeded a machine to help him breathe, Mattie wrote eautiful poetry.

Writing poetry helped Mattie find what he called his eartsong. "Your heartsong is your inner beauty," said attie. "It's the song in your heart that wants you to elp make yourself a better person, and to help other eople do the same. Everybody has one."

inding Your Heartsong

Discovering your vocation is a lot like finding your eartsong. It is finding the unique way that God ants you to make the world a better place. veryone who brings love, peace, and justice to e world helps God increase his reign.

Activity
Connect Your Faith

Your Heartsong
What could your heartsong be? Write and decorate its title in this space.

123

Using Your Gifts

Have students read the paragraph silently.

Heartsongs

Share with students the story of Mattie Stepanek.

- Read aloud Mattie's description of a heartsong.

Finding Your Heartsong

Tell students that Mattie discovered his heartsong by writing poetry, but that other people may have other ways of finding their "inner beauty."

- Discuss with students different ways that they could begin to discover their heartsongs. Possible responses: singing, drawing, volunteering for service projects

Activity

- Distribute art materials such as markers, foil, glue sticks, and stickers.
- If time permits, have each student create a mini-poster to take home.

Quick Review

All Christians can serve God by spreading love, peace, and justice.

 QUICK TIP

Inspiring Stories   Students may be familiar with other stories of people who have faced difficulties with courage, as Mattie Stepanek had.

- Describe the life of the famous writer, speaker, and activist Helen Keller, or that of another person.
- Ask students to tell how people can make a difference in the world while struggling with illnesses or disabilities.

JUSTICE AND PEACE

Disability Awareness   A teaching of Catholic social justice is that no person has less dignity or worth because of a disability.

- Many people with physical challenges provide motivational talks to young people. Your community may have a list of these speakers. Consider inviting one to visit your group.

Catholic Social Teaching: Life and Dignity

Objective: To pray for peace

 **Let Us Pray**

Tell students that they will be praying their own heartsongs.

Meditation on Peace

Prepare

Read Mattie's words about peace.

• Write the phrase *I cannot wait to . . .* on the board or on chart paper.

• Have students write endings.

 Use the *Call to Faith 4* CD, track 10, to rehearse the suggested song.

Gather

Invite students to gather quietly.

Pray

• Follow the order of prayer on page 124.

• Invite students to read their prayers.

• An optional reading is *Matthew 9:35–38.*

• Leader's concluding prayer: **Lord, hear our prayers and help us do good things for the world.**

Meditation on Peace

 **Let Us Pray**

Gather and begin with the Sign of the Cross.

Leader: Let us sit and listen to the words of the Letter to the Colossians.

Reader 1: *Read Colossians 1:2–5.*
Silence

Sing together.

Take, O take me as I am; summon out what I shall be; set your seal upon my heart and live in me.

"Take, O Take Me As I Am" © 1994, Iona Community, GIA Publications, Inc., agent

Reader 2: Let us reflect on peace and listen to words that Mattie Stepanek wrote about peace.

"I cannot wait to become
A peacemaker.
I cannot wait to help
The world overcome
Anger, and problems of evil."
What good things are you eager to do for the world?

Leader: Let us pray.
Bow your heads as the leader prays.

All: **Amen.**

124

 LITURGY LINK

Background Music Meditative activities, such as writing a prayer, are enhanced by quiet background music.

• Music helps create a soothing atmosphere that is conducive to reflection, and it blocks out other distracting noises.

• Use instrumental, slow-paced music, and play it at low volume.

 LECTIONARY LINK

Break Open the Word Read last week's Sunday Gospel. Invite students to think about what the reading means to them as they try to follow Christ's example. For questions related to the weekly Gospel reading, visit our website at **www.osvcurriculum.com.**

 Visit www.osvcurriculum.com for weekly Scripture readings and seasonal resources.

Review and Apply

Wrap-Up

A **Work with Words** Complete each sentence by unscrambling the words.

Jesus announced that God's (grien) _____**reign**_____ was at hand. By this he meant that God's reign of (eceap) _____**peace**_____, (vole) _____**love**_____, and (itcejus) _____**justice**_____ had begun in him, but was still to come in its fullness. All Christians are (leldac) _____**called**_____ by God to cooperate with him in bringing his kingdom to fullness. This calling from God is a (iaotvcno) _____**vocation**_____. All who are baptized can serve their (rspaih) _____**parish**_____ in special ways. Ordained (iesprts) _____**priests**_____ and (eadcnos) _____**deacons**_____ celebrate or assist at the Sacraments and preach the word of God.

B **Check Understanding** Complete the following: Every person is called . . .

_____Responses will vary._____

Activity Live Your Faith

Your Talents Draw the outline of your hand on a separate sheet of paper. On each finger, write one of your talents. Then in the center, write a way that you can use at least one of your talents to bring more peace and justice into the world.

125

Review and Apply

Use the focus questions from the catechist Explore pages to review the lesson concepts.

A **Work with Words** Have students fill in the answers for the scrambled word activity.

B **Check Understanding** Ask each student to write his or her response to the statement.

Activity

- Tell students to think about the things they believe they are good at doing.
- If students have difficulty thinking of talents, give them examples, such as music, dance, academic achievement, or artistic ability.
- Display students' handprints in the classroom.

REACHING ALL LEARNERS

Word Puzzles Scrambled word activities such as the one in the review activity above may be particularly difficult for those students who have dyslexia or other cognitive disabilities.

- Manipulating cutout letter shapes or Scrabble™ tiles may help these students arrive at the answers.
- You may have to provide hints, such as telling the students the first letter of each word.

Family Faith

Remind students to discuss the Family Faith page at home. Encourage students to read the passage from 1 Corinthians.

Activity

- Read aloud the directions, and then use your name to create a sample acrostic.
- Allow students to work together on an acrostic that uses the name of your parish.

People of Faith

Tell students about Blessed Frederic Ozanam.

- Frederic Ozanam wanted to form a community that would serve the people of his time. When Frederic was near death, his confessor told him not to be afraid. Frederic replied, "Why should I fear him who I love so?"
- Remind students to add Blessed Frederic Ozanam to their People of Faith albums.

 Visit **www.osvcurriculum.com** for weekly scripture readings and seasonal resources.

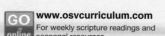

Catholics Believe

- Every person is called by God to a vocation.
- Through your vocation, you can help God increase his reign.

✝ SCRIPTURE

Read *1 Corinthians 12:1–31* to learn more about the spiritual gifts with which God blesses us.

GO online www.osvcurriculum.com
For weekly scripture readings and seasonal resources

Activity
Live Your Faith

Name Acrostics Sit and talk together. Discuss the gifts that you see in each member of your family. Then, using your names, create acrostics that list the gifts of your family. Here is an example:

J oyful
O thers come first
E nthusiastic

Discuss how your family members' gifts are making the world a better place.

▲ **Blessed Frederic Ozanam**
1813–1853

People of Faith

Frederic was born in Milan, Italy. For a time he studied law, but in Paris he discovered a great love for literature. He had a strong faith, and his friends challenged him to find a way to live out his Christian beliefs in his everyday life. Frederic cofounded the Society of Saint Vincent de Paul. This religious association continues today to help those in need, especially those who are poor. Blessed Frederic's feast day is September 8.

 Family Prayer

O God, help us answer your call as Blessed Frederic did, so that we may help you increase your reign of justice, love, and peace. Amen.

In Unit 4 your child is learning about the CHURCH.
126 CCC *See Catechism of the Catholic Church 941, 2046 for further reading on chapter content.*

❓ HOW DID I DO?

My session was

☐ *one of the best ever!* ☐ *pretty good.* ☐ *in need of improvement.*

In what discussions and activities were students most interested?

_____

What activity did I most enjoy teaching?

_____

In what area do I need to improve?

_____

Name _____ Date _____

People of God

Fill in the missing letters to discover some of the roles that the People of God play in the Church. Inside the church shape, fill in the name of someone who serves this role in your parish.

1. CAT __ __ HI __ __

2. M __ __ IC __ __ N

3. SE __ __ E __

4. D __ A __ __ N

5. EU __ __ AR __ STI __

   __ __ NI __ __ ER

6. Y __ __ TH

   MI __ __ ST __ __

7. P __ __ ES __

8. RE __ __ GI __ __ __ LIFE

1. _____ Responses _____   2. _____

3. _____ will vary. _____   4. _____

5. _____   6. _____

7. _____   8. _____

Answers can be found in the back of the Catechist Manual.

Overview

Faith Focus

- All who live their love of God are saints, in whom the Church's holiness shines. *(CCC 828)*
- Mary, the Mother of the Church, is the perfect model of saintly holiness. *(CCC 829)*

Catechism Connection

The *Catechism* notes that canonizing saints gives the faithful hope, as well as models and intercessors. *(CCC 828)*

NDC Link

Human beings come to know themselves, one another, and God through human experiences. Catechesis should follow the example of Jesus, who used ordinary human experiences to show God's presence in our lives and shed light on the mystery of God. (See *NDC*, 29A.)

Resources

BOOK
Saints: Our Friends & Teachers. *
Palencar, Lee. Twenty-Third Publications. Features stories and activities that help students learn about saints.

DVD/VHS
Saints: Gospel Artists (43 min.). Oblate Media. Relates a pilgrimage through Germany and Italy to learn about saints.

*Available at www.osvcurriculum.com

GO online **Catechist Resources**
www.osvcurriculum.com
For interactive lesson planner, chapter resources, and activities

✝ *In the sixth month, the angel Gabriel was sent from God to a town of Galilee called Nazareth, to a virgin betrothed to a man named Joseph, of the house of David, and the virgin's name was Mary. And coming to her, he said, "Hail, favored one! The Lord is with you."*

Luke 1:26–28

Saints

Some people are extraordinary. They rise above the norm, they try harder, and they succeed in the face of adversity. Often you try to be like them because they inspire you. But they are human like you—or else they would be too remote to be inspiring!

These achievers in our community of faith are those the Church honors as saints. They were not perfect. If you read the stories of their lives, you see that they too had moments of doubt and fear. They failed from time to time and even grew despondent. But they continued to say "yes" to God, even in the face of disappointments or great challenges.

Canonized saints are people whom the Church officially recognizes as public examples of virtue and holiness. They are your models, but you must remember that all Christians are called to be saints. They are sanctified by Christ and led by the Holy Spirit. Sainthood is *your* destiny, too.

The Immaculate Conception

The teaching that Mary was immaculately conceived (without sin from the moment of her conception) is directly related to her role as the Mother of God. This dogma was proclaimed by Pope Pius IX in 1854. Mary's freedom from sin made her the perfect mother for Jesus. Her willingness to obey God makes her the perfect model for your Christian discipleship.

Reflect ***How is Mary a model for you? When do you feel favored by the Lord?***

Models of Faith

A unique aspect of Catholic Tradition is the doctrine of the communion of saints. This doctrine includes the spiritual bond that exists between the faithful here on earth and those now in heaven. Saints are friends in the Lord who can guide Christians. Friendship is important to fourth graders; let them know that the saints can provide them with help and support.

- Ask students to name some of the heroes in their lives. Choose a few of these heroes, and identify their admirable qualities. Then ask students to name the qualities in their heroes that would be pleasing to God.

- Consider using some of the many books, videos, and sacramentals that can help students know the saints and learn from their lives.

- Be sure to emphasize Mary, the Church's greatest saint. Invite students to embrace her special example.

Getting Involved

- I admire heroes. Use books, videos, and sacramentals to teach me about the saints.

- I like drama and acting. Include skits and plays in the lessons.

- Sometimes it is hard for me to sit still. Use methods that will allow me to move around and be active.

Growing from Pain

Catechesis, like all endeavors, can bring you rejection, apathy, ridicule, and even betrayal. Catechists must know that great things are often achieved as a result of painful events.

- Painfulness is the practice of turning pain into a learning experience. As a catechist, you may allow pain to touch you, but you should not get lost in it.

- You can learn to recognize pain in others.

- Pain can help you sustain the spirit to teach if you can predict when your words may cause pain to yourself or others and when some of your past patterns need to be changed.

Reflect   **What painful experience has actually improved your ability to sustain your spirit?**

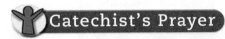

Catechist's Prayer

Jesus Christ, Son of God, be with me this day. I ask all the saints, especially your mother Mary, to surround me with love and guide me with the light of faith. Amen.

	Objectives	Lesson Process	Materials
1 Invite — 10 minutes	**Page 127** **Objective:** To identify beliefs held by faith-filled people	**Let Us Pray:** Psalm 73:1 • Pray the psalm. • Discuss three famous people who made a difference. • Express a statement of personal beliefs.	☐ Board or chart paper
2 Explore — 40 minutes	**Pages 128–129** **Objective:** To learn how saints are models of faith	• Discuss the characteristics of saints. • Read about Saint Catherine and Pope John XXIII. **Activity** Complete the Share Your Faith Activity. **Words of Faith** **saint**	☐ Index cards ☐ Map of the world showing Italy ☐ Pencils or pens
	Pages 130–131 **Objective:** To understand that Mary and the saints are models of holiness	**Scripture:** Luke 1:46–50 • Proclaim the scripture story. • Discuss Mary as a model of holiness. **Activity** Complete the Connect Your Faith Activity. **Words of Faith** **Immaculate Conception , patron saint**	☐ Copies of Activity Master 11 on page 134A ☐ Recording of the *Magnificat* ☐ Crayons or markers
3 Celebrate — 10 minutes	**Page 132** **Objective:** To ask the saints to pray to God for us	**Let Us Pray** • Rehearse the responses. • Gather as a community. • Celebrate a Litany of the Saints. **Hymn:** "Psalm 100" **Activity** Complete the Angelus Activity, page 246 and 247	☐ Hymnals ☐ Music CD ☐ Bible

Wrap Up

Review and Apply

Page 133
• Review the chapter concepts.
• Complete the Live Your Faith Activity.

Family Faith

Page 134
• Introduce the page, and assign it as a family activity.
• Read about Blessed Kateri Tekakwitha.

ACRE Connection, Domain 2—Mary

Home Connection

GO online **www.osvcurriculum.com**
Family Faith activities, feasts and seasonal resources, saint features, and much more

CALL to FAITH e connect

• Online planning tools include chapter background and planner, activity master, customizable test, and more.

• Enhancement activities for each step of the catechetical process, including alternative prayer experiences and blessings.

• Games, activities, interactive review, alternative assessment, and more for children

www.calltofaitheconnect.com

Chapter 11 Models of Faith

Let Us Pray

Leader: Help us learn from those who serve you, O Lord.

"How good God is to the upright,
the LORD, to those who are clean of heart!"

Psalm 73:1

All: Help us learn from those who serve you, O Lord. Amen.

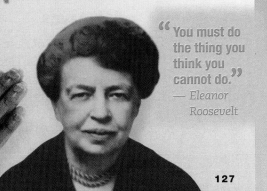

"We must be the change we wish to see."
—Mohandas Gandhi

"...cannot help it when I see injustice. I cannot keep quiet."
—Archbishop Desmond Tutu

"You must do the thing you think you cannot do."
— Eleanor Roosevelt

Activity Let's Begin

I Believe These quotations tell you about the personal beliefs of three famous people who helped change the world. Many who make a difference are as young as you are.

Now think about your beliefs.

• What statement about your own beliefs would you like people to remember? **Responses will vary.**

127

1 Invite

Objective: To identify beliefs held by faith-filled people

Let Us Pray

Have students gather in the prayer space. Proclaim the psalm verse, and invite the entire group to respond.

Activity

• Ask each of three volunteers to read aloud one of the quotes on student page 127. Explain how each person quoted helped make a difference in the world.

• Invite students to mention other famous people and their statements of belief. Responses may include Martin Luther King, Jr.'s "I have a dream" or Jesus' "Love one another."

• Ask students to think of their own statements of belief. Then ask them to share their statements. List their responses on the board or on chart paper.

• Tell students that they will now learn more about followers of Jesus who held strong beliefs and helped change the world.

OPTIONAL ACTIVITY

Quotations Collect inspirational sayings into a book.

• Students can use markers to copy quotations and authors onto pieces of felt or poster board.

• Students may also add pictures.

• Use a hole punch and ribbon to bind the book.

Book of Quotations

Multiple Intelligence: Verbal/Linguistic

CATECHIST BACKGROUND

Famous People Explain that the people quoted cared deeply about human rights.

• Archbishop Desmond Tutu (1931–present) helped those oppressed in South Africa.

• Eleanor Roosevelt (1884–1962) worked for better conditions throughout her adult life.

• Mohandas Gandhi (1869–1948) led the people of India to become an independent nation; he emphasized nonviolent resistance to injustice.

Objective: To learn how saints are models of faith

◎ Focus

What is faith? List students' responses on the board or on chart paper.

Holy Ones of God

Invite students to silently read the paragraph. Define the word *saint*, and have students create cards for their vocabulary packets.

Catherine of Siena

Gather students in a story circle. Show them the location of Italy on the map. Tell students that you are going to read a story about a woman who lived in Italy many years ago.

- Read aloud the biography of Catherine of Siena. Explain that she had a great deal of influence for a woman of her time (1347–1380).

Holy Lives

Ask a volunteer to read aloud the paragraph. Discuss the meaning of *canonized*.

- Ask the discussion question. Affirm students as they share responses.

Explore

Holy Ones of God

◎ Focus What is faith?

The Church honors certain people whose whole lives showed others how to do God's will. These models of faith all helped God bring his reign into the world more fully. The Church calls each of these people a **saint**. Here are the stories of two of them.

A BIOGRAPHY

Catherine of Siena

Catherine wanted to serve God through quiet prayer. But Catherine's world was full of problems. God called her to make a difference.

Catherine lived long ago in Siena, Italy. She was very wise and used words well. Even though it was unusual for a woman of her time, Catherine made public speeches and taught priests. She also cared for those who were sick or in prison.

Catherine spoke out against injustice. She helped leaders in the Church make peace with one another. Christians learn from Catherine that every member of the Church can make a difference.

Catherine's students called her "Mother" and "Teacher." She has been named a Doctor of the Church.

Holy Lives

Catherine of Siena is a canonized saint of the Catholic Church. This means that the Church has officially declared that she led a holy life and is enjoying eternal life with God in heaven.

❓ What do you admire about Catherine?
Possible response: fighting injustice

128

CATECHIST BACKGROUND

Canonization After a candidate's death, bishops send information to the Vatican.

- If a panel recommends it, the pope proclaims the person *venerable*.

- If the candidate is responsible for a miracle, the pope can declare the person *beatified*, or *blessed*.

- If another miracle is confirmed, the pope can declare the candidate a saint.

Good Pope John

Before he was elected pope, John XXIII served soldiers who were wounded in World War I. This experience taught him to work for peace. Later he worked with religious leaders who were not Catholic. He learned to look for things that were the same in their beliefs, rather than for differences.

After he was elected pope, John XXIII called all the world's bishops to Rome to renew and reform the Catholic Church at the Second Vatican Council. He died before it ended, but the council continued. People everywhere mourned the death of the humble, friendly man they called "Good Pope John." Pope John XXIII was named Blessed by the Church in September 2000. This is the last step before a saint is canonized.

What quality of Pope John XXIII do you admire the most? Possible response: peacemaking

Words of Faith

A **saint** is a person who the Church declares has led a holy life and is enjoying eternal life with God in heaven.

Activity — Share Your Faith

Reflect: Think about what makes Saint Catherine and Pope John XXIII models of faith.

Share: Discuss your ideas about them with the class.

Act: Where the circles overlap, write what you know is true of both Saint Catherine and Pope John XXIII. In the circle on the left, write what is true only for Saint Catherine. Write what is true only for Pope John XXIII in the circle on the right.

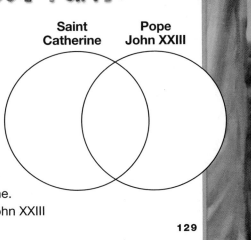

Saint Catherine   Pope John XXIII

129

Good Pope John

Read aloud the biography of Pope John XXIII.

- Ask students what good qualities Pope John demonstrated. peacemaking, understanding, modesty, friendliness

- Then ask the discussion question.

Activity

- Have a student read aloud the directions for the first two parts of the activity. Allow time for students to complete their discussions.

- Draw the Venn diagram on the board or on chart paper, and record students' responses.

Quick Review

Saints are holy people who are models of faith for Catholic Christians.

REACHING ALL LEARNERS

Working in Groups Students of varying learning styles can benefit from completing the activity as a group. In each group, try to include

- a student who is good at recalling information.

- a student who can graphically organize information.

- a student who likes to present information to the whole group.

OPTIONAL ACTIVITY

Saint Catherine and Pope John XXIII Ask volunteers to research Saint Catherine or Pope John XXIII.

- Provide books about the saints or Web site addresses that will get the research started.

- Ask students to report their findings at the next session.

Multiple Intelligence: Verbal/Linguistic

Objective: To understand that Mary and the saints are models of holiness.

 Focus

How is Mary a model of holiness? List students' responses on the board or on chart paper.

Model of Holiness

Read aloud the introductory paragraph.

• Tell students to listen to learn about Mary, the greatest saint of the Catholic Church.

Mary's Song

Ask a proficient reader to proclaim the scripture passage. Tell students that many people still call Mary's Song by its Latin name, the *Magnificat*.

• If possible, play a recording of the Magnificat.

• Read aloud the next two paragraphs. Point out that Mary's Immaculate Conception makes her unique among all the saints.

• Discuss the questions about responsibility.

Model of Holiness

 Focus How is Mary a model of holiness?

There are many saints, but Mary is the perfect model of holiness. God chose Mary to be the mother of Jesus. After Mary said "yes" to being the mother of God's Son, she visited her cousin Elizabeth. Here is how Mary described her joy at the great blessing God had given her.

✝ SCRIPTURE   Luke 1: 46

Mary's Song

"My soul proclaims the greatness of the Lord;
    my spirit rejoices in God my savior.
For he has looked upon his handmaid's lowliness;
    behold, from now on will all ages call
        me blessed.
The Mighty One has done great things for me,
    and holy is his name.
His mercy is from age to age
    to those who fear him."

Luke 1:46–5

God created Mary full of grace. He preserved her from sin from the very first moment of her conception. The Church calls this gift from God Mary's **Immaculate Conception**.

The word *immaculate* means spotless and clean—without sin. The word *conception* means the very moment when a person's life begins. The Catholic Church celebrates the Immaculate Conception of Mary on December 8.

 Have you ever been given a very big responsibility? What did you say or do? Responses will vary.

Madonna and Child by Giambologna

130

✝ SCRIPTURE BACKGROUND

The Magnificat The depth of Mary's faith is shown in a very special way in the Magnificat. The Church models its earthly journey of faith on Mary's journey and constantly repeats the words of the Magnificat, which proclaim the power of God's truth. The Magnificat is recited daily at the liturgy of Vespers.

our Will Be Done

Part of holiness is being able to accept and do the ings that God asks of you. Mary accepted God's will roughout her life. Mary cared for and protected Jesus hen he was a child. She stood by him all through his e. Mary was strong enough to be at the foot of Jesus' oss when he was crucified.

After Jesus ascended into heaven, Mary remained on rth with Jesus' followers. She was there at Pentecost hen the Holy Spirit came to the disciples. Mary is called e Mother of the Church because she is an example of ve and faith for Christians. Even today, she continues to ld all of her Son's followers close to her heart.

Guide for You

When you were baptized, you may have received e name of one of the saints of God. This person your **patron saint**. He or she is your model of ith and prays for you from heaven. You walk in e footsteps of your saint and continue his or er good works in the way you live your life.

Words of Faith

Immaculate Conception is the title for Mary that recognizes that God preserved her from sin from the first moment of her life.

A **patron saint** is a model of faith and a protector for you.

Activity
Connect Your Faith

Time for Holiness Use the clock to show what you do each day. Divide the clock so that it looks like a sliced pie. You may have a narrow slice from seven o'clock to eight o'clock for getting up and preparing for school, but you may have a much larger slice for playing after school. After you have shown your activities for a day, color those that God's presence could make holy.

131

Your Will Be Done

Ask students to read this text silently to find out who was Jesus' most faithful follower.

• Ask students what qualities Mary showed that make her a good model for Christians today. Responses will vary.

• Have students make vocabulary cards for the Words of Faith.

A Guide for You

Read aloud the text.

• Encourage students to find information about their patron saints and share it with the class during the next session.

Activity

• Allow time for students to work.

• Ask for volunteers to share and explain their responses.

Quick Review

Mary is the Church's most important saint and the best model of holiness and faith.

✚ JUSTICE AND PEACE

Peaceful People In 1983 the U.S. Conference of Catholic Bishops wrote a pastoral letter called *The Challenge of Peace.*

• The faithful are to advocate actively for peace by treating all people with justice and understanding.

• Share with students the story of Elizabeth of Portugal or of another peace-making saint.

Catholic Social Teaching: Call to Community

OPTIONAL ACTIVITY

Activity Master 11: Saints and Symbols Distribute copies of the activity found on catechist page 134A.

• Suggest that students use the text and reference sources to complete the activity.

• You may want to send this activity home.

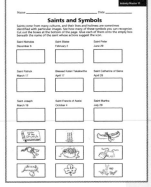

▲ **Activity Master 11**

3 Celebrate

Objective: To ask the saints to pray to God for us

 Let Us Pray

Tell students that they can always call on the saints to pray for them.

Litany of the Saints

Prepare

Review the pronunciation of the names with the reader.

Use the *Call to Faith 4* CD, track 11, to rehearse the suggested song.

Gather

Gather students in the prayer space.

Pray

- Follow the order of prayer on page 132.
- Optional readings are *1 Peter 3:8–9* and *Matthew 5:13–16*.
- Leader's concluding prayer: **God, we thank you for the example of the saints. Help us grow to be more like them in our love for you.**

Celebrate

Litany of the Saints

 Let Us Pray

Gather and begin with the Sign of the Cross.

Leader:	Respond with **Pray for us** after each saint's name.
Reader:	Holy Mary, Mother of God
All:	**Pray for us.**
Reader:	Saint Michael
	Saint John the Baptist
	Saint Joseph
	Saints Peter and Paul
	Saint Mary Magdalene
	Saint Stephen
	Saint Agnes
	Saint Gregory
	Saint Francis
	Saint Dominic
	Saint Catherine
	Saint Teresa
	Saints Perpetua and Felicity
	Saint Martin
Leader:	Let us pray.
	Bow your heads as the leader prays.
All:	**Amen.**

 Sing together.

We are God's people,
the flock of the Lord.

"Psalm 100" © 1969, 1981, 1997, ICEL.

132

 LITURGY LINK

Visual Focus If possible, include a statue of Mary in your prayer space. Encourage students to bring in flowers or draw pictures to show their devotion. Display the items around the statue as a reminder of Mary's special role in faith.

 LECTIONARY LINK

Break Open the Word Read last week's Sunday Gospel. Invite students to think about what the reading means to them as they try to follow Christ's example. For questions related to the weekly Gospel reading, visit our website at **www.osvcurriculum.com**.

GO online Visit www.osvcurriculum.com for weekly Scripture readings and seasonal resources.

Review and Apply

A **Check Understanding** Write responses on the lines below.

1. Name three ways that Catherine of Siena showed her holiness.
   Responses will vary.

2. Why was Blessed John XXIII called Good Pope John?
   Responses will vary.

3. What does it mean to be canonized?
   The Church officially recognizes that someone is a saint.

4. What is meant by Mary's Immaculate Conception?
   She was preserved from sin from the first moment of her life.

5. Why is Mary called the Mother of the Church?
   She is an example of love and faith for Christians.

B **Make Connections** Name two ways that you can grow in holiness.
Responses will vary.

Activity Live Your Faith

Saint Symbols Make a crest for a saint whom you admire. You may need to research more about him or her. On your crest, place a motto and symbols that show the qualities of the saint whom you will try to imitate.

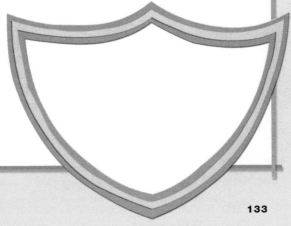

133

Review and Apply

Use the focus questions from the catechist Explore pages to review the lesson concepts.

A **Check Understanding** Have students complete the short-answer activity. Discuss their responses.

B **Make Connections** Ask each student to write his or her response to the statement.

Activity

- Suggest that each student make a crest for one of the saints named during the prayer celebration.
- Make available various books and stories about the saints that students can use for ideas.
- Display the crests.

CULTURAL AWARENESS

Crests Crests, or coats of arms, were symbols of nobility in medieval times. Today crests are associated with family names.

- High Church officials also have symbolic crests or coats of arms.
- The pope's coat of arms includes a tiara, or triple crown, and crossed keys.

Wrap-Up

Family Faith

Remind students to discuss the Family Faith page at home. Encourage students to read the passage from 1 Thessalonians.

Activity

- Read aloud the directions.
- Invite volunteers to bring in their scrapbooks to share with the group.

People of Faith

Tell students about Blessed Kateri Tekakwitha.

- Kateri's life held many challenges. Smallpox killed her parents and left her with severe scarring and reduced vision. She was persecuted by her tribe for becoming a Christian. The name *Tekakwitha* means "one who feels her way along."
- Remind students to add Kateri Tekakwitha to their People of Faith albums. Encourage them to pray the prayer at home with their families.

 Visit **www.osvcurriculum.com** for weekly scripture readings and seasonal resources.

UNIT 4: CHAPTER 11

Family Faith

◎ Catholics Believe

- The Church's holiness shines in the saints. All who live their love of God are saints.
- Mary is the perfect model of holiness, and she is called the Mother of the Church.

✝ SCRIPTURE

Read *1 Thessalonians 4:13–15* for assurance that the saints are with God.

GO online www.osvcurriculum.com
For weekly scripture readings and seasonal resources

Activity
Live Your Faith

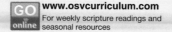

Scrapbook Research a patron saint for your family. You can find information about many saints in your parish library or on the Internet. Also share stories about models of holiness in your own family. Create a scrapbook with drawings and descriptions of all the models of faith you find.

Minister Honored

Models of Holiness

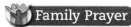

People of Faith

Kateri Tekakwitha is the first Native American to be nearing canonization. She was the daughter of a Mohawk warrior and an Algonquian woman who was Christian. Kateri was born in New York in 1656 and was baptized in 1676. She devoted herself to a life of prayer, penance, and the care of those who were sick or old. After her First Communion in 1677, Kateri's devotion to the Eucharist strengthened her faith. She was named Blessed in 1980. Her feast day is April 17.

▲ **Blessed Kateri Tekakwitha** 1656–1680

👐 Family Prayer

O God, help us grow in holiness as Kateri did. Help us imitate her love for you and her devotion to the Eucharist. Amen.

In Unit 4 your child is learning about the CHURCH.

134 **CCC** *See Catechism of the Catholic Church 828–829, 963, 967–970 for further reading on chapter content.*

❓ HOW DID I DO?

My session was

☐ *one of the best ever!* ☐ *pretty good.* ☐ *in need of improvement.*

In what discussions and activities were students most interested?

_____

What activity did I most enjoy teaching?

_____

In what area do I need to improve?

_____

Name _____ Date _____

Saints and Symbols

Saints come from many cultures, and their lives and holiness are sometimes identified with particular images. See how many of these symbols you can recognize. Cut out the boxes at the bottom of the page. Glue each of them onto the empty box beneath the name of the saint whose actions suggest the icon.

Saint Nicholas

December 6

Saint Blaise

February 2

Saint Peter

June 29

Saint Patrick

March 17

Blessed Kateri Tekakwitha

April 17

Saint Catherine of Siena

April 29

Saint Joseph

March 19

Saint Francis of Assisi

October 4

Saint Martha

July 29

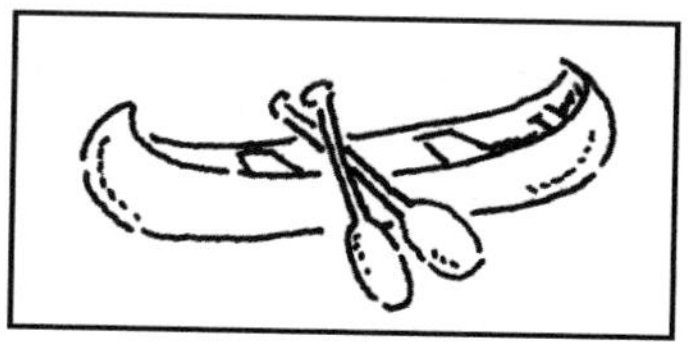

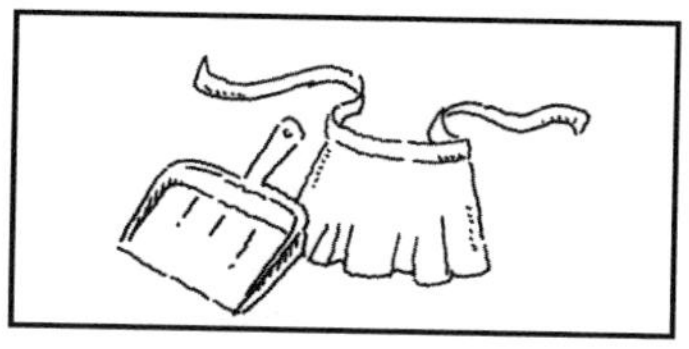

Answers can be found in the back of the Catechist Manual.

Overview

The Church Teaches

CATECHIST FORMATION

Faith Focus

- The Church's leaders interpret Scripture and Tradition, an authority given to them by Jesus. *(CCC 85)*
- The Church is directed by the Holy Spirit as it teaches and guides the People of God. *(CCC 87)*

Catechism Connection

The *Catechism* notes that laypeople have an important part to play in the life of the Church and its ministry. *(CCC 940–943)*

NDC Link

The *Directory* points out that one of the fundamental tasks of catechesis is preparing the faithful to participate in the life and mission of the Church. (See *NDC*, 20.5.)

Resources

📖 **BOOK**
*Catholic Bible Stories for Children.** Ball, Ann with Will, Julianne M. Our Sunday Visitor. Stories of witness, worship, and tradition build on faith formation.

💿 **DVD/VHS**
Peter, Keeper of the Keys (1 hour, 10 min.). Oblate Media. Follows Peter from Galilee to Rome to trace his impact on the early Church.

*Available at www.osvcurriculum.com

GO online **Catechist Resources**
www.osvcurriculum.com
For interactive lesson planner, chapter resources, and activities

✝ *[Jesus] went around all of Galilee, teaching in their synagogues, proclaiming the gospel of the kingdom, and curing every disease and illness among the people.*

Matthew 4:23

The Magisterium and Teaching Authority

Jesus was a teacher. His words, his actions, and his life revealed God. His gift of the Holy Spirit empowered his Apostles and disciples to continue teaching. From these first followers, the vital teaching mission comes to the magisterium of the Church today. The pope and the bishops are entrusted with interpreting the word of God, guarding it from error and misuse, and spreading it throughout the world.

All followers of Jesus make moral choices and take actions that can bear witness to the power of God. As a catechist, though, your responsibility is not only to teach but also to educate yourself. The more you learn about Scripture and Tradition, the better you can share the good news of salvation with the young people you teach.

Precepts of the Church

The precepts of the Catholic Church describe the minimum necessary for Catholics to consider themselves active members of the faith community. Rather than restricting your behavior, the precepts actually encourage you to do more. Following these precepts (loving, praying, worshiping, and living the liturgical year fully) will enrich your spiritual life and enable you to help build a stronger Church community.

Reflect *How can Jesus' teaching style shape your teaching style?*

Church Authority

In their daily lives, fourth graders understand that structure is necessary. They recognize that organizations and groups need procedures and rules to bind them together. Students in your group can apply this concept to the Church.

Your students have gained a historical perspective of the law of God in the Ten Commandments and the Great Commandment. Build on this foundation to teach about the magisterium, through which the Holy Spirit continues to guide the Church.

- Help students recognize the precepts of the Church as rules that hold the faithful together. The precepts make concrete and highlight the behaviors of active Catholics.

- Use games, repetition, or incentives to help students memorize the precepts of the Church.

- Have students work on structured group activities. Students will benefit from the experience of working cooperatively with others.

The Learning Process

- I am interested in the history of my faith. Tell me stories of my faith heritage.

- Role models help me be a better person. Point out people I can follow.

- I like belonging to a group. Teach me ways of being a good member of the Catholic community.

Holy Urgency

Sometimes advice to wait your turn, calm down, and be patient decreases the passion fueling your catechetical commitment. Sustaining your spirit seems to require a mixture of perspective, passion, humility, and self-importance.

Those who sustain their commitments know that their contribution may not compare to other great works but that it is their most important contribution. They will stop at nothing to do it well, and they will not lower their expectations. In maintaining this holy urgency about their work, they protect themselves from the kind of passivity that extinguishes the fire of the spirit to teach.

Reflect **How much passion do you have for your catechetical efforts? What fuels it? What weakens it?**

Catechist's Prayer

Loving God, I thank you for the opportunity to serve by handing on the faith to others and for the Church community that supports me in this task. Amen.

Weekly Planner

Objectives	Lesson Process	Materials
1 Invite — 10 minutes **Page 135** **Objective:** To name the qualities of a good teacher	🎁 **Let Us Pray:** Psalm 43:3 • Pray the psalm verse. • Discuss the qualities of a good teacher. • Complete the Let's Begin Activity.	☐ Board or chart paper
2 Explore — 40 minutes **Pages 136–137** **Objective:** To identify the Church's authority to teach	✝ **Scripture:** Mark 8:27–30 • Proclaim the scripture story. • Discuss the origins of the Church's authority. **Activity** Complete the Share Your Faith Activity.	☐ Pencils or pens ☐ Drawing materials
Pages 138–139 **Objective:** To learn how the Church teaches through its leaders	• Describe the responsibilities of Church members. • Identify the precepts of the Church. **Activity** Complete the Connect Your Faith Activity. **Words of Faith** magisterium , precepts of the Church	☐ Index cards
3 Celebrate — 10 minutes **Page 140** **Objective:** To pray for the grace to be faithful to the teachings of the Church	🎁 **Let Us Pray** • Create streamers. • Gather as a community. • Celebrate a Prayer to the Holy Spirit. 🎵 **Hymn:** "Send Us Your Spirit" **Activity** Complete the Saints Activity, page 228 and 229	☐ Bible ☐ Music CD ☐ Strips of fabric, ribbon, or crepe paper; wooden dowels; tape or glue

Wrap Up

Review and Apply

Page 141
• Review the chapter concepts.
• Complete the Live Your Faith Activity.

Family Faith

Page 142
• Introduce the page, and assign it as a family activity.
• Read about Saint Mary Magdalen Postel.

ACRE Connection, Domain 2—The Role of Church Leaders

Home Connection

GO online **www.osvcurriculum.com**
Family Faith activities, feasts and seasonal resources, saint features, and much more

CALL to FAITH e connect

• Online planning tools include chapter background and planner, activity master, customizable test, and more.

• Enhancement activities for each step of the catechetical process, including alternative prayer experiences and blessings.

• Games, activities, interactive review, alternative assessment, and more for childre

www.calltofaitheconnect.com

Chapter 12 The Church Teaches

Let Us Pray

Leader: God, help us follow in your faithful ways.
"Send your light and fidelity,
that they may be my guide."
Psalm 43:3

All: God, help us follow in your faithful ways.
Amen.

Activity — Let's Begin

A Good Teacher Is . . .

• someone who encourages you to think but allows you to learn from mistakes.

• someone who cares about who you are and what you learn.

• someone who isn't afraid to smile or cry.

• What other statements would you add about good teachers? **Possible responses: someone who listens, someone who is fair**

135

1 Invite

Objective: To name the qualities of a good teacher

Let Us Pray

Invite students to gather in the prayer space. Ask students to close their eyes as you proclaim the psalm verse. Then have students pray the psalm verse as a group.

Activity

• Share a story about one of your favorite teachers. Then encourage students to share stories about their favorite teachers.

• Organize students in three groups. Have a member from each group read aloud one of the bulleted points under "A Good Teacher Is ..."

• Discuss the question in the text. List students' responses on the board or on chart paper.

OPTIONAL ACTIVITY

Teacher Interviews Ask each student to interview a favorite teacher.

• Students can ask questions such as: "What qualities are most important for a teacher?"

• Have each student prepare a sheet to record responses.

Multiple Intelligence: Interpersonal

✠ SCRIPTURE BACKGROUND

Fidelity *Psalm 43:3* personifies light and fidelity as guides to lead the faithful to the Lord. The psalm expresses a longing to be in God's presence.

• Ask students to consider these images in prayer.

• Explain that the word *fidelity* means "faithfulness" or "truth." This knowledge may help students understand the psalm better.

Objective: To identify the Church's authority to teach

 **Focus**

How did Jesus choose Peter as the leader of the Apostles? List students' responses on the board or on chart paper.

Jesus Chooses a Teacher

Ask a volunteer to read aloud the paragraph as an introduction to the scripture story.

You Are the Messiah!

Proclaim the scripture story.

- Ask a volunteer to read aloud the next paragraph. Tell students that Jesus trusted Peter with the authority to teach and govern his Church.

- Ask the question in the text, and invite volunteers to share their responses.

Explore

Jesus Chooses a Teacher

 **Focus** How did Jesus choose Peter as the leader of the Apostles?

The Church is your most important teacher. The Church's authority, or power to teach, was given by Jesus and is guided by the Holy Spirit. Here is a Gospel story about the beginnings of the Church's authority to teach.

✠ SCRIPTURE   Mark 8:2

You Are the Messiah!

*N*ow Jesus and his disciples set out for the villages of Caesarea Philippi. Along the way he asked his disciples, "Who do people say that I am?" They said in reply, "John the Baptist, others Elijah, still others one of the prophets." And he asked them, "But who do you say that I am?" Peter said to him in reply, "You are the Messiah." Then [Jesus] warned them not to tell anyone about him.

Mark 8:27

Peter believed in Jesus and said so. Jesus gave Peter and the other Apostles a share in the authority he had from his Father. Then Jesus sent them out to preach, teach, forgive, and heal in his name.

❓ If Jesus asked you the same question he asked Peter, what would you say? Responses will vary.

Names of Jesus *Messiah* is only one of many titles or names for Jesus.

- See how many others students can remember: Christ, King of the Jews, Lamb of God, Savior, and Good Shepherd are examples.

- Sing hymns that use some of Jesus' different titles.

Multiple Intelligence: Musical

✠ SCRIPTURE BACKGROUND

Jesus Is the Messiah The scripture passage in today's lesson marks an important moment in Jesus' life.

- Jesus is ready to reveal himself to his disciples as the Messiah.

- However, the time is not yet right to share this truth with the general public.

- At this point in Jesus' life, most people regarded him as a prophet, but not as the promised savior.

Peter Denies Jesus

Peter made some mistakes along the way. Much later, the time of Jesus' crucifixion, Peter and the other disciples were very much afraid. In fact, the night before Jesus died, Peter denied three times that he had ever known Jesus. Afterward, he was ashamed of himself and cried bitterly.

Feed My Lambs

But Jesus never lost faith in Peter. After Jesus' death and Resurrection, Jesus was talking to Peter and the other disciples on the shore of a lake. Jesus asked three times whether Peter loved him. Of course, Peter said that he did. Jesus said to him, "Feed my lambs. Feed my sheep." See *John 21:15–17*.

In spite of Peter's earlier denials, Jesus made Peter the chief shepherd of all his flock. When he became the leader, Peter made good decisions for the members of the Church.

Why do you think Jesus asked Peter the same question three times?
Possible response: to let him know how important it was

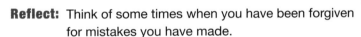

Activity — Share Your Faith

Reflect: Think of some times when you have been forgiven for mistakes you have made.

Share: During a short class prayer, mention the name of someone who has forgiven you.

Act: Using a separate sheet of paper, show a situation in which someone in authority gave you a second chance.

137

Peter Denies Jesus

Explain that although Peter understood that Jesus was the Messiah, he still had more to learn about Jesus.

- Read this paragraph aloud. Emphasize that even though he denied Jesus, Peter later repented and learned from his mistake.

Feed My Lambs

Ask two students to play the parts of Jesus and Peter in a skit for the class. Then ask them to explain what Jesus meant when he said, "Feed my lambs. Feed my sheep." Take care of the people.

- Have students respond to the question that follows the reading.

Activity

- Allow time for students to complete their pictures. If they have trouble thinking of ideas, have them work in pairs or small groups.
- Invite volunteers to share their work.

◎ Quick Review

Jesus chose Peter to be the teacher and leader of his Church and also gave the other Apostles a share in the authority to teach and lead.

★ REACHING ALL LEARNERS

Scripture Skits Students may need some help in transforming scripture stories into skits.

- Students should be able to identify the speakers and their parts.
- They may need your assistance in deciding which actions and lines of dialogue to include and which pieces of background information should be explained by a narrator.

 **Explore**

The Church and You

Objective: To learn how the Church teaches through its leaders

◎ **Focus**

What is your role as a member of the Church? List students' responses on the board or on chart paper.

The Church and You

Read this section aloud. Ask students the name of the current pope and that of your local bishop or archbishop. Be ready to supply the answers.

- Introduce the word *magisterium*. Have each student make a vocabulary card for it.

Your Role

Ask a volunteer to read this section aloud.

- Discuss the question in the text.
- Draw the graphic organizer on the board or on chart paper.
- Ask students to name the one who works through all the people listed in the organizer. Write *Holy Spirit* in the outermost circle with rays.

The Church and You

◎ **Focus** What is your role as a member of the Church?

After Jesus ascended into heaven, Peter and all the disciples were afraid. Then on Pentecost, the Holy Spirit came and gave them courage. They went out and began to preach the good news.

The Apostles, with Peter as their head, were the first leaders of the Church. Jesus founded the Church on the Apostles. He gave them the authority to teach and lead his followers. Today the chief teachers in the Church are the pope and the bishops, the successors of the Apostles. Their authority to teach, called the **magisterium**, goes back to the authority Christ first gave to the Apostles. The Holy Spirit works through the Church's teachers to keep the whole Church faithful to the teachings of Jesus.

Your Role

The Church's mission to share the true message of Jesus is not left to the pope and bishops alone. All members of the Body of Christ have a duty to learn Jesus' message as the Church interprets it and to share it with others. As you do this, you will grow in your love of God and neighbor.

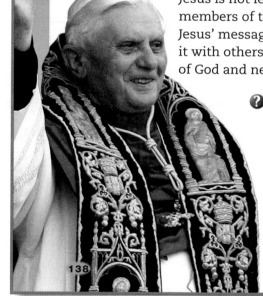

❓ **Who has taught you what the Church teaches?**
Possible responses: family, catechist, priest

138

OPTIONAL ACTIVITY

Write to the Bishop Have students write a group letter to your bishop or archbishop.

- Prepare by brainstorming questions to ask and topics to discuss. For example, students might suggest ways to improve their local church.
- Have students include information about themselves and a statement of support.

Multiple Intelligence: Interpersonal

💡 **QUICK TIP**

Graphic Organizer

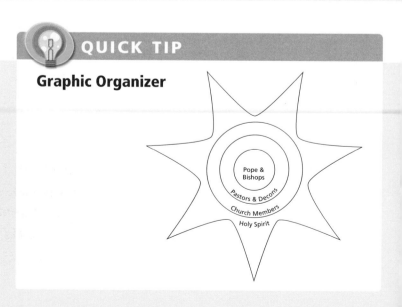

ules for Living

Some of the responsibilities of members of e Catholic Church are summed up in the **recepts of the Church**. The Church's leaders developed ese rules to show you the minimum you should do to e morally and faithfully. As a Catholic, you have a duty live according to the teachings and precepts of the urch.

recepts of the Church

Take part in the Mass on Sundays and holy days. Keep these days holy and avoid unnecessary work.

Celebrate the Sacrament of Reconciliation at least once a year if you have committed a serious sin.

Receive Holy Communion at least once a year during Easter time.

Observe days of fasting and abstinence.

Give your time, gifts, and money to support the Church.

Words of Faith

The **magisterium** is the Church's teaching authority to interpret the word of God found in Scripture and Tradition.

The **precepts of the Church** are some of the minimum requirements given by Church leaders for deepening your relationship with God and the Church.

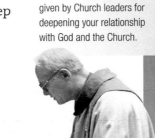

Activity Connect Your Faith

Word Search Find at least six words in this word search puzzle that relate to the teaching authority of the Church.

F	A	I	T	H	O	P	E	A	P
B	P	R	E	C	E	P	T	S	E
H	O	L	Y	S	P	I	R	I	T
A	P	O	S	T	L	E	S	C	E
D	E	B	I	S	H	O	P	S	R

Use three of these words in a sentence about your role in the Church.
Responses will vary.

_____

_____

139

Rules for Living

Tell students that those who lead and teach the Church have written rules to help people live as faithful followers of Jesus.

• Ask a volunteer to read the paragraph aloud.

• Read the definition of the *precepts of the Church,* and have students make vocabulary cards for this term.

Precepts of the Church

Have each of five volunteers read aloud one precept of the Church.

• Organize students in five groups, and assign one precept to each group.

• Have each group tell how fourth graders can obey the assigned precept.

Activity

• Have students complete the word search activity.

 Quick Review

The pope and the bishops have the authority to lead and teach the Church in spreading Jesus' message.

✝ JUSTICE AND PEACE

Authority Catholics depend on the teaching authority of the Church to describe the responsibilities of Christians.

• The Church's teachings are rooted in Scripture and in Jesus' life.

• Pope John Paul II said, the magisterium's duty is to "discern and promote philosophical thinking which is not at odds with faith."

Catholic Social Teaching: Solidarity

3 Celebrate

Objective: To pray for the grace to be faithful to the teachings of the Church

 **Let Us Pray**

Tell students that today they will ask the Holy Spirit for help in being faithful.

Prayer to the Holy Spirit

Prepare

Create streamers from strips of fabric, ribbon, or crepe paper. Attach them to wooden dowels with tape or glue.

• Assign students to Groups 1 and 2.

Use the *Call to Faith 4* CD, track 12, to rehearse the suggested song.

Gather

Form a procession to the prayer space. Have students carry their streamers.

Pray

• Follow the order of prayer on page 140.

• An optional scripture reading is *Acts 2:1–13.*

• Leader's concluding prayer: **Lord, may your Holy Spirit help us and those you have chosen to lead us.**

Celebrate

Prayer to the Holy Spirit

 **Let Us Pray**

Gather and begin with the Sign of the Cross.

 Sing together the refrain.

Come Lord Jesus,
send us your Spirit,
renew the face of the earth.
Come Lord Jesus,
send us your Spirit,
renew the face of the earth.

"Send Us Your Spirit" © 1981, 1982, 1987, GIA Publications, Inc.

Group 1: Come, Holy Spirit, fill the hearts of your faithful. And kindle in them the fire of your love.

All: *Sing refrain.*

Group 2: Send forth your Spirit and they shall be created. And you shall renew the face of the earth.

All: *Sing refrain.*

Lord, by the light of the Holy Spirit you have taught the hearts of your faithful. In the same Spirit, help us desire what is right and always rejoice in your consolation. We ask this through Christ our Lord. Amen.

Leader: Let us pray.
Bow your heads as the leader prays.

All: **Amen.**

The Pentecost by Juan de Juanes

140

 LITURGY LINK

The Holy Spirit Discuss with students common symbols and imagery for the Holy Spirit, such as water, fire, a cloud, and a dove.

• Tell students that the streamers in this celebration recall the image of the Holy Spirit as wind or as the breath of God.

• Remind students that prayer gestures such as waving streamers should be done respectfully.

 LECTIONARY LINK

Break Open the Word Read last week's Sunday Gospel. Invite students to think about what the reading means to them as they try to follow Christ's example. For questions related to the weekly Gospel reading, visit our website at **www.osvcurriculum.com**.

 Visit www.osvcurriculum.com for weekly Scripture readings and seasonal resources.

140 Chapter 12

A **Work with Words**   Complete each sentence with the correct term from the Word Bank.

WORD BANK

precepts
Holy Spirit
authority
live
   according to
Church
magisterium

1. Some of the rules that the Church gives to help you grow closer to Jesus are called the _____precepts_____ of the Church.

2. Jesus gave the Church the _____authority_____ to teach and lead the Body of Christ.

3. You have the duty to _____live according to_____ the rules and laws of the Church.

4. The _____magisterium_____ is the teaching authority of the Church.

5. The Church and the magisterium are guided by the _____Holy Spirit_____.

B **Check Understanding**   List two of the precepts of the Church. How do they help you become a better member of the Church?

Responses will vary.
_____
_____
_____

Activity Live Your Faith

More About Peter   Find in the Bible the story of Peter's denial of Jesus *(Mark 14:66–72)* and the story of Jesus and Peter as they talked on the shore *(John 21:1–19)*. Think of a creative way to retell one of these stories—a radio play, a song, or a skit. Perform your story for the class.

141

Review and Apply

Use the focus questions from the catechist Explore pages to review the lesson concepts.

A **Work with Words**   Have students fill in the answers for the review. Tell them to use each term only once.

B **Check Understanding**   Ask each student to write his or her response to the question.

Activity

• Have students work in small groups to complete this activity.

• Remind those groups performing radio plays or skits to assign roles. Point out that most plays require a narrator.

• Allow time for groups to rehearse their performances.

• Have each group present its story.

OPTIONAL ACTIVITY

Activity Master 12: Precepts Poem   Distribute copies of the activity found on catechist page 142A.

• The activity will reinforce the precepts of the Church.

• As an alternative, you may wish to send this activity home with students.

▲ Activity Master 12

Family Faith

Remind students to discuss the Family Faith page at home. Tell students to read the passage from Nehemiah.

Activity

- Read aloud the directions.
- Brainstorm with students some suggestions for their families to consider.

People of Faith

Tell students about Saint Mary Magdalen Postel.

- Mary Magdalen Postel believed that she was called to establish her own order. "I want to teach the young and inspire them with the love of God," she said, "and help the poor and relieve their misery."
- Remind students to add Saint Mary Magdalen Postel to their People of Faith albums. Encourage them to pray the prayer with their families.

 Visit **www.osvcurriculum.com** for weekly scripture readings and seasonal resources.

UNIT 4: CHAPTER 12

Family Faith

◎ Catholics Believe

- Jesus gave the leaders of the Church the authority to interpret Scripture and Tradition for the faithful.
- The Holy Spirit directs the Church in teaching and guiding the People of God.

✝ SCRIPTURE

Read *Nehemiah 8:1–12* to see how the ancient Israelites kept the Sabbath.

GO online www.osvcurriculum.com For weekly scripture readings and seasonal resources

Activity

Live Your Faith

Sunday Suggestions As a family, choose ways to observe the Church precept to keep Sunday holy. Create a list of *dos* and *don'ts*. For example:

- **Do** go to Mass.
- **Do** visit relatives.
- **Do** have a family picnic.
- **Don't** spend the day shopping at the mall.
- **Don't** make sports more important than God.

Encourage one another to practice these suggestions on the next Sunday. Discuss the experience.

▲ Saint Mary Magdalen Postel 1756–1846

People of Faith

Mary Magdalen Postel was educated in a Benedictine convent, where she dedicated herself to God. At eighteen she opened a school for girls in France just before the French Revolution broke out. During the revolution her school was closed, and Mary Magdalen became a leader who sheltered fugitive priests. After the revolution Mary Magdalen Postel continued to work in the field of religious education. Her teachings became well known. Saint Mary Magdalen's feast day is July 16.

In Unit 4 your child is learning about the CHURCH.

142 **CCC** *See Catechism of the Catholic Church 85–87 for further reading on chapter content.*

🙌 Family Prayer

Saint Mary Magdalen, pray for us that we may open our hearts and minds to learn more as we grow in faith and in our love for God. Amen.

❓ HOW DID I DO?

My session was

☐ *one of the best ever!* ☐ *pretty good.* ☐ *in need of improvement.*

In what discussions and activities were students most interested?

_____

What activity did I most enjoy teaching?

_____

In what area do I need to improve?

_____

Name _____ Date _____

Precepts Poem

Color and decorate this miniposter, and display it where you will see it often. The first letter of each line spells an important word for Catholics to remember.

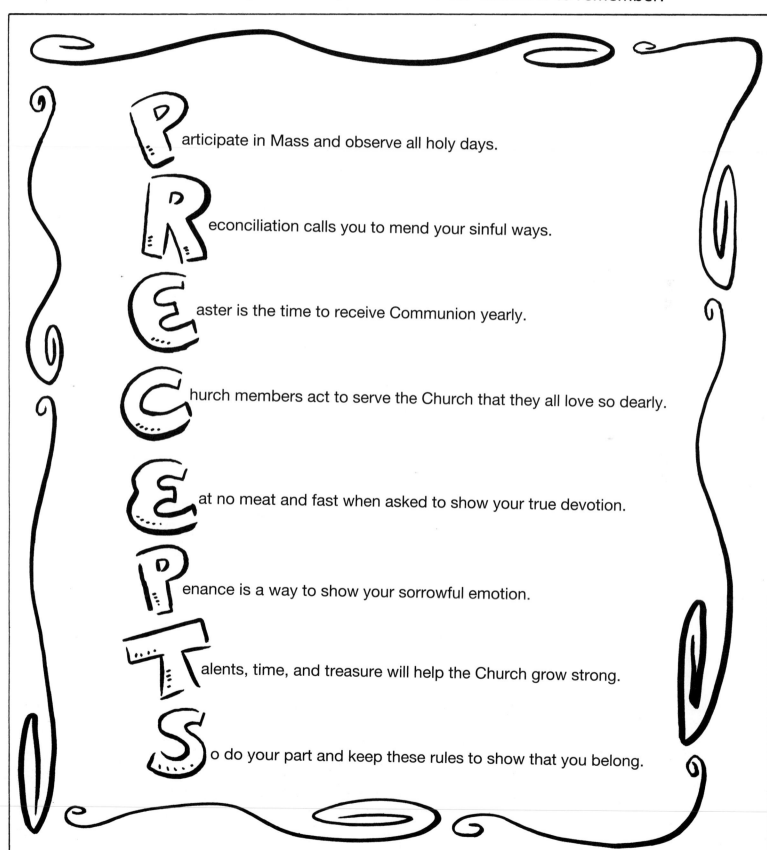

Participate in Mass and observe all holy days.

Reconciliation calls you to mend your sinful ways.

Easter is the time to receive Communion yearly.

Church members act to serve the Church that they all love so dearly.

Eat no meat and fast when asked to show your true devotion.

Penance is a way to show your sorrowful emotion.

Talents, time, and treasure will help the Church grow strong.

So do your part and keep these rules to show that you belong.

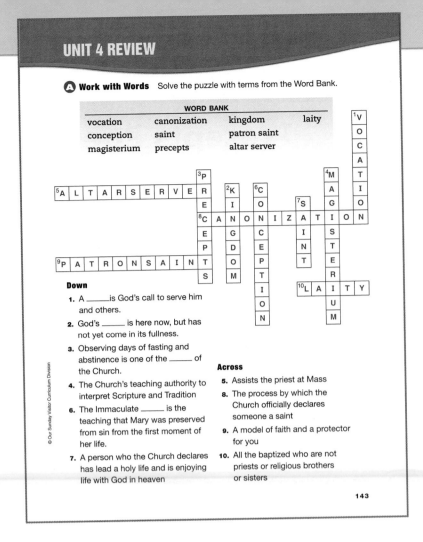

A Work with Words Solve the puzzle with terms from the Word Bank.

WORD BANK

vocation	canonization	kingdom	laity
conception	saint	patron saint	
magisterium	precepts	altar server	

Down

1. A _____ is God's call to serve him and others.
2. God's _____ is here now, but has not yet come in its fullness.
3. Observing days of fasting and abstinence is one of the _____ of the Church.
4. The Church's teaching authority to interpret Scripture and Tradition
6. The Immaculate _____ is the teaching that Mary was preserved from sin from the first moment of her life.
7. A person who the Church declares has lead a holy life and is enjoying life with God in heaven

Across

5. Assists the priest at Mass
8. The process by which the Church officially declares someone a saint
9. A model of faith and a protector for you
10. All the baptized who are not priests or religious brothers or sisters

© Our Sunday Visitor Curriculum Division

143

Unit Review

The Unit Review is designed to prepare students for the Unit Assessment. This page focuses on vocabulary words and the main concepts presented in the chapters.

Each review contains various sections that will appeal to the many different learning styles of your students. There are puzzles to engage students' attention, as well as true-false, multiple-choice, short-answer, and fill-in-the-blank exercises.

Direct students to complete the review, and check their responses. Determine areas in which students still need practice, and review those sections of the unit.

Notes

Name _____ Date _____

The Church Teaches

(A) Work with Words   Match each description in Column 1 with the correct word in Column 2.

Column 1

Column 2

_____ **1.** the teaching authority of the Church

a. magisterium

_____ **2.** assists the priest at Mass

b. deacon

_____ **3.** some of the duties of Catholics

c. laity

_____ **4.** person who called the Second Vatican Council

d. precepts of the Church

_____ **5.** an ordained minister who proclaims God's word and does works of charity

e. Pope John XXIII

_____ **6.** God's kingdom of peace, justice, and love

f. Immaculate Conception

_____ **7.** baptized Church members who have not received Holy Orders or consecrated their lives to God

g. reign of God

_____ **8.** belief that Mary was free from all sin from the first moment of her life

h. altar server

(B) Check Understanding   Circle the letter of the choice that best completes the sentence.

9. Saint Catherine of Siena is an example to all _____.

 a. that writing letters is useful
 b. of how hard life can be
 c. of how women were treated
 d. that every Church member can contribute

10. A way for me to carry out the precepts of the Church is by _____.

 a. attending religion class
 b. completing my homework
 c. participating in Sunday Mass
 d. taking care of my pet

11. The Second Vatican Council was a special type of Church _____.

 a. teaching
 b. leader
 c. meeting
 d. office

Answers can be found in the back of the Catechist Manual.

Name _____ Date _____

12. A person and his or her patron saint share a _____.

    a. name

    b. country

    c. virtue

    d. birthday

13. The perfect model of holiness is _____.

    a. Peter

    b. Mary, Mother of the Church

    c. Jeremiah

    d. the Bible

14. When God calls a person to do good, he is showing that person his or her _____.

    a. reign

    b. authority

    c. vocation

    d. precepts

15. The title *Blessed* in front of a name means that the person _____.

    a. is on the way to being a canonized saint

    b. was ordained to the deaconate or priesthood

    c. preached to and blessed many people

    d. prayed every day for special blessings

(C) Make Connections Use the five terms below to write a one-paragraph response to the question.

    parish   sisters   vocation   Church   peace

16–20. What choices will you face as an adult when you want to make choices about serving God?

_____

_____

_____

_____

_____

_____

_____

ASSESSMENT

Answers can be found in the back of the Catechist Manual.

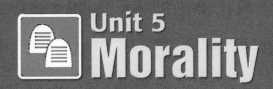

Unit 5
Morality

In this unit you will...

learn that all human life is sacred. God created humans to live in strong, loving families and communities. These communities are called to respect life and live in the truth. We learn basic ways of respecting human life by practicing the Fourth through Tenth Commandments.

Chapter 13

Chapter 14

Chapter 15

? **What do you think you will learn in this unit about faithful living?**

144

UNIT 5 OPENER

Preview Unit Theme

Tell students that Unit 5 is about Morality.

- Read aloud the text on page 144 of the student edition. Tell students they will learn more about these things in the next three chapters.

- Ask students what they think "sacred" means.

- Invite volunteers to share ways they can show respect for life.

Chapter 13

Overview

Family Love
CATECHIST FORMATION

✝ *Set me as a seal on your heart,*
as a seal on your arm;
For stern as death is love,
relentless as the nether world is devotion;
its flames are a blazing fire.

Song of Songs 8:6

The Marriage Covenant

The Catholic Church gives much importance to the covenant of marriage, basing its teachings on both Scripture and Tradition. The wedding feast appears in the Old Testament as a symbol of the union of God and his people. In the New Testament, the feast symbolizes the union of Christ and his Church. Matrimony is more than a human institution.

The love of a husband and wife echoes the love of God for humans. Marriage is a relationship of love and commitment for a lifetime. In marriage, human love and commitment are bonded with the eternal love and covenant of God.

Family Life

Marriage is the foundation of family and community life. Parents are coworkers with God in creating new life. The family is a blessing to both parents and children. Parents nurture and guide their children, passing on the faith. Children remind their parents of the calling to share God's love. Together, family members support one another in mutual love. Families are the basic unit of society and of the Christian community. Strength and stability in family life promote strength and stability among the People of God.

Reflect   How has your family help you grow in faith?

Family Love

Fourth graders' families are very important to them. Your students may want to talk about families in general and their families in particular. Most will think their own families' behavior, morality, and customs are the norm for everyone. The challenge is to help your students think of family not just personally, but in a universal or sacred sense.

- Teach the fourth, sixth, and ninth commandments as positive actions that keep families strong and united.

- Although students of this age do not have the maturity or resources to solve the many problems that families face today, they can understand that God wants to work in and through families.

- Help students see how their words and actions can powerfully affect their families. A kind word or a generous act by a family member of any age can strengthen the family.

Families

- My family is very important to me. Help me appreciate my family's strengths.

- I know that there are many types of families. I like reading stories about families and how they are special.

- I know that all families sometimes have problems. Be sensitive about asking me to share personal information.

Keeping Company

Sustaining your spirit requires a community of voices. Some voices cheer you on and unconditionally support you. Other voices ask you to reevaluate and extend your thinking.

We tend to let our relationships and networks develop naturally. If instead you intentionally keep company with colleagues, friends, and family who provide challenging and supportive voices, you gain the confidence to sustain your spirit.

Keeping company with prophets and cheerleaders, mystics and managers, sergeants and social workers allows you to create and maintain a kind of invisible community that is pulsating instead of passive.

Reflect **Does the company you keep comfort and challenge you? If so, list three voices and the roles they play in sustaining your spirit.**

Catechist's Prayer

Loving God, be with the families of the students I teach. Heal what needs to be healed. Strengthen what needs to be strengthened. Help me appreciate these students as your children. Amen.

Weekly Planner

Objectives	Lesson Process	Materials
1 Invite — 10 minutes	**Page 145** **Objective:** To express the power of family love	**Let Us Pray:** Psalm 128:1 • Pray the psalm. • Read about God's love for families. • Discuss family love.	☐ Board or chart paper
2 Explore — 40 minutes	**Pages 146–147** **Objective:** To understand the importance of family members' supporting one another	**Scripture:** Luke 2:41–52 • Read and discuss the fable about family unity. • Examine the Holy Family in Scripture. **Activity** Complete the Share Your Faith Activity.	☐ A small bundle of sticks ☐ Pencils or pens ☐ Paper
	Pages 148–149 **Objective:** To identify ways that families can keep the fourth, sixth, and ninth commandments	• Discuss how the commandments call families to act. • Discuss faithfulness and God's love for families. **Activity** Complete the Connect Your Faith Activity. **Words of Faith** obey, vows, modesty	☐ Index cards ☐ Copies of Activity Master 13 on page 152A
3 Celebrate — 10 minutes	**Page 150** **Objective:** To pray for families	**Let Us Pray** • Rehearse the music. • Gather as a community. • Celebrate a Prayer of Petition. **Hymn:** "All Grownups, All Children" **Activity** Complete the Gifts of the Holy Spirit Activity, page 236 and 237	☐ Music CD ☐ Bible

Wrap Up

Review and Apply

Page 151
• Review the chapter concepts.
• Complete the Live Your Faith Activity.

Family Faith

Page 152
• Introduce the page, and assign it as a family activity.
• Read about Saints Anne and Joachim.

ACRE Connection, Domain 3—Sacrament of Matrimony

Home Connection

GO online www.osvcurriculum.com
Family Faith activities, feasts and seasonal resources, saint features, and much more

• Online planning tools include chapter background and planner, activity master, customizable test, and more.

• Enhancement activities for each step of the catechetical process, including alternative prayer experiences and blessings.

• Games, activities, interactive review, alternative assessment, and more for children

www.calltofaitheconnect.com

Chapter 13 Family Love

Invite

🙌 Let Us Pray

Leader: God, may we always share your happiness with those we love.

"Happy are all who fear the LORD, who walk in the ways of God."

Psalm 128:1

All: God, may we always share your happiness with those we love. Amen.

Activity — Let's Begin

All Shapes and Sizes God loves each family, no matter what its shape or size. He wants each family member to be a sign of his love within the family.

• Who in your family has shown you God's love? **Responses will vary.**

145

1 Invite

Objective: To express the power of family love

🙌 Let Us Pray

Ask children to move to your classroom prayer space. In the space, have a crucifix and a Bible opened to the psalm. Tell students about the meaning of "fear the Lord," as discussed below. Play quiet music. Then read aloud the psalm verse, and have the class read aloud the response.

Activity

• Draw a large circle on the board or on chart paper. Above the circle, write *All Types of Families*. Inside the circle, list different family types (for example, two parents, single parent, foster parents, adopted children, extended family, stepchildren).

• Read aloud the text.

• Direct students' attention to the question, and give them time to respond. Invite volunteers to share their responses.

OPTIONAL ACTIVITY

Ways to Show Love Brainstorm with students a list of ways to show their love for their families.

• Record students' responses on the board or on chart paper.

• Encourage students to use one of the suggestions to show their love for their families.

Multiple Intelligence: Interpersonal

✴ CATECHIST BACKGROUND

Fear The phrase "fear the Lord" may confuse or have negative connotations for students.

• Point out that "fear" in this context does not mean being afraid of something or being scared that someone will cause harm. Instead, it refers to profound respect and awe.

• Tell students that this word should remind them of the reverence and respect that are owed to God and the respect owed to their parents and teachers.

Objective: To understand the importance of family members' supporting one another

 **Focus**

What makes families strong? List students' responses on the board or on chart paper.

Families in God's Plan

Ask students what is good about being part of a family and what is sometimes difficult.

- Record responses.
- Read aloud the introduction.

The Bundle of Sticks

Gather students into a circle. Bring a bundle of sticks to use as a prop.

- Read aloud the first part of the fable. Allow each student to try to break the bundle. Continue with the story, allowing each student to break a single stick.
- Discuss the questions that follow the story.

Explore

Families in God's Plan

 Focus What makes families strong?

God's plan for humans includes living in families. The following story shares an important lesson about living as a family.

A FABLE

The Bundle of Sticks

Some brothers and sisters were quarreling among themselves, so their father asked them to bring him a handful of sticks. He tied the sticks together in a bundle. Then the father placed the bundle in the hands of each child in turn and said, "Break it into pieces." None of the children could break the bundle.

Then the father separated the sticks and handed one to each child. The children broke the individual sticks easily. Their father told them, "If you are divided among yourselves, you will be broken as easily as these individual sticks. But if you unite to help one another, you will be strong, like the bundle of sticks. You will not be overcome by attempts to divide you."

Based on an Aesop fable

 What is the lesson of this fable? Name a time when your family has learned the same lesson.

Possible response: Families are stronger when everyone works together. Responses to the second part will vary.

146

⭐ **REACHING ALL LEARNERS**

Adaptations If you have a student with developmental or cognitive disabilities, ask what adaptations have been implemented in the school setting.

- Special chairs, large-print texts, and headphones are examples of adaptive equipment that might be used.
- Consider having an aide help.

Family Unity

God created humans to live in families. Like the
[fa]ther in the story, God wants families to be strong, to
[pr]otect one another, and to live in peace and love.

The fourth, sixth, and ninth commandments
[pr]ovide basic laws about family love and respect.
[T]he fourth commandment is this: Honor your father
[a]nd mother. Jesus is the perfect example for living
[ou]t this commandment.

✝ SCRIPTURE   Luke 2:41–52

Jesus and His Family

When Jesus was twelve, he went to Jerusalem
[w]ith his family to celebrate Passover. As Mary and
[Jo]seph were returning home, they realized that Jesus
[w]as not with them. They finally found him talking
[w]ith the teachers in the Temple. Mary told Jesus
[h]ow worried they had been, and Jesus returned to
[N]azareth with his parents.

Jesus was obedient as he grew in wisdom and
[a]ge. His actions were pleasing to God and to all
[w]ho knew him.

Based on Luke 2:41–52

Why is it important to obey your parents?

Responses will vary.

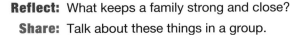

Activity — Share Your Faith

Reflect: What keeps a family strong and close?

Share: Talk about these things in a group.

Act: Imagine that your group is working on a new TV
series about families. Come up with a name for the
series and titles for three episodes.

147

Family Unity

Ask a volunteer to read aloud these
two paragraphs.

• Invite a volunteer to recite the
fourth commandment.

Jesus and His Family

Have a proficient reader proclaim the
scripture story.

• Tell students to listen carefully and
think of how Mary and Joseph felt
when Jesus was missing and when
they found him.

• Discuss the questions in the text.

Activity

• Direct students' attention to the
activity. Ask when they have seen
strong families on TV and what
makes those families strong.

• Students can work on the activity in
groups of three or four. Invite them
to share the name of their series
and their episode titles.

◎ Quick Review

**God meant humans to live as
families. Love holds families together.**

✝ SCRIPTURE BACKGROUND

The Holy Family This passage points out that Jesus'
family was faithful to the religious practices of the
time—in this case, traveling to the Temple for Passover.

• The students may be concerned that Mary and
Joseph could lose Jesus. Families in biblical times
traveled in caravans, the men in one group and
the women in another. Children traveled in either
group. Both Mary and Joseph probably thought
that Jesus was with the other's group.

Objective: To identify ways that families can keep the fourth, sixth, and ninth commandments

 **Focus**

What do the commandments teach about family love? **List students' responses on the board or on chart paper.**

Commandments for Families

Read aloud the first paragraph.

- Say that these instructions tell what children are to do for their parents.

- Have students read to learn what responsibilities parents have.

Faithful Love

Have students read silently.

- Tell students that *covet* means to want something that belongs to someone else.

- Have students make vocabulary cards for *obey* and *vows*.

Commandments for Families

Focus What do the commandments teach about family love?

Faith Fact

About 260,000 Catholic marriages are celebrated each year in the United States.

The fourth commandment teaches you to honor your parents and guardians. You honor them when you

- listen to and **obey** them in all that is good.
- show gratitude for all that they do for you.
- respect and care for them as they grow older.
- respect people in authority.

Parents and guardians provide for your needs, serve as good role models, and share their faith with you. They help you grow in faith, make good choices, and decide your vocation.

Faithful Love

The sixth commandment is this: You shall not commit adultery. The ninth is this: You shall not covet your neighbor's wife. These commandments are about the faithful love and commitment between married couples.

When a man and woman marry, they make solemn promises called **vows**. They promise to love and honor each other always and to welcome the gift of children.

Part of being faithful is respecting the vows of other married couples and not acting in ways that could weaken their marriage. Adultery means being unfaithful to these vows. The grace of the Sacrament of Matrimony strengthens the couple to be faithful and true.

❓ **What does it mean to be a good role model? Who has been a good role model for you?**
Responses will vary.

148

Activity Master 13: Blessing Prayer Distribute copies of the activity found on catechist page 152A.

- As a class, brainstorm some marital symbols that students may want to include.

- As an alternative, you may wish to send this activity home.

Activity Master 13

▲ **Activity Master 13**

CATECHIST BACKGROUND

Adultery Parents will probably prefer that you do not discuss the sexual meaning of adultery with students of this age.

- Explain adultery as breaking a vow or as acting in ways that weaken a marriage.

- Students will understand comparisons between marriages and friendship. They will almost certainly have witnessed (or experienced) someone's attempt to break up a friendship.

aithfulness and You

The sixth and ninth commandments apply to
everyone. You can live out these commandments by
keeping promises to family, friends, and God. You can
practice **modesty** by dressing, talking, and acting in
ways that honor your own dignity and that of others.
You can respect that the differences between males and
females are gifts from God.

amily Disappointments

Sometimes it is hard for families to live as God
intends. Arguments, hurts, and disappointments can
keep families from being signs of God's love. Parents and
children sometimes hurt one another. Some families are
hurt through separation, divorce, or even death.

But God continues to love all families and to help
them grow stronger. Every time families are signs
of love, they reflect the love that exists within the
Holy Trinity.

What can families do to be signs of God's love?
Possible responses: sharing, forgiving

Words of Faith

To **obey** is to do things or
act in certain ways that are
requested by those in
authority.

Vows are solemn
promises that are made to
or before God.

Modesty is the virtue that
helps people dress, talk,
and act in appropriate
ways.

Activity · Connect Your Faith

Build with Solid Blocks The family is the building block of
the Christian community and of society. In the
blocks, write at least six qualities of good
friendships and family love. Tell how your family
shows one of these qualities to others.

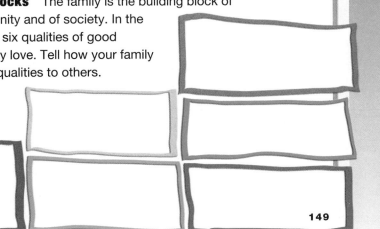

149

Faithfulness and You

Have students read this paragraph
silently.

- Ask students how they have been
  faithful in their friendships.
- Then ask why faithfulness is so
  important in relationships.
  Responses will vary.

Family Disappointments

Read aloud or summarize this section
for students.

- Spend time on the question.
- Be sensitive to family privacy issues.

Activity

- Ask students to complete the
  activity.
- Invite volunteers to draw their
  building blocks on the board or on
  chart paper.

Quick Review

The fourth, sixth, and ninth
commandments help families grow in
love. God loves all families, even
when they have problems.

Objective: To pray for families

 **Let Us Pray**

Tell students that today they will pray for families everywhere.

Prayer of Petition

Prepare

Choose readers for the prayer.

• Ask students to draw their families or write names of family members.

Use the *Call to Faith 4* CD, track 13, to rehearse the suggested song.

Gather

Gather students in the prayer space with their pictures or lists. Ask them to think about their families as they pray.

Pray

• Follow the order of prayer on page 150.

• Alternative readings are *Sirach 3:2–6, 12–14,* or *Colossians 3:12–21.*

• Leader's concluding prayer: **God— Father, Son, and Holy Spirit— through the love that exists among you, we ask that you strengthen and bless family life.**

Celebrate

Prayer of Petition

 **Let Us Pray**

Gather and begin with the Sign of the Cross.

Leader: God, from you every family learns to love. We ask you to strengthen our families.

All: **Hear us, O Lord.**

Reader 1: May parents and those who care for us be blessed in their commitment to love their children and each other.

All: **Hear us, O Lord.**

Reader 2: May all children find support and security in their families.

All: **Hear us, O Lord.**

Reader 3: May all families discover your gift of faithful love.

All: **Hear us, O Lord.**

Leader: Let us pray.

Bow your heads as the leader prays.

All: **Amen.**

 Sing together.

All grownups, all children,
all mothers, all fathers
are sisters and brothers
in the fam'ly of God.

"All Grownups, All Children"
© 2000, GIA Publications, Inc.

150

 LITURGY LINK

Prayer Leaders Preparing leaders for prayer is important in setting the tone for a prayer celebration.

• Make sure that each student can read and pronounce the words correctly.

• Review when to sit, stand, or use proper gestures.

• Students' participation now may inspire them to serve in liturgical ministries in the future.

 LECTIONARY LINK

Break Open the Word Read last week's Sunday Gospel. Invite students to think about what the reading means to them as they try to follow Christ's example. For questions related to the weekly Gospel reading, visit our website at **www.osvcurriculum.com**.

 GO online Visit www.osvcurriculum.com for weekly Scripture readings and seasonal resources.

Review and Apply

A Work with Words Complete each sentence with the correct term from the Word Bank.

God made humans to live as

_____families_____ who love and respect one another. By following the

_____fourth_____ commandment, children _____honor_____ and obey their parents and guardians. The

_____sixth_____ and ninth commandments are about being _____faithful_____ in marriage, keeping promises, and practicing

_____modesty_____.

WORD BANK

faithful
modesty
fourth
families
sixth
honor

B Make Connections Write three ways you will follow the fourth commandment this week.

Responses will vary.

_____

_____

_____

Activity — Live Your Faith

Be Positive Write three bumper sticker slogans that can help families live the fourth, sixth, and ninth commandments. Think of positive phrases to help people remember what to do.

151

Review and Apply

Use the focus questions from the Explore pages to review the lesson concepts.

A Work with Words Have students use terms from the Word Bank to complete each sentence. Ask a student to read aloud the completed paragraph.

B Make Connections Ask each student to write his or her response to the statement. Remind students to put their responses into action in the coming week.

Activity

• Read aloud the directions, and give students time to complete the activity.

• Ask volunteers to share one slogan each.

JUSTICE AND PEACE

Strong Families The Church calls on society to strengthen families.

• Remind students of the power of forgiveness, hugs, kind words, and loving actions.

• Encourage students to use these techniques every day.

Catholic Social Teaching: Call to Community

Family Faith

Remind students to discuss the Family Faith page at home. Encourage students to read the passage from Galatians.

Activity

- Read aloud the directions for the activity.
- Brainstorm with students possible coupons, such as "I will do my chores today without complaining."

People of Faith

Tell students about Saints Anne and Joachim [jō′ə•kim].

- Saints Anne and Joachim are usually portrayed as being childless until old age. According to legend, both fasted and prayed until an angel appeared, saying that Anne would conceive.
- Remind students to add Saints Anne and Joachim to their People of Faith albums. Encourage them to pray the prayer at home with their families.

 Visit **www.osvcurriculum.com** for weekly scripture readings and seasonal resources.

UNIT 5: CHAPTER 13
Family Faith

Catholics Believe

- God created humans to live in strong, loving families.
- The fourth, sixth, and ninth commandments provide basic laws of family love and respect.

✝ SCRIPTURE

Read *Galatians 6:9–10* to find out about love in the family of faith.

GO online www.osvcurriculum.com
For weekly scripture readings and seasonal resources

Activity
Live Your Faith

Make Coupons Discuss with your family something you shared with your class this week. Then talk about the importance of showing love to one another. Make coupons that can be given to family members at appropriate times.

Example:

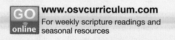

> ~ COUPON ~
> Good for one hug.

People of Faith

Little is known about the parents of Mary. Legend says that **Anne** and **Joachim** had wanted a child for a long time. When Mary was born, they took her to the Temple and dedicated her to God. Anne and Joachim raised Mary to respect others, to be faithful to God, and to follow God's ways in all things. Saint Anne is the patron of women who are childless and women who are pregnant. Saint Anne is often pictured teaching Mary to read. The feast day of Saints Anne and Joachim is July 26.

▲ **Saints Anne and Joachim**
first century B.C.

🎁 Family Prayer

Saints Anne and Joachim, pray for our families, that we may become signs of God's loving and forgiving presence to one another and to the world. Amen.

In Unit 5 your child is learning about MORALITY.

152 **CCC** See Catechism of the Catholic Church 2197–2200, 2204–2206, 2380–2381, 2521–2524 for further reading on chapter content.

❓ HOW DID I DO?

My session was

☐ *one of the best ever!* ☐ *pretty good.* ☐ *in need of improvement.*

In what discussions and activities were students most interested?

_____

What activity did I most enjoy teaching?

_____

In what area do I need to improve?

_____

Name _____ Date _____

Blessing Prayer

This prayer is the closing blessing of the marriage rite. Decorate the prayer with a colorful border. Cut it out, roll it into a scroll, and tie it with a brightly colored ribbon. Present it to a married couple whom you know.

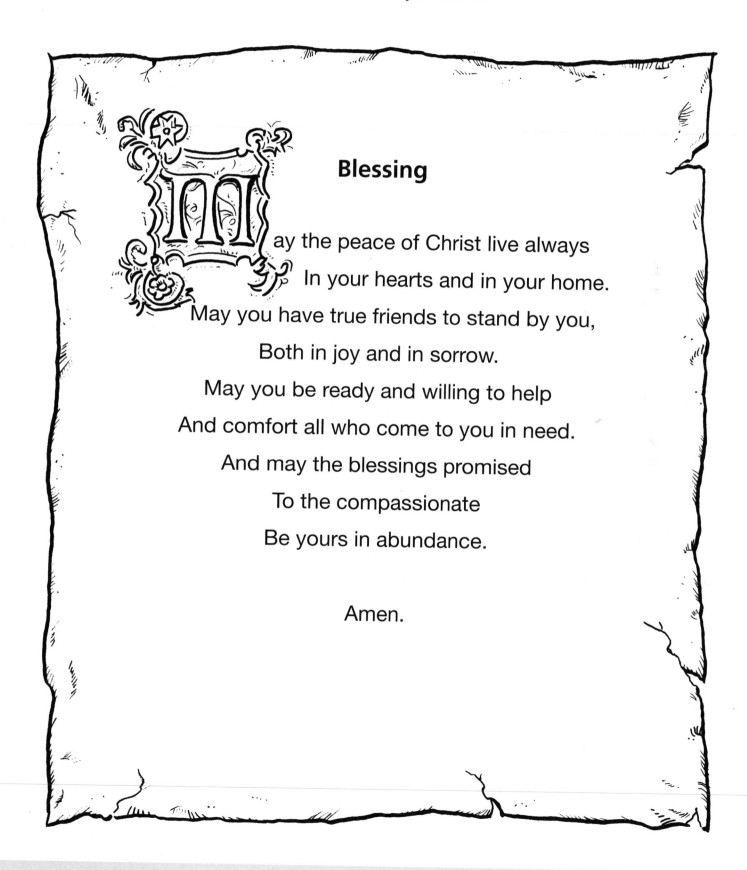

Blessing

ay the peace of Christ live always

In your hearts and in your home.

May you have true friends to stand by you,

Both in joy and in sorrow.

May you be ready and willing to help

And comfort all who come to you in need.

And may the blessings promised

To the compassionate

Be yours in abundance.

Amen.

Overview

Faith Focus

- All human life is sacred because it comes from God. *(CCC 2258)*
- The fifth commandment forbids any action that takes a human life. *(CCC 2268)*

Catechism Connection

The *Catechism* explains that war and hatred are also against the fifth commandment. *(CCC 2303–2304)*

NDC Link

Catechesis on the Seventh and Tenth Commandments leads students to focus on social and economic justice issues and helps prepare them to work for the rights of others. (See *NDC*, 45G.)

Resources

BOOKS

Saint Maximilian Kolbe: Mary's Knight. Jablonski, Patricia E. Pauline Books. Captures the life of the saint who died at Auschwitz.

How Do We Protect the Living? Heubsch, Bill. [Growing Faith Project series] Twenty-Third Publications. Centers on Church teaching about the Fifth Commandment.

 Catechist Resources For interactive lesson planner, chapter resources, and activities www.osvcurriculum.com

✝ *"You have heard that it was said to your ancestors, 'You shall not kill; and whoever kills will be liable to judgment.' But I say to you, whoever is angry with his brother will be liable to judgment."*

Matthew 5:21–22

Respect for Life

You have a choice to make regarding life. You can cooperate with God in creating, sustaining, and protecting life, or you can choose to kill. Your mandate to protect life stems from the fact that all life is a gift from God. Humans are the stewards, not the owners, of life.

Respect for human life is a broad category that includes society's approach to those who are elderly, ill, poor, or otherwise marginalized. Abortion, homicide, suicide, war, and other life-and-death concerns are grave matters that must be seen in the light of faith and the commandments.

Acting on the Challenge

The Church has many profound teachings that challenge the faithful on issues related to life. Catholics are called to examine their consciences and take actions that promote respect for human life and dignity. The use of force is to be the last resort in any situation. Violence against those who are innocent and defenseless (as in abortion) is never acceptable.

Reflect   How do I show respect for life?

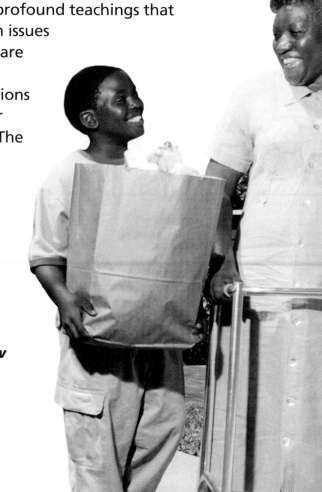

Respect for Life

Learning what respect for life means will give your students much to consider. Some issues, such as suicide or abortion, may not have touched their lives yet. However, the present is a teachable moment. Children will appreciate having guidance on difficult moral issues.

- Help your students understand that anger, hatred, and fighting are ways that people fail to show respect for life.

- Explain to students that showing respect for their own lives means taking good care of their bodies and nourishing both mind and spirit with the word of God.

FOURTH GRADERS SAY

Attitudes

- I don't always want to compete. Use cooperative games and projects with my group.

- I am becoming aware of the world around me. Tell me about current events affecting respect for life.

- I need role models. Tell me about people who show respect for life and who love justice.

SUSTAINING YOUR SPIRIT

Keeping Sabbath

Keeping Sabbath means taking time to worship and rest. Our fast-paced secular world puts pressure on us and makes it easy to feel overwhelmed. Sometimes we lose sight of the values and virtues we hold most sacred.

Sustaining your spirit requires more than keeping the right company, living with complexity, and turning pain into thoughtfulness. It requires rest and worship that allows us to remember who we are and whose we are. Keeping Sabbath through worship and rest allows us to reflect on and renew our relationship with God, our moral life, and the spiritual resources available to us as children of God in a community of faith.

Reflect **How can you improve the way you worship and rest?**

Catechist's Prayer

O Creator, with the tenderness of a mother you loved me into being. With the strong arms of a loving father, you protect me. Thank you for the gift of my life. Amen.

Weekly Planner

	Objectives	Lesson Process	Materials
1 Invite	**10 minutes** **Page 153** **Objective:** To understand the sacredness of life	**Let Us Pray:** Psalm 36:10 • Pray the psalm. • Read the poem and answer the question. • Discuss the sacredness of life.	☐ Music CD
2 Explore	**40 minutes** **Pages 154–155** **Objective:** To understand the fifth commandment	**Scripture:** Deuteronomy 30:19–20 • Explore the life and work of Alfred Nobel. • Discuss respect for life. **Activity** Complete the Share Your Faith Activity.	☐ Board or chart paper ☐ Pencils or pens ☐ Art supplies
	Pages 156–157 **Objective:** To learn ways of keeping the fifth commandment	**Scripture:** Matthew 5:43–45 • Discuss how to keep the fifth commandment. • Discuss ways to care for your body. **Activity** Complete the Connect Your Faith Activity. **Words of Faith** murder	☐ Copies of Activity Master 14 on page 160A
3 Celebrate	**10 minutes** **Page 158** **Objective:** To pray for help to choose God's way	**Let Us Pray:** 1 Peter 3:9–12 • Rehearse the music. • Gather as a community. • Pray a Celebration of the Word. **Hymn:** "Jesu, Jesu" **Activity** Complete the Paschal Candle Activity, page 232 and 233	☐ Hymnals ☐ Music CD ☐ Bible

Wrap Up

Review and Apply

Page 159
• Review the chapter concepts.
• Complete the Live Your Faith Activity.

Family Faith

Page 160
• Introduce the page, and assign it as a family activity.
• Read about Saint Maximilian Kolbe.

Home Connection

ACRE Connection, Domain 5—Life and Dignity of the Human Person

GO online **www.osvcurriculum.com**
Family Faith activities, feasts and seasonal resources, saint features, and much more

• Online planning tools include chapter background and planner, activity master, customizable test, and more.

• Enhancement activities for each step of the catechetical process, including alternative prayer experiences and blessings.

• Games, activities, interactive review, alternative assessment, and more for children

www.calltofaitheconnect.com

Chapter 14 Choosing Life

 Let Us Pray

Leader: God, we thank you for your precious gifts of life and light.

"For with you is the fountain of life,
and in your light we see light."

Psalm 36:10

All: God, we thank you for your precious gifts of life and light. Amen.

 **Activity** **Let's Begin**

If I Can Stop One Heart from Breaking

If I can stop one heart from breaking,
I shall not live in vain;
If I can ease one life the aching,
Or cool one pain,
Or help one fainting robin
Unto his nest again,
I shall not live in vain.

Emily Dickinson

• What are your thoughts about making your life worthwhile?
Responses will vary.

153

 **1 Invite**

Objective: To understand the sacredness of life

 Let Us Pray

Play soft music as students gather in the prayer space. Softly and reverently pray the psalm several times as students draw. Explain that students will draw images that the psalm brings to mind. Have volunteers explain their drawings.

Activity

• Have a volunteer read aloud the poem. Ask students what they think is meant by *I shall not live in vain*. Possible response: I will have done something important.

• Discuss the question in the text. Explain that *worthwhile* means "worth living" or "meaningful."

• Tell the students that each of them shares in God's precious gift of life.

REACHING ALL LEARNERS

Poetry Many learning styles can be addressed by poetry.

• Students strong in verbal learning will enjoy the way words combine to convey meaning.

• Those who learn visually will appreciate concrete images, such as the fainting robin.

• Interpersonal learners may respond to the powerful emotions that poetry can evoke.

• Auditory learners will enjoy the rhythm of the words.

CATECHIST BACKGROUND

Poet Emily Dickinson is one of the most famous American poets. Born in Amherst, Massachusetts, in 1830, she wrote more than 1,800 poems.

• Many of her poems focus on issues that affect all people, such as life, love, death, and belief.

• Suggest to students that they memorize an appropriate poem of Dickinson's.

Objective: To understand the fifth commandment

 **Focus**

How do you respect life? List students' responses on the board or on chart paper.

Respect Life

Read aloud or summarize this introduction.

A Change of Heart

Tell students that they will read about a man who decided to devote his life to peace and good works.

• Ask students why a rich, successful man would want to change his life.

• Have volunteers take turns reading the biography.

• Ask students what the term *merchant of death* means. Nobel made money from his invention of dynamite, which was used to kill.

• Explain that death notices in newspapers summarize a person's life. Discuss the question that follows the biography.

Respect Life

 Focus How do you respect life?

Living a worthwhile life means respecting and caring for others' lives. Here is a true story about a man who made a choice to respect life.

BIOGRAPHY

A CHANGE OF HEART

About eighty years ago Alfred Nobel picked up the morning paper and, to his horror, read his own death notice! The newspaper had reported his death by mistake. Nobel read the bold heading, "Dynamite King Dies." In the article he was described as a merchant of death.

Nobel was saddened. Although he had made a fortune by inventing dynamite, he did not want to be remembered as a "merchant of death." From then on, he devoted his energy and money to works of peace and the good of humankind.

Today, Alfred Nobel is remembered as the founder of the Nobel Prizes, especially the Peace Prize. These prizes reward and encourage people who work for the good of others.

❓ **If your death notice were written accidentally today, what could it say about your respect for the lives of others?**
Responses will vary.

Nobel Peace Prize winners

154

 CATECHIST BACKGROUND

Alfred Nobel The story of Alfred Nobel tells of an exceptional person who recognized his potential for doing good rather than harm.

• By promoting and rewarding efforts for peace, he improved the lives of countless people.

• Nobel's story exemplifies respect for the dignity of human life.

OPTIONAL ACTIVITY

Nobel Peace Prize Winners Suggest that students learn more about the lives of people who have won the Nobel Peace Prize.

• Mother Teresa was honored for her work in India.

• Nelson Mandela worked for equality for all people in South Africa.

• Albert Schweitzer was a medical missionary in Africa.

Multiple Intelligence: Verbal/Linguistic

The Fifth Commandment

Alfred Nobel changed the direction of his life and began supporting work that gave life to others. He was a clear example of respect for the fifth commandment: you shall not kill.

All human life is sacred, and all actions that support and protect life support the fifth commandment. At the end of his life Moses told the people to remember that God's law was life for them.

SCRIPTURE

I call heaven and earth today to witness against you: I have set before you life and death, the blessing and the curse. Choose life, then, that you and your descendants may live, by loving the LORD, your God, heeding his voice, and holding fast to him. For that will mean life for you. . . .

Deuteronomy 30:19–20

Path to Life

God's laws show the path to life and happiness. The fifth commandment reminds you of the fundamental respect for life that is owed to every person. Because every life comes from God, every human life is sacred from the moment of conception until the time of death.

Activity

Share Your Faith

Reflect: Think about someone you know who deserves a prize for the way that he or she respects life.

Share: Share with a partner what this person does to respect life.

Act: Design a medal to honor the person you chose. Write his or her name on the line.

_____

155

Introduce this part of the lesson by reading aloud these two paragraphs.

- Ask a volunteer to stand and proclaim the Scripture.
- Ask students what life-and-death decisions people must make daily. Possible responses: to cross streets safely, to follow safety rules at home

A Path to Life

Ask students to read the text silently to learn more about why life is sacred.

Activity

- Read the directions aloud.
- Remind students that their medals can include both words and symbols.
- Invite volunteers to share their medals with the class and explain why they chose a particular person.

◉ Quick Review

The fifth commandment says to respect and protect all human life. Human life is sacred because it comes from God.

OPTIONAL ACTIVITY

Collage Distribute old magazines.

- Tell students to look for pictures that show respect for life, such as building homes, eating healthful foods, and caring for those who are sick.
- Have students make a collage on poster board.

Multiple Intelligence: Visual/Spatial

Explore

Keeping the Fifth Commandment

 Focus How do you keep the fifth commandment?

 **Objective:** To learn ways of keeping the fifth commandment

Focus

How do you keep the fifth commandment? List students' responses on the board or on chart paper.

Keeping the Fifth Commandment

Have students read these paragraphs.

- Discuss the meaning of the word *murder*.

Respect for the Body

Read aloud this paragraph.

- Draw the graphic organizer on the board or on chart paper. Explain that the words branching from the center are actions that harm life. Ask volunteers to name other actions that harm life.
- Ask the discussion question.

All human life is sacred, including the life of the unborn and the elderly. The life of an unborn child is most fragile, and it is deserving of the greatest respect and care. Thus, the intentional ending of the life of an unborn child is a grave sin.

The taking of one's own life is suicide. It is seriously contrary to God's gift of life and love. However, one's responsibility may be lessened by certain factors. **Murder**, the intentional killing of an innocent person, is seriously sinful because it contradicts Jesus' law of love. To kill in self-defense, however, is justified, if it is the only way to protect one's own life.

The Catholic Church teaches that the death penalty, or capital punishment, is almost always wrong. Alternatives such as life in prison without parole, are preferred.

Respect for the Body

The Church teaches that your body and soul are united. You are a temple in which God's Spirit dwells. The fifth commandment teaches you to respect your body and those of others. Eating healthful foods and getting enough exercise are important to protect your life and health. At your age, using alcohol is an offense against the fifth commandment. The use of tobacco and illegal drugs is harmful to the body. Tempting or encouraging others to disrespect the gift of life is wrong, too.

❓ **What can you do to help others respect life?**
Responses will vary.

156

OPTIONAL ACTIVITY

Activity Master 14: Respect Your Body Distribute copies of the activity found on catechist page 160A.

- Tell students that this activity will remind them not to harm their bodies.
- As an alternative, you may wish to send this activity home with students.

▲ **Activity Master 14**

QUICK TIP

Graphic Organizer

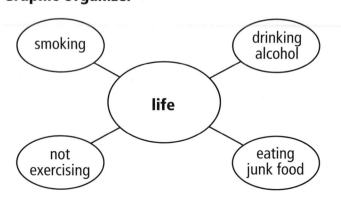

Jesus' Message

Jesus said that even anger can be sinful if it is not controlled; anger can harden into hatred. Hatred can lead to revenge, or getting back at someone for something that has happened, or to violence.

It can be difficult to show love and respect for those who bully or treat you unfairly. Jesus calls you to love this way.

Words of Faith

Murder is the intentional killing of an innocent person.

✝ SCRIPTURE   Matthew 5:43–45

Love of Enemies

You have heard that it was said, "You shall love your neighbor and hate your enemy." But I say to you, love your enemies, and pray for those who persecute you, that you may be children of your heavenly Father, for he makes his sun rise on the bad and the good, and causes rain to fall on the just and unjust.

Matthew 5:43–45

What did Jesus mean when he said that God makes his sun rise on the bad and the good?

Possible response: God treats everyone equally.

Activity — Connect Your Faith

Choose Life   Circle one life-giving action that you will practice today.

- Protect unborn children.
- Let go of anger.
- Forgive your enemies.
- Set a good example for others.
- Show respect for your body by eating healthful foods.

157

Jesus' Message

Tell students to read these two paragraphs to learn how the fifth commandment relates to anger, hatred, and revenge.

Love of Enemies

Have a strong reader proclaim the Scripture.

- Discuss the question in the text.
- Invite students to share times when they have been able to avoid hatred or revenge, even when they were provoked.
- Remind students that forgiveness is a way to show love to others, even to enemies.

Activity

- Allow time for students to complete the activity.
- Encourage them to state practical ways to perform these actions.

◎ Quick Review

The fifth commandment forbids harm to life because all human life is sacred. This means that humans must treat their bodies with respect.

✝ SCRIPTURE BACKGROUND

Sermon on the Mount   This passage from the Gospel according to Matthew is taken from the Sermon on the Mount, in which Jesus preaches to his disciples how to live an ethical life.

- Jesus taught that laws such as "love your enemies" cannot be achieved by humans alone but through the grace of God.
- Almost every section of this sermon is repeated elsewhere in the New Testament.

 Let Us Pray

Objective: To pray for help to choose God's way

 Let Us Pray

Tell students that they will ask for help in obeying the fifth commandment.

Celebration of the Word

Prepare

Choose readers who will set a respectful tone for the prayer.

 Use the *Call to Faith 4* CD, track 14, to rehearse the suggested song.

Gather

Have students sit in a circle in the prayer space.

Pray

- Follow the order of prayer on page 158.
- Leader's concluding prayer: **Lord, we know that protecting life is within our power. Help us find the strength to do what is right.**

Celebrate

Celebration of the Word

 Let Us Pray

Gather and begin with the Sign of the Cross.

Reader 1: A reading from the First Letter of Peter.
Read 1 Peter 3:9–12.
The word of the Lord.

All: **Thanks be to God.**

Reader 2: When we are given the choice to walk away or to stay and fight,

All: **Help us choose your way, O Lord.**

Reader 3: When we are given the choice to stay angry or to forgive,

All: **Help us choose your way, O Lord.**

Reader 4: When we are given the chance to help those who are sick, disabled, or elderly,

All: **Help us choose your way, O Lord.**

Leader: Let us pray.
Bow your heads as the leader prays.

All: **Amen.**

 Sing together.

Jesu, Jesu, fill us with your love, show us how to serve the neighbors we have from you.

"Jesu, Jesu."© 1969, Hope Publishing Co.

 **LITURGY LINK**

Reflection Ask students to close their eyes. In a soft voice, encourage them to relax.

- Have students reflect on questions about showing respect for life.
- Pause so that students can think about how these questions apply to their lives.

LECTIONARY LINK

Break Open the Word Read last week's Sunday Gospel. Invite students to think about what the reading means to them as they try to follow Christ's example. For questions related to the weekly Gospel reading, visit our website at **www.osvcurriculum.com**.

 GO online Visit **www.osvcurriculum.com** for weekly Scripture readings and seasonal resources.

Review and Apply

A **Check Understanding**   Complete the following statements.

1. The fifth commandment says this:

   You shall not kill
   _____.

2. One way you can follow the fifth commandment is by

   Possible responses: taking care of my body,
   not physically hurting others

3. One serious sin against the fifth commandment is

   Possible responses: murder, suicide, taking the life
   of an unborn child

4. All human life is _____ **sacred** _____.

5. Hatred can lead to _____ **revenge or violence** _____.

B **Make Connections**   Write brief answers to these questions.

What new lesson did Jesus give about the fifth commandment?

Love your enemies.
_____.

How do you show that you respect life?

Responses will vary.
_____.

Activity Live Your Faith

Brainstorm   What are three steps you can take to control your anger when you are in a difficult situation? Write them here. **Responses will vary.**

159

Review and Apply

Use the focus questions from the catechist Explore pages to review the lesson concepts.

A **Check Understanding**   Have students complete each sentence.

B **Make Connections**   Ask each student to write his or her response to the questions.

• Ask volunteers to share their answers.

Activity

• Ask students to respond to the question.

• Create a master list of students' responses on the board or on chart paper.

JUSTICE AND PEACE

Human Dignity   All human life is sacred and equal in dignity because it comes from God.

• Help students develop awareness of the factors that affect the respect a person receives from society.

• Society often rewards external factors that should not influence the respect a person receives.

Catholic Social Teaching: Life and Dignity

Family Faith

Remind students to discuss the Family Faith page at home. Encourage students to read the passage from Isaiah.

• If students have completed the Optional Activity about Nobel prize winners, tell them to use their reports as a basis for their letters.

People of Faith

Tell students about Saint Maximilian Kolbe.

• As a priest, a journalist, and a prisoner in the death camp at Auschwitz, Maximilian Kolbe worked for human rights. The condemned man whose place Kolbe took was present at the saint's canonization ceremony.

• Remind students to add Saint Maximilian Kolbe to their People of Faith albums. Encourage them to pray the prayer with their families.

 Visit **www.osvcurriculum.com** for weekly scripture readings and seasonal resources.

UNIT 5: CHAPTER 14

Family Faith

Catholics Believe

■ All human life is sacred because it comes from God.

■ The fifth commandment forbids anything that takes a human life.

✝ SCRIPTURE

Read *Isaiah 9:1–6* to find out about the Prince of Peace.

GO online www.osvcurriculum.com
For weekly scripture readings and seasonal resources

Activity

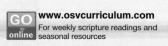
Live Your Faith

Write a Letter of Thanks   Research the life and work of a recent Nobel Peace Prize winner who is still alive. Find out about the person's contribution and how he or she has worked for peace. Write a letter to the person, thanking him or her for choosing life.

▲ **Saint Maximilian Kolbe 1894–1941**

People of Faith

Maximilian Kolbe was ordained a Franciscan priest and was devoted to Our Lady of the Immaculate Conception. During World War II he was imprisoned at Auschwitz. While in prison, Maximilian encouraged other prisoners to hold fast to God's love. He volunteered to take the place of a young father condemned to execution by the Nazis. He chose life even as he gave his own for another. Maximilian was named a saint in 1982. His feast day is August 14.

In Unit 5 your child is learning about MORALITY.

160 **CCC** *See Catechism of the Catholic Church 2258, 2268–2269 for further reading on chapter conten*

👥 Family Prayer

Saint Maximilian Kolbe pray for us that we may be faithful to God's love and always choose the path of life and hope. Amen.

❓ HOW DID I DO?

My session was

☐ *one of the best ever!*   ☐ *pretty good.*   ☐ *in need of improvement.*

In what discussions and activities were students most interested?

_____

What activity did I most enjoy teaching?

_____

In what area do I need to improve?

_____

Name _____ Date _____

Respect Your Body

Think about the things that can harm your body. Draw a symbol for each of the following items, and then draw and color the barred circle "No" symbol over each drawing. Next, write a personal pledge saying what you will do to show respect for your body.

Junk food

Smoking

Not using safety equipment

Fighting

Staying up too late

Alcohol

I will respect my body by

_____

_____

_____

Signed _____

Overview

Faith Focus

- Because God himself is Truth, his people are called to live in truth. *(CCC 2465)*
- Living in truth truly sets one free. *(CCC 1741)*

Catechism Connection

The *Catechism* explains that humans are naturally drawn toward the truth. *(CCC 2467)*

NDC Link

The ongoing faith formation of the catechists on human, spiritual, and intellectual levels helps set the stage for those they catechize so that they may understand and be led to the religious, liturgical, moral, and community life of the Church. (See *NDC*, 55E.)

Resources

BOOK
A Thomas More Source Book. Wegemer, Gerard B. and Smith, Stephen W. (editors). Catholic University of America Press. Brings together classic texts by and about this great saint.

DVD and CD
Move! Pray! Celebrate! Our Sunday Visitor Curriculum Division. "Spirit Be with Us" (4:06 min.). A prayer for strength on our faith journey.

*Available at www.osvcurriculum.com

 Catechist Resources For interactive lesson planner, chapter resources, and activities www.osvcurriculum.com

 Who may go up the mountain of the LORD? Who can stand in his holy place? "The clean of hand and pure of heart, who are not devoted to idols, who have not sworn falsely."

Psalm 24:3–4

Truth

Truth is central to your relationship with God. The Bible often refers to truth: The truth will set you free *(John 8:32)*; Jesus calls himself "the truth" *(John 14:6)*; Christians are called to follow the Spirit of truth *(John 16:13)*. To become one with Jesus, you must speak the truth.

The benefits of candor and sincerity are many. Truth builds community by creating trust. It nurtures love by strengthening communication and respect. The covenant between God and humans, reflected in human relationships, depends on the constancy of truth.

False Witness

Lying is more than not telling the truth. People bear false witness both by what they say and do and by what they refuse to say and do. Humans witness to falsehood whenever they are *not* witnessing to the truth, that is, to God.

Lying destroys reputations, relationships, and lives. Gossip and slander are all too common forms of this sin. False witness aimed at deliberately leading another into error or danger is especially grave. It tarnishes the honor of both the hearer and the liar and steps far away from the gospel call to speak the truth.

Honesty is the best policy. I cannot tell a lie. The truth will set you free.

Reflect **How does my life show that I respect truth?**

Truthfulness

Fourth grade is a good time to highlight the importance of being consistently truthful. Relationships with family and friends depend on the presence of trust. Encourage your students to make the connection between how honest they are and the trust people give them.

- Affirm students when they are truthful, and encourage them to affirm one another's truthfulness.

- Help them learn to measure the morality of choices through role-playing or acting out scenarios about truthfulness.

- Help students feel comfortable telling the truth by creating a classroom environment that is open, positive, and fair.

Using Words

- I will follow models of truthfulness. Be sure that you are always truthful with me.

- I know that mean words can hurt. Teach me ways to affirm others.

- I need to know what you expect of me when I'm doing a project. Please give clear directions.

Challenges and Practices

Some challenges in catechesis are adaptive challenges in which changes are required to sustain your spirit. Some adaptive challenges are obvious, while others erode the ability to sustain your spirit.

The best way to respond to adaptive challenges is with specific practices that

- are intentional ways of doing something instead of simply trying to hold on.

- are proactive responses instead of reactive responses.

- require discipline or courage.

Reflect **What is the greatest challenge you face in sustaining your spirit, and how do you deal with it?**

Catechist's Prayer

Dear God, there is no greater joy than to walk in your ways. In your words and actions I find truth. Lead me to follow you and find freedom for my spirit and purpose in my life. Amen.

Weekly Planner

	Objectives	**Lesson Process**	**Materials**

1 Invite

10 minutes

Page 161
Objective:
To recognize the importance of living in truth

🙌 **Let Us Pray:** Psalm 86:11
_____
• Pray the psalm.
• Discuss mottos or sayings about telling the truth.
• Have students write their own sayings.

☐ Pencils or pens
☐ Paper

---

2 Explore

40 minutes

Pages 162–163
Objective:
To explain what witnessing to the truth means

• Discuss the story of Thomas More.
• Explain what a martyr is.
 Activity Complete the Share Your Faith Activity.
Words of Faith martyr

☐ Board or chart paper
☐ A map of the world showing the location of England

Pages 164–165
Objective:
To articulate ways to obey the eighth commandment

✝ **Scripture:** John 8:31–32, 14:6
_____
• Reflect on Jesus' teachings about truth.
• Identify ways of living the truth.
 Activity Complete the Connect Your Faith Activity.
Words of Faith reparation

☐ Copies of Activity Master 15 on page 168A

---

3 Celebrate

10 minutes

Page 166
Objective:
To ask the Spirit of Truth for guidance

🙌 **Let Us Pray**
_____
• Gather as a community.
• Rehearse the music.
• Celebrate a Prayer of Petition.
🔥 **Hymn:** "Send Down the Fire"
_____
 Activity Complete the Prayer to the Holy Spirit Activity, page 240 and 241

☐ Hymnals
☐ Music CD
☐ Bible

Wrap Up

Review and Apply

Page 167
• Review the chapter concepts.
• Complete the Live Your Faith Activity.

Family Faith

Page 168
• Introduce the page, and assign it as a family activity.
• Read about Saint Joan of Arc.

ACRE Connection, Domain 5—Personal Morality

Home Connection

GO online **www.osvcurriculum.com**
Family Faith activities, feasts and seasonal resources, saint features, and much more

• Online planning tools include chapter background and planner, activity master, customizable test, and more.

• Enhancement activities for each step of the catechetical process, including alternative prayer experiences and blessings.

• Games, activities, interactive review, alternative assessment, and more for children

www.calltofaitheconnect.com

Chapter 15 Live in Truth

Let Us Pray

Leader: Lord God, may we always be honest in our praise of you.

"Teach me, LORD, your way
that I may walk in your truth,"

Psalm 86:11

All: Lord God, may we always be honest in our praise of you.
Amen.

nesty is the best policy.
annot tell a lie.
e truth will set you free.

Activity · Let's Begin

It's the Truth! Look at the sayings on the board.

• Create your own saying about the importance of telling the truth. **Responses will vary.**

1 Invite

Objective: To recognize the importance of living in truth

Let Us Pray

Have students gather in the prayer space. Read aloud the Leader part, and have everyone join in to read the All response.

Activity

• Tell students that a motto is a saying that a person may choose to help guide his or her life.

• Read aloud It's the Truth!

• Help students compose additional sayings about telling the truth. Praise them for their efforts.

• Ask students when it might be hard to tell the truth. Possible response: when it gets you into trouble Discuss what can happen when a person does not tell the truth. Possible responses: People don't trust you. You commit a sin.

OPTIONAL ACTIVITY

Posters About Truth People who are stopped in traffic often pass the time by reading billboards.

• Have students use their sayings to create "billboards" (poster size) that promote telling the truth.

• If possible, display the posters in public areas.

Multiple Intelligence: Visual/Spatial

CULTURAL AWARENESS

Jewish Proverbs A proverb is a brief popular saying that expresses the beliefs of a culture or religion. The Jewish religion has many proverbs that deal with the value of truth and honesty. Two such proverbs are

• A half-truth is a whole lie.

• What you don't see with your eyes, don't invent with your mouth.

Objective: To explain what witnessing to the truth means

 **Focus**

How do people witness to the truth? List students' responses on the board or on chart paper.

Honest Choices

Read aloud the introduction. Tell students to listen to find out what Thomas More's dilemma was.

Thomas More

Show students the location of England on a map. Explain that kings and queens were very powerful during the sixteenth century.

- Read aloud the letter.
- Ask students to identify the two choices that Thomas More faced. to support the king and live or to support the Catholic Church and die
- Guide students in discussing the question in the text. Do not require students to reveal embarrassing or sinful choices.

Honest Choices

 **Focus** How do people witness to the truth?

Thomas More, an important official in England in the sixteenth century, was imprisoned for refusing to tell a lie. Thomas had an important decision to make. In a letter to his daughter, he discussed his dilemma.

A LETTER

THOMAS MORE

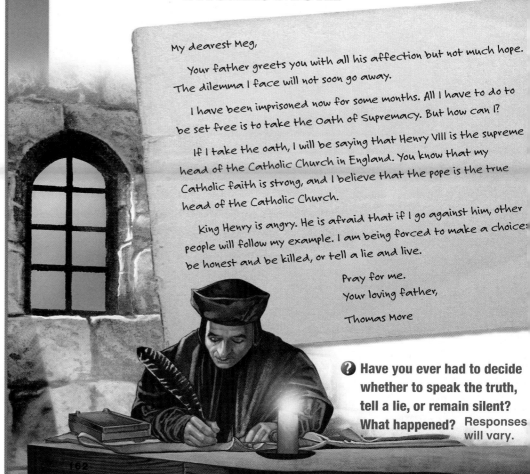

My dearest Meg,

Your father greets you with all his affection but not much hope. The dilemma I face will not soon go away.

I have been imprisoned now for some months. All I have to do to be set free is to take the Oath of Supremacy. But how can I?

If I take the oath, I will be saying that Henry VIII is the supreme head of the Catholic Church in England. You know that my Catholic faith is strong, and I believe that the pope is the true head of the Catholic Church.

King Henry is angry. He is afraid that if I go against him, other people will follow my example. I am being forced to make a choice: be honest and be killed, or tell a lie and live.

Pray for me.
Your loving father,

Thomas More

❓ **Have you ever had to decide whether to speak the truth, tell a lie, or remain silent? What happened?** Responses will vary.

162

 REACHING ALL LEARNERS

Student Pairs Arrange students with different learning styles in pairs.

- Pair a visual learner with a student strong in movement skills to work on a skit.
- For a storybook activity, pair an artist and a student with strong language skills.

OPTIONAL ACTIVITY

Famous Martyrs Perform an Internet search, and print pictures and stories of martyrs.

- Have students cut out the pictures and mount them on construction paper.
- Then have students glue the appropriate story to the back of each picture.
- Share the stories in a "wall of fame" gallery.

Multiple Intelligence: Visual/Spatial

ving the Truth

Thomas More chose to remain true to his beliefs and eak the truth. As a result, the king had him killed, but e Catholic Church named him a saint. Many saints d heroes have suffered torture and death for the sake the truth of their faith. A person who stays faithful to rist and suffers and dies rather than denying the uth is called a **martyr**. Martyrs live the truth by cking up their words with actions.

You probably will not be called on to be a martyr. But ery follower of Jesus is called to live in the truth. By ur actions you show your faithfulness to Jesus and the uth of his message.

Words of Faith

A **martyr** is someone who gives up his or her life to witness to the truth of the faith.

Activity

Share Your Faith

uth-telling

Reflect: Think about why it is always best to tell the truth.

Share: With a partner, list ten reasons for truth-telling.

Act: List words for a song about truth-telling.

_____ _____ _____

163

Living the Truth

Have students read these two paragraphs to learn about people who stand up for truth.

- Tell students that the Church recognizes many martyrs as saints.
- Explain that early Christians who were killed because of their beliefs are also considered martyrs. Over the centuries, many Catholics have died for their faith.
- Ask why Thomas More and others were willing to give up their lives to witness to the truth. Possible responses: They wanted to remain faithful to Christ; they knew that the truth was important.

Activity

- Have students work individually or in pairs to write songs.
- Ask volunteers to share their work.

◎ Quick Review

Followers of Jesus are called to live in the truth. Martyrs are people who die for the truths of faith.

✚ JUSTICE AND PEACE

Martyr for Human Rights Politics and religious social teachings intersect in the realm of human rights.

- These include the right to life, economic rights, and political rights (voting and religious freedom).
- Archbishop Oscar Romero gave his life for human rights.

≡VOTE≡

Catholic Social Teaching: Rights and Responsibilities

Objective: To articulate ways to obey the eighth commandment

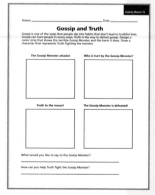 **Focus**

What does the eighth commandment call you to do? List students' responses on the board or on chart paper.

The Eighth Commandment

Read aloud the text. Ask students to underline the eighth commandment.

- Remind students that Jesus said that everyone is our neighbor.

- Point out that his response means that Jesus might say that the eighth commandment is "You shall not bear false witness against anyone."

- Organize students into groups of three or four to discuss the question.

Explore

The Eighth Commandment

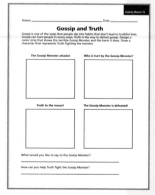 **Focus** What does the eighth commandment call you to do?

God is the source of all truth. His word and his law c people to live in the truth. The eighth commandment says this: You shall not bear false witness against your neighbor.

The eighth commandment forbids lying, or purposel not telling the truth. Lying can take many forms. If a person lies in court when under oath, he or she comm perjury, or false witness. Gossip is talking about anothe person behind his or her back. Gossip may or may not a lie, but all gossip can harm the good reputation of another person.

All lies are unjust and unloving. All require **reparatio** or repair. Reparation may be as simple as an apology, o it may take more work, such as trying to help a person get back the reputation you have hurt.

❓ **What are some ways you can repair th damage to another person when you have not told the truth?**

Possible responses: Tell the truth, apologize, stand up for the person who may be in trouble.

164

OPTIONAL ACTIVITY

Activity Master 15: Gossip and Truth Distribute copies of the activity found on catechist page 168A.

- Have students design their comic strips and share them with the class.

- As an alternative, you may wish to send this activity home with students.

▲ Activity Master 15

💡 **QUICK TIP**

Truth and the Media Students need to develop critical thinking skills regarding the media and truth.

- Discuss stories that harm a person's reputation. Do they judge a person prematurely or unfairly?

- Teach students to bring fairness and charity to the evaluation of issues of truth in the media.

Jesus Is the Truth

Living in the spirit of the eighth commandment is more than not lying. You must choose to be truthful in words and actions. When you are truthful, you are living as a follower of Jesus, who always told the truth.

✠ SCRIPTURE — John 8:31–32, 14:6

The Truth Will Set You Free

Jesus . . . said . . . , "If you remain in my word, you will truly be my disciples, and you will know the truth, and the truth will set you free. . . . I am the way and the truth and the life. No one comes to the Father except through me."

John 8:31–32, 14:6

People trusted what Jesus did and said. When you are truthful, people trust you. When you promise to tell the truth, you have a special duty. Let your "yes" mean "yes" and your "no" mean "no." Telling the truth will set you free to follow Jesus and to live in love.

Words of Faith

Reparation is action taken to repair the damage done by sin.

Activity — Connect Your Faith

Live the Truth   Read the following list, and mark an X if a statement talks about living in truth and an O if it does not. For each statement marked with an O, tell one way the person could make up for his or her wrong choice.

- **X** Juanita heard an unkind story about a classmate. She did not repeat it.
- **O** Scott bragged falsely about how good he was at sports.
- **O** Samantha told her parents that she was going to the library, but instead she went to the park.
- **X** Maria discovered that her friend had shoplifted. She did not tell her other friends.

165

Jesus Is the Truth

Ask students to explain the difference between being truthful and not lying. Have students read silently to learn the answer.

The Truth Will Set You Free

Choose a proficient reader to proclaim the Scripture.

- Discuss what Jesus meant when he said, "The truth will set you free."
- Read aloud the paragraph following the Scripture. Tell students that having people trust you is a good consequence of being truthful.

Activity

- Read each situation aloud, and have students record their answers.
- Discuss as a group ways to make the wrong choices right.

◎ Quick Review

The eighth commandment forbids lying. You must make up for the harm done by any lies you tell. Jesus said, "The truth will set you free."

✠ SCRIPTURE BACKGROUND

Truth   *John 14:6* ("I am the way and the truth and the life") is part of the Last Supper Discourses.

- As one of the last lessons Jesus gave his disciples, this message is of extreme importance.
- With his next words, Jesus specifies *how* he is the way and the truth and the life: "No one comes to the Father except through me."

Objective: To ask the Spirit of Truth for guidance

 Let Us Pray

Tell students that *Spirit of Truth* is another name for the Holy Spirit.

Prayer of Petition

Prepare

Choose a leader for the prayer service, and rehearse the response.

 Use the *Call to Faith 4* CD, track 15, to rehearse the suggested song.

Gather

Invite students into the prayer space, and sit with them in a circle.

Pray

- Follow the order of prayer on page 166.
- You may wish to sing the third verse as well as the refrain of "Send Down the Fire."
- For a scripture reading, consider *Psalm 15; Proverbs 12:17, 19, 22; John 1:14–18;* or *John 18:37–38.*

Celebrate

Prayer of Petition

 **Let Us Pray**

Gather and begin with the Sign of the Cross.

Leader:	Whenever we are afraid to tell the truth,
All:	**Spirit of Truth, guide us!**
Leader:	Whenever we are tempted to gossip,
All:	**Spirit of Truth, guide us!**
Leader:	Whenever we are faced with choices about telling the truth,
All:	**Spirit of Truth, guide us!**
Leader:	Whenever we falsely judge another,
All:	**Spirit of Truth, guide us!**
Leader:	God of all truth, whenever we face choices about telling the truth, guide us to your light. Give us strength to make good choices. We ask this in Jesus' name. Amen.

 Sing together.

Send down the fire of your justice, Send down the rains of your love; Come, send down the Spirit, breathe life in your people, and we shall be people of God.

"Send Down the Fire" ©2001, GIA Publications, Inc.

166

 LITURGY LINK

Reminders of the Spirit   Consider enhancing the prayer service connection to the Holy Spirit by encouraging students to wear red clothes or accessories to class.

- Point out that red is associated not only with the Holy Spirit, but also with enthusiasm, or zeal.

 **LECTIONARY LINK**

Break Open the Word   Read last week's Sunday Gospel. Invite students to think about what the reading means to them as they try to follow Christ's example. For questions related to the weekly Gospel reading, visit our website at **www.osvcurriculum.com**.

 Visit www.osvcurriculum.com for weekly Scripture readings and seasonal resources.

Review and Apply

A **Check Understanding** Circle True if a statement is true, and circle False if a statement is false. Correct any false statements.

1. A martyr is someone who gives up his or her life to witness to Jesus and the truth of the faith.

   (True)　　False _____

2. Three sins against the eighth commandment are false witness, perjury, and love.

   True　　(False) **replace love with gossip** _____

3. Reparation is repairing a wrong.

   (True)　　False _____

4. The eighth commandment is "You shall not kill."

   True　　(False) **"You shall not bear false witness against your neighbor."**

5. Only martyrs are called to live in truth.

   True　　(False) **All Christians are called to live in truth.** ___

B **Make Connections** Write a response on the lines below. What did Jesus mean when he said, "The truth will set you free"?

Responses will vary. _____

_____

Activity

Live Your Faith

Mini-dramas Work with a group.

- Create a skit in which a person hurts another or damages another's reputation by telling a lie.

- Show how the person makes reparation for the wrong that he or she has done.

167

Review and Apply

Use the focus questions from the Explore pages to review the lesson concepts.

A **Check Understanding** Have students circle the answers and correct the false statements.

B **Make Connections** Ask students to write their responses to the question. Invite volunteers to share their responses.

Activity

- Organize students into small groups.

- On several slips of paper, write examples of how students hurt one another by telling lies; you might brainstorm these with students.

- Have each group choose a slip of paper and create a skit to present to the class.

OPTIONAL ACTIVITY

Truth Pageant Invite students to stage a pageant about truth, lies, and the eighth commandment.

- Ask groups of students to personify one character: lying, perjury, gossip, reparation, or apology.

- Have each group write and perform a short song telling about the character, its effects, and how it relates to truth.

Multiple Intelligence: Musical

Family Faith

Remind students to discuss the Family Faith page at home. Encourage students to read the passage from Proverbs.

Activity

- Read aloud the directions before sending the page home with students.
- Invite volunteers to share the results of their family discussions at your next session.

People of Faith

Tell students about Saint Joan of Arc.

- Joan of Arc was born to a family of farmers during the Hundred Years' War. As a child, she began to have visions. She respected these saintly messengers and prayed about their words. Joan is a model of faith whom students can admire.
- Remind students to add Saint Joan to their People of Faith albums. Encourage them to pray the prayer at home with their families.

 Visit **www.osvcurriculum.com** for weekly scripture readings and seasonal resources.

UNIT 5: CHAPTER 15
Family Faith

Catholics Believe

- Because God is truth, his people are called to live in the truth.
- The eighth commandment forbids lying.

✝ SCRIPTURE

Read *Proverbs 12:12–26* to learn more about the rewards that await those who are honest.

GO online www.osvcurriculum.com
For weekly scripture readings and seasonal resources

Activity
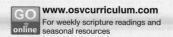
Live Your Faith

Truth Talk As a family, take time this week to talk about the following questions:
- How do you handle a situation in which being honest would hurt someone?
- When is it right to tell on someone, and when is it wrong?
- How can you help one another live in truth?

▲ Saint Joan of Arc 1412–1431

People of Faith

Joan of Arc was true to God's will and truth. She had visions and heard voices that told her to lead an army to fight for truth and save France from invaders. She bravely told the truth about her visions and voices and saved France in many battles. However, Joan was accused of being against the Church and of being a witch. She was burned at the stake when she was still a teenager. Joan was named a saint in 1920, and her feast day is May 30.

Family Prayer

Saint Joan of Arc, pray for us that we may grow strong in our faith and have the courage to speak and live the truth. Amen.

In Unit 5 your child is learning about MORALITY.
168 CCC *See Catechism of the Catholic Church 1741, 2465–2470 for further reading on chapter conte*

? HOW DID I DO?

My session was

☐ *one of the best ever!* ☐ *pretty good.* ☐ *in need of improvement.*

In what discussions and activities were students most interested?

_____

What activity did I most enjoy teaching?

_____

In what area do I need to improve?

_____

Name _____ Date _____

Gossip and Truth

Gossip is one of the ways that people slip into habits that don't lead to truthful lives. Gossip can hurt people in many ways. Truth is the way to defeat gossip. Design a comic strip that shows the terrible Gossip Monster and the harm it does. Draw a character that represents Truth fighting the monster.

The Gossip Monster attacks!

Who is hurt by the Gossip Monster?

Truth to the rescue!

The Gossip Monster is defeated!

What would you like to say to the Gossip Monster?

_____

How can you help Truth fight the Gossip Monster?

_____

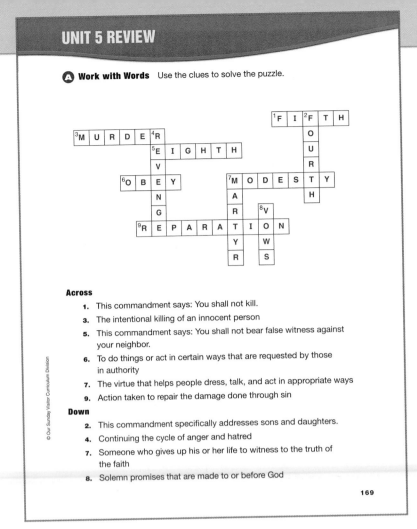

A Work with Words Use the clues to solve the puzzle.

Crossword answers:
- ¹F I F T H
- ²F O U R T H
- ³M U R D E ⁴R
- ⁵E I G H T H
- ⁴R E V E N G E
- ⁶O B E Y
- ⁷M O D E S T Y
- ⁷M A R T Y R S
- ⁸V O W S
- ⁹R E P A R A T I O N

Across

1. This commandment says: You shall not kill.
3. The intentional killing of an innocent person
5. This commandment says: You shall not bear false witness against your neighbor.
6. To do things or act in certain ways that are requested by those in authority
7. The virtue that helps people dress, talk, and act in appropriate ways
9. Action taken to repair the damage done through sin

Down

2. This commandment specifically addresses sons and daughters.
4. Continuing the cycle of anger and hatred
7. Someone who gives up his or her life to witness to the truth of the faith
8. Solemn promises that are made to or before God

169

© Our Sunday Visitor Curriculum Division

Unit Review

The Unit Review is designed to prepare students for the Unit Assessment. This page focuses on vocabulary words and the main concepts presented in the chapters.

Each review contains various sections that will appeal to the many different learning styles of your students. There are puzzles to engage students' attention, as well as true-false, multiple-choice, short-answer, and fill-in-the-blank exercises.

Direct students to complete the review, and check their responses. Determine areas in which students still need practice, and review those sections of the unit.

Notes

Name _____ Date _____

Faithful Living

(A) **Work with Words**   Circle the letter of the choice that best completes the sentence.

1. The virtue that helps people dress, talk, and act properly is _____.

    a. thrift

    b. modesty

    c. obedience

    d. truthfulness

2. A martyr is a person who _____.

    a. asks God for help in difficult times

    b. tries to be a peacemaker

    c. gives up his or her life for the faith

    d. gives advice to Church officials

3. Lying under oath is called _____.

    a. testimony

    b. gossip

    c. prejudice

    d. perjury

4. Gossip harms people _____.

    a. whether it is true or untrue

    b. only if the story is about them

    c. who do not pray

    d. who show respect for creation

5. Truthfulness leads to _____.

    a. pride

    b. good grades

    c. forgiveness

    d. trust

6. The fourth through the tenth commandments guide people in loving _____.

    a. themselves

    b. the saints

    c. their neighbor

    d. God

7. I fail to obey the fifth commandment when I _____.

    a. let go of harmful anger

    b. use tobacco or drugs

    c. eat healthful foods and exercise

    d. avoid violence

Name _____ Date _____

Complete each sentence with the correct word from the Word Bank.

8–11. One of the major messages of the commandments is that life is God's gift and that humans are to treasure it. This is why _____, intentionally killing an innocent person, is wrong. For the same reason, _____ is sinful when it leads you to wishing serious harm to another person. Because God loves humans, he will grant them _____. People must also remember to make _____ for their sins against life.

WORD BANK
reparation
forgiveness
hatred
murder

B Check Understanding Match each description in Column 1 with the correct term in Column 2.

Column 1

_____ **12.** remind people to honor marriage

_____ **13.** sacred promises

_____ **14.** one who wanted to be remembered for good works

_____ **15.** says that life is sacred

_____ **16.** encourages people to tell the truth

_____ **17.** a martyr who remained true to his beliefs

Column 2

a. Alfred Nobel

b. eighth commandment

c. sixth and ninth commandments

d. vows

e. Thomas More

f. fifth commandment

C Make Connections Use the three terms below to write a one-paragraph response.

parents   authority   respect

18–20. Explain what the fourth commandment means for children and how you live it out.

_____

_____

_____

_____

_____

_____

Answers can be found in the back of the Catechist Manual.

Unit 6
Sacraments

In this unit you will....

learn about the Paschal mystery and how it is celebrated in the seasons of the liturgical year and through the Sacraments. Christ instituted the Sacraments as signs of God's love and presence, and to give us grace. The Eucharist is the heart of the Church's life. The Sacraments of Healing are about conversion, forgiveness, and healing.

 Chapter 16
 Chapter 17
 Chapter 18

 What do you think you will learn in this unit about the Paschal mystery?

170

UNIT 6 OPENER

Preview Unit Theme

Tell students that Unit 6 is about the Sacraments.

- Read aloud the text on page 170 of the student edition. Tell students they will learn more about these things in the next three chapters.

- Ask students why they think the Paschal Mystery is so important to us.

- Invite volunteers to name the Sacraments of Healing.

Overview

The Church Year
CATECHIST FORMATION

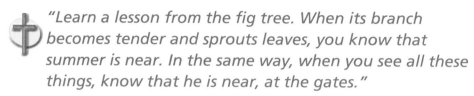

Faith Focus

- Throughout the Church year, the faithful celebrate the Paschal Mystery. *(CCC 1067)*
- The liturgical seasons include Advent, Christmas, Lent, Easter, and Ordinary Time. *(CCC 1171)*

Catechism Connection

The *Catechism* notes that the liturgy is to be celebrated by the entire Body of Christ as a community. *(CCC 1140)*

NDC Link

Catechesis prepares us for active participation in the liturgy by helping us understand its nature, rites, and symbols. It also springs from the liturgy in that it helps us worship God and reflect on the experience of the words, signs, and rituals. (See *NDC*, 33.)

Resources

BOOK
To Everything There Is a Season. Daly, Jude (illustrator). Eerdmans Books for Young Readers. The timeless words from Ecclesiastes are illustrated.

DVD/VHS
Following Jesus through the Church Year (74 min.). Twenty-Third Publications. Introduces the purpose and meaning of the liturgical seasons.

GO online **Catechist Resources**
For interactive lesson planner, chapter resources, and activities
www.osvcurriculum.com

"*Learn a lesson from the fig tree. When its branch becomes tender and sprouts leaves, you know that summer is near. In the same way, when you see all these things, know that he is near, at the gates.*"

Matthew 24:32–33

Liturgical Seasons

The rhythm of the liturgical seasons matches the cycle of life. During the Church year, the faithful experience the anticipation of Advent; rejoice at the Savior's birth on Christmas; live faithfully in Ordinary Time; grow reflective in Lent; and know suffering, death, and rising to new life in Christ through the Triduum and Easter. Catholics do not simply watch this drama unfold; they are drawn into the reality of God's continuing presence in their lives. This presence is reinforced as Catholics recall Christ's life and the Paschal Mystery at every Mass.

The Paschal Mystery

The mystery began with consecrated Bread and Wine on Holy Thursday evening. It moved through suffering on a cross to the miracle of an empty tomb on Easter morning. As Jesus revealed himself to the disciples on Easter evening, the mystery moved to joy in the knowledge that Jesus had saved all humans from sin and death and made his followers full participants in new life. Through the Sacrament of Baptism and the Paschal Mystery, all Church members become true sons and daughters of the heavenly Father.

Reflect **How do you show your belief in the Paschal Mystery?**

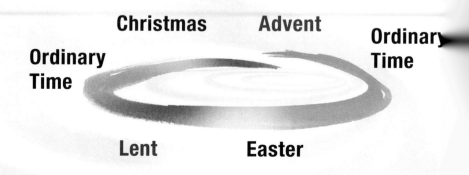

Christmas Advent

Ordinary Time

Ordinary Time

Lent Easter

The Liturgical Year

The Church has a cycle called the liturgical year. The extent of the cycle may not be clear to students. However, they probably have bits and pieces of understanding. All of your students know about Christmas. They also know about Lent and Easter, although they may not yet know the sacred significance of the events or the particulars of the Triduum and the Easter Season.

- Help students order the liturgical year in their minds. During the course of the lesson, present the liturgical year as a cycle of seasons.

- Show students where each part of the liturgical year falls on the calendar.

- Identify colors, feasts, liturgical practices, readings, and music for each part of the liturgical year.

- Encourage students to keep the seasons in their hearts as they journey through the life of Jesus.

How I Learn

- I like to learn through movement. Incorporate gestures into class activities.

- Sometimes I just don't know the answers. Help me discover them.

- To put information in order, I may need to see it as well as hear it. Help me learn both auditorily and visually.

Moments of Grace

Catechesis puts you in touch with the longings and dreams of those around you. It is an important spiritual task to listen to and truly hear the inner voices of students and their parents. You may see the unspoken pain in someone's eyes. You may hear important questions that shy souls are afraid to ask.

The practice of collecting moments of grace is a way to stay in touch with the spiritual nature of your work by deliberately paying attention. You can collect moments of grace by noticing when people invite you to come to know them better or let you get a glimpse of their vulnerability. Moments of grace are collected when you realize that the present is sacred and the ordinary is holy.

Reflect **What moments of grace have sustained your spirit in the past?**

Catechist's Prayer

Jesus, you walked the journey of life loving others generously. By learning and teaching about you, may I know the Father's will in my life. Amen.

Weekly Planner

Objectives	Lesson Process	Materials

1 Invite

10 minutes

Page 171
Objective:
To understand the concept of a life cycle

🙏 **Let Us Pray:** Psalm 19:2

- Pray the psalm verse.
- Describe a life cycle.
- Identify changes in each season.

2 Explore

40 minutes

Pages 172–173
Objective:
To explore how the Paschal Mystery is celebrated in the Eucharist and remembered throughout the liturgical year

✝ **Scripture:** Ecclesiastes 3:1–8

- Proclaim the scripture reading.
- Identify the Paschal Mystery.
- Describe the liturgical year.
- **Activity** Complete the Share Your Faith Activity.

Words of Faith Paschal Mystery, liturgical year

- ☐ Board or chart paper
- ☐ Pencils or pens
- ☐ Index cards
- ☐ Recordings of "Parables" (OCP), or "Turn, Turn, Turn" by the Byrds

Pages 174–175
Objective:
To articulate the seasons of the Church year

- Compare the liturgical seasons to the seasons of nature.
- Describe each of the seasons of the Church year.
- **Activity** Complete the Connect Your Faith Activity.

Words of Faith Triduum

- ☐ A calendar
- ☐ Copies of Activity Master 16 on page 178A

3 Celebrate

10 minutes

Page 176
Objective:
To praise God for the gift of his Son

🙏 **Let Us Pray**

- Rehearse the music.
- Gather as a community.
- Celebrate a Prayer of Praise.
- 🎵 **Hymn:** "Shout for Joy"

- **Activity** Complete the Triduum Triptychs Activity, page 230 and 231

- ☐ Bible
- ☐ Hymnals
- ☐ Music CD
- ☐ Banners or colored ribbons

Wrap Up

Review and Apply

Page 177
- Review the chapter concepts.
- Complete the Live Your Faith Activity.

Family Faith

Page 178
- Introduce the page, and assign it as a family activity.
- Read about Saint Bede.

ACRE Connection, Domain 3—Liturgical Year

Home Connection

GO online **www.osvcurriculum.com**
Family Faith activities, feasts and seasonal resources, saint features, and much more

CALL to FAITH e connect

- Online planning tools include chapter background and planner, activity master, customizable test, and more.
- Enhancement activities for each step of the catechetical process, including alternative prayer experiences and blessings.
- Games, activities, interactive review, alternative assessment, and more for childr[...]

www.calltofaitheconnect.com

Chapter 16 The Church Year

 Let Us Pray

Leader: Creator God, we rejoice in the beauty and variety of your creation.

"The heavens declare the glory of God;
    the sky proclaims its builder's craft."

Psalm 19:2

All: Creator God, we rejoice in the beauty and variety of your creation. Amen.

Activity Let's Begin

The Life Cycle   All living things follow a pattern. They come to life, they grow and develop, and finally they die. This pattern is called a life cycle. Every year as the seasons change, you see changes in the world around you. The change of seasons affects you, too.

• Tell about one seasonal change that happens where you live. **Responses will vary.**

171

Objective: To understand the concept of a life cycle

 Let Us Pray

Have students move to your classroom prayer space. In the space, have a crucifix and a Bible opened to the psalm. Pray the psalm verse with enthusiasm. Encourage students to reflect on the beauty and wonder of creation as they respond.

Activity

• Read aloud The Life Cycle.

• Enhance students' understanding by describing the simple life cycle of the butterfly from egg to caterpillar to cocoon to butterfly.

• Discuss seasonal changes that happen where students live.

• Ask students how their family patterns of activity change throughout the year. Possible responses: camping in summer, sports in autumn, and planting in spring

• Tell students that the Church has a cycle of seasons to celebrate God's presence in people's lives.

 QUICK TIP

Classroom Environment   Your classroom environment can make students aware of changes that occur throughout the year.

• If you have a bulletin board, appoint a group of students to help you change it seasonally.

• Encourage students to bring in seasonal items, such as flowers or autumn leaves, to decorate the room or your prayer space.

Objective: To explore how the Paschal mystery is celebrated in the Eucharist and remembered throughout the liturgical year

 **Focus**

What is the Paschal mystery? List students' responses on the board or on chart paper.

The Cycle of Life

Tell students that just as they notice the changing seasons, a poet observed and wrote in the Bible about different times and events of life.

The Right Time

Organize students into two groups, and have the groups face each other. Have them proclaim the Scripture aloud, with the first group reading the first line of each couplet and the other group reading the second line.

- You may want to have students listen to a recording of these verses: "Parables" (OCP), or "Turn, Turn, Turn" by the Byrds.
- Discuss the question in the text.

Explore

The Cycle of Life

 Focus What is the Paschal mystery?

Your life is full of cycles and seasons. As you grow in faith, you will notice them more. A wise man once wrote a poem about the cycle of life. It is in the Bible.

✝ **SCRIPTURE** Ecclesiastes 3:1–8

The Right Time

There is an appointed time for everything, and a time for every affair under the heavens.

A time to be born, and a time to die;
  a time to plant, and a time to uproot the plant.

A time to kill, and a time to heal;
  a time to tear down, and a time to build.

A time to weep, and a time to laugh;
  a time to mourn, and a time to dance.

A time to scatter stones, and a time to
    gather them;
  a time to embrace, and a time to be far
    from embraces.

A time to seek, and a time to lose;
  a time to keep, and a time to cast away.

A time to rend, and a time to sew;
  a time to be silent, and a time
    to speak.

A time to love, and a time to hate;
  a time of war, and a time of peace.

Ecclesiastes 3:1–8

❓ **What do you think the poet wants you to understand?** Possible response: There is a time for everything.

172

⭐ **REACHING ALL LEARNERS**

Kinesthetic Learners Some students may better understand the poem from Ecclesiastes if they act it out.

- As they pantomime, draw their attention to the pairs of opposites in each couplet.
- Confirm students' understanding of the poem by asking them to state its message in their own words.

✝ **SCRIPTURE BACKGROUND**

Ecclesiastes This passage stresses that God has a plan that humans do not fully understand, and that all aspects of life are under his loving providence.

- Joy and sorrow are part of the human condition for individuals as well as for society as a whole.
- The verses following this excerpt urge people to appreciate the gifts that God has given them.

The Paschal Mystery

Jesus experienced the natural cycle of life, but his life cycle did not end with his death on the cross. God the Father raised Jesus from the dead. Then Jesus ascended to join his Father in heaven. The suffering, death, Resurrection, and Ascension of Jesus are called the **Paschal mystery**. This mystery reveals that Jesus saved all humans from the power of sin and everlasting death.

The Church celebrates this mystery in every Sacrament and especially at every Eucharist. Every Sunday you gather with the parish community to celebrate the new life that Jesus' Resurrection gives you.

The Liturgical Year

From week to week at Sunday Mass, you may notice different readings, hymns, and colors. These mark the seasons of the Church's year, called the **liturgical year**. The liturgical year begins on the first Sunday of Advent, usually around December 1, and ends with the feast of Christ the King.

❓ **What signs of the present liturgical season do you see?** Responses will vary.

Words of Faith

The **Paschal mystery** is the mystery of Jesus' suffering, death, Resurrection, and Ascension.

The **liturgical year** is the cycle of feasts and seasons that make up the Church's year of worship.

Activity — Share Your Faith

Reflect: Reflect on the things you did last week.

Share: With a partner, share some of the best times and worst times you had last week.

Act: In the boxes below, sketch a symbol for the "times" of your life. If Monday was a happy time, draw a symbol to show that you were happy. Use different symbols to represent your "times."

SUNDAY	MONDAY	TUESDAY	WEDNESDAY	THURSDAY	FRIDAY	SATURDAY

173

The Paschal Mystery

Tell students to listen to learn what the Paschal mystery is.

- Read aloud the text.
- Stress the importance of the Mass as a celebration of the Paschal mystery.

The Liturgical Year

Have students read the text and make vocabulary cards for *Paschal mystery* and *liturgical year*.

- Ask the question in the text. Discuss the changes that occur in a parish church. Write three headings on the board or on chart paper— *Readings, Music,* and *Environment*. List the way these items change.

Activity

- Allow time for students to reflect and complete the activity.
- Invite volunteers to share responses.

Quick Review

The Paschal mystery is Jesus' cycle of life, death, and new life. The Paschal mystery is celebrated in the Mass and in the seasons of the Church year.

OPTIONAL ACTIVITY

Seasonal Predictions Before each liturgical season, have students predict changes that they expect in the parish church.

- Prompt their predictions with questions about colors, decorations, and so on.
- At the start of a new season, walk through the parish church and check predictions.

Multiple Intelligence: Mathematical/Logical

Objective: To articulate the seasons of the Church year

 Focus

What are the seasons of the Church year? List students' responses on the board or on chart paper.

The Seasons

Review the meaning of *Paschal mystery.*

- Summarize the first paragraph.
- Tell students that the meaning of the Paschal mystery is celebrated each year within the seasons that the Church celebrates.

Advent

Have students read the text silently.

- Point out the Advent Season on a calendar.

Christmas

Have students read the text and note the length of this season on the calendar.

- Discuss the question in the text.

Explore

The Seasons

 Focus What are the seasons of the Church year?

Just as the seasons of the year mark the cycles of life and death in nature, the seasons of the liturgical year mark and celebrate the events of the Paschal mystery.

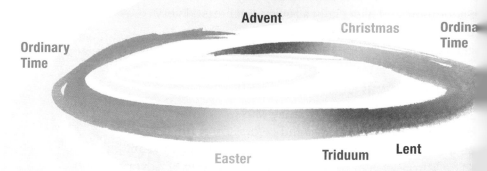

Ordinary Time — Advent — Christmas — Ordinary Time — Ordinary Time — Easter — Triduum — Lent

Advent

Advent is the beginning of the Church year. The four weeks before Christmas are a time of preparation for the coming of Jesus. The Church asks the Holy Spirit to help people welcome Jesus into their hearts every day. The seasonal color is violet, a sign of waiting.

Christmas

The Christmas Season lasts from Christmas Eve through the Sunday after Epiphany, which is twelve days after Christmas. It is a time to be joyful and to thank God the Father for sending his Son to become one of us. White and gold colors are reminders to celebrate the gift of Jesus.

❓ **How do your family and parish prepare for Christmas?**
Responses will vary.

174

✝ **JUSTICE AND PEACE**

Protecting Life Catholics are called to be in harmony with the cycle of life by protecting and preserving God's creation. The Jubilee Pledge calls all of Jesus' disciples to "advocate for public policies that protect human life, promote human dignity, preserve God's creation, and build peace."

Catholic Social Teaching: Care for Creation

Lent

Lent lasts for forty days. It begins on Ash Wednesday and ends on Holy Thursday. Lent is a time to prepare for Easter by following Jesus more closely. The seasonal color of violet is used as a sign of penance.

Triduum

The Easter Season is preceded by a three-day celebration of the Paschal mystery called the **Triduum**. It starts with the celebration of the Lord's Supper on Holy Thursday and ends with evening prayer on Easter Sunday.

Easter

The Easter Season continues for fifty days until Pentecost. It is a time to remember your Baptism and to give thanks for the Resurrection of Jesus that saved all people from the power of sin and everlasting death. White or gold colors are used during this season as a sign of great joy.

Ordinary Time

Ordinary Time is a season in two parts. The first is between the Christmas Season and the First Sunday of Lent. The second is between the Easter Season and Advent. Ordinary Time is the time to remember the works of Jesus and listen to his teachings. The color green is used during this season as a sign of hope and growth.

❓ **What is your favorite liturgical season?**

Words of Faith

Triduum is a celebration of the passion, death, and Resurrection of Christ. In the Church year, the Triduum begins on Holy Thursday evening and concludes on Easter Sunday night.

Activity Connect Your Faith

Remember His Love On the chart of seasons on the opposite page, design symbols to illustrate the saving actions of Jesus that are celebrated in each Church season.

175

Lent

Read aloud the section on Lent.

- Discuss with students the mood of the Church during the Lenten Season. solemn

Triduum/Easter

Read these sections aloud.

- Ask students what they should remember during this season.
- Have each student make a vocabulary card for *Triduum*.

Ordinary Time

Have students read to learn about the parts of the Church year not covered by special feasts and seasons.

Activity

- Brainstorm with students a list of appropriate symbols.
- Have volunteers share their work.

 Quick Review

The seasons of Advent, Christmas, Lent, Triduum, Easter, and Ordinary Time make up the Church year.

CATECHIST BACKGROUND

Triduum Describe the Triduum liturgies.

- The Evening Mass of the Lord's Supper on Holy Thursday recalls the first Eucharist.
- The Celebration of the Lord's Passion on Good Friday memorializes Jesus' sacrifice and victory on the cross.
- On Saturday, The Easter Vigil begins the celebration of the Resurrection, which culminates on Easter Sunday.

OPTIONAL ACTIVITY

Activity Master 16: Seasons and Feast Days Distribute copies of the activity found on catechist page 178A.

- Provide lectionaries or a liturgical calendar to help students complete the activity.
- As an alternative, you may wish to send this activity home with students.

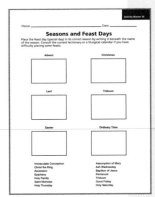

▲ Activity Master 16

Objective: To praise God for the gift of his Son

 **Let Us Pray**

Tell students that today they will express the joy of the Paschal mystery.

Prayer of Praise

Prepare

Choose a leader for the celebration, and rehearse the refrain.

- Provide banners or ribbons, if possible.

 Use the *Call to Faith 4* CD, track 16, to rehearse the suggested song.

Gather

Process to the prayer space.

Pray

- Follow the order of prayer on page 176.
- Optional Bible readings are *Psalm 33:1–5* and *Luke 24:1–8.*
- Leader's concluding prayer: **Our Father, we praise and thank you for the gift of your Son.**

Celebrate

Prayer of Praise

 Let Us Pray

Gather and begin with the Sign of the Cross.

 *Sing together the refrain.*

Shout for joy, joy, joy! Shout for joy, joy, joy!
God is love, God is light, God is everlasting!

"Shout for Joy" © 1982, Jubilate Hymns, Ltd.

Leader:	God, our good Father, you sent Jesus, your Son, to rescue us from the power of sin and everlasting death. This is our song.
All:	*Sing refrain.*
Leader:	Jesus, you came into this world of darkness as the light. Your words of love touched those who were sick and weak. You forgave sinners and freed them from shame. This is our song.
All:	*Sing refrain.*
Leader:	Jesus, you died on the cross, a sacrifice of love to set us free from our sins. This is our song.
All:	*Sing refrain.*
Leader:	Jesus, you were raised from the dead and ascended into heaven. You sent the Spirit to be with us always. We hope to share eternal life with you. This is our song.
All:	*Sing refrain.*
Leader:	Let us pray.
	Bow your heads as the leader prays.
All:	**Amen.**

176

 LITURGY LINK

Procession   When worship involves stopping and starting movements, a brief rehearsal is helpful.

- Show and tell students where they will process and at what pace to move.
- Remind them to leave enough space so that they do not bump into one another.

 LECTIONARY LINK

Break Open the Word   Read last week's Sunday Gospel. Invite students to think about what the reading means to them as they try to follow Christ's example. For questions related to the weekly Gospel reading, visit our website at **www.osvcurriculum.com.**

 GO online Visit **www.osvcurriculum.com** for weekly Scripture readings and seasonal resources.

Review and Apply

A **Work with Words** Match each description in Column 1 with the correct term in Column 2.

Column 1

_____d_____ **1.** A time of fasting and penance

_____b_____ **2.** Celebrates the birth of Jesus

_____e_____ **3.** Focuses on the Resurrection of Jesus

_____a_____ **4.** Prepares for the coming of Jesus

_____c_____ **5.** The suffering, death, Resurrection, and Ascension of Jesus

Column 2

a. Advent

b. Christmas

c. Paschal mystery

d. Lent

e. Easter

B **Check Understanding** Write responses on the lines below. What is the focus of Ordinary Time? What liturgical color is used?

Possible responses: Jesus' life, remembering his teachings, green

Activity Live Your Faith

What Season Is It? Recall the liturgical season the Church is currently celebrating.

• Decide what you can do to celebrate this season now.

• Make a plan for the coming week.

177

Review and Apply

Use the focus questions from the catechist Explore pages to review the lesson concepts.

A **Work with Words** Have students complete the matching activity. Tell them that they will use each letter only once.

B **Check Understanding** Have students answer the questions. Discuss their responses.

Activity

• Involve the whole group in making a plan to celebrate the current liturgical season.

• Help students think of appropriate songs, prayers, and activities.

• If time permits, implement some of the suggestions the next time the group meets.

OPTIONAL ACTIVITY

The Lectionary Ask your Director of Religious Education (DRE) to obtain a lectionary from the church.

• Demonstrate how the readings are organized according to the liturgical year.

• Ask students to locate the scripture readings for the current week.

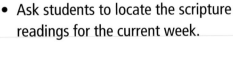

Multiple Intelligence: Visual/Spatial

Family Faith

Remind students to discuss the Family Faith page at home. Encourage students to read the passage from Psalms.

- Read aloud the directions for the family activity.
- Remind students that signs of the seasons can be seen and felt in urban areas as well as in suburban and rural areas.

People of Faith

Tell students about Saint Bede.

- A humble man of high character, Saint Bede is said to have been interested in cooking, carpentry, and music. Although living among mostly illiterate people, he was able to preserve much of the ancient classical and Christian culture.
- Remind students to add Saint Bede to their People of Faith albums. Encourage them to pray the prayer at home with their families.

 Visit **www.osvcurriculum.com** for weekly scripture readings and seasonal resources.

Catholics Believe

- The Church year celebrates the Paschal mystery.
- The seasons of the liturgical year include Advent, Christmas, Lent, Easter, and Ordinary Time.

SCRIPTURE

Read *Psalm 148:1–14* to praise the beauty of God's many wonderful creations.

GO online **www.osvcurriculum.com** For weekly scripture readings and seasonal resources

Activity
Live Your Faith

Notice Signs of the Season Take a family walk or hike to look for signs of the season. Listen to the sounds, look for changes, and take in the beauty of God's creation. Discuss how these signs of the season in nature reflect the liturgical season as well. Pray a simple prayer of thanks as you list each sign of the season. Then celebrate with a snack or meal.

▲ Saint Bede
673–735

People of Faith

Bede was born in Sunderland, England. After he became a monk, Bede studied the Scriptures. He wrote many lessons about the Bible and explained ways to reform the Church. Bede also became an expert in the history of the English Church. When he realized that he was dying, Bede worked hard and finished translating the Gospel of John into English. The feast day of Saint Bede is May 25.

Family Prayer

O God, help us grow closer to you by our worship at the Eucharist, our learning of our Catholic faith, and our devotion to prayer. Amen.

In Unit 6 your child is learning about SACRAMENTS.
178 CCC See Catechism of the Catholic Church 1067–1068, 1168–1171 for further reading on chapter content.

 ## HOW DID I DO?

My session was

☐ *one of the best ever!* ☐ *pretty good.* ☐ *in need of improvement.*

In what discussions and activities were students most interested?

_____

What activity did I most enjoy teaching?

_____

In what area do I need to improve?

_____

Name ________________________ Date ____________

Seasons and Feast Days

Place the feast day (special day) in its correct season by writing it beneath the name of the season. Consult the current lectionary or a liturgical calendar if you have difficulty placing some feasts.

Advent

Christmas

Lent

Triduum

Easter

Ordinary Time

Immaculate Conception
Christ the King
Ascension
Epiphany
Holy Family
Saint Nicholas
Holy Thursday

Assumption of Mary
Ash Wednesday
Baptism of Jesus
Pentecost
Triduum
Good Friday
Holy Saturday

Answers can be found in the back of the Catechist Manual.

Overview

Faith Focus

- The Church recognizes seven sacraments. *(CCC 1210)*
- The Sacrament of the Eucharist is at the heart of Christian life. *(CCC 1407)*

Catechism Connection

The *Catechism* explains that the Eucharist unites all believers on earth with those in heaven. *(CCC 1370)*

NDC Link

Catechesis prepares for and leads to the liturgy, as well as springs from it. Liturgical catechesis leads to a deeper understanding of the meaning of the liturgy and the sacraments. (See *NDC*, 33.)

Resources

 BOOK
*Catholic Bible Stories for Children.** Ball, Ann with Will, Julianne M. Our Sunday Visitor. Stories of witness, worship, and tradition build on faith formation.

DVD/VHS
This Sacred Meal (21 min.). Twenty-Third Publications. A catechist shares the meaning of the Eucharist with an RCIA candidate.

*Available at www.osvcurriculum.com

GO online **Catechist Resources**
www.osvcurriculum.com
For interactive lesson planner, chapter resources, and activities

 The cup of blessing that we bless, is it not a participation in the blood of Christ? The bread that we break, is it not a participation in the body of Christ?

1 Corinthians 10:16

Signs and Symbols

Signs and symbols are staples of communication. People use signs to welcome and to warn. Symbols can be as disparate as birthday candles and wedding rings. Signs and symbols point to realities that are greater and richer than the symbols themselves. Sacraments bring about these realities.

Spiritual realities are manifested through symbols as well. The sacraments are filled with symbols of many types. These include signs of the physical world: fire, water, light, and darkness; rituals taken from daily actions: washing, eating, and drinking; and ancient signs from God's earliest covenants: anointing and the laying on of hands. In all these ways and more, the Church celebrates the origin of the sacraments in Jesus. Through the sacraments, believers are enveloped in the mystery of God.

Eucharist

Eucharist is a word with many levels of meaning. When translated literally, it means "thanksgiving." When you celebrate the Eucharist, you share a sacred meal, offer yourself in sacrifice in union with Christ, remember the saving actions of Jesus, and praise and thank God for acting on your behalf.

At the very heart of the faith, Catholics are first, finally, and always people of the Eucharist.

Reflect How does the Eucharist increase your participation in the Body of Christ?

Signs of God's Presence

The sacraments are rituals that celebrate life, bring Christ's life into the present, and encourage Catholics to live as Jesus did. When you teach about the sacraments, tell students that these are the ways Catholics root their lives in the actions of Jesus.

- Teach with concrete symbols. Bring in a Bible, water, a candle, oil, and a stole as tangible reminders of God's desire to be present in the lives of his people.

- To help students understand the concept, ask them to think of times when they have seen someone "live the sacraments"—for example, a family member caring for a relative who is elderly.

- Remind students that the Lord wants them to be a physical presence of his love in the world.

Working with Others

- I like to be helpful. Show me ways to serve others.

- I am growing aware of the community around me. Tell me about services for people in need.

- I enjoy social activities. Include classroom activities that let me talk and work with others.

Remember Who You Are

You can be overwhelmed by the religious, educational, and emotional expectations of others. Unless you adapt to the challenge of superhuman expectations, you may become fatigued and ineffective.

You may not be able to change others' superhuman expectations of you, but you can practice remembering who you are. This means intentionally reclaiming what you do best and what you care most about.

Remembering who you are encompasses including tasks in your life that come naturally, so that you preserve those sources of fulfillment.

Reflect *Which of your natural talents or interests do you need to remember and reclaim?*

 Catechist's Prayer

Loving God, the signs of your presence are all around me.
Help me see them with new eyes and understand them afresh.
Amen.

Weekly Planner

Objectives	Lesson Process	Materials

1 Invite

10 minutes

Page 179
Objective:
To recognize that symbols can be reminders of special people

Let Us Pray: Psalm 104:31
- Pray the psalm.
- Discuss the meaning of the story.
- Share memories of special people.

2 Explore

40 minutes

Pages 180–181
Objective:
To learn how the sacraments are effective signs of God's presence

Scripture: John 14:6–7
- Proclaim the scripture story.
- Articulate what the seven sacraments celebrate.
- **Activity** Complete the Share Your Faith Activity.

Words of Faith sacraments

Materials:
- ☐ Index cards
- ☐ Board or chart paper
- ☐ Pens or pencils

Pages 182–183
Objective:
To learn that the Eucharist is a call to live as Jesus did

Scripture: 22:17–20
- Compare the Last Supper and the Eucharist.
- Discuss how the Eucharist calls people to live.
- **Activity** Complete the Connect Your Faith Activity.

Words of Faith Eucharist

Materials:
- ☐ Self-stick notes

3 Celebrate

10 minutes

Page 184
Objective:
To pray to thank God

Let Us Pray
- Rehearse the music.
- Gather as a community.
- Celebrate a Prayer of Thanks.
- **Hymn:** "Song of the Body of Christ"

Activity Complete the Act of Contrition Activity, page 242 and 243

Materials:
- ☐ Bible
- ☐ Hymnals
- ☐ Music CD

Wrap Up

Review and Apply

Page 185
- Review the chapter concepts.
- Complete the Live Your Faith Activity.

Family Faith

Page 186
- Introduce the page, and assign it as a family activity.
- Read about Saint Margaret Mary Alacoque.

ACRE Connection, Domain 3—Sacraments

Home Connection

GO online **www.osvcurriculum.com**
Family Faith activities, feasts and seasonal resources, saint features, and much more

CALL to FAITH e connect

- Online planning tools include chapter background and planner, activity master, customizable test, and more.
- Enhancement activities for each step of the catechetical process, including alternative prayer experiences and blessings.
- Games, activities, interactive review, alternative assessment, and more for child

www.calltofaitheconnect.com

Chapter 17 — The Seven Sacraments

Let Us Pray

Leader: Lord, we see your mightiness in the works you have done.

"May the glory of the LORD endure forever; may the LORD be glad in these works!"

Psalm 104:31

All: Lord, we see your mightiness in the works you have done. Amen.

Activity — Let's Begin

I Will Remember Juana's favorite time of year is spring. Every spring Juana and her *abuela,* or grandmother, would garden together. This spring was different. Abuela died during the winter, and Juana missed her very much.

One day Juana walked past the flower bed and noticed buds on the green shoots. "Those are the flowers from the bulbs Abuela and I planted in the fall!" she thought. "When I see them, I will remember that she is living with God now."

- What things remind you of the special people in your life when they are not with you? **Responses will vary.**

179

 **1 Invite**

Objective: To recognize that symbols can be reminders of special people

 **Let Us Pray**

Have students gather in the prayer space. Invite them to pray the psalm verse together, loudly and joyfully.

Activity

- Invite a student to read aloud the story.
- Ask why the flowers in Juana's garden were signs to her that her *abuela* was living with God. Responses will vary.
- Discuss the question that follows the story. Allow each student time to share. Tell students that remembering people is a sign of love.

OPTIONAL ACTIVITY

Signs After students discuss the question on the page, suggest that they write poems that remind them of the special people in their lives.

- Choose one poem, and ask students to sing it to the tune of a popular song.

Multiple Intelligence: Musical

 CULTURAL AWARENESS

Dia de los Muertos People from Hispanic cultures often assemble home altars, which are decorated for November 1, Dia de los Muertos (Day of the Dead).

- This is a day for remembering loved ones who have died.
- The altars often feature the loved one's pictures, favorite foods, flowers, and belongings.

Objective: To learn how the sacraments are effective signs of God's presence

 **Focus**

What is a sacrament? List students' responses on the board or on chart paper.

God's Love Is Present

Read aloud the introductory paragraphs.

- Ask students what signs of God's presence they have seen today and what the signs tell them. Responses will vary.

- Ask students to listen as you tell them about a special sign that God sent to the whole world. Then proclaim the scripture verses.

- Encourage students to memorize *John 14:6–7* to help them remember that Jesus is the way to the Father.

- Read aloud the remaining paragraph.

- Have student partners discuss the question. Then ask the pairs to share their answers with the class.

Explore

 Faith Fact

When Germans and Saracens were about to invade Assisi, Saint Clare stood atop the city's walls, holding the Blessed Sacrament as a protection. When the invaders saw her, they ran away.

God's Love Is Present

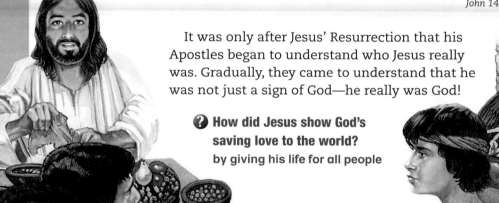 **Focus** What is a Sacrament?

The flowers in Juana's garden were signs to her that her *abuela* still lived with God and was loved by him. God the Father sent Jesus into the world as a sign of his love for all people. He pointed the way to God for all who followed him.

Jesus welcomed people like Peter and Zacchaeus, and they changed their lives for him. Jesus showed people God the Father's forgiveness. He healed some and called others to serve God's people. Through Jesus' words and actions, many people experienced God's saving love. Jesus made God and his love present.

Jesus said this to his Apostles at the Last Supper.

✝ **SCRIPTURE**

No one comes to the Father except through me. If you know me, then you will also know my Father. From now on you do know him and have seen him.

John 14:6–

It was only after Jesus' Resurrection that his Apostles began to understand who Jesus really was. Gradually, they came to understand that he was not just a sign of God—he really was God!

❓ **How did Jesus show God's saving love to the world?**
by giving his life for all people

180

 CATECHIST BACKGROUND

Symbol   A symbol is something visible that allows people to look beyond the message of their senses to a deeper meaning.

- The symbols used in liturgies—candles, bread, wine, oil, water, and so on—are connections between God's creation and humans, his loyal followers who use the symbols.

 SCRIPTURE BACKGROUND

John 14:6–7   These verses are preceded by an appeal to believe in Jesus, not only because of his words, but also because of his deeds.

- *John 14:6–7* emphasizes that Jesus is the means of salvation.

- By knowing Jesus, Christians will know God the Father, because the Father and the Son are one God with the Spirit in the Trinity.

Signs of God's Love

Jesus told his followers that he would always be with them and that they would continue his saving work. One of the ways that Jesus is with his people today is through the seven **Sacraments**. The Sacraments are actions of the Holy Spirit at work in Christ's Body, the Church. Jesus is present in the Sacraments.

The Church has named seven Sacraments that have their origins in Jesus. Each one celebrates a way that Jesus' saving work continues in the world.

The Seven Sacraments

Baptism	New life in Christ
Confirmation	Strengthening through the Holy Spirit
Eucharist	Unity and salvation in Christ through the Body and Blood of Christ
Reconciliation	Conversion and forgiveness through Christ
Anointing of the Sick	Healing in Christ
Holy Orders	Ministry to Christ's Body, the Church
Matrimony	Marriage covenant as a sign of Christ's covenant with his Church

Activity

Share Your Faith

Reflect: Think of someone you love.

Share: Sketch a sign that reminds you of the person. Explain the sign to the class as you say the name.

Act: With your classmates, play a game matching the signs and names.

181

Signs of God's Love

Introduce the page by saying that Jesus promised that he would be with his followers even after he died.

- Read aloud the paragraph. Have students listen to find out how Jesus is present with his followers today.
- Ask volunteers to share experiences of celebrating the sacraments.
- Have students read the second paragraph silently.
- Have students read the definition of *sacraments* silently, and ask them to make vocabulary cards for *sacraments*.
- Call students' attention to the chart of the sacraments.

Activity

- Allow time for students to sketch their signs.
- Ask students to talk about their sketches.
- Tell students to play the matching game.

Quick Review

Jesus is with his people today through the Church's seven sacraments.

★ REACHING ALL LEARNERS

Assistance When the lesson calls for a hands-on activity, you may wish to assign partners to students who have special needs.

- Most students like to maintain a degree of independence.
- Do not assume that help is needed; ask the student whether he or she would like help and, if so, how much and what kind.

Objective: To learn that the Eucharist is a call to live as Jesus did

 **Focus**

What is the heart of Christian life? List students' responses on the board or on chart paper.

Eucharist

Tell students that they will now focus on the Sacrament of the Eucharist.

The Last Supper

Proclaim the Scripture.

- As an alternative, you may wish to use "The Last Supper" in *Guided Meditations for Children* (Jane Reehorst BVM, Our Sunday Visitor Curriculum Division, page 220).

- Ask where students have heard these words of Jesus before. at Mass

Breaking of the Bread

Have students read silently to learn more about the Eucharist.

- Discuss the question.

Explore

Eucharist

 **Focus** What is the heart of the Christian life?

Jesus often ate meals with his friends. On the night before he died, Jesus shared a meal with his Apostles and asked them to remember him always.

✝ SCRIPTURE — Luke 22:17–2

The Last Supper

Then [Jesus] took a cup, gave thanks, and said, "Take this and share it among yourselves; for I tell you [that] from this time on I shall not drink of the fruit of the vine until the kingdom of God comes." Then he took the bread, said the blessing, broke it, and gave it to them, saying, "This is my body, which will be given for you; do this in memory of me." And likewise the cup after they had eaten, saying, "This cup is the new covenant in my blood, which will be shed for you."

Luke 22:17–

Breaking of the Bread

After Jesus was raised from the dead and returne to the Father, his followers gathered weekly for a special meal. They called this meal the "breaking of the bread." They believed, as Catholics do today, tha Jesus was present when they broke bread together. Today this meal is called the **Eucharist**, or Mass.

❓ **When did you first receive Jesus in Holy Communion Tell what you remember about the day.**
Responses will vary.

182

✝ SCRIPTURE BACKGROUND

The Institution Narratives The institution of the Sacrament of the Eucharist is related in this important passage, as well as in verses from the Gospels according to Matthew and Mark.

- *Matthew 26:26–29* states that Christ's blood "will be shed on behalf of many for the forgiveness of sins."

- *Mark 14:22–25* does not have the phrase "for the forgiveness of sins."

The Eucharist

The word *Eucharist* means "thanksgiving." At the beginning of Mass, you ask God's mercy because of your sins. Your venial sins can be forgiven through your celebration of the Eucharist. You listen to God's word. You thank God the Father for the great gift of his Son. When you receive Jesus in Holy Communion, you are united with the other members of the Body of Christ.

Living the Eucharist

When Jesus told the Apostles to "do this in memory of me," he did not mean only that they should break bread together. He meant that they should live their lives as he did. Living the Eucharist means loving, welcoming, and forgiving others. You live the Eucharist when you share with those who do not have what you do.

? **What are some ways that you can live the Eucharist?** Possible responses: give to charity, follow Jesus' example, show love

Words of Faith

Eucharist is the Sacrament through which Catholics are united with the life, death, and Resurrection of Jesus.

Activity Connect Your Faith

Dinner Guests Think of people you would like to have as company for dinner at your house, and write their names on the chairs. In the space on the table, write what you might do to welcome them and show them the love of Jesus.

183

The Eucharist

Have students read this paragraph to learn the meaning of the word *Eucharist* and what happens during the celebration of the sacrament.

• Ask students to make vocabulary cards for *Eucharist.*

Living the Eucharist

Ask students what the words *Living the Eucharist* mean. Accept all reasonable responses.

• Explain that Jesus is present to his followers in the Eucharist and that he expects them to live a certain way. Then read aloud the paragraph.

• Discuss the question in the text.

Activity

• Read aloud the directions for the activity.

• Invite volunteers to share responses.

◎ Quick Review

The Eucharist unites Jesus with his followers. Living the Eucharist means continuing Jesus' work in the world.

✚ JUSTICE AND PEACE

Eucharist The U.S. Conference of Catholic Bishops calls Catholics to be "engaged and challenged, encouraged and empowered" to live the faith every day (*Sharing Catholic Social Teaching*, p. 9).

• Give each student a self-stick note on which to write one way that he or she might bring Christ's love to the world.

Catholic Social Teaching: Call to Community

OPTIONAL ACTIVITY

Unselfish Acts In the Eucharist, the faithful are called to give of themselves for others.

• Distribute newspapers.

• Ask students to find articles that describe people who sacrificed to help others.

• Encourage students to perform unselfish acts, such as helping with chores instead of playing.

Multiple Intelligence: Interpersonal

3 Celebrate

> **Objective:** To pray to thank God

 **Let Us Pray**

Tell students that today they will pray to thank God for his love.

Prayer of Thanks

Prepare

Choose a reader for the celebration. Today, you will be the leader.

 Use the *Call to Faith 4* CD, track 17, to rehearse the suggested song.

Gather

Move into the prayer space.

Pray

- Follow the order of prayer on page 184.
- Optional Bible readings are *Ephesians 1:3–10* and *James 1:22–25*.
- Leader's concluding prayer: **Jesus, we thank you for your loving sacrifice. Help us live in the spirit of the Eucharist.**

Celebrate

Prayer of Thanks

 **Let Us Pray**

Gather and begin with the Sign of the Cross.

Reader:	The Lord be with you.
All:	**And with your spirit.**
Reader:	Lift up your hearts.
All:	**We lift them up to the Lord.**
Reader:	Let us give thanks to the Lord our God.
All:	**It is right and just.**

 Sing together.

We come to share our story,
  we come to break the bread,
We come to know our rising from the dead.

"Song of the Body of Christ" © 2001, GIA Publications, Inc.

Reader:	Because you love us, you gave us this great and beautiful world.
All:	*Sing refrain.*
Reader:	Because you love us, you sent Jesus your Son to bring us to you.
All:	*Sing refrain.*
Leader:	Let us pray. *Bow your heads as the leader prays.*
All:	**Amen.**

184

 LITURGY LINK

Offering When members of the assembly bring forward the gifts, everyone is reminded of the need to offer themselves to God.

- Perhaps an offering could be part of your prayer celebration.

- Invite students to bring nonperishable food items when they gather for prayer.

LECTIONARY LINK

Break Open the Word Read last week's Sunday Gospel. Invite students to think about what the reading means to them as they try to follow Christ's example. For questions related to the weekly Gospel reading, visit our website at **www.osvcurriculum.com**.

 GO online Visit **www.osvcurriculum.com** for weekly Scripture readings and seasonal resources.

Review and Apply

A **Check Understanding**   Circle True if a statement is true, and circle False if a statement is false. Correct any false statements.

1. There are eight Sacraments.
   True   (False)   **There are seven.**

2. Jesus is present in all of the Sacraments.
   (True)   False _____

3. The early Christians did not celebrate the Eucharist.
   True   (False)   **Early Christians gathered weekly for the Eucharist.**

4. Eucharist means "thanksgiving."
   (True)   False _____

5. When you live the Eucharist, you continue Jesus' work in the world.
   (True)   False _____

B **Make Connections**   Why are the Sacraments called saving actions?

Responses will vary.

_____
_____
_____
_____
_____

Activity   Live Your Faith

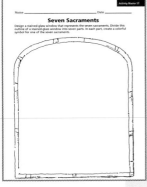

Make a Eucharist Poster   Create a poster for your parish bulletin board for people to see as they come to Mass.

• Title the poster "Living the Eucharist."

• On the poster, draw several ways people can live the Eucharist.

185

Review and Apply

Using the focus questions from the catechist Explore pages, review the lesson concepts.

A **Check Understanding**   Have students label the statements as true or false and correct any false statements.

B **Make Connections**   Then ask each student to write his or her response to the question. Have volunteers share their responses.

Activity

• Allow time for students to begin the activity.

• You may wish to use this time for a planning session for the activity, with the poster to be completed later.

OPTIONAL ACTIVITY

Activity Master 17: Seven Sacraments   Distribute copies of the activity found on catechist page 186A.

• This activity reviews sacraments and the idea of symbols.

• As an alternative, you may wish to send this activity home with students.

▲ **Activity Master 17**

Family Faith

Remind students to discuss the Family Faith page at home. Encourage students to read the psalm.

Activity

• Invite a volunteer to read aloud the directions.

• Remind students to take their lists with them the next time they attend Mass.

People of Faith

Tell students about Saint Margaret Mary Alacoque.

• The devotion to the Sacred Heart did not begin with Saint Margaret Mary Alacoque; the observance dates back to the thirteenth century. Devotion grew, however, through Margaret Mary and her visions.

• Remind students to add Saint Margaret Mary Alacoque to their People of Faith albums. Encourage them to pray the prayer at home.

 Visit **www.osvcurriculum.com** for weekly scripture readings and seasonal resources.

UNIT 6: CHAPTER 17

Family Faith

Catholics Believe

■ The seven Sacraments are signs, instituted by Christ, that give grace.

■ The Sacrament of the Eucharist is at the heart of Christian life.

✝ **SCRIPTURE**

Read *Psalm 107* as a way to give thanks to God for his blessings.

GO online www.osvcurriculum.com
For weekly scripture readings and seasonal resources

Activity

Live Your Faith

Create a Thank-you List In the Eucharistic Prayer you hear the words "Lift up your hearts" and "Let us give thanks to the Lord our God." Make a list of things for which you offer thanks to God. Remember these things the next time you participate in the Eucharist.

People of Faith

Margaret Mary Alacoque was born into a peasant family in France. When she joined a convent, Margaret Mary developed a deep prayer life. She had several visions in which Jesus told her about his loving heart. Devotion to the Sacred Heart of Jesus, which includes participating in Mass and receiving the Eucharist on the first Friday of each month, developed and grew in the Church because of her inspiration. Her feast day is October 16.

▲ **Saint Margaret Mary Alacoque 1647–1690**

Family Prayer

Saint Margaret Mary Alacoque, pray for us that we may deepen our prayer lives and our devotion to the Eucharist. Amen.

In Unit 6 your child is learning about SACRAMENTS.
186 **CCC** *See Catechism of the Catholic Church 1210, 1407 for further reading on chapter content.*

? HOW DID I DO?

My session was

☐ *one of the best ever!* ☐ *pretty good.* ☐ *in need of improvement.*

In what discussions and activities were students most interested?

_____

What activity did I most enjoy teaching?

_____

In what area do I need to improve?

_____

Name _____ Date _____

Seven Sacraments

Design a stained-glass window that represents the seven sacraments. Divide this outline of a stained-glass window into seven parts. In each part, create a colorful symbol for one of the seven sacraments.

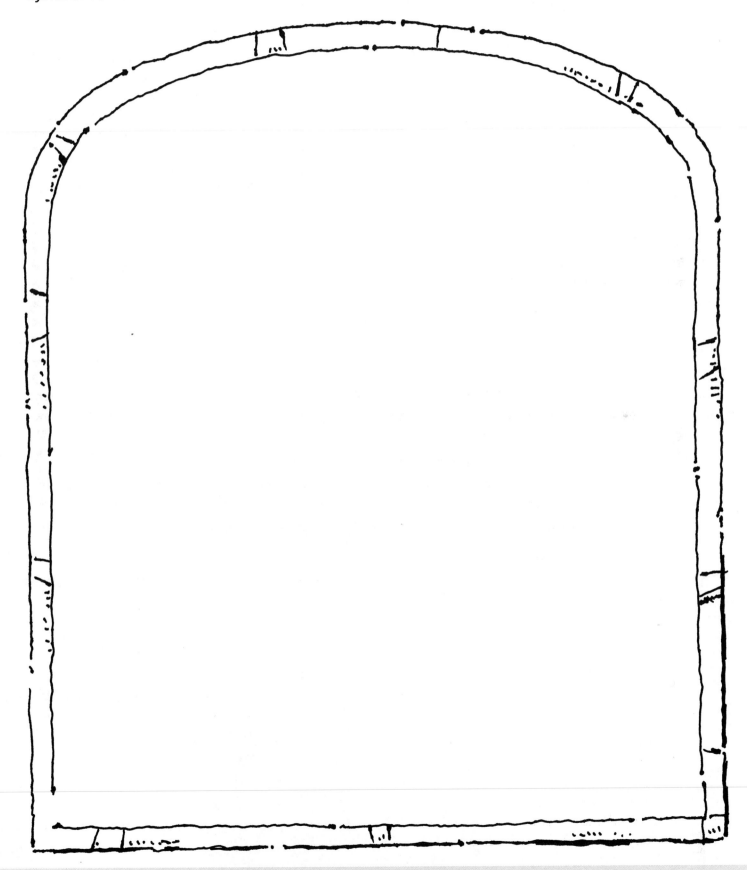

Overview

Faith Focus

- **God offers forgiveness to all who seek it.** *(CCC 1489)*
- **The Sacrament of Penance and Reconciliation and the Sacraments of Anointing of the Sick celebrate God's healing love.** *(CCC 1421)*

Catechism Connection

The *Catechism* calls Jesus Christ the "physician of our souls and bodies." *(CCC 1421)*

NDC Link

The *Directory* explains that catechesis is enhanced by recognizing various ethnic and cultural expressions of rituals and customs throughout the liturgical year. (See *NDC*, 37A.)

Resources

BOOK
70 Sacrament Starters for Children. * Twenty-Third Publications. Offers creative ways to celebrate and learn about each of the seven sacraments.

DVD/VHS
*Inspired: Stories and Songs Inspired by the Scriptures.** Our Sunday Visitor Curriculum Division. "The Nosy Neighbor" (8:35 min.). Uses an interesting perspective to convey how people felt about a miracle.

*Available at www.osvcurriculum.com

GO online Catechist Resources
www.osvcurriculum.com
For interactive lesson planner, chapter resources, and activities

 And all this is from God, who has reconciled us to himself through Christ and given us the ministry of reconciliation.

2 Corinthians 5:18

The Healing Sacraments

The Church's Sacraments of Healing are Penance and the Anointing of the Sick. Humans are fallible and fragile on many levels. On one level, their bodies grow older and deteriorate; debilitating illnesses may come gradually or suddenly. On another level, people sometimes choose to do an immoral act because it is easier or because they do not want to appear "different." They sin, and their consciences grow callous.

God's plan for humans, body and soul, flesh and spirit, is to be whole and well. He knows your physical and spiritual weaknesses and responds by offering you his healing grace. Jesus was a healer. He gave his Church the mission of continuing his healing ministry by the power of the Holy Spirit. The Sacraments of Healing make you strong as you travel forward on your journey of faith.

Forgiving and Reconciling

Forgiving and reconciling are closely related, but quite distinct. Forgiveness involves letting go of sin and accepting God's forgiveness. It means getting past hurt and anger; it is the choice to change your thoughts, attitudes, and actions toward another person. Reconciliation means restoring the relationship. Reconciliation brings friends, families, and even nations together again. When you reconcile, you reconnect to others —and to God, whose arms are always open and ready to receive you.

Reflect **When do you feel the need to reconnect with God?**

Forgiveness

Fourth graders have a strong sense of right and wrong and want things to be "fair." They understand making up after an argument when both parties agree to do so. It is unusual, however, for a fourth grader to reach out with forgiveness to someone who has not asked to be forgiven. God's forgiveness, based on mercy, may not seem logical to fourth graders.

- Use examples from Jesus' life to show how forgiving Jesus was.

- Challenge students to imagine ways they can follow Jesus' example of forgiveness in their own lives.

- The Sacrament of Penance and Reconciliation is a real way for students to experience God's love and forgiveness. Encourage them to celebrate this sacrament regularly.

- Review the ritual with them. Schedule a time for your group to celebrate the sacrament.

Learning to Forgive

- Fairness is important to me. Make sure that everyone knows the rules.

- Sometimes it is not easy for me to forgive. Remind me when I forget.

- Using signs like the sign of peace helps me understand the meaning of forgiveness. Include them in our lessons.

Accepting Mediocrity

Acceptance of mediocrity is the quietest and most harmful of all the challenges you face. Accepting mediocrity makes you ineffective and may eventually lead to apathy.

Whether mediocrity is found in colleagues who have lowered expectations, materials that are inadequate, or environments that are in disrepair, its lullaby is the same: "It's good enough."

Testimony is the courageous practice of making a public statement—to one person or many, with words or with actions—that "It's not good enough for me." Even if you don't know how to improve a situation, truthfully testifying that something is not good enough strengthens the fire of your spirit.

Reflect **To what area of mediocrity might you now need to apply the practice of Testimony?**

 Catechist's Prayer

Generous God, your love for me is immeasurable. Help me remember all of the forgiveness and mercy you have offered me. Amen.

Weekly Planner

	Objectives	Lesson Process	Materials

1 Invite

10 minutes

Page 187
Objective:
To consider the meaning of forgiveness

🎁 **Let Us Pray:** Psalm 25:6
- Pray the psalm verse.
- Discuss and define *forgiveness*.
- Complete sentences regarding forgiveness.

2 Explore

40 minutes

Pages 188–189
Objective:
To recognize whom God forgives

✝ **Scripture:** Luke 19:1–10
- Read the story of Zacchaeus.
- Reflect on Jesus' actions toward outcasts.
- **Activity** Complete the Share Your Faith Activity.

Words of Faith Sacrament of Reconciliation

Materials:
- ☐ Board or chart paper
- ☐ Index cards
- ☐ Pencils or pens

Pages 190–191
Objective:
To identify how the Church celebrates forgiveness and healing

✝ **Scripture:** John 9:1–38
- Learn about the Sacrament of Reconciliation.
- Proclaim a scripture story about healing.
- **Activity** Complete the Connect Your Faith Activity.

Words of Faith absolution, penance, Sacrament of the Anointing of the Sick

Materials:
- ☐ Copies of Activity Master 18 on page 194A

3 Celebrate

10 minutes

Page 192
Objective:
To pray for the peace of forgiveness

🎁 **Let Us Pray**
- Rehearse the music.
- Gather as a community.
- Celebrate a Prayer for Peace.
- 🎵 **Hymn:** "Go Now in Peace"

- **Activity** Complete the Reconciliation Activity, page 232 and 233

Materials:
- ☐ Hymnals
- ☐ Music CD
- ☐ Flashlights (optional)
- ☐ Bible

Wrap Up

Review and Apply

Page 193
- Review the chapter concepts.
- Complete the Live Your Faith Activity.

Family Faith

Page 194
- Introduce the page, and assign it as a family activity.
- Read about Matt Talbot.

ACRE Connection, Domain 3—Sacraments of Healing

Home Connection

GO online www.osvcurriculum.com
Family Faith activities, feasts and seasonal resources, saint features, and much more

- Online planning tools include chapter background and planner, activity master, customizable test, and more.
- Enhancement activities for each step of the catechetical process, including alternative prayer experiences and blessings.
- Games, activities, interactive review, alternative assessment, and more for children

www.calltofaitheconnect.com

Chapter 18 Healing and Reconciliation

Let Us Pray

Leader: Merciful God, be always with us as we pray.
"Remember your compassion and love,
O Lᴏʀᴅ;
for they are ages old."

Psalm 25:6

All: Merciful God, be always with us as we pray. Amen.

 **Activity** **Let's Begin**

Forgiveness How would you complete these sentences?

• Forgiveness is easy when . . .

• Forgiveness is difficult when . . .

• I can always forgive . . .

• When I forgive, I . . .

• When I am forgiven, I . . .
Responses will vary.

1 Invite

Objective: To consider the meaning of forgiveness

Let Us Pray

Invite students to gather in the prayer space. Review with them what the word *compassion* means. Together, repeat the psalm verse slowly and prayerfully.

Activity

• Organize students in groups of three. Have the groups discuss each statement about forgiveness.

• Invite representatives of the groups to report on their discussions.

• Tell students that forgiveness is one kind of healing. Say that the Church offers many kinds of healing, including forgiveness.

 OPTIONAL ACTIVITY

Forgiveness Tell students that Christians embody forgiveness by showing a spirit of compassion.

• Point out that the Lord's Prayer both asks forgiveness and reminds Christians to forgive.

• Have students make bookmarks that say "Forgive us as we forgive others." Ask students to use their bookmarks as they read this chapter.

Multiple Intelligence: Interpersonal

 JUSTICE AND PEACE

Catholic Teaching In *Communities of Salt and Light,* the U.S. Conference of Catholic Bishops calls the pursuit of justice and peace "an essential part" of what being Catholic means.

• Apply the concepts to the wider world.

• Point out the need for forgiveness when you see it in neighborhood or world events.

Catholic Social Teaching: Call to Community

Healing and Reconciliation 187

Objective: To recognize whom God forgives

 Focus

Who is forgiven? List students' responses on the board or on chart paper.

God's Forgiveness

Have students silently read the introductory paragraph. As they listen to the story, ask them to think about how Jesus changed Zacchaeus.

The Story of Zacchaeus

Read aloud the story.

- Ask students why Zacchaeus was unpopular. He cheated people.

- Ask students how Zacchaeus changed after he met Jesus. He repaid those he had cheated and gave money to those who were poor.

- Point out that Jesus offered friendship, and that this led to the change in Zacchaeus.

- Discuss the questions.

Explore

God's Forgiveness

 Focus Who is forgiven?

Jesus showed God's forgiveness to others through words and actions. In this story, Jesus meets a wealt[h] tax collector who decides to become his follower.

✝ SCRIPTURE   Luke 1[9]

The Story of Zacchaeus

One day Jesus was passing through the town of Jeri[cho]. Zacchaeus, a rich tax collector, wanted to see Jesus a[nd] learn about him. Zacchaeus was short, so he climbed [a] tree to see past the crowd.

Jesus noticed Zacchaeus in the tree. He said, "Zacchaeus, come down quickly, for today I must sta[y at] your house." Zacchaeus came down happily.

The crowd complained, saying that Jesus should n[ot] stay with Zacchaeus because Zacchaeus was a sinne[r.]

Zacchaeus told Jesus that he would give money to those who were poor. He offered to give anyone he had cheated four times the amount of money that he owed to that person.

"Today salvation has come to this house," said Jesus. "For the Son of Man has come to seek and to save what was lost."

Based on Luke 19:1–10

❓ **Who has taught you the most about forgiveness? What did the person or persons say or do?** Responses will vary.

188

✝ SCRIPTURE BACKGROUND

Zacchaeus The rich tax collector in this story, Zacchaeus, provides a contrast to the rich young man who would not follow Jesus because he would not give up his possessions.

- Zacchaeus got rich by cheating people.

- After encountering Jesus, he exemplifies a right attitude toward wealth.

Turn to God

God is always ready and waiting to forgive. When you decide to turn away from sin and turn back toward God, you are experiencing conversion. God welcomes you back, just as Jesus welcomed Zacchaeus.

During his life Jesus forgave many people in his Father's name. After his Resurrection, Jesus told his disciples that he would send the Holy Spirit, who would give them the power to forgive sins. Today the Church continues to celebrate God's forgiveness in the **Sacrament of Reconciliation**. Sometimes this is called Penance or Confession. In this Sacrament, you receive God's forgiveness of sins through the Church. The grace of this Sacrament strengthens you to make peace with those whom you may have hurt.

Words of Faith

The **Sacrament of Reconciliation** celebrates God's mercy and forgiveness and a sinner's reconciliation with God and with the Church through the absolution of the priest.

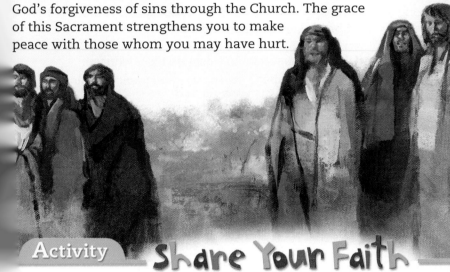

Activity

Share Your Faith

Reflect: Think of someone who has forgiven you. Why did you need forgiveness?

Share: In groups discuss ways to show you are sorry and make peace with others.

Act: List two ways that you can be more forgiving of others.

Responses will vary.

Turn to God

Read aloud the first paragraph to reinforce the message of the story of Zacchaeus.

- Point out the word *conversion*. Tell students that it means "a change of heart."
- Ask students who in the story experienced conversion. Zacchaeus
- Have students read the second paragraph silently to learn how the Church continues Jesus' actions.
- Have students make vocabulary cards for the *Sacrament of Penance and Reconciliation* to add to their packets.

Activity

- Allow ample time for this activity because it applies the lesson on forgiveness directly to students' lives.

Quick Review

Jesus showed God's love and forgiveness to Zacchaeus. The Church offers God's forgiveness through the Sacrament of Penance.

REACHING ALL LEARNERS

Partner Reading   When students read independently, pair a more proficient reader with a less proficient reader. Proficient readers can read aloud while their partners follow along.

- Remind readers to use inside voices.
- Have students who followed along state the most important ideas.

OPTIONAL ACTIVITY

Forgiveness Booklets   Help students make small booklets by stapling folded sheets of paper together.

- Have students write about times when they have experienced or granted forgiveness.
- Ask students to illustrate their stories.

Multiple Intelligence: Visual/Spatial

Objective: To identify how the Church celebrates forgiveness and healing

 Focus

How does the Church celebrate forgiveness and healing? List students' responses on the board or on chart paper.

The Sacraments of Healing

Tell students that there is more to learn about how the Church celebrates God's forgiveness.

• Have students read the paragraph silently.

• Point out that God will forgive any sins you confess if you experience real conversion the way Zacchaeus did.

• Discuss the question in the text.

Repairing the Harm

Have students read the paragraph to learn what must be done after celebrating the sacrament.

• Have students make vocabulary cards for *absolution* and *penance*.

The Sacraments of Healing

 Focus How does the Church celebrate forgiveness and healing?

Celebrating the Sacrament of Reconciliation is a public sign that you are willing to turn away from sin and toward the love of God and the community. When you confess your sins to a priest, you ask for God's forgiveness through the power the Holy Spirit gives to the Church. God will forgive all sins, even mortal sins, if you are truly sorry and want to change your heart. When the priest says the words of **absolution**, you know that God has taken your sins away.

❷ **Why is it important to celebrate the Sacrament of Reconciliation?** to help you turn away from sin and toward God

Repairing the Harm

God forgives your sins, but the effects of your sins are still in the world. You must do what you can to repair the harm your sin has caused. Part of making up for your sin is to do the **penance** that the priest gives you.

190

OPTIONAL ACTIVITY

Activity Master 18: What Will Help? Distribute copies of the activity found on catechist page 194A.

• Provide drawing materials so that students can complete the activity.

• As an alternative, you may wish to send this activity home with students.

▲ **Activity Master 18**

God's Healing Love

Today the Church anoints the sick or dying through the **Sacrament of the Anointing of the Sick**. This Sacrament strengthens those who celebrate it and reminds them of God's healing love. God's love and forgiveness are available to all who turn to him.

In Jesus' time, people thought that sickness was God's punishment for someone's sin. But Jesus taught a different message.

✝ SCRIPTURE   John 9:1–38

The Man Born Blind

One day Jesus saw a man who had been blind from birth. His disciples asked him, "Why is this man blind? Is it because of his own sin or that of his parents?"

Jesus answered, "Neither he nor his parents sinned; it is so that the works of God might be made more visible through him."

Jesus rubbed clay on the man's eyes and told him to go to a certain place and wash it off. When the man did, he could see!

Many did not believe that Jesus had done this. When the man came back, Jesus asked the man, "Do you believe in the Son of Man? . . . You have seen him and the one speaking with you is he."

The man answered, "I do believe, Lord."

Based on *John 9:1–38*

Activity | Connect Your Faith

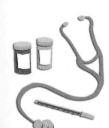

Think About Healing In the space below, name an illness that you've had or that someone you know has had. Then add the people and medicines or other things God has provided for healing.

Responses will vary.

_____

191

Words of Faith

Words of **absolution** are spoken by the priest during the Sacrament of Reconciliation.

Penance is the name for the prayer, offering, or good works the priest gives you in the Sacrament of Reconciliation.

The **Sacrament of the Anointing of the Sick** brings Jesus' healing touch to strengthen, comfort, and forgive the sins of those who are seriously ill or close to death.

God's Healing Love

Have students read the first paragraph to learn about the Sacrament of the Anointing of the Sick.

- Read aloud the second paragraph. Draw the graphic organizer on the board or on chart paper. Ask how students can build their relationships with God. Write their answers on the bridge.

The Man Born Blind

Assign parts, and have students proclaim the Scripture as a readers' theater.

Activity

- Assign the activity.
- Invite volunteers to share their responses.

◎ Quick Review

Reconciliation and the Anointing of the Sick are sacraments that celebrate God's forgiveness and healing.

✝ SCRIPTURE BACKGROUND

Healing The New Testament contains many stories of healing by Jesus and his disciples.

- The Gospels include *Matthew 8:14–15* (the cure of Peter's mother-in-law); *Mark 1:40–45* (the cleansing of a leper); *Luke 8:40–56* (the revival of Jairus's daughter); and *John 11:1–44* (the raising of Lazarus).

- In the Acts of the Apostles, Jesus' followers continue his healing ministry. (See *Acts 3:1–10, 5:12–16, 9:32–43,* and *20:7–12.*)

💡 QUICK TIP

Graphic Organizer

The Church

me — Pray — Value Jesus — Read Scripture — Accept forgiveness — Celebrate sacraments — Grace — **The Trinity**

Celebrate

Objective: To pray for the peace of forgiveness

 Let Us Pray

Tell students that this prayer reflects the concern of Saint Francis for peace in the world.

Prayer for Peace

Prepare

Select four readers.

 Use the *Call to Faith 4* CD, track 18, to rehearse the suggested song.

Gather

Move to the prayer space. If lights are lowered, use flashlights to read.

Pray

• Follow the order of prayer on page 192.

• Optional readings are *1 Corinthians 12:12–31* and *1 John 4:7–12*.

• Leader's concluding prayer: **Lord, grant us the peace of your forgiveness. May we also forgive others and bring peace to them.**

Prayer for Peace

 **Let Us Pray**

Gather and begin with the Sign of the Cross.

Reader 1: Merciful Father, we are together on earth, alone in the universe.

All: **Grant us peace, Lord.**

Reader 2: Look at us and help us love one another. Teach us to understand one another, just as you understand us.

All: **Grant us peace, Lord.**

Reader 3: Make our souls as fresh as the morning. Make our hearts as innocent as a baby's.

All: **Grant us peace, Lord.**

Reader 4: May we forgive one another and forget the past. And may we have peace within—and in our world today and forever.

All: **Grant us peace, Lord.**

Leader: Let us pray.
Bow your heads as the leader prays.

All: **Amen.**

Sing together.

Go now in peace.
Go now in peace.
May the love of God
surround you ev'rywhere,
ev'rywhere you may go.

"Go Now in Peace" ©1976 Hinshaw Music, Inc.

 LITURGY LINK

Setting the Atmosphere Candles have always been used in Catholic worship. To establish a mood that encourages refelctive prayer, use low lighting. Candlelight tends to quiet the atmosphere.

• Turn off most or some of the lights in the room, and use candlelight if local laws allow it.

• If very low lighting can be achieved, use flashlights or a small lamp to provide adequate lighting for readers.

LECTIONARY LINK

Break Open the Word Read last week's Sunday Gospel. Invite students to think about what the reading means to them as they try to follow Christ's example. For questions related to the weekly Gospel reading, visit our website at **www.osvcurriculum.com**.

 GO online Visit www.osvcurriculum.com for weekly Scripture readings and seasonal resources.

Review and Apply

Work with Words Use the clues to solve the puzzle.

Down

1. Welcoming someone back after a wrong has been done

2. These separate you from God and others.

3. This is done for those who are very sick or dying.

5. When you tell the priest your sins, you are really _____ to God.

Across

4. The Sacrament that celebrates God's forgiveness of sins

6. When the priest says this, you know that God has taken your sins away.

7. Deciding to turn away from sin and turn back to God

8. This helps you make up for your sins.

9. _____ is always ready to forgive you.

10. Another name for Reconciliation

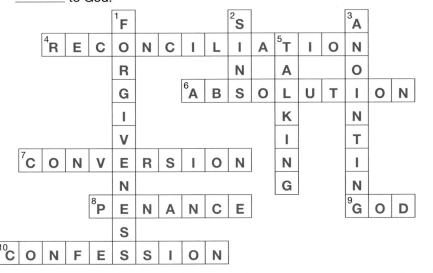

Crossword solution:
- 1 Down: F (FORGIVING)
- 2 Down: S (SINS)
- 3 Down: A (ANOINTING)
- 4 Across: RECONCILIATION
- 5 Down: SAYING
- 6 Across: ABSOLUTION
- 7 Across: CONVERSION
- 8 Across: PENANCE
- 9 Across: GOD
- 10 Across: CONFESSION

Review and Apply

Use the focus questions from the catechist Explore pages to review the lesson concepts.

Work with Words Have students fill in the answers for the crossword puzzle. Remind them that they can refer back to the text. Review the answers.

Activity

- Provide art materials so that students can make and decorate their cards.
- Allow time for students to complete the activity.

Activity Live Your Faith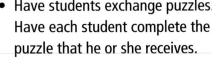

Share Forgiveness Think of a friend or family member who needs to hear a message of forgiveness from you. Create a card with a handwritten message, and deliver it to that person.

193

OPTIONAL ACTIVITY

Puzzles Students enjoy creating their own puzzles.

- They might enjoy using their vocabulary cards to create a review of previous chapters.
- Have students exchange puzzles. Have each student complete the puzzle that he or she receives.

Multiple Intelligence: Mathematical/Logical

Family Faith

Remind students to discuss the Family Faith page at home. Encourage students to read the passage from the Gospel of Matthew.

Activity

- Read aloud the instructions for the yarn game.
- Play a round of the game with students so that they will be able to teach it to their families.

People of Faith

Tell students about Matt Talbot.

- As part of his practice to maintain his sobriety, Matt Talbot prayed faithfully each day and reconciled with many people he had hurt. Matt gave God credit for his conversion and sobriety.
- Remind students to add Matt Talbot to their People of Faith albums. Encourage them to pray the prayer at home with their families.

 GO online Visit **www.osvcurriculum.com** for weekly scripture readings and seasonal resources.

UNIT 6: CHAPTER 18
Family Faith

⊚ Catholics Believe

- God's forgiveness is offered to all who seek it.
- The Sacraments of Reconciliation and the Anointing of the Sick celebrate God's healing love.

✝ SCRIPTURE

Read *Matthew 18:21–35* to learn from Jesus how we should forgive.

GO online www.osvcurriculum.com For weekly scripture readings and seasonal resources

Activity
Live Your Faith

Play the Yarn Game Gather your family in a circle with a ball of yarn. Hold the end of the yarn in one hand and the ball in the other. Hold your end of the yarn and toss the ball to another person. Tell that person you are sorry for something that you did to him or her. Then that person repeats the action with someone else. Repeat the process until you weave a web of forgiveness with the yarn. Pray the Act of Contrition together.

People of Faith

▲ Venerable Matt Talbot 1856–1925

Matt Talbot was born in Dublin, Ireland, to a family that was poor. As he grew up he developed a drinking problem. After years of heavy drinking, Matt decided to become sober. He had hurt and disappointed many of his friends and family members, but he asked their forgiveness. He prayed and practiced self-sacrifice. Matt gave most of his lumberyard wages to people who were poor or hungry. He made a better life for himself and many other people.

In Unit 6 your child is learning about SACRAMENTS.

194 **CCC** *See Catechism of the Catholic Church 1420–1421, 1489–1490 for further reading on chapter content.*

🙌 Family Prayer

O God, give us the grace to overcome our shortcomings, and teach us to be self-sacrificing, as Matt Talbot was. Amen.

❓ HOW DID I DO?

My session was

☐ *one of the best ever!* ☐ *pretty good.* ☐ *in need of improvement.*

In what discussions and activities were students most interested?

_____

What activity did I most enjoy teaching?

_____

In what area do I need to improve?

_____

Name _____ Date _____

What Will Help?

For each picture in the left-hand column, draw a kind of healing that will help the situation.

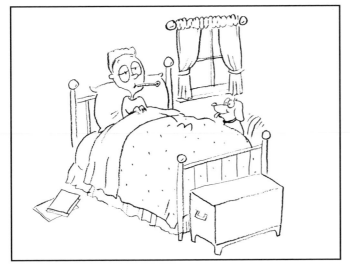

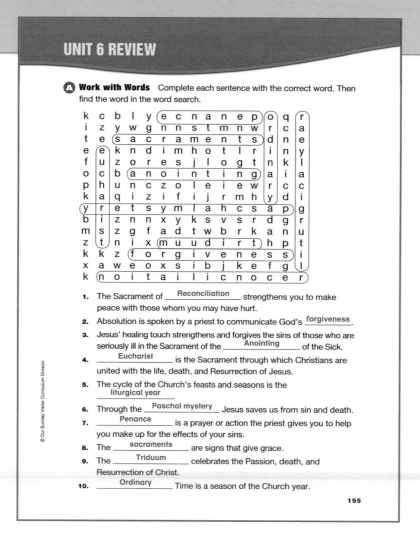

A **Work with Words** Complete each sentence with the correct word. Then find the word in the word search.

```
k  c  b  l  y  e  c  n  a  n  e  p  o  q  r
i  z  y  w  g  n  n  s  t  m  n  w  r  c  a
t  e  s  a  c  r  a  m  e  n  t  s  d  n  e
e  e  k  n  d  i  m  h  o  t  l  r  i  n  y
f  u  z  o  r  e  s  j  l  o  g  t  n  k  l
o  c  b  a  n  o  i  n  t  i  n  g  a  i  a
p  h  u  n  c  z  o  l  e  i  e  w  r  c  c
k  a  q  i  z  i  f  i  j  r  m  h  y  d  i
y  r  e  t  s  y  m  l  a  h  c  s  a  p  g
b  i  z  n  n  x  y  k  s  v  s  r  d  g  r
m  s  z  g  f  a  d  t  w  b  r  k  a  n  u
z  t  n  i  x  m  u  u  d  i  r  t  h  p  t
k  k  z  f  o  r  g  i  v  e  n  e  s  s  i
x  a  w  e  o  x  s  i  b  j  k  e  f  g  l
k  n  o  i  t  a  i  l  i  c  n  o  c  e  r
```

1. The Sacrament of ___Reconciliation___ strengthens you to make peace with those whom you may have hurt.

2. Absolution is spoken by a priest to communicate God's ___forgiveness___.

3. Jesus' healing touch strengthens and forgives the sins of those who are seriously ill in the Sacrament of the ___Anointing___ of the Sick.

4. ___Eucharist___ is the Sacrament through which Christians are united with the life, death, and Resurrection of Jesus.

5. The cycle of the Church's feasts and seasons is the ___liturgical year___.

6. Through the ___Paschal mystery___ Jesus saves us from sin and death.

7. ___Penance___ is a prayer or action the priest gives you to help you make up for the effects of your sins.

8. The ___sacraments___ are signs that give grace.

9. The ___Triduum___ celebrates the Passion, death, and Resurrection of Christ.

10. ___Ordinary___ Time is a season of the Church year.

© Our Sunday Visitor Curriculum Division

195

Unit Review

The Unit Review is designed to prepare students for the Unit Assessment. This page focuses on vocabulary words and the main concepts presented in the chapters.

Each review contains various sections that will appeal to the many different learning styles of your students. There are puzzles to engage students' attention, as well as true-false, multiple-choice, short-answer, and fill-in-the-blank exercises.

Direct students to complete the review, and check their responses. Determine areas in which students still need practice, and review those sections of the unit.

Notes

Name _____ Date _____

The Paschal Mystery

(A) Work with Words   Match each description in Column 1 with the correct term in Column 2.

Column 1

_____ **1.** the cycle of Church feasts and seasons

_____ **2.** strengthens the sick and reminds them of God's love

_____ **3.** the first season of the Church year

_____ **4.** sacramental covenant that a man and a woman celebrate

_____ **5.** forgives sins confessed to a priest

_____ **6.** liturgical season whose colors are white and gold

Column 2

a. Matrimony

b. Christmas

c. Sacrament of the Anointing of the Sick

d. Sacrament of Reconciliation

e. Advent

f. liturgical year

(B) Check Understanding   Circle the letter of the choice that best completes the sentence or answers the question.

7. Which of the following is **NOT** part of the Paschal mystery?

    a. Jesus' birth

    b. Jesus' death

    c. Jesus' Resurrection

    d. Jesus' Ascension

8. Which statement is **NOT** true of the sacraments?

    a. They were given by Jesus.

    b. The Holy Spirit works within them.

    c. They are a sign that Jesus is still with us

    d. They are private prayers

9. The Sacrament of Penance and Reconciliation celebrates our _____.

    a. baptismal anointing

    b. original sin

    c. kinship and priesthood

    d. conversion and forgiveness through Christ

10. The word *Eucharist* literally means _____.

    a. bread and wine

    b. Body and Blood of Jesus

    c. thanksgiving

    d. sacrifice

Name _____ Date _____

11. The first Christians called the Eucharist the _____.

    a. breaking of the bread   **c.** distributing of the food

    b. cutting of the loaf   **d.** dinner for Christians

12. Which of these is an example of penance?

    a. remembering a friend's birthday   **c.** keeping my room clean

    b. apologizing to someone I have hurt   **d.** reading a story to a child

Complete each sentence with the correct term from the Word Bank.

13. The period from Holy Thursday to Easter Sunday is

the _____.

14. Two separate periods of the Church year are

called _____.

15. _____ is the season from Ash Wednesday to
Holy Thursday.

16. In the Sacrament of Reconciliation, a person receives _____, and his or her
personal sins are forgiven.

17. _____ celebrates Jesus' rising from the dead to new life.

WORD BANK
Lent
Triduum
Easter
absolution
Ordinary Time

C **Make Connections** Use the three terms below to write a paragraph that
describes how you celebrate the Eucharist on Sunday.

    participate   meal   give

18–20. _____

_____

_____

_____

_____

_____

_____

_____

_____

_____

ASSESSMENT

Unit 7
Kingdom of God

In this unit you will...

learn that our mission is to promote the kingdom of God. We do this by proclaiming the gospel and being a sign of Christ to others. We are called to be generous stewards of our possessions and to work for the good of all people. How we live our lives now, matters. We try to live justly so that we can live forever with God in heaven.

Chapter **19**

Chapter **20**

Chapter **21**

What do you think you will learn in this unit about being judged on love?

196

UNIT 7 OPENER

Preview Unit Theme

Tell students that Unit 7 is about the Kingdom of God.

- Read aloud the text on page 196 of the student edition. Tell students they will learn more about these things in the next three chapters.

- Ask students how they think we can be signs of Christ.

- Invite volunteers to share ways they can be good stewards.

A Generous Spirit
CATECHIST FORMATION

Faith Focus

- **God entrusted the earth to the care of humans.** *(CCC 299)*
- **The goods of the earth are meant for the benefit of the whole human family.** *(CCC 2402)*

Catechism Connection

The *Catechism* notes that the proper attitude toward possessions requires temperance, justice, and solidarity. *(CCC 2407)*

NDC Link

The *Directory* points out that like the earliest disciples, catechists are invited to imitate Jesus in teaching the faith, in living lives of holiness, and in being examples of Christian life. (See *NDC*, 53, 54B8.)

Resources

BOOKS
Four Feet, Two Sandals. Williams, Karen and Mohammed, Khadra. Eerdmans Books for Young Readers. Two refugees share a pair of sandals and develop a deep friendship.

Teaching Self-Discipline to Children. Vasiloff, Barbara. Twenty-Third Publications. "Sharing." Provides a framework to use in the classroom for countering greed.

 Catechist Resources
For interactive lesson planner, chapter resources, and activities
www.osvcurriculum.com

 A good name is more desirable than great riches, and high esteem, than gold and silver.

*Rich and poor have a common bond:
the LORD is the maker of them all.*

Proverbs 22:1–2

Envy and Greed

Most desires, such as the desire for food, shelter, and loving relationships, are good and natural. When belongings are at the top of a person's priorities, however, desire for them often becomes extreme. Greed implies fulfilling one's own desires without any consideration of other people's needs or wishes.

The sin of envy is a close relative of greed. Admiration for another, and even emulation, is normal. Growing unhappy at another person's success is envy. Clearly, greed and envy oppose the love and generosity to which Jesus has called his followers. Greed and envy offer nothing but dissatisfaction and an insatiable appetite for material goods and worldly pleasures. Following Jesus leads to joy and fulfillment.

Generosity

What can humans give to God, who has everything? They can offer nothing and yet everything—they offer him all they are by opening their hearts. By not allowing the desire for material goods to control them, people are free to be centered on the real treasure—God. All humans are part of his family and must share the resources of the earth with all, in justice and solidarity.

***Reflect** How do you demonstrate generosity in your daily life?*

A Generous Spirit

As fourth graders' moral thinking develops, so will their ability to make good moral decisions. This chapter lays the groundwork for a proper attitude toward material goods. It is a great challenge to be charitable and a greater one to give unselfishly to others in order to work for the kingdom of God.

- Envy is a huge issue for many students at this age. Challenge your students to move beyond this tendency by reflecting on the gifts they have been given.

- Encourage generosity and imaginative thinking about solutions to social problems that result from poverty and injustice by having students plan and take part in a charitable activity, such as a food or clothing drive.

FOURTH GRADERS SAY

People Skills

- I am beginning to be able to solve interpersonal problems. Show me new strategies to try.

- I am learning to be generous. Show me how to share time and attention.

- I enjoy working with others. Help me share responsibility for group prayer.

SUSTAINING YOUR SPIRIT

Coming to the Balcony

Pursuing catechetical excellence is increasingly complex. The challenges erode your willingness to shift, evaluate, and grow. As a result, you may find yourself doubting your effectiveness.

In *Leadership Without Easy Answers*, Ronald Heifetz proposes the practice of Coming to the Balcony: occasionally rising above the dance floor to get a better view of the dynamics, interactions, and pace making up the complexity of your catechetical dance. When Coming to the Balcony, seek the Wisdom of the Ratio, which can be found not by choosing one approach over the other but by determining when you are doing too much or not enough of different approaches.

Reflect **How can you practice Coming to the Balcony?**

Catechist's Prayer

Gracious God, you grant me a beating heart, a thinking mind, and a giving nature. Give me one more gift—a grateful spirit to appreciate the gifts of each day. Amen.

Weekly Planner

	Objectives	Lesson Process	Materials
1 Invite — 10 minutes	**Page 197** **Objective:** To develop an awareness of unselfish giving	**Let Us Pray:** Psalm 73:1 • Pray the psalm verse. • Learn about the giveaway custom. • Discuss giving up certain possessions.	
2 Explore — 40 minutes	**Pages 198–199** **Objective:** To explain what Jesus taught about possessions	• Discover through the story of King Midas the harm of greed. • Read and discuss the first beatitude. **Activity** Complete the Share Your Faith Activity.	☐ Pencils or pens ☐ Board or chart paper
	Pages 200–201 **Objective:** To describe how to live the seventh and tenth commandments	**Scripture:** Mark 12:41–44 • Discuss the importance of charity and justice. • Recognize generosity in the widow's contribution. **Activity** Complete the Connect Your Faith Activity. **Words of Faith** envy, greed	☐ Copies of Activity Master 19 on page 204A
3 Celebrate — 10 minutes	**Page 202** **Objective:** To pray for God's generosity	**Let Us Pray** • Practice the responses. • Gather as a community. • Celebrate a Prayer for Help. **Hymn:** "For Your Gracious Blessing" **Activity** Complete the Apostles' Creed Activity, page 240 and 241	☐ Hymnals ☐ Music CD ☐ Bible

Wrap Up

Review and Apply

Page 203
• Review the chapter concepts.
• Complete the Live Your Faith Activity.

Family Faith

Page 204
• Introduce the page, and assign it as a family activity.
• Read about Catherine de Hueck Doherty.

ACRE Connection, Domain 5—Solidarity

Home Connection

GO online www.osvcurriculum.com
Family Faith activities, feasts and seasonal resources, saint features, and much more.

• Online planning tools include chapter background and planner, activity master, customizable test, and more.

• Enhancement activities for each step of the catechetical process, including alternative prayer experiences and blessings.

• Games, activities, interactive review, alternative assessment, and more for child

www.calltofaitheconnect.com

A Generous Spirit

Let Us Pray

Leader: Kindly God, your generous spirit amazes all your children.
"How good God is to the upright,
the Lord, to those who are clean of heart!"
Psalm 73:1

All: Kindly God, your generous spirit amazes all your children.
Amen.

Activity Let's Begin

The Giveaway Some Native Americans have a custom called *giveaway*. Instead of receiving gifts on his or her birthday, a person thinks of some personal possession that someone else has admired during the year. Then the person celebrating the birthday gives that possession to the person who has admired it. Native Americans say that this custom helps them show how grateful they are for the gifts of life and good fortune.

• What do you own that someone else has admired?

• How difficult would it be for you to give that possession away? Why?
Responses will vary.

Objective: To develop an awareness of unselfish giving

Let Us Pray

Invite students to gather in the prayer space. In the space, have a crucifix and a Bible opened to the psalm. Pray aloud the psalm, and ask students to respond.

Activity

• Help students learn about a Native American custom by reading aloud The Giveaway.

• Discuss the questions that follow an explanation of the custom.

• Explain to students that generosity means giving freely. Remind them that having a generous spirit enhances human understanding of what it means to be made in the image and likeness of God.

OPTIONAL ACTIVITY

Give a Gift Your students may want to imitate the Native American custom described on this page.

• Encourage them to look through things that they have made for art class or craft projects.

• Have them consider who would enjoy owning these things or find them useful.

• Suggest that students give away their projects.

Multiple Intelligence: Interpersonal

CULTURAL AWARENESS

The Giveaway This is not just a birthday custom.

• Native American families use the giveaway as a year-long custom to honor the memory of a loved one.

• Many charitable programs that involve Native Americans' helping one another are based on or named after the custom of the giveaway.

Objective: To explain what Jesus taught about possessions

 **Focus**

What does Jesus want you to know about riches? List students' responses on the board or on chart paper.

Desire for Riches

Tell students that they are about to hear a story from ancient Greece. Point out that some of them may have heard this tale before.

King Midas

Invite volunteers to play the roles of Bacchus, Midas, the old man, and Midas's daughter. Read the story aloud as the students pantomime the action.

- Ask how Midas showed generosity. by taking care of the old man **Discuss** what happened when Midas was offered a reward for his generosity. He became too greedy.

- Ask how King Midas hurt himself. by putting his possessions first

- Discuss the question that follows the story.

Explore

Desire for Riches

 **Focus** What does Jesus want you to know about riches?

Many cultures have stories that explore how much is too much. Here is one from ancient Greece.

A STORY

KING MIDAS

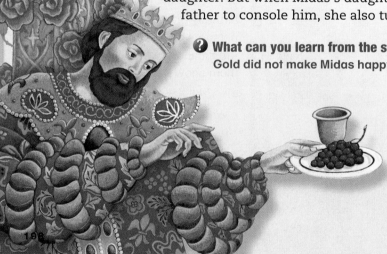

Long ago and far away there lived in Greece a king named Midas. One day an old man wandered into King Midas's rose garden. Midas had his servants feed and care for the man.

Midas escorted the old man back to his home. The god Bacchus was pleased with the care Midas had given the man. Bacchus granted Midas one wish. Midas wished that everything he touched would turn to gold. And his wish was granted!

When he reached his palace, Midas ordered a feast to celebrate his good fortune. But when Midas tried to eat, his food turned to gold when he touched it. Midas soon grew hungry and thirsty, and he complained to his daughter. But when Midas's daughter hugged her father to console him, she also turned to gold!

 What can you learn from the story of Midas?
Gold did not make Midas happy.

OPTIONAL ACTIVITY

Midas Touch Choose a student to be King Midas. Have that student gently tap another student on the shoulder. To avoid "turning to gold," the tapped student then must name an act of generosity. That student then taps another student. Continue playing until all students have had a chance to name an act of generosity.

Multiple Intelligence: Interpersonal

CATECHIST BACKGROUND

King Midas The story of Midas has been used for centuries to explain the consequences of greed.

- Jesus used the image of a treasure in his stories. This treasure is symbolic, representing salvation or God's kingdom.

- King Midas never discovers this kind of treasure, but Jesus' followers do.

Poor in Spirit

King Midas did not think of the consequences of his wish. Because Midas put his desire for riches first, he hurt himself and others.

Everything that God made is good. People are good. The things that people create with love and care are good. But Jesus taught that possessions are not the most important things. Do you remember the story found in *Matthew 19:16–22* about the rich young man? Jesus loved him and wanted him to be happy.

❓ **What did Jesus tell the rich young man to do?**
give away all that he owned

First Things First

Sometimes people need to leave behind their material possessions in order to have the time and energy to do good. The Apostles left their homes, families, and jobs in order to follow Jesus and help him spread God's word.

The first beatitude says, "Blessed are the poor in spirit, for theirs is the kingdom of heaven" (*Matthew 5:3*). Those who do not become too attached to their possessions are able to work for love and peace in the world and help bring about God's kingdom.

Faith Fact

In the Bible, the word *blessed* means "favored with the blessings of God."

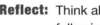 **Activity** Share Your Faith

Reflect: Think about right and wrong choices for the following situations.

- A video game that you want is on an outdoor table during a sidewalk sale.
- Someone else wins an award that you wanted.

Share: In a small group, role-play one of these situations, showing how you could make a good choice.

Act: Write what you would do to make a good choice in the other situation. Why would this be a good choice?

199

Poor in Spirit

Restate the lesson from the story by reading aloud the first paragraph.

- Ask students to read the second paragraph silently to discover what Jesus taught about possessions.
- Invite volunteers to share what they remember about Jesus and the rich young man *(Matthew 19:16–22)*. Discuss the question.

First Things First

Tell students to read silently to learn which beatitude talks about the right attitude toward possessions and dependence upon God.

Activity

- Organize students into groups of two or three. Allow time for them to plan and present their role-plays.
- Invite volunteers to share their responses to the question.

⊚ Quick Review

Everything God made is good, but being too attached to possessions makes it difficult for people to love.

⭐ **REACHING ALL LEARNERS**

Role-plays Putting themselves in another's place is enjoyable and instructive for fourth graders.

- Students who are particularly strong in social skills, word activities, and movement will have a chance to shine when performing skits.
- Praise students for the ingenuity of their solutions, not for the quality of their acting.

Objective: To describe how to live the seventh and tenth commandments

 **Focus**

What do the seventh and tenth commandments teach you? List students' responses on the board or on chart paper.

Living a Generous Life

Ask which commandments tell about the right attitude to have toward material possessions.

• Have students read to find the answer.

• Review the meanings of *envy* and *greed*. Ask students to give examples of these types of behavior.

An Open Heart

Explain that almost everyone feels greed or envy at times. Point out that students can overcome these feelings.

• Tell them to read to learn how to be happy for their own gifts and to appreciate those of others.

• Discuss the question in the text.

Explore

Living a Generous Life

 **Focus** What do the seventh and tenth commandments teach you?

There are two commandments that help you have the right attitude about material possessions. The seventh commandment says this: You shall not steal. The tenth commandment says this: You shall not covet your neighbor's goods.

Theft, greed, and envy are all sins against the seventh and tenth commandments. Theft is taking what is not yours. When you have **envy**, you resent or are sad because someone else possesses something that you really want. Envy harms the Body of Christ because it divides God's people rather than bringing everyone together. **Greed** is the desire to gain earthly possessions without concern for what is reasonable or right.

An Open Heart

Humility, a spirit of generosity, and trust in God's care can help overcome envy and greed. If you are happy with what you have received, then you can be happy for the good fortune of others. Caring too much for things usually brings unhappiness and disappointment.

Because everything comes from God, all people have a right to what they need to live comfortably. As a member of the Body of Christ you are called to share your possessions with others, especially those who do not have food, shelter, or decent clothing.

❓ **In what ways are people your age tempted to be envious or greedy?** Possible responses: by being shown fancy clothes, video games, or bikes

---

 JUSTICE AND PEACE

Save Resources In *Economic Justice for All,* the U.S. Conference of Catholic Bishops ask Catholics to "examine our way of living in light of the poor" (#75).

• Ask students to name resources that people consume.

• Then ask students to name resources that should be conserved.

Catholic Social Teaching: Option for the Poor

Called to Stewardship

The seventh and tenth commandments require you to be generous with others. Being generous means giving more than is necessary.

God created the world for all creatures and called humans to stewardship. As stewards, or caretakers, people are called to use natural resources well and protect the environment for everyone now and in the future; to respect all life as a gift from God; and to share time, money, and talent to help others.

Words of Faith

To **envy** is to resent or be sad from wanting for yourself what belongs to others.

Greed is the desire to acquire earthly goods without limit or beyond one's means.

✚ SCRIPTURE   Mark 12:41–44

The Widow's Contribution

Jesus watched people put money into the temple treasury. Many rich people put in large sums of money. A poor widow put in two small coins worth only a few cents. Jesus said to his disciples, "I say to you, this poor widow put in more than all the others. They contributed their extra money, but the widow has given all she had."

Based on *Mark 12:41–44*

❓ **How did the widow contribute more than the rest?**
She gave everything she had.

❓ **Who do you know who has a generous spirit?**
Responses will vary.

Activity — Connect Your Faith

Be a Good Steward Sketch a design for a stewardship ad that shows you or your group giving your time, talent, or treasure for the good of others. Encourage other people in your parish to share in similar ways.

201

Called to Stewardship

Read aloud the first paragraph as a review of the lesson so far.

- Invite a volunteer to read aloud the next paragraph. Remind students of the meaning of *stewardship*.

The Widow's Contribution

Invite a proficient reader to proclaim the scripture story.

- Discuss the questions.

Activity

- Ask students to use public service ads as a model.
- Tell students to complete the activity and then share their ads.

◎ Quick Review

The seventh and tenth commandments deal with generosity and stewardship.

✚ SCRIPTURE BACKGROUND

The Generous Widow The story of the widow's contribution comes right after Jesus' denunciation of some of the scribes.

- Jesus says of the scribes, "They devour the houses of widows and, as a pretext, recite lengthy prayers. They will receive a very severe condemnation" (*Mark 12:40*).

- He then praises the widow. Jesus says that God prefers a sincere heart to an empty show.

OPTIONAL ACTIVITY

Activity Master 19: Good Stewards Distribute copies of the activity found on catechist page 204A.

- Have students fill in the chart with information about the gifts God has given them.

- As an alternative, you may wish to send this activity home with students.

▲ Activity Master 19

3 Celebrate

Objective: To pray for God's generosity

 Let Us Pray

Tell students that God is generous in offering help so that we may be generous, too.

Prayer for Help

Prepare

Choose readers for the prayer, and provide time for preparation.

 Use the *Call to Faith 4* CD, track 19, to rehearse the suggested song.

Gather

Gather students in a circle in the prayer space.

Pray

- Follow the order of prayer on page 202.
- Optional Bible readings are *Matthew 6:1–4, Matthew 19:16–30,* or *Luke 12:16–21.*

Celebrate

Prayer for Help

 **Let Us Pray**

Gather and begin with the Sign of the Cross.

Leader: God our Father, please hear our prayer. Help us see your Son in others.

All: **So that we may give freely and generously.**

Reader 1: Help us appreciate what we have been given.

All: **So that we may show gratitude to those who have been generous to us.**

Reader 2: Help us be happy when others have received gifts.

All: **So that we may be good friends to them.**

Reader 3: Help us remember others.

All: **So that we are willing to share our possessions.**

Leader: We ask for your guidance and continued love in Jesus' name by the grace of the Holy Spirit.

All: **Amen.**

Sing together.

For your gracious blessing, for your wondrous word, for your loving kindness, we give thanks, O God.

"For Your Gracious Blessing," Traditional.

202

 LITURGY LINK

Scripture Cycles The Gospel readings at Mass are rotated in a three-year cycle.

- The Gospel according to Matthew is read during Year A, the Gospel according to Mark in Year B, and the Gospel according to Luke in Year C.
- The Gospel according to John is read every year during the seasons of Christmas, Lent, and Easter, and sometimes during Ordinary Time.

 LECTIONARY LINK

Break Open the Word Read last week's Sunday Gospel. Invite students to think about what the reading means to them as they try to follow Christ's example. For questions related to the weekly Gospel reading, visit our website at **www.osvcurriculum.com**.

GO online Visit www.osvcurriculum.com for weekly Scripture readings and seasonal resources.

A **Work with Words**   Complete the following statements.

1. The ___seventh commandment___ states that you should not steal.

2. The responsibility to care for all of God's creation is ___stewardship___.

3. The ___tenth commandment___ states that you should not desire what others have.

4. When you ___envy___ someone, you are resentful or sad that he or she possesses something that you want.

5. The unlimited gathering of material possessions is ___greed___.

B **Check Understanding**   Explain how caring too much about possessions can get in the way of helping you cooperate with God's kingdom.

Responses will vary.

___

___

Activity — Live Your Faith

Suggest Changes   In each column, list several changes you would like to see happen for your family, friends, or community. Then make a resolution to help bring about one of these changes.

Community Center

Family	Friends	Community
_____	_____	_____
_____	_____	_____
_____	_____	_____

Review and Apply

Use the focus questions from the Explore pages to review the lesson concepts.

A **Work with Words**   Have students complete each statement. Review their responses.

B **Check Understanding**   Ask students to write a response to the statement. Encourage volunteers to share their responses.

Activity

• Assign each student a partner, and allow time for the pairs to discuss ideas for the activity.

• Have students fill in their charts individually.

• Encourage students to implement their changes. Suggest that they start with their family and friends.

OPTIONAL ACTIVITY

Generosity in the Media   Tell students that newspapers occasionally run stories about people who have worked for justice by sharing.

• Encourage students to look for such stories and share them with the class.

Multiple Intelligence: Verbal/Linguistic

Wrap-Up

Family Faith

Remind students to discuss the Family Faith page at home. Encourage students to read the passage from 2 Corinthians.

Activity

- Invite a volunteer to read aloud the directions for the home activity.
- If time permits, begin a discussion of ways to show a generous spirit.

People of Faith

Tell students about Catherine de Hueck Doherty.

- Catherine de Hueck Doherty is considered a pioneer in implementing the Church's social teachings. Share her words with the group: "Preach the Gospel with your life—without compromise." Discuss what this quotation means.
- Remind students to add Catherine de Hueck Doherty to their People of Faith albums. Encourage them to pray the prayer at home.

 Visit **www.osvcurriculum.com** for weekly scripture readings and seasonal resources.

UNIT 7: CHAPTER 19
Family Faith

Catholics Believe

- The commandments call you to be generous and to have the right attitude toward possessions.
- The goods of the earth are meant for the benefit of the whole human family.

✝ SCRIPTURE

Read *2 Corinthians 9:6–9* to find out how the Corinthians were challenged to be generous.

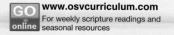 **www.osvcurriculum.com** For weekly scripture readings and seasonal resources

Activity
Live Your Faith

Start a New Custom Talk about the *giveaway* story at the beginning of this chapter.

- How hard would it be to add this custom to a birthday or to another celebration?
- In what other ways could you express a generous spirit toward others?

Choose one way, and decide how you will act on it as a family.

People of Faith

Catherine de Hueck Doherty was a Russian noblewoman who moved to Canada. She saw poverty in the world around her and decided to act. She founded the first Friendship House, a welcoming place for those who are poor. She then started Madonna House, a farm that combines prayer and a simple lifestyle. Since her death in 1985, Madonna Houses and Friendship Houses have continued to spread in the United States and Canada.

▲ Catherine de Hueck Doherty 1900–1985

🙌 Family Prayer

Jesus, help us imitate Catherine de Hueck Doherty's caring spirit as we learn how to share what we have with those in need. Amen.

In Unit 7 your child is learning about the KINGDOM OF GOD.

204 CCC See Catechism of the Catholic Church 299, 2402–2405 for further reading on chapter content

---

❓ HOW DID I DO?

My session was

☐ *one of the best ever!* ☐ *pretty good.* ☐ *in need of improvement.*

In what discussions and activities were students most interested?

_____

What activity did I most enjoy teaching?

_____

In what area do I need to improve?

_____

Name _____ Date _____

Good Stewards

Fill in the chart to show the gifts that God has given you, why each gift is important, and how you are taking care of it. You can include material gifts, such as water, clothing, and toys, as well as spiritual gifts, such as virtues and talents.

My Gift	Why It Is Important	How I Care for It

Now draw a picture of yourself being a good steward of one of these gifts.

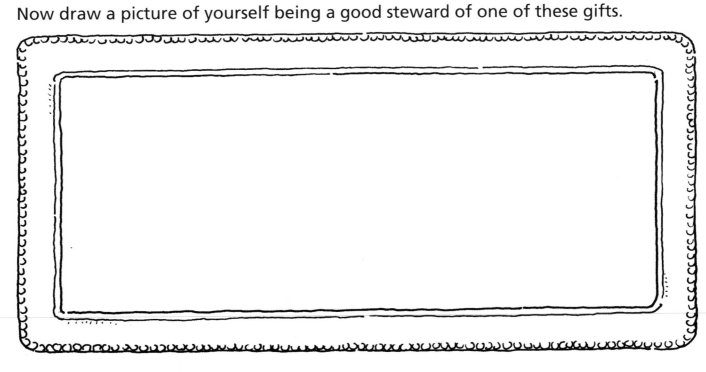

Faith Focus

- Humans share in God's plan by proclaiming the gospel and working for the common good. *(CCC 849)*
- Working for justice is the mission of all the faithful. *(CCC 1807)*

Catechism Connection

The *Catechism* reminds lay people that they have a mission to promote holiness within the human community. *(CCC 942)*

NDC Link

Catechists are witnesses to Jesus, evangelizers, and missionaries. They do not simply instruct students about Christ; they lead them to him. (See *NDC*, 55E.)

Resources

BOOK
*To Act Justly.** Neuberger, Anne. Twenty-Third Publications. "A Story of Saint Paul Miki and Companions." For use as a group reading to show the devotion of missionaries.

DVD/VHS
Many Faces in God's House (17 min.). USCCB. Rejoices in the cultural diversity of Catholicism.

*Available at www.osvcurriculum.com

GO online Catechist Resources
For interactive lesson planner, chapter resources, and activities
www.osvcurriculum.com

 I planted, Apollos watered, but God caused the growth. Therefore, neither the one who plants nor the one who waters is anything, but only God, who causes the growth. . . . For we are God's co-workers; you are God's field, God's building.

1 Corinthians 3:6–7, 9

Diversity and Justice

Differences are part of the beauty of creation. If all roses were red and all birds blue, their beauty would be lost in their sameness. Christians are called to be grateful for human diversity as well, because it is part of God's plan. The Church teaches that people with various talents and backgrounds, as well as people of different ethnicities, genders, and ages, share a birthright as God's children. Instead of merely tolerating diversity, Catholics are called to celebrate it.

By recognizing the value of diversity, you also recognize that you must respect people who are different from you. This respect leads to treating others justly. Justice, in turn, leads to harmony among people.

Mission

Mission is one of the duties of Christianity. Spreading the good news of salvation is an act of love that is guided by the Holy Spirit. Its hallmarks are respectful dialogue, acts of compassion, and the humble awareness that God is in charge. Rooted in prayer, the Christian mission welcomes all of God's children.

Reflect How are you God's "co-worker" in the world?

Mission

The ministry of Catholic missionaries provides a lens through which students can see that the Catholic Church is unified in its mission, yet it is as diverse as the various cultures of the world.

Many missionaries are examples of unselfish love for others. Many give up personal comfort and security to serve others in living the message of the gospel. Fourth graders can begin to do this, too—moving outside their "comfort zone" to offer help and forgiveness to other young people their age.

- Point out to students that missionaries spread the good news by doing the things that Jesus did—healing, teaching, and bringing hope—as well as by telling his story and repeating his message.

- Remind them that acceptance and tolerance of various cultures has helped Catholicism spread throughout the world.

Reaching Out

- I want to work for justice. Show me ways to work for it in the classroom.

- I like new sights and sounds. Include videos in class presentations.

- I often stay with one group of friends. Use different techniques for forming groups.

Confession

Psychologists tell us that we unconsciously create enemies to avoid responsibility for a problem, to bond closer with the colleagues on our side, or to better define who we are. In catechetics, we can make such an imagined enemy out of parents, the pastor, or a certain group of students.

The struggle to sustain your spirit is difficult enough without carrying such a burden. The courageous practice of Confession enables you to let go of the illusion of an enemy and freely carry on the noble work of catechetics. Your virtuous act of Confession can help you refrain from contributing to the enemy illusion.

Reflect **What enemy comes to your mind as you consider the practice of Confession?**

 Catechist's Prayer

Risen Lord, I am blessed to be embraced by your generous love. Continue to form me in your ways of compassion and concern for others. Amen.

Weekly Planner

Objectives	Lesson Process	Materials
1 Invite — 10 minutes **Page 205** **Objective:** To explore how people are alike and different	🫙 **Let Us Pray:** Psalm 133:1 • Pray the psalm verse. • Explore differences and likenesses. • Have students share with a partner similarities and differences.	☐ Paper ☐ Pencils or pens ☐ Copies of Activity Master 20 on page 212A
2 Explore — 40 minutes **Pages 206–207** **Objective:** To describe how the Catholic faith is brought to people worldwide	• Read about mission work in Bolivia. • Discuss the role of missionaries. **Activity** Complete the Share Your Faith Activity.	☐ Board or chart paper ☐ A world map showing the location of Bolivia ☐ Art materials
Pages 208–209 **Objective:** To explain the Church's mission to the world	✝ **Scripture:** Matthew 28:18–20 • Discuss the meaning of Jesus' mission. • Describe the diversity of people in the Church. **Activity** Complete the Connect Your Faith Activity. **Words of Faith** mission , justice , diversity	☐ Index cards ☐ Newspaper headlines
3 Celebrate — 10 minutes **Page 210** **Objective:** To pray to spread the good news of Jesus	🫙 **Let Us Pray** • Practice the responses. • Gather as a community. • Celebrate a Prayer of Praise. 🎵 **Hymn:** "Psalm 117: Go Out to All the World" **Activity** Complete the Mission Activity, page 228 and 229	☐ Hymnals ☐ Music CD ☐ Bible

Wrap Up

Review and Apply

Page 211
• Review the chapter concepts.
• Complete the Live Your Faith Activity.

Family Faith

Page 212
• Introduce the page, and assign it as a family activity.
• Read about Cesar Chavez.

ACRE Connection, Domain 2—The Church's Mission

Home Connection

GO online www.osvcurriculum.com
Family Faith activities, feasts and seasonal resources, saint features, and much more

CALL to FAITH e connect

• Online planning tools include chapter background and planner, activity master, customizable test, and more.
• Enhancement activities for each step of the catechetical process, including alternative prayer experiences and blessings.
• Games, activities, interactive review, alternative assessment, and more for child...

www.calltofaitheconnect.com

Chapter 20 The Church in the World

 Let Us Pray

Leader: Giving God, thank you for the world you made and all the people who share it.

"How good it is, how pleasant,
    where the people dwell as one!"
Psalm 133:1

All: Giving God, thank you for the world you made and all the people who share it. Amen.

Activity Let's Begin

Different, Yet the Same Look around you. You are surrounded by differences. The people sitting in the room with you have different hairstyles, different eye colors, and different skin tones. They have different last names and may have different cultural backgrounds.

And yet, with all these differences, you all belong to the same human family.

• With a partner, name all of the things that are the same for both of you. Then name all the ways that the two of you are different. Describe the most important thing that is the same for both of you and then the most important difference between you.

205

Invite

 **1 Invite**

Objective: To explore how people are alike and different

 **Let Us Pray**

Ask students to gather in the prayer space. Choose a student to read aloud the psalm, and invite everyone to respond.

Activity

• Discuss which is more important: the ways people are different or the ways they are the same.

• Invite a student to read aloud Different, Yet the Same.

• Assign partners for the activity. Have each pair of partners use a Venn diagram to record similarities and differences. Pairs can then use the diagram during the class discussion.

OPTIONAL ACTIVITY

Activity Master 20: Diversity Bingo Distribute copies of the activity found on catechist page 212A.

• This game allows students to find out more about one another.

▲ **Activity Master 20**

QUICK TIP

Venn Diagram A Venn diagram is often used to compare and contrast two things.

• For this activity, have students record common traits where the circles overlap.

• In the areas that do not overlap, students should record their differences.

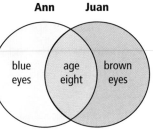

The Church in the World 205

Objective: To describe how the Catholic faith is brought to people worldwide

Focus

How does the Church include different cultures? List students' responses on the board or on chart paper.

The Church in Bolivia

Show students the location of Bolivia on a world map.

A Floating Church

Slowly read aloud the text, pausing to answer any questions.

• Have students tell how the priest in Bolivia is like Saint Paul. The priest travels to spread the word of God.

The People

Have students continue listening as you read aloud.

• Discuss the question.

• Distribute paper and drawing materials. Suggest that students sketch life in Bolivia and something in your parish that is similar.

The Church in Bolivia

Focus How does the Church include different cultures?

In the following story told by a Maryknoll missionary, you will find some ways that the Church in Bolivia is like your parish and some ways that it is different from your parish.

A REAL-LIFE STORY

A Floating Church

Our Parish boat

I work with other missionaries in the jungle region of northeast Bolivia. We travel in our parish boat to visit the people who live far apart along the Beni River. Most of the people work deep in the jungle. Some work with rubber trees, and others harvest Brazilian nuts. On our way up the river, we tell whoever is home to gather their neighbors together for Mass, Baptisms, and marriages on the day we will return downstream. When we return, the people gather near the river. There we baptize people, celebrate Mass, and perform marriages.

The People

The people are happy to have us come and celebrate the sacraments with them. Ninety-five percent of Bolivians are Catholic. Their ancestors were converted to Christianity a long time ago. Many of the people we meet along the river still speak their native Indian languages. The people we meet also bring some of their native customs into their religious life.

❓ **What about the missionaries' experience in Bolivia is different from the experience in your parish?**
Possible response: Priests do not travel by boat.

 206

A Worldwide Mission Most dioceses have a world missions office.

• Check with the world missions office in your diocese for resources appropriate for students.

• Ask whether speakers are available.

• Share literature and musical recordings from other Catholic missions.

Multiple Intelligence: Musical

Maryknoll Maryknoll, one of the most active Catholic missionary orders, was established in 1911.

• Today there are over 550 Maryknoll priests and brothers and approximately 700 Maryknoll sisters, as well as lay missionaries.

The Mission

My coworkers and I have learned the languages of the people. We spend time talking and listening to the people. We are able to help them take care of their health in a clinic, and we educate them in a school. We have helped them set up a type of company called a *cooperative*, which is owned by the people who use its services. For example, we helped the farmers set up a cooperative so that they could get fair prices for their rubber and nut crops.

Bolivia has a lot of troubles. Once there was an uprising in a town, and one of the government people asked me to be mayor for four months. Another time I was arrested with another priest. We were put in jail because we had helped the people form a cooperative.

Our outdoor clinic

The Beni River

Activity

Share Your Faith

Reflect: Think about how the "floating church" is the same as your parish church.

Share: With a partner, use examples from the story to describe how the Church includes different cultures.

Act: Write one thing that you can do to support people in the Church who come from different cultures.

Responses will vary.

207

The Mission

Continue reading the text aloud.

- Explain that a cooperative helps people share what they produce and keeps money in their community. People in power may be afraid that with the help of a cooperative, people will become educated and seek civil rights.

- Ask why Catholic missionaries might help set up cooperatives. Possible response: so people can work together and improve the quality of life

- Stress that missionaries build strong communities where people can have what they need to live.

Activity

- Brainstorm with students ways the Church helps the people in Bolivia. Encourage students to include some of these examples in their descriptions.

- Ask volunteers to share responses.

Quick Review

The Church welcomes all cultures. Missionaries help others by sharing the word of God and by providing social services.

REACHING ALL LEARNERS

See Bolivia Students with different learning styles will understand the story better if they can see the country and conditions in which the people live.

- Work with your parish or local librarian to find a videotape about Bolivia.

- Select a few minutes of the tape with scenes similar to those described in the student text.

BOLIVIA

Objective: To explain the Church's mission to the world

 **Focus**

How does the Church reach out to the world? List students' responses on the board or on chart paper.

To the Whole World

Read aloud the text.

- Summarize it by saying that the missionaries in Bolivia are following in the footsteps of Jesus and obeying his instructions.

Go Forth

Proclaim the scripture story.

- Read aloud the rest of the text to introduce the word *mission*. Have students make cards to add to their vocabulary packets.

- Ask students what Catholics and Christians in communities around the world have in common. They are followers of Jesus.

- Discuss the question in the text.

Explore

To the Whole World

 **Focus**   How does the Church reach out to the world?

Catholic missionaries bring the Catholic faith to people all over the world. They are careful to respect and include the customs of different groups in prayer and worship.

The missionaries in Bolivia are preaching the gospel of Jesus in word and deed. Before Jesus ascended into heaven, he gave his Apostles this command.

Faith Fact

There are over 92,000 Catholic missionaries working around the world.

✝ SCRIPTURE   Matthew 28:18–2

Go Forth

"All power in heaven and on earth has been given to me. Go, therefore, and make disciples of all nations, baptizing them in the name of the Father, and of the Son, and of the holy Spirit, teaching them to observe all that I have commanded you. And behold, I am with you always, until the end of the age."

Matthew 28:18–20

Jesus wanted his followers to go out to all places. Today, no matter where you go in the world, you will find followers of Jesus. In every country, you will find communities of Catholics and other Christians. Every one of these communities and all of the followers of Jesus are called to continue the **mission** of Jesus.

❓ **How do you live out the mission of Jesus?** Possible responses: by helping those who are poor, by spreading his message

208

✝ SCRIPTURE BACKGROUND

The Commissioning   The commissioning of the Apostles in *Matthew 28:18–20* comes after Jesus' death and Resurrection; the text emphasizes baptizing new followers.

- Similar passages occur in *Mark 16:14–18* and *John 20:19–22.*

- These passages indicate that the Church, through its leaders and members, continues Jesus' work.

OPTIONAL ACTIVITY

Celebrate Diversity   Celebrate diversity with students.

- Point out that the ancestors of most Americans came from other countries.

- Invite each student to show his or her family's original home country on a map.

Multiple Intelligence: Interpersonal

Jesus' Universal Mission

Jesus' universal, or worldwide, mission on earth was to share God's love with all people. When you read the Scriptures, you see that Jesus reached out to all people, especially people who were poor and those who were left out by others. Jesus healed, forgave, and loved people, especially those people who were considered sinners. Jesus treated everyone with dignity and respect. Jesus' mission was one of **justice**.

Diversity in the Church

There are differences in the way the people of other countries and cultures practice their faith. Even in your parish you may notice a **diversity**, or variety, in the ways that people express their faith. These differences do not divide the Church. They make it better. The Church is united because of its faithfulness to the common belief handed down from the Apostles through their successors, the bishops. The Church is united in the celebration of the Mass, in the Sacraments, in prayer, and when people in every culture help bring justice to the world. You bring justice to the world by working to give others what is rightfully theirs.

❓ What cultural practices does your parish or family have? Responses will vary.

Words of Faith

To be sent on a **mission** means to be sent to share the Good News of Jesus and the kingdom of God.

Justice is the virtue of giving to God and people what is due them.

Diversity means variety, especially among people.

Activity

Connect Your Faith

Tell the World Write a newspaper headline that tells one way that you can bring justice to the world now or in the future.

_____

_____

209

Jesus' Universal Mission

Have students read silently.

- Ask them to tell what Jesus' mission was.

Diversity in the Church

Read aloud the text.

- Draw the graphic organizer, and write ways that the Catholic Church is diverse worldwide. Possible responses: countries, languages
- Point out that amidst the diversity, Catholics are united through the same faith.
- Discuss what unites the Church.
- Have students make vocabulary cards for *justice* and *diversity*.
- Encourage discussion of the question.

Activity

- If possible, show students sample headlines.
- Ask students to share their work.

◎ Quick Review

The Catholic Church celebrates diversity and carries out its mission of sharing God's message.

💡 QUICK TIP

Graphic Organizer

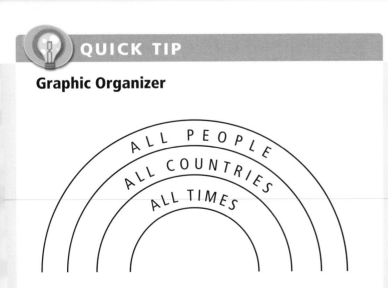

ALL PEOPLE
ALL COUNTRIES
ALL TIMES

3 Celebrate

Objective: To pray to spread the good news of Jesus

 Let Us Pray

Tell students that they will have a chance today to share some good news about Jesus.

Prayer of Praise

Prepare

Choose a leader for the prayer.

• Ask each student to write good news about Jesus to share.

🔥 Use the *Call to Faith 4* CD, track 20, to rehearse the suggested song.

Gather

Gather students in the prayer space. Have them bring their statements.

Pray

• Follow the order of prayer on page 210.
• Allow students time to read statements.
• Optional Bible readings are *Mark 16:14–18* and *John 20:19–22.*

Celebrate

Prayer of Praise

 Let Us Pray

Gather and begin with the Sign of the Cross.

Sing together.

Go out to all the world, and tell the Good News.

"Psalm 117: Go Out to All the World" © 1969, 1981, and 1997, ICEL.

Leader: Lord, all the nations praise you. All the people of the world glorify you.

All: God our loving Father, we thank you for the gift of your Son, Jesus. We thank you for the beautiful diversity of our world. All nations and people show us your greatness. Fill us with your Spirit so that we can bring the Good News of Jesus to all whom we meet. Amen.

210

 LITURGY LINK

Movement in Prayer As an alternative to each student's writing a statement on a sheet of paper, have students write statements about the good news of Jesus on a paper banner.

• During the celebration, have a student bring the banner to the center of the prayer area and pass it to the next student, continuing to pass the banner while the rest of the group sings.

 LECTIONARY LINK

Break Open the Word Read last week's Sunday Gospel. Invite students to think about what the reading means to them as they try to follow Christ's example. For questions related to the weekly Gospel reading, visit our website at **www.osvcurriculum.com.**

GO online Visit www.osvcurriculum.com for weekly Scripture readings and seasonal resources.

Review and Apply

A **Work with Words** Complete each sentence by unscrambling the word in parentheses.

1. Jesus' (sonsimi) _____**mission**_____ was to share God's love with all people.

2. The Church is one, made up of a great (vidityers) _____**diversity**_____ of members.

3. The mission of every person in the Church is to bring the good news of Jesus to the (lorwd) _____**world**_____.

4. The virtue of (tcjuise) _____**justice**_____ challenges followers of Jesus to work to provide for the needs and rights of others.

5. Missionaries must (serpcet) _____**respect**_____ the culture and customs of the local people.

B **Check Understanding** Write a response on the lines below. How can you bring justice to the world?

**Possible response: Treat people with dignity and respect.**

_____

_____

Activity — Live Your Faith

Share Good News Take the good news statement that you created for the prayer service, print it on a card, and decorate it. How can you share this good news with someone this week? Write your idea, and act on it in the coming week.

To Do
- ☐ _____
- ☐ _____
- ☐ _____
- ☐ _____
- ☐ _____

211

Review and Apply

Use the focus questions from the catechist Explore pages to review the lesson concepts.

A **Work with Words** Have students fill in the answers by unscrambling the words in parentheses. Review their answers.

B **Check Understanding** Ask students to respond to the question. Invite volunteers to share their responses.

Activity

- Give students time to complete the activity.
- Discuss the question with the entire group in order to help students develop their ideas.

JUSTICE AND PEACE

Different Cultures The Church emphasizes that we are one human family, whatever our differences.

- Emphasize to students the call to inclusiveness.
- Discuss ways to promote dignity as well as opportunity for all.

Catholic Social Teaching: Solidarity

Wrap-Up

Family Faith

Remind students to discuss the Family Faith page at home. Encourage students to read the passage from Ephesians.

Activity

- Read aloud the directions for the home activity.
- Name some other faith traditions for students, such as Protestant, Jewish, Hindu, Muslim, Buddhist, and Shinto.

People of Faith

Tell students about Cesar Chavez.

- The difficulties of Cesar Chavez as a migrant worker continued as he struggled to support his own children. He developed the vision of a true leader, and Robert F. Kennedy called him "one of the heroic figures of our time."
- Remind students to add Cesar Chavez to their People of Faith albums. Encourage them to pray the prayer at home with their families.

 Visit **www.osvcurriculum.com** for weekly scripture readings and seasonal resources.

◎ Catholics Believe

- The mission of the People of God is to proclaim the Gospel and to work for the good of all people.
- The Church is made up of people of many cultures, but all are united by their belief in Christ.

✝ SCRIPTURE

Read *Ephesians 4:7–16* to find out about unity in diversity.

GO online www.osvcurriculum.com
For weekly scripture readings and seasonal resources

Activity

Live Your Faith

Research Religious Traditions Share your experiences of different religious traditions. If possible, go online with a family member to research the religious traditions from a culture other than your own. Plan a special family time to tell what you discovered.

People of Faith

▲ **Cesar Chavez**
1927–1993

As a child, **Cesar Chavez** was a migrant farm worker. As an adult, he improved working conditions for migrant workers and started the United Farm Workers union. Cesar had a deep Christian faith. He also followed the nonviolent teachings of Mohandas Gandhi and of Martin Luther King, Jr. He and other protesters often went to Mass together before they began a march. He organized strikes and boycotts to get fair wages for farm workers.

🙌 Family Prayer

Dear God, give us a sense of justice and the courage to carry out your mission of justice in our world as Cesar Chavez did. Amen.

In Unit 7 your child is learning about the KINGDOM OF GOD.

212 **CCC** *See Catechism of the Catholic Church 849, 858–859, 1807, 1934–1938 for further reading on chapter content.*

HOW DID I DO?

My session was

☐ *one of the best ever!* ☐ *pretty good.* ☐ *in need of improvement.*

In what discussions and activities were students most interested?

_____

What activity did I most enjoy teaching?

_____

In what area do I need to improve?

_____

Name _____ Date _____

Diversity Bingo

How diverse is your group? Find out by having another student sign a box which has a phrase that accurately describes him or her. See how many boxes you can fill.

plays baseball	has brown eyes	likes pizza	sings well
wears glasses	was born in another country	is an only child	has a nickname
can do a handstand	has curly hair	has a pet	likes reading
has a sister	speaks another language	plays soccer	knows how to cook

I Want to See God
CATECHIST FORMATION

Faith Focus

- At the end of time, all will be raised from the dead. *(CCC 681)*

- When that happens, all will come to Christ for final judgment. *(CCC 682)*

Catechism Connection

The *Catechism* states that although Christ's reign is already present in the Church, at the last judgment it will be fulfilled. *(CCC 671)*

NDC Link

Catechesis can provide liberation through knowledge that salvation is here as well as yet to come. Christians are loved by God and are not alone and should spread the Good News to others. (See *NDC*, 25C.)

Resources

BOOK
The Catholic Kid's Guide to Stewardship. Johnson, Elizabeth. Twenty-Third Publications. Stories and suggestions for designing service projects related to the works of mercy.

GO **Catechist Resources**
online For interactive lesson planner, chapter resources, and activities
www.osvcurriculum.com

 "I will not leave you orphans; I will come to you. In a little while the world will no longer see me, but you will see me, because I live and you will live."

John 14:18–19

Last Judgment

Individually, humans will stand accountable before God at the time of death. The last judgment refers to a different reality than this individual judgment. Scripture speaks of a time when Jesus will return. At this second coming, all humanity will stand before God. All humans will face the truth of their lives and their relationships with him and others.

No one knows when Jesus will return in glory. However, at that time the harmony and intimacy lost in the garden of Eden will be reestablished and surpassed. Therefore, the last judgment is not a time of fear; it is a time of completion.

Knowing that humans are accountable raises levels of anxiety but also gives hope. Imperfections, pain, and disappointments will cease. "So faith, hope, love remain, these three; but the greatest of these is love" (*1 Corinthians 13:13*). This will truly be the kingdom come.

Gifts of the Holy Spirit

The Holy Spirit, the third Person of the Trinity, motivates and guides the Church. The Spirit is generous, supplying humans with the gifts they need. These gifts are wisdom, understanding, counsel, fortitude, knowledge, piety, and fear of the Lord. These are the seeds of a person's moral decisions, prayer, love for others, and worship of God. Like seeds, they grow only with attention and nurturing.

Reflect **What gifts of the Spirit do you want to develop more fully?**

The Last Judgment

This concept is a challenging one to present to fourth graders. Some students may have experienced the death of a loved one. These students may already have developed an image of heaven or eternal life. Other students will not have had this personal experience. For them, death and what comes after may be a very abstract concept. Accept students' varying degrees of comprehension.

- Students will benefit from having language to talk about final judgment and eternal life.

- Discuss the kingdom that God is preparing for the faithful, referring to *Matthew 25:34–40*. It will help students anticipate with patience and hope the life of the world to come.

- Use many examples when teaching about the gifts of the Holy Spirit so that students will understand that these gifts can change lives.

Difficult Topics

- The idea of death is puzzling and sometimes scary. Help me see that it is part of life.

- Sometimes religious concepts are difficult to understand. Explain them simply and patiently.

- I sometimes like to write or draw what I learn instead of talking about it. Add these activities to my lessons.

The Promise to Become

Your commitment to catechesis has enabled others to address their promise to become the kind of person God has called them to be. You have given them opportunities to gain knowledge, develop attitudes, and identify behaviors. These things can help them respond spiritually to the Call to Faith.

Reflect **Circle any of the following to revisit and cultivate as you continue to follow your vocational commitments.**

Engagement with Others	Coming to the Balcony
Habits of Mind	Confession
Keeping Company	Moments of Grace
Motivations	Vocational Seasons
Remembering Who You Are	Blessed Assurance

Catechist's Prayer

Faithful God, thank you for sustaining me throughout the school year. Thank you for my students and the joy they have brought me. Amen.

Weekly Planner

	Objectives	Lesson Process	Materials
1 Invite — 10 minutes	**Page 213** **Objective:** To imagine what heaven is like	**Let Us Pray:** Psalm 34:15 • Pray the psalm verse. • Read a story about a child's ideas of heaven. • Discuss ideas of heaven.	
2 Explore — 40 minutes	**Pages 214–215** **Objective:** To describe the gifts of the Holy Spirit	• Relate the concept of heaven. • Discuss each gift of the Holy Spirit. **Activity** Complete the Share Your Faith Activity. **Words of Faith** heaven	☐ Board or chart paper ☐ Copies of Activity Master 21 on page 220A ☐ Pencils or pens
	Pages 216–217 **Objective:** To understand the teachings about the particular and last judgments	**Scripture:** Matthew 25:34–40 • Describe the judgments and God's kingdom. • Discuss ways to prepare for heaven. **Activity** Complete the Connect Your Faith Activity. **Words of Faith** particular judgment, last judgment	☐ Markers or colored pencils
3 Celebrate — 10 minutes	**Page 218** **Objective:** To pray with hope for the coming of the kingdom	**Let Us Pray** • Practice the music. • Gather as a community. • Pray a Prayer for the Kingdom. **Hymn:** "We Come to Share Our Story" **Activity** Complete the Way of the Cross Activity, page 244 and 245	☐ Hymnals ☐ Music CD ☐ Bible

Wrap Up

Review and Apply

Page 219
• Review the chapter concepts.
• Complete the Live Your Faith Activity.

Family Faith

Page 220
• Introduce the page, and assign it as a family activity.
• Read about the Korean saints and martyrs.

ACRE Connection, Domain 4—Kingdom of God

Home Connection

GO online www.osvcurriculum.com
Family Faith activities, feasts and seasonal resources, saint features, and much more

• Online planning tools include chapter background and planner, activity master, customizable test, and more.

• Enhancement activities for each step of the catechetical process, including alternative prayer experiences and blessings.

• Games, activities, interactive review, alternative assessment, and more for chil

www.calltofaitheconnect.com

Chapter 21
I Want to See God

 **Let Us Pray**

Leader: God, teach us to live so that we may share eternal life with you.

"Turn from evil and do good;
seek peace and pursue it."
Psalm 34:15

All: God, teach us to live so that we may share eternal life with you. Amen.

 Activity *Let's Begin*

With Jesus Jessie sat with her mother in the car. Her mother wiped away Jessie's tears and said, "I will miss your Grandma Ruth, too. But she is happy and in heaven with Jesus."

When they arrived at the funeral home, Jessie gazed around the room where the body of her grandmother lay. Sweet-smelling flowers filled the room, and soft music played. With a huge gasp, Jessie declared, "Oh, so this is heaven!"

• What do you think heaven is like?
Responses will vary.

213

1 Invite

Objective: To imagine what heaven is like

 Let Us Pray

Invite students to gather in the prayer space. Pray the psalm verse with students. Play reflective music as they think about how to do good and seek peace.

Activity

• Tell students that they will hear a story about a girl who thought she knew what heaven looked like. Then read aloud the story.

• Ask why the girl thought that the funeral home was heaven. Possible responses: It was beautiful; her grandmother was there.

• Have students describe their ideas of heaven.

• Tell students that it is natural to wonder what death and heaven will be like.

OPTIONAL ACTIVITY

Children's Literature A book that may be helpful with this lesson is *That Summer*, by Tony Johnston (Harcourt, 2002). It tells the story of the final illness of a boy, through the eyes of his brother. Before using this book, consider personal situations within the class.

Multiple Intelligence: Verbal/Linguistic

QUICK TIP

Visions of Heaven For now, accept all students' ideas of heaven and affirm their creativity.

• Some students may respond with a traditional view of heaven with angels, clouds, and harps.

• Students who are knowledgeable about and interested in the natural world may picture heaven as a beautiful landscape or a lovely garden.

Objective: To describe the gifts of the Holy Spirit

 Focus

How do the gifts of the Holy Spirit help you live in friendship with God? List students' responses on the board or on chart paper.

Being with God

Compare students' ideas of heaven with the idea of sharing life with God and all holy people forever. Then read aloud the text.

- Point out that there is much about heaven that people will need to wait to understand. Whatever it is like, heaven will be an experience of love and peace.

- Ask what students think will be the best thing about heaven.

- Point out that Baptism and Confirmation, which help people grow in friendship with God, are sacraments of the Spirit.

Being with God

 Focus How do the gifts of the Holy Spirit help you live in friendship with God?

Heaven is not a room with sweet-smelling flowers. It is not a place in the sky among the clouds. **Heaven** is the life that all holy people will share with God forever.

To spend eternity with God, you first must grow in friendship with God. Through the Holy Spirit, God has given you gifts that will help you grow in friendship with him and with others. You receive the gifts of the Holy Spirit at Baptism, and in Confirmation these gifts are strengthened in you. These seven powerful gifts help you follow Jesus more closely. They open your heart so that the Holy Spirit can guide you to make good and unselfish choices.

THE GIFT OF	HELPS YOU
WISDOM	• see yourself as God sees you and act as God wants you to act • live in the image and likeness of God
UNDERSTANDING	• get to know God, yourself, and other people better • see why you sometimes make wrong choices • learn to make better choices • learn to forgive more freely
COUNSEL (or right judgment)	• give good advice to others • hear the Holy Spirit, who speaks to you through your conscience and through the good advice and good example of others

214

OPTIONAL ACTIVITY

Windsock Give students the following directions.

- Draw a symbol for the Holy Spirit on construction paper. Roll the paper into a cylinder and tape the sides together.

- Write one gift of the Spirit on each of seven strips of colored paper. Tape them to the windsock.

Multiple Intelligence: Visual/Spatial

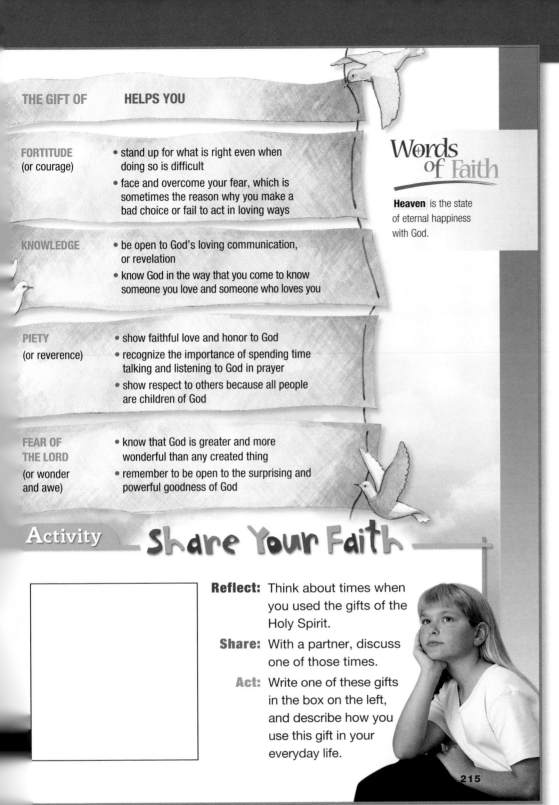

THE GIFT OF	HELPS YOU
FORTITUDE (or courage)	• stand up for what is right even when doing so is difficult • face and overcome your fear, which is sometimes the reason why you make a bad choice or fail to act in loving ways
KNOWLEDGE	• be open to God's loving communication, or revelation • know God in the way that you come to know someone you love and someone who loves you
PIETY (or reverence)	• show faithful love and honor to God • recognize the importance of spending time talking and listening to God in prayer • show respect to others because all people are children of God
FEAR OF THE LORD (or wonder and awe)	• know that God is greater and more wonderful than any created thing • remember to be open to the surprising and powerful goodness of God

Words of Faith

Heaven is the state of eternal happiness with God.

Activity

Share Your Faith

Reflect: Think about times when you used the gifts of the Holy Spirit.

Share: With a partner, discuss one of those times.

Act: Write one of these gifts in the box on the left, and describe how you use this gift in your everyday life.

215

Gifts of the Spirit

Direct students' attention to the chart on pages 214–215.

• Tell students that this chart tells how the gifts of the Holy Spirit help you grow in friendship with God.

• Work through the chart with students, reading each banner shape as a sentence: "The gift of . . . helps you . . ."

• Stop after each sentence and ask students how that gift might be used by someone their age.

• Remind students that using these gifts will help them prepare for the joy of being with God in heaven.

Activity

• Give students time to complete the activity individually.

• Ask volunteers to share a time when they used a gift of the Holy Spirit.

Quick Review

Heaven is not a place; it is eternal life and happiness with God. The gifts of the Holy Spirit help people make good choices.

OPTIONAL ACTIVITY

Activity Master 21: Gifts of the Spirit Distribute copies of the activity found on catechist page 220A.

• The distinction between gifts such as knowledge and wisdom may be challenging. Remind students to refer to their texts.

▲ Activity Master 21

REACHING ALL LEARNERS

The Gifts of the Spirit Visual learners will benefit from seeing the gifts of the Holy Spirit listed and displayed in the classroom. Write each gift and a brief definition on chart paper, and post it where students can refer to it throughout the lesson.

Objective: To understand the teachings about the particular and last judgments

 **Focus**

How does a person prepare for the last judgment? List students' responses on the board or on chart paper.

The Last Judgment

Tell students that everyone may choose to accept or reject God's grace and the gifts of the Holy Spirit. Then read aloud the first paragraph of the text.

- Point out that God welcomes all who love him above all things and love their neighbor as themselves.

- Summarize the second paragraph. Tell students that those who choose to reject God are separated from him forever. Tell students that permanent separation from God is called *hell.*

- Ask students to read the third paragraph to learn what will happen to all people at the end of time.

Explore

The Last Judgment

 **Focus** How does a person prepare for the last judgment?

The gifts of the Holy Spirit help you turn away from selfish actions and prepare you to be with God forever. All through your life you have the choice of accepting or rejecting the grace offered through Jesus. At the time of your death, God will judge how well you have accepted his gifts. This is called the **particular judgment**.

Jesus asks you to love God above all things and your neighbor as yourself. If you remain in God's grace and friendship by following his law, the everlasting happiness of heaven will eventually be yours. Some people sin greatly and reject God's covenant of love. They refuse his grace and forgiveness. These sinners will be separated forever from God because of their own choices. That separation is called hell.

At the end of time, all people who have ever lived will rise again and appear before God for judgment. This **last judgment** will not change each person's particular judgment. Rather, it will mark the coming of God's kingdom in its fullness. This is the time when Christ will come again in glory.

Preparing for Heaven

When you live with the particular and last judgments in mind, you will try to work every day for the justice, love, and peace of God's reign. As you do so, you a preparing to live forever with God. Jesus told his followers what would happen o the day of the last judgment.

 JUSTICE AND PEACE

Judgment Scripture and the teachings of the Church point out that we will be judged by our actions.

- Students often think about judgment in terms of what they have done wrong.

- Help students reflect on how they live their faith in right words, actions, and examples.

Catholic Social Teaching: Rights and Responsibilities

The Last Judgment

"Then the king will say to those on his right, '. . . . Inherit the kingdom prepared for you. . . . For I was hungry and you gave me food, I was thirsty and you gave me drink, a stranger and you welcomed me, naked and you clothed me, ill and you cared for me, in prison and you visited me.' Then the righteous will answer him and say, 'Lord, when did we see you hungry and feed you, or thirsty and give you drink? When did we see you a stranger and welcome you, or naked and clothe you? When did we see you ill or in prison, and visit you?' And the king will say to them in reply, 'Amen, I say to you, whatever you did for one of these least brothers of mine, you did for me.' "

Matthew 25:34–40

Words of Faith

Particular judgment is the individual judgment by God at the time of your death.

The **last judgment** will occur at the end of time when Jesus returns to judge all who have ever lived. Then, all will fully see and understand God's plan for creation.

? **Who is the king in this story?** Jesus

? **Who are the righteous in this story?**
those who have helped others as Jesus taught

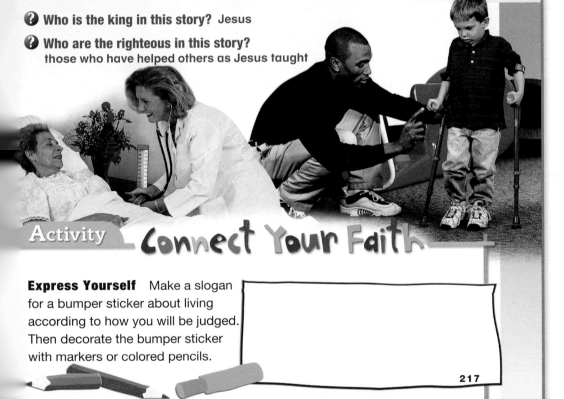

Activity

Connect Your Faith

Express Yourself Make a slogan for a bumper sticker about living according to how you will be judged. Then decorate the bumper sticker with markers or colored pencils.

217

Preparing for Heaven

Tell students to read the text silently.

- Ask them to underline or write the words that tell how to prepare for heaven. Work every day for the justice, love, and peace of God's reign.

The Last Judgment

Say that Jesus described the last judgment for his followers.

- Proclaim the scripture passage.
- Discuss the questions.

Activity

- Plan time for students to write their slogans.
- Ask for volunteers to share their work with the class.

Quick Review

People are judged on how well they have helped others and followed God's will. Particular judgment occurs after a person dies. The last judgment happens at the end of time, when Jesus comes in glory.

OPTIONAL ACTIVITY

Collage Distribute magazines and newspapers.

- Ask students to find pictures or articles that show the good actions described in *Matthew 25:34–40*.
- Have students glue their pictures and articles on poster board.
- Tell them to use words from the Scripture to make a border for the collage.

Multiple Intelligence: Visual/Spatial

SCRIPTURE BACKGROUND

Scripture *Matthew 25:34–40* is followed by a similar passage in which those who have not obeyed God are sent to "eternal punishment."

- If you want to share verses 41–46, consider whether students are mature enough for the images in the passage.
- If you share the passage with students, explain it carefully.

Objective: To pray with hope for the coming of the kingdom

 Let Us Pray

Tell students they will have a chance to share favorite stories about Jesus.

Prayer for the Kingdom

Prepare

Ask individuals or small groups to select favorite stories about Jesus for the prayer celebration. Remind students to listen respectfully.

Use the *Call to Faith 4* CD, track 21, to rehearse the suggested song.

Gather

Gather students in a circle.

Pray

- Follow the order of prayer on page 218.
- An optional Bible reading is *Matthew 22:1–14.*

Celebrate

Prayer for the Kingdom

 **Let Us Pray**

Gather and begin with the Sign of the Cross.

Leader: Lord Jesus, you sometimes described heaven as a feast or a banquet. Help us remember the gift of your life and teaching that we have shared together this year. Be with us as we remember and pray.

Share a story of Jesus that you remember from this year. Then pray together.

All: Lord Jesus, we long to see your face. May your kingdom come into our hearts and into our world. Open our hearts to those who are poor, sick, imprisoned, lonely, and suffering. Make us one Body in Christ through the gifts of your Spirit. Help us ready ourselves for the banquet of heaven. Amen.

Sing together.

We come to share our story,
Venimos a decir del misterio,
we come to break the bread.
y partir el pan de vida.
We come to know our rising from the dead.
Venimos a saber de nuestra eternidad.

"We Come to Share Our Story" © 1989, GIA Publications, Inc.

218

 LITURGY LINK

Circle Gathering This prayer, with its sharing of stories, is a good one for the group to share in a circle.

- Have students bring their books.
- Invite students to think about their stories of Jesus for a "centering" time.
- Then, when you are ready to begin the prayer, ask students to turn to page 218.

 LECTIONARY LINK

Break Open the Word Read last week's Sunday Gospel. Invite students to think about what the reading means to them as they try to follow Christ's example. For questions related to the weekly Gospel reading, visit our website at **www.osvcurriculum.com**.

 Visit www.osvcurriculum.com for weekly Scripture readings and seasonal resources.

Review and Apply

Wrap-Up

A **Work with Words** Complete each statement with the correct gift of the Holy Spirit.

1. Josh gives his best friend good advice, telling him not to shoplift. _____**counsel**_____

2. Kim didn't do her homework, but she decides to tell her teacher the truth. _**fortitude, or courage**_

3. Tasha was ready to steal a CD. When she remembered what was talked about in religion class, she put the CD back. _____**understanding**_____

4. Madison is overwhelmed with the beauty of the night sky and she thinks of God. _**fear of the Lord, or awe and wonder**_

5. Amelia is struggling with a decision. She thinks about what Jesus would do. _____**wisdom**_____

B **Check Understanding** In your own words, explain what will happen at the last judgment.

**Responses will vary.**

_____

Activity Live Your Faith

Describe Your Life How do you want to be remembered by others after you leave your life on earth? In the space below, write a sentence that describes your life.

_____
_____
_____
_____
_____

219

Review and Apply

Use the focus questions from the catechist Explore pages to review the lesson concepts.

A **Work with Words** Have students fill in the gifts of the Holy Spirit.

B **Check Understanding** Ask students to write a response to the statement. Discuss their responses.

Activity

- Invite students to share how they remember loved ones who have died.

- Then allow time for them to write about how they would like to be remembered.

- Ask volunteers to share their responses.

OPTIONAL ACTIVITY

Vocabulary Games Students have been using the Words of Faith to make vocabulary cards.

- Create games to review words as the year ends.

- Students could play a quiz game or a memory game by matching words and definitions.

- Students can help in designing the word games.

absolution

Multiple Intelligence: Verbal/Linguistic

Wrap-Up

Family Faith

Remind students to discuss the Family Faith page at home. Encourage students to read the passage from the Gospel according to Mark.

Activity

- Invite a student to read aloud the directions for the activity.
- Show an example of a newspaper story featuring people who are suffering.

People of Faith

Tell students about the Korean saints and martyrs.

- Christianity was brought to Korea not by missionaries but by Korean laypeople. The Catholic Church in Korea flourished largely because of the tenacity of the lay community.
- Remind students to add the Korean saints and martyrs to their People of Faith albums. Encourage them to pray the prayer at home with their families.

 Visit **www.osvcurriculum.com** for weekly scripture readings and seasonal resources.

UNIT 7: CHAPTER 21

Family Faith

◉ Catholics Believe

- The Church teaches that at the end of time, all will be raised from the dead.
- After being raised from the dead, all will come into the presence of Christ to be judged.

✝ SCRIPTURE

Read *Mark 7:31–37* to learn a story about Jesus' powerful ability to heal those who are suffering.

GO online www.osvcurriculum.com
For weekly scripture readings and seasonal resources

Activity
Live Your Faith

Think of Ways to Help As a family, brainstorm ways in which people in the world are suffering. Look for newspaper articles and stories on the news. When you gather for dinner, pray for a person or about a situation in which there is suffering. Discuss how your family could help. If there is no direct action you can take, keep that person or situation in your family's prayers each day this week.

▲ **Korean Saints and Martyrs 1839–1867**

People of Faith

On May 6, 1984, the Church canonized 103 Korean people. These saints ranged in age from thirteen-year-old **Peter Yu Tae-chol** to seventy-two-year-old **Mark Chong**. Each of these people sacrificed his or her life for the sake of Jesus and the Catholic faith. Eleven of the martyrs were priests. Many of these saints were the first Christians in Korea, among them **Yi Sung-hun**, founder of the first Church community in that country. The feast day for these saints and martyrs is September 20.

In Unit 7 your child is learning about the KINGDOM OF GOD.

220 **CCC** *See Catechism of the Catholic Church 681–682 for further reading on chapter content.*

🙌 Family Prayer

Saints and martyrs of Korea, pray for us that we will be strong in our faith even when it is difficult to do so. Pray that we may live wisely and lovingly to prepare to meet God at the end of time. Amen.

❓ HOW DID I DO?

My session was

☐ *one of the best ever!* ☐ *pretty good.* ☐ *in need of improvement.*

In what discussions and activities were students most interested?

_____

What activity did I most enjoy teaching?

_____

In what area do I need to improve?

_____

Name _____ Date _____

Gifts of the Spirit

Write each gift of the Holy Spirit in the first column next to its description in the middle column. Then in the third column, write an example of how you use the gift.

FORTITUDE	WISDOM	KNOWLEDGE	COUNSEL
PIETY	UNDERSTANDING		FEAR OF THE LORD

Gift	Description	I use this gift when I . . .
	Helps you see yourself as God sees you and act as God wants you to act	
	Helps you give good advice	
	Helps you come to know God, yourself, and others	
	Helps you be open to God's loving communication	
	Helps you recognize that God is greater and more wonderful than any created thing	
	Helps you show love and honor to God	
	Helps you stand up for what is right	

Work with Words   Complete each sentence with the correct term.

1. To _____ resent _____ or want for yourself what belongs to others is called envy.

2. Variety, especially among people, is known as _____ diversity _____.

3. The _____ last judgment _____ will occur at the end of time, when Jesus returns to judge all who have ever lived.

4. The virtue of giving to God and people what is due them is called _____ justice _____.

5. _____ Greed _____ is the desire to acquire earthly goods without limit or beyond one's means.

6. The _____ poor in spirit _____ are those who do not become too attached to their possessions and are able to help bring about God's reign.

7. To share the good news of Jesus and the kingdom of God, people are sent on a _____ mission _____.

8. _____ Stewardship _____ is the responsibility to care for all of God's creation.

9. The state of eternal happiness with God is known as _____ heaven _____.

10. _____ Particular judgment _____ is the individual judgment by God at the time of a person's death.

221

Unit Review

The Unit Review is designed to prepare students for the Unit Assessment. This page focuses on vocabulary words and the main concepts presented in the chapters.

Each review contains various sections that will appeal to the many different learning styles of your students. There are puzzles to engage students' attention, as well as true-false, multiple-choice, short-answer, and fill-in-the-blank exercises.

Direct students to complete the review, and check their responses. Determine areas in which students still need practice, and review those sections of the unit.

Notes

Name _____ Date _____

Judged on Love

(A) Work with Words   Match each description in Column 1 with the correct term in Column 2.

Column 1

_____ **1.** helps you give good advice to others

_____ **2.** helps you show love and honor to God

_____ **3.** helps you see yourself as God sees you

_____ **4.** helps you be open to God's revelations

_____ **5.** helps you be aware of God's power

Column 2

a. wisdom

b. counsel

c. knowledge

d. piety

e. fear of the Lord

(B) Check Understanding   Circle the letter of the choice that best completes the sentence.

6. Thinking of the last judgment should remind people to _____.

    a. fear the unknown

    b. work for justice and peace

    c. compete with others

    d. spend time in church

7. One sin against the seventh commandment is _____.

    a. theft

    b. murder

    c. idolatry

    d. lying

8. One sin against the tenth commandment is _____.

    a. adultery

    b. envy

    c. disobeying one's parents

    d. lying

9. A virtue that helps you follow the seventh commandment is _____.

    a. humility

    b. obedience

    c. trust

    d. both a and c

10. One virtue that helps you follow the tenth commandment is _____.

    a. honesty

    b. obedience

    c. generosity

    d. peace

ASSESSMENT

Answers can be found in the back of the Catechist Manual.

Name _____ Date _____

11. Jesus' mission for Christians is to _____.

    a. make disciples of all nations   **c.** give everyone a Bible

    b. have everyone be happy always   **d.** teach themselves about him

12. Justice is _____.

    a. found only in courts   **c.** a virtue for adults

    b. a work of mercy   **d.** giving people what is due them

13. An example of appreciating diversity is _____.

    a. eating a well-balanced meal   **c.** learning about another culture

    b. sharing school supplies   **d.** writing a letter to your grandmother

14–17. Complete the paragraph with the correct terms from the Word Bank.

After humans die, they meet God and have their lives judged.

This is the _____. Then their souls will go to

_____, where they will be with God always,

or to _____, where they will never see him.

At the end of time, all souls will meet for the last judgment,

when Jesus will come again in glory. This will be the fulfillment

of _____.

WORD BANK
particular judgment
God's kingdom
hell
heaven

C **Make Connections** Write a brief response to the statement.

18–20. Describe three specific ways in which you are preparing for your mission in life.

_____

_____

_____

_____

_____

_____

_____

_____

ASSESSMENT

    Answers can be found in the back of the Catechist Manual.

CATHOLIC SOURCE BOOK

HOW TO USE Topics covered in each of the sections will enrich the content in the student book. During class time, you may wish to invite students to use the Catholic Source Book to clarify or discuss some of the topics of interest in a given lesson.

ACTIVITIES In the first five sections of the teacher edition for the Catholic Source Book, you will find Optional Activities for each page of the student book. These activities are located beneath the reproduced student pages in your teacher edition.

You may wish to use these during class as enrichment activities, or, if appropriate, as homework.

GLOSSARY The Glossary section contains all of the Words of Faith found in the student book as well as other important faith words that are introduced in the text.

Encourage your students to refer to the Catholic Source Book when they want to learn more about a topic.

The Catholic Source Book for *Call to Faith*—which includes the four pillars of the Catechism of the Catholic Church—is organized in six sections.

Scripture	p. 222
Creed	p. 226
Liturgy	p. 230
Morality	p. 234
Prayer	p. 239
Glossary	p. 242

CATHOLIC SOURCE BOOK

Scripture

The Books of the Bible

The Catholic version of the Bible contains seventy-three books—forty-six in the Old Testament and twenty-seven in the New Testament.

The Old Testament

The Pentateuch

Genesis	Leviticus	Deuteronomy
Exodus	Numbers	

Faith Fact

Before the invention of the printing press, the Bible had to be copied by hand. Many times when copying the text, monks would also illuminate, or illustrate, Scripture passages.

The Historical Books

Joshua	2 Kings	Judith
Judges	1 Chronicles	Esther
Ruth	2 Chronicles	1 Maccabees
1 Samuel	Ezra	2 Maccabees
2 Samuel	Nehemiah	
1 Kings	Tobit	

The Wisdom Books

Job	Ecclesiastes	Sirach
Psalms	Song of Songs	(Ecclesiasticus)
Proverbs	Wisdom	

© Our Sunday Visitor Curriculum Division

The Prophetic Books

Isaiah	Hosea	Nahum
Jeremiah	Joel	Habakkuk
Lamentations	Amos	Zephaniah
Baruch	Obadiah	Haggai
Ezekiel	Jonah	Zechariah
Daniel	Micah	Malachi

The New Testament

The Gospels

Matthew
Mark
Luke
John

The Acts of the Apostles

The New Testament Letters

Romans	1 Thessalonians	James
1 Corinthians	2 Thessalonians	1 Peter
2 Corinthians	1 Timothy	2 Peter
Galatians	2 Timothy	1 John
Ephesians	Titus	2 John
Philippians	Philemon	3 John
Colossians	Hebrews	Jude

Revelation

© Our Sunday Visitor Curriculum Division

222

223

Faith Fact

Each of the Gospel writers has a symbol. Matthew is represented by a winged man, Mark is represented by a winged lion, Luke is represented by a winged ox, and John is represented by an eagle.

About the Old Testament

The Pentateuch is the first five books of the Old Testament. The word pentateuch means "five containers." In the beginning the pentateuch was written on leather or papyrus and each book was kept in a separate container. Jewish people call these books the Torah. The books of the pentateuch tell of the beginning of human relationship with God. They also tell the story of God's loving actions for humans.

The Wisdom books of the Old Testament provide guidance in human behavior. Wisdom is a spiritual gift that allows a person to know God's purpose and plan. They remind us that God's wisdom is always greater than human knowledge.

Many prophets were authors of Old Testament books. A prophet is a person sent by God to call people back to their covenant with God.

The Formation of the New Testament

The New Testament was formed in three stages:
1. The life and teaching of Jesus—Jesus' whole life and teaching proclaimed the good news.
2. The oral tradition—After the Resurrection the Apostles preached the good news. Then the early Christians passed on what the Apostles had preached. They told and retold the teachings of Jesus and the story of his life, death, and Resurrection.
3. The four Gospels and other writings—The stories, teachings, and sayings of Jesus were collected and written down in the Gospels according to Matthew, Mark, Luke, and John. The actions and lessons of the early Church were recorded in the Acts of the Apostles and the New Testament letters.

How to Locate Bible Passages

To practice finding a particular Bible passage, use the example of *Matthew 8:23–27*.

Matthew is the name of a book in the Bible. The chapter number always comes directly after the name of the book, so 8 is the chapter number. The numbers 23–27 refer to the verses. To find this passage, go to the table of contents in your Bible. Find the page number for the Gospel according to Matthew, and turn to that page. The chapter number will be at the top of the page. Turn the pages to find Chapter 8. When you reach Chapter 8, look for the smaller numbers within the passage. These are the verse numbers. Find verse 23. This is where you will begin reading. Continue reading through verse 27, the last verse in the passage.

Matthew is the name of the book in the Bible.

The numbers *23–27* refer to the verses.

The Covenant

The covenant is the sacred agreement joining God and humans in relationship. When God made the covenant with Noah after the flood, he promised never to destroy the earth again. God renewed the covenant with Abram (Abraham), promising that Abraham's descendants would be as numerous as the stars. Years later, when the descendants of Abraham were slaves in Egypt, God used Moses to lead the people away in the *Exodus*, or "the road out." At Mount Sinai the covenant was renewed with Moses. God guided the Israelites to the Promised Land. In return, the Israelites were called to love only God and to follow his Law, the Ten Commandments. Finally, through the Paschal mystery—Jesus' life, death, and Resurrection—the covenant was fulfilled and a new covenant was created. The new covenant is open to all who remain faithful to God.

224

225

OPTIONAL ACTIVITY

Old Testament Passages   Prepare a list of citations from the Old Testament, and have students find these citiations in their Bibles.

- Ask students to write the main idea of each passage next to its citation.
- Then have students compare their findings with a partner.

OPTIONAL ACTIVITY

Oral Tradition   Organize students in small groups, and invite each member to share a pleasant memory about a friend who has moved, a relative who has passed away, or someone (even a pet) who is no longer physicaly present in the student's life.

- Ask students to share appropriate family stories that they hear at Christmas or Thanksgiving gatherings.
- Explain that the disciples told similar stories about Jesus.

Creed

The Holy Trinity

God is revealed in three Persons: God the Father and Creator, God the Son and Savior, God the Holy Spirit and Guide. Each of the Persons of the Trinity is separate from the other Persons. However, the Father, Son, and Holy Spirit are one and the same God. The Holy Trinity is the central mystery of the Catholic faith.

The mission of God the Son and God the Holy Spirit is to bring people into the love of the Trinity—the perfect love that exists in the Father, Son, and Holy Spirit.

Faith Fact

The Holy Trinity is represented by many symbols, including the equilateral triangle, three interwoven circles, a circle of three fish, and the shamrock.

God the Father

God created all things. The beauty of creation reflects the beauty of the Creator. He cares for and loves all. In his divine providence, God guides everything toward himself.

God the Son

Jesus is the Son of God. The Church has many important teachings about him. The **Incarnation** is a basic mystery of the Catholic faith and is the belief that God became man. Jesus Christ became man in order to save all people from the power of sin and everlasting death. Jesus was truly man and yet was truly God. Jesus became human, being born of the Virgin Mary. Except for sin, Jesus had all the experiences of being human.

Through the teachings of Jesus, people come to know about the kingdom of God and how to live for God's reign. From the Sermon on the Mount and other teachings, people learn to live in love. Jesus did not reject sinners, but instead called them to turn away from sin and back to God. Jesus taught everyone how to live the Ten Commandments—by loving God and all of his creation.

226

Jesus' **Resurrection** showed him as the Messiah, the Savior. By his death Jesus conquered sin. By rising from the dead, Jesus conquered death and so saved all humans from the power of sin and everlasting death.

The Ascension happened forty days after the Resurrection, when Jesus ascended to heaven to join the glory of God the Father. At the Ascension Jesus commanded the Apostles to continue his mission by teaching and guiding people toward God's kingdom. The sending of the Holy Spirit on Pentecost is the final part of Jesus' act of salvation.

God the Holy Spirit

The Holy Spirit continues to guide people in the Christian life. Through the teachings of Jesus, Christians learned how to live in love. Through the strength and wisdom of the Holy Spirit, they are able to lead this life of love. The Holy Spirit breathes into the faithful his fruits and his gifts. The fruits—such as piety, peace, and joy—and the gifts—such as wisdom, courage, and reverence—help humans turn toward God and cooperate in bringing about the kingdom of God.

The **Immaculate Conception** means that Mary was preserved from original sin from the first moment of conception. The Feast of the Immaculate Conception is December 8. On this date the Catholics of Paraguay celebrate the feast day of the Virgin of Caacupé. Centuries ago, the Virgin Mary appeared in the Paraguayan countryside. A church was built in the place where she had appeared, and many pilgrims to that church have experienced miracles. Today December 8 is as special a celebration to the Catholics of Paraguay as Christmas is. Many Paraguayans honor Mary every year by making a pilgrimage, or long walk, to the church of the Virgin of Caacupé.

227

OPTIONAL ACTIVITY

The Holy Trinity   Have students make three-dimensional symbols for the Holy Trinity.

- Allow students to use known symbols or to create symbols of their own.
- Provide students with construction paper, scissors, staplers, and glue. Display the completed Trinity symbols.

OPTIONAL ACTIVITY

Mary   Assign stories about Mary for students to read. Reading such stories will help students reflect on Mary's faith in God.

- Encourage students to retell some of the stories to the group.
- Possible stories from the Gospel according to Luke include *Luke 1:26–38, 1:39–56, 2:1–14, 2:22–38,* and *2:41–52.*

Church

Church **authority** is based on the command from Jesus to his Apostles to make disciples of people everywhere, teaching them to live as Jesus taught and baptizing them in the name of the Father, Son, and Holy Spirit. (See *Matthew 28:18–20*.) Authority also comes from the Holy Spirit as the Spirit of Truth that guides the Church. The official teaching authority of the Church is the **magisterium,** which is made up of the pope and the bishops. The magisterium teaches with the authority given by Jesus and the guidance of the Holy Spirit.

Mission

The Church has the mission to help bring justice to everyone. The principles of social justice are respect for all persons, equality for all persons, and oneness in the family of God with responsibility for one another. These principles can be accomplished with the fair distribution of goods, fair wages for work, and fair resolution in conflicts.

Pope

The pope's title of "Servant of the Servants" began with Pope Gregory the Great. It is stated at Mark 10:44 *"[W]hoever wishes to be first among you will be the slave of all."*

Faith Fact

The many titles for the Pope include: Bishop of Rome, Vicar of Christ, Supreme Pontiff of the Universal Church, Patriarch of the West, Primate of Italy, Successor of St. Peter, Prince of the Apostles, Servant of the Servants of God, and Sovereign of Vatican City.

© Our Sunday Visitor Curriculum Division

228

Saints

Canonization is the process by which the Church recognizes faithful people as saints. During each of the three stages of becoming a saint, the faithful person has a different title—first Venerable, then Blessed, and finally Saint.

Last Things

Purgatory

At death some people are not ready for heaven and God's eternal friendship. However, they have not broken their relationship with God. These souls are given time in purgatory. *Purgatory* means "purifying." Purgatory helps the soul prepare for life with God. The soul becomes more faithful and loving.

Particular judgment

When people die, they are judged by how well they have lived and loved. This judgment is called particular judgment. Souls will be given reward or punishment at this time.

General judgment

General judgment, or the last judgment, will occur at the Second Coming of Christ. This judgment represents God's triumph over evil. General judgment will mark the arrival of God's kingdom in its fullness. General judgment will happen to all people, living and dead. However, this judgment will not change the particular judgment received by each soul.

© Our Sunday Visitor Curriculum Division

229

OPTIONAL ACTIVITY

Mission   Supply students with news articles on social justice issues.

- Ask each student to read an article and tell the group how the article illustrates real-world applications of social justice.
- Help students identify in their articles any of the principles of social justice found on page 298.

OPTIONAL ACTIVITY

Saints   Direct each student to research the life of a saint. The research should focus on the saint's contribution to his or her local faith community or to the wider Church.

- Ask students to illustrate their saints' contributions.
- Put the illustrations together to make a bulletin board.

Liturgy — The Liturgical Year

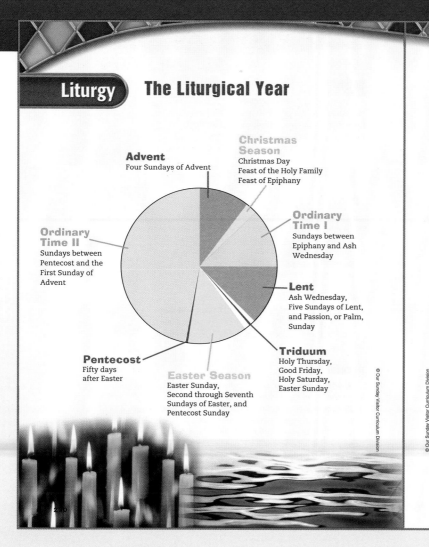

Advent
Four Sundays of Advent

Christmas Season
Christmas Day
Feast of the Holy Family
Feast of Epiphany

Ordinary Time I
Sundays between Epiphany and Ash Wednesday

Lent
Ash Wednesday, Five Sundays of Lent, and Passion, or Palm, Sunday

Triduum
Holy Thursday, Good Friday, Holy Saturday, Easter Sunday

Easter Season
Easter Sunday, Second through Seventh Sundays of Easter, and Pentecost Sunday

Pentecost
Fifty days after Easter

Ordinary Time II
Sundays between Pentecost and the First Sunday of Advent

© Our Sunday Visitor Curriculum Division

230

Order of Mass

The Mass follows a pattern, with some differences according to the feast or season of the liturgical year. The main parts of the Mass are the Liturgy of the Word and the Liturgy of the Eucharist. Here is an outline of the order of Mass:

Introductory Rites
- Entrance Chant
- Greeting
- Rite for the Blessing and Sprinkling of Water
- Penitential Act
- *Kyria*
- *Gloria*
- Collect

Liturgy of the Word
- First Reading (usually from the Old Testament)
- Responsorial Psalm
- Second Reading (from New Testament Letters)
- Gospel Acclamation
- Dialogue at the Gospel
- Gospel Reading
- Homily
- Profession of Faith (Creed)
- Prayer of the Faithful

Liturgy of the Eucharist
- Preparation of the Gifts
- Invitation to Prayer
- Prayer over the Offerings
- Eucharistic Prayer
  Preface Dialogue
  Preface
  Preface Acclamation
  Consecration
  Mystery of Faith
  Concluding Doxology
- Communion Rite
  The Lord's Prayer
  Sign of Peace
  Lamb of God
  Invitation to Communion
  Communion
  Prayer After Communion

Concluding Rite
- Greeting
- Blessing
- Dismissal

Faith Fact

The Eucharist is known by several different names. These include the Blessed Sacrament, Holy Communion, the Bread of Heaven, Breaking of Bread, the Lord's Supper, Holy Sacrifice, Holy Mass, and the Body of Christ.

© Our Sunday Visitor Curriculum Division

231

The Sacraments

The Catholic Church celebrates seven Sacraments, or signs, of Jesus' presence. There are three groups of Sacraments.

Sacraments of Initiation	Baptism Confirmation Eucharist
Sacraments of Healing	Reconciliation Anointing of the Sick
Sacraments of Vocation and Service	Matrimony Holy Orders

Holy Water

Holy water is water that has been blessed. It is used during the Sacrament of Baptism as well as for the blessing of people or objects. Fonts of holy water are placed at the entrances of churches so that people may bless themselves and recall the meaning of Baptism as they make the Sign of the Cross.

The Paschal Candle

The Paschal candle is a symbol of Christ and of Easter. This candle is lit from the Easter fire during the Easter Vigil. Throughout the fifty days of the Easter Season, the candle burns during the liturgy. After the Easter Season it is used during baptisms and funerals as a symbol of the Resurrection.

232

The Sacrament of Reconciliation

The Sacrament of Reconciliation is also known as the Sacrament of Penance or the Sacrament of Confession. In this Sacrament, sin is forgiven and the one who has sinned is reconciled with God, with himself or herself, and with the Church community. The essential elements for Reconciliation are

- contrition (sorrow for the sin)
- confession
- absolution by the priest
- satisfaction (attempting to correct or undo the wrong done). The priest can never reveal what he is told during a confession. The priest's silence is called the *sacramental seal* or the *seal of confession*.

Celebrating the Sacrament

Communal Rite of Reconciliation

1. Greeting
2. Celebration of the Word
3. Homily
4. Examination of Conscience
5. General Confession of Sin
6. The Lord's Prayer
7. Individual Confession of Sins, Acceptance of a penance, and Absolution
8. Closing Prayer

Individual Rite of Reconciliation

1. Welcome
2. Reading from Scripture
3. Confession of Sins and Acceptance of a Penance
4. Act of Contrition
5. Absolution
6. Closing Prayer

233

OPTIONAL ACTIVITY

Paschal Candle Point out to students that the Paschal candle reminds the faithful that Christ is their source of illumination—that he is the Light of the World.

- Supply students with large candles and decorating supplies.
- Ask each student to decorate a candle. Decorations should reflect either that Christ is a light in their lives or themes of the Easter season.

OPTIONAL ACTIVITY

Reconciliation Ask each student to compose an Act of Contrition.

- Reinforce the absolute confidentiality of students' confessions.
- Point out that even civil laws respect the seal of the confessional.

The Beatitudes

The Beatitudes are sayings of Jesus that show us the way to true happiness in God's kingdom. The Beatitudes are listed in the Gospel according to Matthew (*Matthew 5:3–10*), see Chapter 7.

Faith Fact

The eight points on the Maltese Cross represent the Beatitudes.

The New Commandment

Jesus also gave his followers a new commandment: "love one another. As I have loved you, so you also should love one another." (*John 13:34*)

The Ten Commandments

THE TEN COMMANDMENTS

THE TEN COMMANDMENTS	THEIR MEANING
1. I am the Lord your God. You shall not have strange Gods before me.	Keep God first in your life.
2. You shall not take the name of the Lord your God in vain.	Always use God's name in a reverent way.
3. Remember to keep holy the Lord's day.	Attend Mass and rest on Sunday.
4. Honor your mother and father.	Obey your father and mother.
5. You shall not kill.	Care for yourself and others.
6. You shall not commit adultery.	Be respectful of every person.
7. You shall not steal.	Respect other people and their property.
8. You shall not bear false witness against your neighbor.	Respect others by always telling the truth.
9. You shall not covet your neighbor's wife.	Don't be jealous of other people's relationships.
10. You shall not covet your neighbor's goods.	Don't be jealous of what other people have.

© Our Sunday Visitor Curriculum Division

234

Conscience

Conscience is the gift from God that helps you know the difference between right and wrong. Conscience helps you choose what is right. It involves free will and reason working together. You must form your conscience properly. If not formed properly, your conscience can lead you to choose what is wrong.

Forming your conscience is a lifelong process. It involves practicing virtues and avoiding sin and people or situations that may lead you to sin. You can turn to good people for advice, to Church teachings for guidance, and to God for help in educating your conscience.

Examining Your Conscience

For help with examining your conscience, use the following steps:

1. Pray for the Holy Spirit's help in making a fresh start.

2. Look at your life in the light of the Beatitudes, the Ten Commandments, the Great Commandment, and the precepts of the Church.

3. Ask yourself these questions: Where have I fallen short of what God wants for me? Whom have I hurt? What have I done that I knew was wrong? What have I not done that I should have done? Have I made the necessary changes in bad habits? What areas am I still having trouble with? Am I sincerely sorry for all my sins?

© Our Sunday Visitor Curriculum Division

235

OPTIONAL ACTIVITY

The Ten Commandments   Ask each student to copy the Ten Commandments on a sheet of art paper.

- Invite students to decorate their papers so that they resemble scrolls and to display them in a prominent place at home.

- During the next session, challenge students to recite from memory the Ten Commandments.

OPTIONAL ACTIVITY

Conscience   Have students work in small groups to compose questions that will be used in an examination of conscience.

- Assign group members to read the Ten Commandments, the Beatitudes, or the precepts of the Church and to use these as a basis for their questions.

- Remind students that a regular examination of conscience helps ensure continued growth in faith.

Law

Laws are rules that help people live as members of a community and behave in an acceptable manner.

Divine law is the eternal law of God. It includes physical law and moral law. The law of gravity is an example of physical. A moral law is one that humans understand through reasoning (you may not steal) and through divine revelation (keep holy the Lord's Day).

Natural moral law consists of those decisions and duties that all humans accept as right. For example, people everywhere understand that no one may kill another unjustly. Everyone must obey natural moral law.

Precepts of the Church

The following precepts are important duties of all Catholics.

1. Take part in the Mass on Sundays and holy days. Keep these days holy and avoid unnecessary work.
2. Celebrate the Sacrament of Reconciliation at least once a year.
3. Receive Holy Communion at least once a year during Easter Season.
4. Fast and abstain on days of penance.
5. Give your time, gifts, and money to support the Church.

Corporal Works of Mercy

These works of mercy help care for the physical needs of others.

Feed the hungry.
Give drink to the thirsty.
Clothe the naked.
Shelter the homeless.
Visit the sick.
Visit the imprisoned.
Bury the dead.

Faith Fact

Pope John XXIII listed food, clothing, shelter, health care, rest, and social services as basic human needs. All people have a right to those basic needs.

© Our Sunday Visitor Curriculum Division

236

Human Dignity

God's image is his likeness that is present in you because you are his creation. You are called to respect the dignity of all people because everyone is made in God's image.

Freedom

Freedom means you are able to choose and act with few limitations.

Free will

Free will is the gift from God that allows humans to make their own choices. Because you are free to choose between right and wrong, you are responsible for your choices and actions.

Grace

God gives you two types of grace. **Sanctifying grace** is the gift of God's life in you. It gives you the desire to live and act within God's plan. **Actual grace** is the gift of God's life in you that helps you think or act in a particular situation according to God's plan. Actual grace opens you to understanding and strengthens your will.

Gifts of the Holy Spirit

You receive the gifts of the Holy Spirit through the Sacraments of Baptism and Confirmation. These gifts help you grow in relationship with God and others.

Wisdom	Knowledge
Understanding	Reverence *(Piety)*
Right judgment *(Counsel)*	Wonder and awe *(Fear of*
Courage *(Fortitude)*	*the Lord)*

© Our Sunday Visitor Curriculum Division

237

Corporal Works of Mercy   Have students create a mural that illustrates the Corporal Works of Mercy.

- Help students generate ideas for the mural by providing them with examples of the Corporal Works of Mercy from the parish bulletin, diocesan newspaper, or other media.

Gifts of the Holy Spirit   Have students work together in small groups to write prayers to the Holy Spirit.

- Each group's prayer should include a request for an increase in one of the gifts of the Holy Spirit.
- Pray one of these prayers during the opening prayer of each session.

Sin

Sin is a turning away from God and a failure to love others. Sin affects both the individual and the community. A person may be sorry for his or her sin, ask forgiveness for it, accept punishment for it, and resolve to do better. In this case, the experience may actually help the person develop as a Christian and avoid sin in the future. However, a person who makes a habit of sin will harm his or her development, set a poor example, and bring sorrow to others. Society suffers when people disobey God's law and the just laws of society. There are many types of sin.

Original Sin is the human condition of weakness and the tendency toward sin that resulted from the first humans' choice to disobey God. Baptism restores the relationship of loving grace in which all people were created.

Actual sin is any thought, word, act, or failure to act that goes against God's law. Sin is always a choice, never a mistake.

Mortal sin separates you from God. A mortal sin is an act, such as murder. There must be a deliberate choice to commit the act; it is never an accident.

Venial sin does not destroy your relationship with God, but it does weaken the relationship. Venial sin often comes from bad habits. It can lead to mortal sin.

Social sin happens when one person's sins affect the larger community. Poverty and racism are examples of social sin.

Faith Fact

The word *virtue* means "strength." Practicing virtue can give you the strength to make loving choices.

Virtue

Virtues are good qualities or habits of goodness. These are the two types of virtues:

Theological Virtues	Cardinal Virtues
Faith	Prudence (careful judgment)
Hope	Fortitude (courage)
Love	Justice (giving people their due)
	Temperance (moderation, balance)

238

© Our Sunday Visitor Curriculum Division

The Sign of the Cross

In the name of the Father, and of the Son, and of the Holy Spirit. Amen.

The Lord's Prayer

Our Father,
who art in heaven,
hallowed be thy name;
thy kingdom come;
thy will be done on earth
as it is in heaven.
Give us this day our
daily bread;
and forgive us our
trespasses
as we forgive those who trespass
against us;
and lead us not into temptation,
but deliver us from evil. Amen.

Hail Mary

Hail, Mary, full of grace,
the Lord is with you!
Blessed are you among women,
and blessed is the fruit of your womb, Jesus.
Holy Mary, Mother of God,
pray for us sinners,
now and at the hour of our death. Amen.

Glory to the Father (Doxology)

Glory to the Father, and to the Son, and to the Holy Spirit:
as it was in the beginning, is now, and will be forever. Amen.

239

© Our Sunday Visitor Curriculum Division

OPTIONAL ACTIVITY

Virtues Have students create bookmarks that incorporate the symbols of the theological virtues (faith: a cross; hope: an anchor; love: a heart).

- Provide students with appropriate art supplies.
- You may also wish to have students brainstorm symbols for the cardinal virtues to use for the bookmarks.

OPTIONAL ACTIVITY

The Lord's Prayer Have students suggest reverent gestures to accompany the phrases of the Lord's Prayer.

- After students have practiced using their gestures while saying the prayer, have them share the gestures with parents or another group of students.
- Use the gestures as part of the Lord's Prayer during future prayer services.

Apostles' Creed

I believe in God, the Father almighty,
Creator of heaven and earth,
and in Jesus Christ, his only Son, our Lord,

At the words that follow, up to and including the Virgin Mary, all bow.

who was conceived by the Holy Spirit,
born of the Virgin Mary,
suffered under Pontius Pilate,
was crucified, died and was buried;

he descended into hell;
on the third day he rose again from the dead;
he ascended into heaven, and is seated at the right hand of God the Father almighty;
from there he will come to judge the living and the dead.

I believe in the Holy Spirit,
the holy catholic Church,
the communion of saints,
the forgiveness of sins,
the resurrection of the body,
and life everlasting. Amen.

Faith Fact

Amen means "So be it." Isn't that the perfect way to end a conversation with God?

Nicene Creed

I believe in one God,
the Father almighty,
maker of heaven and earth,
of all things visible and invisible.
I believe in one Lord Jesus Christ,
the Only Begotten Son of God,
born of the Father before all ages.
God from God, Light from Light,
true God from true God,
begotten, not made,
consubstantial with the Father;
through him all things were made.
For us men and for our salvation
he came down from heaven,

At the words that follow up to and including and became man, all bow.

and by the Holy Spirit was incarnate of the Virgin Mary,
and became man.
For our sake he was crucified under Pontius Pilate,
he suffered death and was buried,
and rose again on the third day
in accordance with the Scriptures.
He ascended into heaven and is seated at the right hand of the Father.
He will come again in glory to judge the living and the dead

and his kingdom will have no end.
I believe in the Holy Spirit,
the Lord, the giver of life,
who proceeds from the Father and the Son,
who with the Father and the Son is adored and glorified,
who has spoken through the prophets.
I believe in one, holy, catholic and apostolic Church.
I confess one Baptism for the forgiveness of sins
and I look forward to the resurrection of the dead
and the life of the world to come. Amen.

© Our Sunday Visitor Curriculum Division

240

I Confess / Confieor

I confess to almighty God
and to you, my brothers and sisters,
that I have greatly sinned,
in my thoughts and in my words,
in what I have done
and in what I have failed to do,

Gently strike your chest with a closed fist.

through my fault, through my fault,
through my most grievous fault;

Continue:

therefore I ask blessed Mary ever-Virgin,
all the Angels and Saints,
and you, my brothers and sisters,
to pray for me to the Lord our God.

Prayer to the Holy Spirit

Come, Holy Spirit, fill the hearts of your faithful.
And kindle in them the fire of your love.
Send forth your Spirit and they will be created.
And you will renew the face of the earth.
Let us pray.
Lord, by the light of the Holy Spirit you have taught the hearts of your faithful. In the same Spirit help us to relish what is right and always rejoice in your consolation. We ask this through Christ our Lord. Amen.

Memorare

Remember, most loving Virgin Mary, never was it heard that anyone who turned to you for help was left unaided. Inspired by this confidence, though burdened by my sins, I run to your protection for you are my mother. Mother of the Word of God, do not despise my words of pleading but be merciful and hear my prayer. Amen.

© Our Sunday Visitor Curriculum Division

241

Apostles' Creed   Tell students that the Apostles' Creed is a summary of Christian beliefs. It contains the truths taught by the Apostles, and it highlights what we believe as Catholics. At some Masses with younger children, we profess the Apostles' Creed.

The language in the Apostles' Creed was updated when we began to implement the English translation of the Third Edition of the Roman Missal in November 2011.

- Have students write this prayer in the middle of a piece of paper.
- Provide them with colored pencils and markers to add illustrations or drawings around the text to create an "illuminated" manuscript page.
- Encourage students to work in pairs to memorize this prayer.

Prayer to the Holy Spirit   Invite students to create banners or other liturgical art that reflects the imagery of this prayer.

- Encourage students to pray this prayer before taking a test or in other situations in which the Spirit's wisdom or guidance would be especially welcome.

Act of Contrition

My God, I am sorry for my sins with all my heart.
In choosing to do wrong
and failing to do good,
I have sinned against you
whom I should love above all things.
I firmly intend, with your help,
to do penance,
to sin no more,
and to avoid whatever leads me to sin.
Our Savior Jesus Christ
suffered and died for us.
In his name, my God, have mercy.

Faith Fact

Contrition is the sorrow
that rises up in the soul,
making you repent past sins
and plan not to sin again.
To repent is to turn back
from the sin and ask God's
mercy.

Grail Prayer

Lord Jesus,
I give you my hands to do your work.
I give you my feet to go your way.
I give you my eyes to see as you do.
I give you my tongue to speak your words.
I give you my mind that you may think in me.

Above all, I give you my heart
that you may love in me your Father
and all mankind.
I give you my whole self that
you may grow in me,
so that it is you, Lord Jesus,
who will live and work and pray in me. Amen.

© Our Sunday Visitor Curriculum Division

Prayer for Our Lady of Guadalupe Day

(December 12)
Loving God,
you bless the peoples of the Americas
with the Virgin Mary of Guadalupe
as our patron and mother.
Through her prayers
may we learn to love one another
and to work for justice and peace.
Amen.

Lady of Guadalupe,	pray for us
La morena of Tepeyac,	comfort us
Mother of the faithful,	defend us
Refuge of the oppressed,	strengthen us
Hope of the immigrant,	cheer us
Light of the traveler,	guide us
Friend of the stranger,	welcome us
Shelter of the poor and needy,	sustain us
Patron of the Americas,	unite us
Mother of many children,	watch over us
Star of the morning,	waken us to the coming of your Son, Jesus Christ, who arose from you the sun of justice and is Lord for ever and ever. Amen.

© Our Sunday Visitor Curriculum Division

242

243

OPTIONAL ACTIVITY

Act of Contrition   Tell students that the Act of Contrition is a prayer of sorrow. Through it we tell God we are sorry and want to do better, and we ask him to help us avoid temptation.

- Talk about the difference between someone just saying "I am sorry," and someone showing that he or she is really sorry.
- Have students write a prayer of sorrow in their own words.
- Encourage them to share their prayers with their families.

OPTIONAL ACTIVITY

Litany for Our Lady of Guadalupe   A Litany is a form of prayer used in church services and processions consisting of a number of petitions. Pray the litany—the second half of the Prayer for Our Lady of Guadalupe Day—together as a class.

- Explain the format of the litany to students.
- Ask them to use their books to follow along with the prayer.
- As the leader, read all of the first column text.
- Each time you finish your line, pause so that the students can give the appropriate response from the second column.

The Way of the Cross

The First Station: Jesus is condemned to death.
The Second Station: Jesus bears his cross.
The Third Station: Jesus falls the first time.
The Fourth Station: Jesus meets his mother.
The Fifth Station: Simon of Cyrene helps Jesus carry his cross.
The Sixth Station: Veronica wipes the face of Jesus.
The Seventh Station: Jesus falls a second time.
The Eighth Station: Jesus meets the women of Jerusalem.
The Ninth Station: Jesus falls a third time.
The Tenth Station: Jesus is stripped of his garments.
The Eleventh Station: Jesus is nailed to the cross.
The Twelfth Station: Jesus dies on the cross.
The Thirteenth Station: Jesus is taken down from the cross.
The Fourteenth Station: Jesus is placed in the tomb.

Faith Fact

In the devotion known as the Way of the Cross, "stations" represent stops along the way of Jesus' journey from Pilate's court all the way to the tomb. Walking in a church from one station to the next and really focusing on each picture or image of the passion of Christ can inspire prayer from the heart.

The Mysteries of the Rosary

The Joyful Mysteries	The Luminous Mysteries
The Annunciation	The Baptism of Jesus
The Visitation	The Wedding at Cana
The Nativity	The Proclamation of the Kingdom
The Presentation in the Temple	The Transfiguration
The Finding in the Temple	The Institution of the Eucharist
The Sorrowful Mysteries	**The Glorious Mysteries**
The Agony in the Garden	The Resurrection
The Scourging at the Pillar	The Ascension
The Crowning with Thorns	The Descent of the Holy Spirit
The Carrying of the Cross	The Assumption of Mary
The Crucifixion and Death	The Coronation of Mary in Heaven

Litany of St. Joseph

Lord, have mercy.	Lord, have mercy.
Christ, have mercy.	Christ, have mercy.
Lord, have mercy.	Lord, have mercy.
Good Saint Joseph,	pray for us.
Descendant of the House of David	pray for us.
Husband of Mary,	pray for us.
Foster father of Jesus,	pray for us.
Guardian of Christ,	pray for us.
Support of the holy family,	pray for us.
Model of workers,	pray for us.
Example to parents,	pray for us.
Comfort of the dying,	pray for us.
Provider of food to the hungry,	pray for us.
Companion of the poor,	pray for us.
Protector of the church,	pray for us.

Merciful God,
grant that we may learn from Saint Joseph
to care for the members of our families
and share what we have with the poor.
We ask this through Christ our Lord. Amen.

© Our Sunday Visitor Curriculum Division

244

245

OPTIONAL ACTIVITY

The Way of the Cross The Stations of the Cross (also known as the Way of the Cross, the Way of Sorrows, or simply, The Way) refers to the depiction of the final hours of Jesus and the devotion commemorating the Passion. The celebration of the Way of the Cross is especially common on the Fridays of Lent, and particularly Good Friday.

- Arrange to take students to the church to follow the stations.

- Emphasize that they should show respect and behave in an appropriate manner.

- Provide students with the scriptural prayers to pray at each station or encourage them to make up their own prayers.

OPTIONAL ACTIVITY

The Mysteries of the Rosary Symbols that represent the Joyful Mysteries include green leaves or white rosettes. Scriptural passages and meditations that apply to these mysteries include: the Annunciation (humility), Luke 1:26–38; the Visitation (charity), Luke 1:39–45; the Nativity (poverty), Luke 2:1–20; the Presentation (obedience) Luke 2:22–35; and the Finding of Jesus in the Temple (piety), Luke 2:41–52.

- Divide the class into five groups and assign each group one of the Joyful Mysteries.

- Provide each group with the scriptural passages from Luke that apply to their mystery, as well as the concept to meditate on.

- Have volunteers within the groups read the passages aloud.

- Encourage groups to think about the meditations and then discuss how these ideas apply to the mysteries they read about.

How to Pray the Rosary

1. Pray the Sign of the Cross and say the Apostles' Creed.
2. Pray the Lord's Prayer.
3. Pray three Hail Marys.
4. Pray the Glory to the Father.
5. Say the first mystery; then pray the Lord's Prayer.
6. Pray ten Hail Marys while meditating on the mystery.
7. Pray the Glory to the Father.
8. Say the second mystery; then pray the Lord's Prayer. Repeat 6 and 7 and continue with the third, fourth, and fifth mysteries in the same manner.
9. Pray the Hail, Holy Queen.

Faith Fact

As the Mother of Jesus, the Son of God, Mary is called the Mother of God, the Queen of all Saints, and the Mother of the Church. There are many prayers and practices of devotion to Mary. One of the most popular is the Rosary. It focuses on the twenty mysteries that describe events in the lives of Jesus and Mary.

Hail, Holy Queen

Hail, holy Queen, Mother of mercy,
hail, our life, our sweetness, and our hope.
To you we cry, the children of Eve;
to you we send up our sighs,
mourning and weeping in this land of exile.
Turn, then, most gracious advocate,
your eyes of mercy toward us;
lead us home at last
and show us the blessed fruit of your womb,
        Jesus:
O clement, O loving, O sweet Virgin Mary.
Salve, Regina

Angelus

V. The angel spoke God's message to Mary,
R. and she conceived of the Holy Spirit.
Hail, Mary . . .

V. "I am the lowly servant of the Lord:
R. let it be done to me according to your word."
Hail, Mary . . .

V. And the Word became flesh,
R. and lived among us.
Hail, Mary . . .

V. Pray for us, holy Mother of God,
R. that we may become worthy of the promises of Christ.

Let us pray.

Lord,
fill our hearts with your grace:
once, through the message of an angel
you revealed to us the incarnation of your Son;
now, through his suffering and death
lead us to the glory of his resurrection.

We ask this through Christ our Lord.
Amen.

246

247

OPTIONAL ACTIVITY

Hail, Holy Queen   Talk with students about the unique role Mary played in salvation history as the Christ-bearer.

- Using index cards, have students create prayer cards, printing the last two lines of the Hail, Holy Queen in the center of the card.

- Ask them to discuss names or titles that we use most often for Mary: Blessed Mother, Virgin, Mother of God, Madonna, and so on.

- Have them add these names decoratively around the edges of their prayer cards.

- Students can use these cards when they pray for Mary's intercession.

OPTIONAL ACTIVITY

Angelus   In this prayer, the angel of the Lord spoke God's message to Mary. Through quiet prayer and contemplation, we can attempt to discern God's special messages to us.

- Have students create images of personal angel messengers.

- Provide them with the appropriate art supplies and simple outlines of an angel to copy if they wish.

- Have them include a small banner across the bottom of the angel.

- After a few moments of silent prayer, ask them to write in the banner one word or a short phrase that they feel that God may be asking them to focus on or work on. (This could include ideas such as Family, Friends, Be More Forgiving, Love Others.)

Act of Faith

O God, we firmly believe that you are one God in three divine Persons, Father, Son, and Holy Spirit; we believe that your divine Son became man and died for our sins, and that he will come to judge the living and the dead. We believe these and all the truths that the holy Catholic Church teaches because you have revealed them, and you can neither deceive nor be deceived.

Act of Hope

O God, relying on your almighty power and your endless mercy and promises, we hope to gain pardon for our sins, the help of your grace, and life everlasting, through the saving actions of Jesus Christ, our Lord and Redeemer.

Act of Love

O God, we love you above all things, with our whole heart and soul, because you are all good and worthy of all love. We love our neighbor as ourselves for the love of you. We forgive all who have injured us and ask pardon of all whom we have injured.

Holy, Holy, Holy Lord

In English
Holy, Holy, Holy Lord God of hosts.
Heaven and earth are full of your glory.
Hosanna in the highest.
Blessed is he who comes in the name of the Lord.
Hosanna in the highest.

In Latin
Sanctus, Sanctus, Sanctus
Dominus Deus Sabaoth.
Pleni sunt coeli et terra gloria tua.
Hosanna in excelsis.

Benedictus qui venit in nomine Domini.
Hosanna in excelsis.

Agnus Dei (Lamb of God)

In English
Lamb of God, you take away the
  sins of the world,
  have mercy on us.
Lamb of God, you take away the
  sins of the world,
  have mercy on us.
Lamb of God, you take away the
  sins of the world,
  grant us peace.

In Latin
Agnus Dei, qui tollis peccata mundi:
miserere nobis.
Agnus Dei, qui tollis peccata mundi:
miserere nobis.
Agnus Dei, qui tollis peccata mundi:
dona nobis pacem

Faith Fact

As members of the Catholic Church, we usually pray in the language that we speak, but we sometimes pray in Latin, the common language of the Church. The following are a couple of the common prayers of the Church in both English and Latin.

© Our Sunday Visitor Curriculum Division

248

249

OPTIONAL ACTIVITY

Act of Love Believing in God and loving him are not the same as recognizing his presence. Recognizing his presence is not always easy because God usually makes his presence known to us in the quiet of our hearts. Deep within our souls, we can recognize God's presence in truth, beauty, and love.

- Explain to students that we often have to make an effort to hear God's voice in the "noisy," busy worlds we live in.

- Have them list five "noises" or things that might make it hard for them to recognize God's presence or hear his voice.

- Ask volunteers to share some of the elements from their lists, and encourage the group to offer suggestions for quieting those noises.

OPTIONAL ACTIVITY

Agnus Dei **(Lamb of God)** The reference to Jesus as the Lamb of God in this litany prayer comes from John 1:29 and Revelation 5:6–13, as well as other Scripture passages.

- Have students write the Latin version of Lamb of God on prayer cards.

- Have them draw peace symbols around the edges of the card.

- Encourage them to memorize the Latin verses.

You may wish to play for students "The Supper of the Lamb," Track 12 of *And With Your Spirit* by John Burland, to familiarize them with the new language in the English translation of the Third Edition of the Roman Missal.

Faith in Action!
CATHOLIC SOCIAL TEACHING

Care for God's Creation

All elements of God's creation should work in harmony. Our task is to recognize that harmony and live within it. When we work in harmony with creation, we take and use only what is appropriate. If we consider ourselves true stewards of creation, we will not take more than we need of anything. This discipline must extend to manufactured products, because the process of making them also results in waste and pollution.

The Catholic Church calls us

- to use resources for the benefit of all creatures.
- to act as trustees, not owners, of the world's goods.
- to show our respect for God through our management of the environment.

Reflect **How can you model caring for creation in the classroom?**

Catholic Social Teaching Document

"God destined the earth and all it contains for all people and nations so that all created things would be shared fairly by all humankind under the guidance of justice tempered by charity."

From *Gaudium et Spes (Pastoral Constitution on the Church in the Modern World)*, Pope Paul VI, 1965

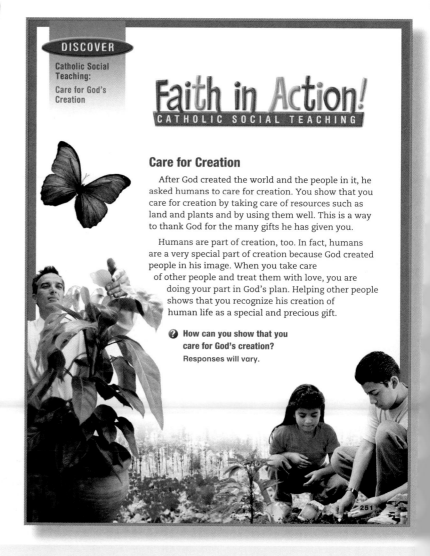

Discover Catholic Social Teaching

Let Us Pray God, thank you for the gift of creation. Help us share it.

Care for Creation

Invite students to read and summarize the two paragraphs.

- Point out the photographs of the man caring for the tree and the family planting a small garden. Ask what these pictures reveal about creation. They reveal that even small gardens bring beauty to the world.

How can you show that you care for God's creation? Emphasize specific, practical actions.

Connect with the Call to Justice

More Than Just a Garden

Challenge a volunteer to point out Michigan on a map or globe.

- Read the first paragraph, and then have students predict the outcome.
- Test the predictions by reading.
- Discuss why the parishioners did not garden on Sundays. to keep the Third Commandment
- Invite students to share their own gardening experiences. Point out that gardening can be hard work, but that it also is rewarding.
- Call attention to the photographs as you discuss aspects of gardening.

More Than Just Food

Read aloud the last paragraph.

❷ **How did the parishioners show care for God's creation?** Encourage responses that mention caring for plants and caring for other people.

Serve Your Community

Kinds of Care

Point out that both plants and humans are part of creation, and that both need care in order to survive and grow.

- Arrange students in pairs, and have them work on the first two questions.
- Discuss the third question with the entire class.

Make a Difference

Read aloud the directions, and begin planning the planting and sharing activity in class.

- Once each week, note any progress and affirm students' efforts.
- When the project is completed, point out that in addition to caring for the plants, students showed care for the recipients by visiting them.

Faith in Action!
CATHOLIC SOCIAL TEACHING

Life and Dignity of the Human Person

We are called by God to respect life when making decisions involving life, death, hunger, poverty, war, and peace. Many of the problems we see in the world today arise from a failure to protect and respect the image of God in ourselves and others.

The Catholic Church calls us

- to realize that all human life is sacred and that all people are worthy of dignity and respect.
- to recognize that the Fifth Commandment is also a mandate to promote and preserve life.
- to be aware that ignoring the call to respect human life and dignity leads to grave personal and social sin.

*Reflect   **What is my personal value system?***

Catholic Social Teaching Document

"The Catholic Church proclaims that human life is sacred and that the dignity of the human person is the foundation of a moral vision for society. Our belief in the sanctity of human life and the inherent dignity of the human person is the foundation of all the principles of our social teaching."

From *Sharing Catholic Social Teaching*, U.S. Conference of Catholic Bishops, 1999

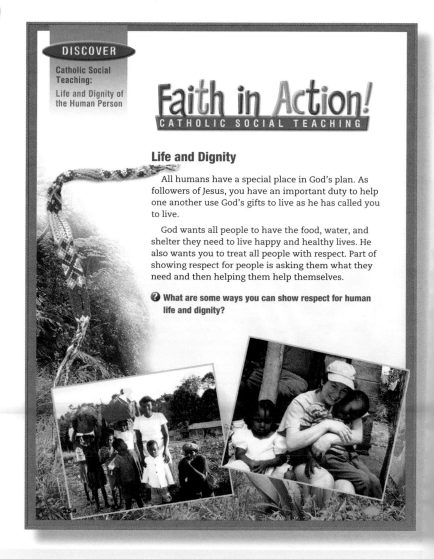

DISCOVER
Catholic Social Teaching: Life and Dignity of the Human Person

Faith in Action!
CATHOLIC SOCIAL TEACHING

Life and Dignity

All humans have a special place in God's plan. As followers of Jesus, you have an important duty to help one another use God's gifts to live as he has called you to live.

God wants all people to have the food, water, and shelter they need to live happy and healthy lives. He also wants you to treat all people with respect. Part of showing respect for people is asking them what they need and then helping them help themselves.

❓ **What are some ways you can show respect for human life and dignity?**

Discover Catholic Social Teaching

🙌 **Let Us Pray**   Loving God, thank you for all the gifts you have given us. Teach us to use them wisely.

Life and Dignity

Read aloud the two paragraphs as a summary of the lesson.

- Direct students' attention to the photographs on the page. Tell students that these pictures show people working to promote human life and dignity.

❓ **What are some ways you can show respect for human life and dignity?** Use an example to start the discussion.

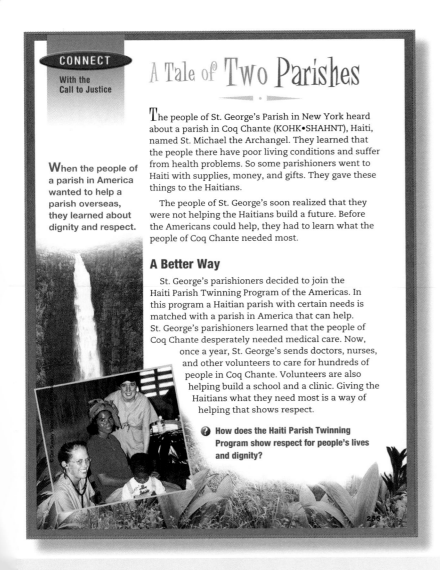

CONNECT With the Call to Justice

A Tale of Two Parishes

The people of St. George's Parish in New York heard about a parish in Coq Chante (KOHK•SHAHNT), Haiti, named St. Michael the Archangel. They learned that the people there have poor living conditions and suffer from health problems. So some parishioners went to Haiti with supplies, money, and gifts. They gave these things to the Haitians.

When the people of a parish in America wanted to help a parish overseas, they learned about dignity and respect.

The people of St. George's soon realized that they were not helping the Haitians build a future. Before the Americans could help, they had to learn what the people of Coq Chante needed most.

A Better Way

St. George's parishioners decided to join the Haiti Parish Twinning Program of the Americas. In this program a Haitian parish with certain needs is matched with a parish in America that can help. St. George's parishioners learned that the people of Coq Chante desperately needed medical care. Now, once a year, St. George's sends doctors, nurses, and other volunteers to care for hundreds of people in Coq Chante. Volunteers are also helping build a school and a clinic. Giving the Haitians what they need most is a way of helping that shows respect.

❓ **How does the Haiti Parish Twinning Program show respect for people's lives and dignity?**

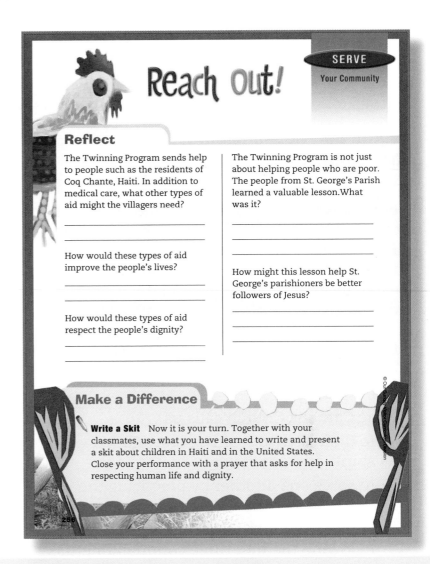

SERVE Your Community

Reach Out!

Reflect

The Twinning Program sends help to people such as the residents of Coq Chante, Haiti. In addition to medical care, what other types of aid might the villagers need?

_____

How would these types of aid improve the people's lives?

_____

How would these types of aid respect the people's dignity?

_____

The Twinning Program is not just about helping people who are poor. The people from St. George's Parish learned a valuable lesson. What was it?

_____

How might this lesson help St. George's parishioners be better followers of Jesus?

_____

Make a Difference

Write a Skit Now it is your turn. Together with your classmates, use what you have learned to write and present a skit about children in Haiti and in the United States. Close your performance with a prayer that asks for help in respecting human life and dignity.

Connect with the Call to Justice

A Tale of Two Parishes

Show students the location of Haiti on a map or globe. Tell them that Haiti is one of the poorest nations in the world.

- Read aloud the first two paragraphs of the story.
- Ask students to consider why the people of St. George's Parish wanted to make life easier for the people of Coq Chante.
- Ask why simply sending money and gifts to the Haitians was not a real answer to their problems.

A Better Way

Have students read the next paragraph silently.

❓ **How does the Haiti Parish Twinning Program show respect for people's lives and dignity?**
Emphasize that respecting human life and dignity is one of the most important duties that Christians have.

Serve Your Community

Reflect

Ask a volunteer to read aloud the text in the first column.

- Have students write responses and share answers.
- Repeat this procedure with the second column.

Make a Difference

Organize students in groups to plan their skit.

- Tell students that their skit should provide information about people in Coq Chante and how Americans are helping them.
- If possible, arrange for students to present their skit to another class, at a school assembly, or to a group of parents and families.

CATHOLIC SOCIAL TEACHING

Rights and Responsibilities of the Human Person

This principle emphasizes the balance between what is due to people and what their responsibilities are. Humans are entitled to life and the means to sustain it: food, shelter, and medical care. They are also entitled to sustenance for their intellect in the form of education and employment. Because humans live in community with other people, they must help ensure these rights for others. They also have a responsibility to honor God for these gifts.

The Catholic Church calls us

- to find ways to reaffirm one another spiritually.
- to serve one another by practicing the Corporal Works of Mercy.
- to deepen our relationship with God by following the first three commandments.

Reflect   How does my teaching style affirm the rights of my students?

Catholic Social Teaching Document

"In our teaching, the human person is not only sacred but social. How we organize our society—in economics and politics, in law and policy—directly affects human dignity and the capacity of individuals to grow in community. The obligation to 'love our neighbor' has an individual dimension, but it also requires a broader social commitment to the common good."

From *Economic Justice for All,* U.S. Conference of Catholic Bishops, 1986, Introduction, paragraph 14

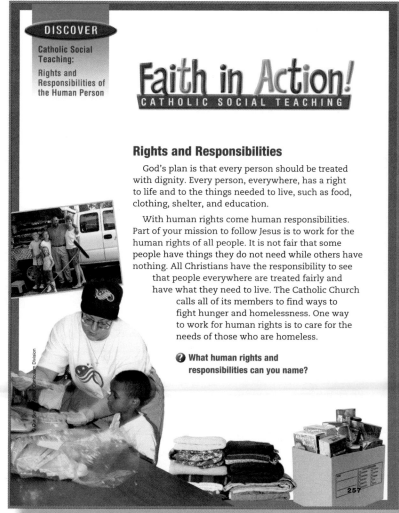

Rights and Responsibilities

God's plan is that every person should be treated with dignity. Every person, everywhere, has a right to life and to the things needed to live, such as food, clothing, shelter, and education.

With human rights come human responsibilities. Part of your mission to follow Jesus is to work for the human rights of all people. It is not fair that some people have things they do not need while others have nothing. All Christians have the responsibility to see that people everywhere are treated fairly and have what they need to live. The Catholic Church calls all of its members to find ways to fight hunger and homelessness. One way to work for human rights is to care for the needs of those who are homeless.

❷ **What human rights and responsibilities can you name?**

Discover Catholic Social Teaching

🙌 **Let Us Pray**   God, help us enjoy the rights you have given us. Help us know our responsibilities.

Rights and Responsibilities

Invite a volunteer to read aloud the first paragraph.

- Ask students how Jesus cared for people's rights.
- Invite students to discuss the responsibilities they have.
- Say that all Christians have responsibilities to God's family. Then read aloud the rest of the text.
- Ask students how we fulfill our responsibilities to other people. by making certain that they have what they need

❷ **What human rights and responsibilities can you name?** Tell students that young people share in these rights and responsibilities.

CONNECT
With the Call to Justice

Mealtime on the Streets

God calls people to share what they have with others. Let's look at what one parish did to help care for others.

MOBILE LOAVES & FISHES
Miracles on Wheels

It is a winter night in Texas. People who are homeless, cold, and hungry are huddled in corners and in doorways. Suddenly, a truck appears. The doors open and people begin to give out sandwiches, hot drinks, and warm blankets. Who are these people?

This is the work of Mobile Loaves and Fishes. In the summer of 1998, six parishioners from St. John Neumann Church began planning the project. They had heard about a church that gave out blankets and coffee to the homeless, and they decided to do the same. Soon after, they distributed 75 sack lunches to citizens who were homeless.

A Good Idea Grows

The project grew quickly. Parishioners began to give money, volunteer their time, and offer their prayers. By spring the parish had its own truck and was distributing food seven nights a month. Soon the deliveries were up to 15 nights a month. By 2002 more than 2,000 volunteers were sending four trucks into the streets every night. In 2003 the Mobile Loaves and Fishes program served over 100,000 meals, and the project is still growing. That's what can happen when you start with an idea, a commitment, and a group of caring people!

❓ Why do you think the project is called "Mobile Loaves and Fishes"?

© Our Sunday Visitor Curriculum Division

258

SERVE
Your Community

Reach out!

Donations

Sharing Food

One way to work for human rights is to gather food for a local food bank. Your class will have a lot to do to get ready. Check off each task as you complete it.

☐ Find a food bank nearby, and ask what kinds of foods are needed.

☐ Decide when and where you will collect the food.

☐ Decide how you will let people know about your food drive.

☐ Get containers for the food, and encourage class members to collect it.

☐ Arrange to have the food delivered to the food bank.

☐ Make cards to thank those who have donated food.

☐ Think about how to collect food other times during the year.

Make a Difference

Do Your Part Decide how you can help.

Which of the project jobs could I do best? _____

Do I have my own money that I can use to buy food? _____

Can I earn money to buy food for the poor? _____

© Our Sunday Visitor Curriculum Division

259

Connect with the Call to Justice

Mealtime on the Streets
Invite students to close their eyes and picture what is happening as you read aloud the first paragraph.

• Ask students to imagine how homeless people might feel about getting things from the truck.

• Ask a volunteer to read aloud the second paragraph.

A Good Idea Grows
Ask students to predict what happens with the project. Then read aloud the next paragraph.

• Ask students what effect the project has on homeless people. It meets some of their daily needs.

• Ask them how they think the people who volunteer might feel as they work on this project.

❓ Why do you think the project is called "Mobile Loaves and Fishes"? You may wish to read aloud Luke 9:10–17.

Serve Your Community

Sharing Food
Check with your DRE before starting this service project to resolve any scheduling problems or other issues.

• After sharing the food drive idea with students, ask which Corporal Works of Mercy the class would be performing.

• Extend the list of tasks, and display it to the class. Work with students to assign the tasks appropriately. For many jobs, you will need the assistance of other adults.

Make a Difference
Have students write individual answers to the questions.

• If possible, have at least a few students go along to deliver the food to the food bank.

• Ask them to report on their experience.

Faith in Action!
CATHOLIC SOCIAL TEACHING

Dignity of Work and the Rights of Workers

Work, whether it is done by volunteers or paid employees, elevates the workers. Through our work, we share in God's plan for creation by making resources into something new. Workers have an obligation to use their time and talents for God and their employers. However, workers also have rights that are defended by the Church. These include safe working conditions, reasonable hours, and fair wages.

The Catholic Church calls us

- to serve God and one another through our work.
- to work cooperatively to achieve good for ourselves and the human community.
- to respect the achievements of all workers, no matter what their jobs are.

Reflect **How do I show respect for the work of my students and my colleagues?**

Catholic Social Teaching Document

"Work remains a good thing, not only because it is useful and enjoyable, but also because it expresses and increases the worker's dignity. Through work we not only transform the world, we are transformed ourselves, becoming 'more a human being.'"

From *On Human Work (Donders Translation),* US Conference of Catholic Bishops, #9

DISCOVER
Catholic Social Teaching: The Dignity of Work and the Rights of Workers

Faith in Action!
CATHOLIC SOCIAL TEACHING

The Dignity of Work

Work is more than just a way to make money or complete a task—God calls you to discover your unique gifts and talents and to use them in your work. When you do this, your work becomes part of God's continuing work of creation. Through work, people can see that they have dignity as gifted children of God.

❷ **When have you used your gifts and talents alongside others?**

Respecting All Workers

One kind of work is no more important than another. Each person's work can help his or her community and the people who live there. How much a job pays is not important. Every worker and every kind of work is important and worthy of respect.

❷ **What kinds of work do you respect most? Why?**

© Our Sunday Visitor Curriculum Division

Discover Catholic Social Teaching

🎁 **Let Us Pray** God, thank you for all our talents. Help us use them to do your work.

The Dignity of Work
Have a volunteer read aloud this paragraph.

Respecting All Workers
Read aloud this section of the text.

- Discuss how all workers deserve respect because they share in God's creative work.
- Discuss how the photographs show the dignity of each worker.

❷ **When have you used your gifts and talents alongside others? What kinds of work do you respect most? Why?** Allow ample time for discussion. Affirm responses that indicate an awareness that all legitimate work deserves respect.

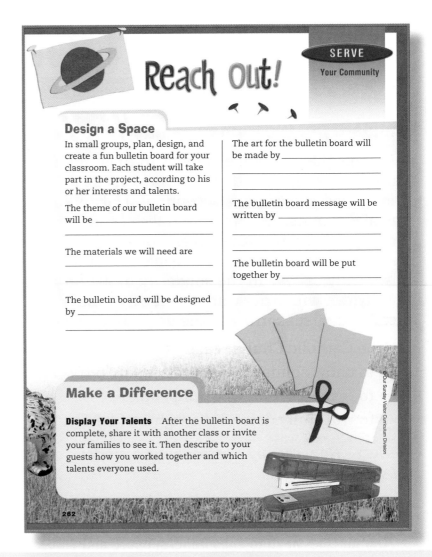

Connect with the Call to Justice

A School of Talents

Call attention to the photographs of the decorated classrooms.

- Tell the class that students at a school decorate the rooms.

Together Is Better

Have students read the next paragraphs silently.

- Ask the class how the students at St. Charles School worked to change their world. They redesigned the art room into a different place each year.

- Ask the class what kinds of skills students used when they decorated the room. They used creative and organizational skills.

❓ **What do students learn during their project?** Point out that some of the workers on these projects were fourth graders like your students.

Serve Your Community

Design a Space

Introduce the project idea.

- Organize the class in groups to complete the activity.

- Assist students with organizing their groups.

- Permit students to work together to resolve any differences. However, be available to them as a consultant.

- Have members from each group report on their experiences.

Make a Difference

Ask volunteers to greet guests, explain your project, and give credit to the participants.

- End the lesson by thanking students for their hard work and reminding them to thank God for all of their talents and abilities.

Faith in Action!
CATHOLIC SOCIAL TEACHING

Solidarity of the Human Family

We *know* that everyone belongs to the human family. However, we do not always act as though we know it. We accept political and racial divisions, refer to *us* and *them,* and are quick to distinguish ourselves from others. We seldom reflect on needs and goals of all humans. If we truly believe in the solidarity of the human family, we will avoid wars, meet everyone's needs, and feel sorrow at the death of any child.

The Catholic Church calls us
- to show solidarity with the family of God.
- to respect the lives of all people.
- to truthfully defend the rights of others.

Reflect **How can my classroom be a model of solidarity?**

Catholic Social Teaching Document

"Our parishes need to encourage, support, and sustain lay people in living their faith in the family, neighborhood, marketplace, and public arena. . . . The most challenging work for justice is not done in church committees, but in the secular world of work, family life, and citizenship."

From *Communities of Salt and Light,* 1992, page 7

DISCOVER

Catholic Social Teaching: Solidarity of the Human Family

Faith in Action!
CATHOLIC SOCIAL TEACHING

Solidarity

When you look at the word *solidarity*, you can see the word *solid*. To stand in solidarity with others means to stand strong, or solid, next to them, helping them with their problems and sharing their joys. United, both groups of people become brothers and sisters in the one family of God.

The Call to Unity

Sometimes it may be difficult to see God's plan for solidarity and unity. Countries fight one another in wars. Family members argue. Even friends sometimes walk away angry. But Christians are called to look for ways to grow in unity and peace. Bringing people together to solve problems is one way.

❷ How can you help your family live in unity?

❷ How can you help the world live in solidarity?

263

Discover Catholic Social Teaching

🎁 Let Us Pray   God, help us know that we are all your children. Help us show that we are one in you.

Solidarity

Ask a volunteer to read aloud the paragraph.

- Ask students when they have stood up for a family member or friend.
- Discuss their reasons for doing so and the results.

The Call to Unity

Invite another volunteer to read aloud this paragraph.

- Discuss what it means to stand in solidarity with other people. Responses will vary.

❷ **How can you help your family live in unity? How can you help the world live in solidarity?** List students' responses on the board or on chart paper.

Sisters in Spirit

Having a sister parish is a big responsibility and a great blessing. The adopting parish promises to help its sister parish. In turn, the adopted parish promises to help its new friends. The parishes of St. Ignatius Catholic Church in California and San Antonio Parish in El Salvador have adopted each other and become sister parishes.

God calls people to help one another in times of need. Let's see how one parish found a way to help another.

Sisters in Action

When an earthquake struck El Salvador, many homes were damaged or destroyed. Men, women, teens, and children were needed to help rebuild. A group of parishioners from St. Ignatius traveled to El Salvador. Their friends at San Antonio Parish welcomed them warmly.

The parishioners of San Antonio were busy rebuilding their homes. Every family member, even children, helped make new bricks from mud. The people showed their friends from California how to make and bake the bricks.

The parishioners of St. Ignatius stood in solidarity by helping their sister parishioners build homes. San Antonio parishioners stood in solidarity by sharing their homes and hearts with the St. Ignatius parishioners. The parishes are now one family in spirit, friendship, and faith.

❷ **What did the people of each parish learn from their sister parish?**

© Our Sunday Visitor Curriculum Division

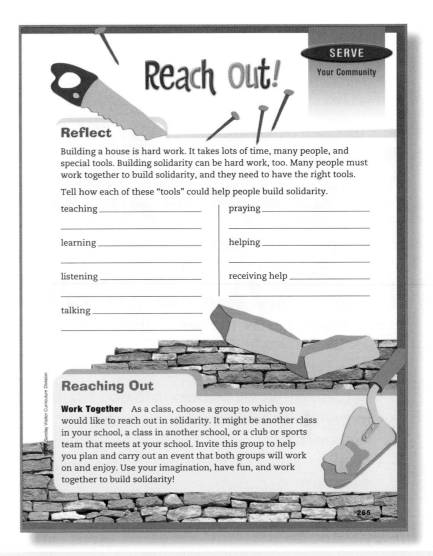

Reach Out!

Reflect

Building a house is hard work. It takes lots of time, many people, and special tools. Building solidarity can be hard work, too. Many people must work together to build solidarity, and they need to have the right tools.

Tell how each of these "tools" could help people build solidarity.

teaching _____ praying _____

learning _____ helping _____

listening _____ receiving help _____

talking _____

Reaching Out

Work Together As a class, choose a group to which you would like to reach out in solidarity. It might be another class in your school, a class in another school, or a club or sports team that meets at your school. Invite this group to help you plan and carry out an event that both groups will work on and enjoy. Use your imagination, have fun, and work together to build solidarity!

Sunday Visitor Curriculum Division

Connect with the Call to Justice

Sisters in Spirit

Indicate on a map or a globe the location of El Salvador. Tell students that El Salvador is a very poor country in Central America.

- Ask students what it means to be a sister. Discuss how sisters help one another because they love one another.
- Summarize the first paragraph.

Sisters in Action

Read the first sentence in this section.

- Ask students to predict what will happen.
- Finish reading aloud the text to test the predictions.

❷ **What did the people of each parish learn from their sister parish?** Emphasize that each parish gained something from the other.

Serve Your Community

Reflect

Have students work in groups to trade ideas about how the "tools" build solidarity.

Reaching Out

Solicit suggestions for groups with whom the class might work and projects for the combined groups to do together. You may wish to discuss suggestions with your DRE before making a final decision.

- Plan and carry out the activity.
- Ask students to evaluate this experience in writing. Have them tell what they learned about solidarity.

Faith in Action!
CATHOLIC SOCIAL TEACHING

Call to Family, Community, and Participation

The obligation of Christians is stated simply: They are called to belong. They are not *asked* to belong. They are called—as to a vocation—to be responsible for family members and to participate as members of communities. Furthermore, Christians cannot deny anyone else's call to active participation. They must allow others to serve our communities and answer the call to help.

The Catholic Church calls us

- to realize that we all belong to God's family.
- to find unity and community in the sacraments.
- to make peace with community members when rifts occur.

Reflect   *How do I answer the call to community in my classroom?*

Catholic Social Teaching Document

"These fundamental duties can be summarized in this way: basic justice demands the establishment of minimum levels of participation in the life of the human community for all persons."

From *Economic Justice for All,* U.S. Conference of Catholic Bishops, 1986, #77

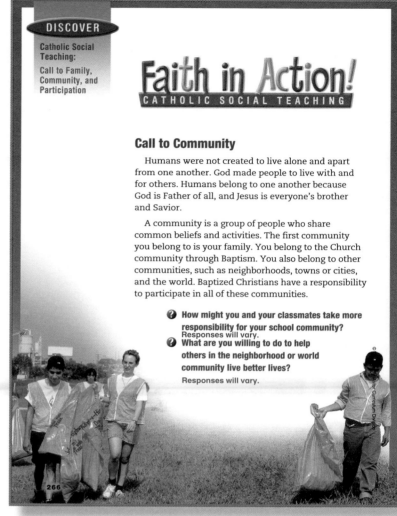

DISCOVER

Catholic Social Teaching:
Call to Family, Community, and Participation

Faith in Action!
CATHOLIC SOCIAL TEACHING

Call to Community

Humans were not created to live alone and apart from one another. God made people to live with and for others. Humans belong to one another because God is Father of all, and Jesus is everyone's brother and Savior.

A community is a group of people who share common beliefs and activities. The first community you belong to is your family. You belong to the Church community through Baptism. You also belong to other communities, such as neighborhoods, towns or cities, and the world. Baptized Christians have a responsibility to participate in all of these communities.

❷ **How might you and your classmates take more responsibility for your school community?**
Responses will vary.
❷ **What are you willing to do to help others in the neighborhood or world community live better lives?**
Responses will vary.

266

Discover Catholic Social Teaching

Let Us Pray   God our Father, thank you for our community. Help us keep it a place where your love is alive.

Call to Community

Invite volunteers to read aloud the two paragraphs in this section.

- Explain the call to community by having students reflect on all of the people who help them in the parish and school communities.
- Use the photographs to further the concept of community.

❷ **How might you and your classmates take more responsibility for your school community? What are you willing to do to help others in the neighborhood or world community live better lives?** Commend students for their insights and suggestions.

Neighborhood Problems

God's love is revealed in families and communities. Let's see how one community joined together to make their city better.

Crime and drugs were entering Connecticut. Children attending a local middle school were no longer safe coming to school. The neighborhood was falling apart. Something had to be done.

"But what could one person do?" a resident asked himself. Alone, he could do little. But together with his neighbors, he could do great things. The man and his neighbors, who belong to St. Rose of Lima parish, knew that they could work together to solve some of the community's problems.

Neighborhood Solutions

Before long, other churches and organizations joined the effort. For more than ten years, ECCO, Elm City Congregations Organized, has done amazing things for local residents.

Working with the local police, members of ECCO have put drug pushers out of business. They have helped change the laws that allowed liquor stores near schools. Now children at Clemente Middle School can safely enjoy recess outside.

The group begun by the St. Rose of Lima parishioners has also made sure that clean and decent housing is available. Above all, the group members have learned the importance of working together to make a better community for everyone.

❓ **How did ECCO members show that they took responsibility for their community?**

267

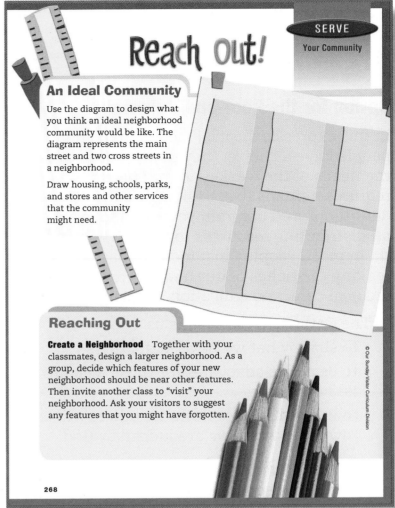

Reach Out!

An Ideal Community

Use the diagram to design what you think an ideal neighborhood community would be like. The diagram represents the main street and two cross streets in a neighborhood.

Draw housing, schools, parks, and stores and other services that the community might need.

Reaching Out

Create a Neighborhood Together with your classmates, design a larger neighborhood. As a group, decide which features of your new neighborhood should be near other features. Then invite another class to "visit" your neighborhood. Ask your visitors to suggest any features that you might have forgotten.

268

Connect with the Call to Justice

Neighborhood Problems

Locate Connecticut on a map or globe.

- Set the scene for this story by reading aloud the first two paragraphs.
- Ask students to predict how the problems could be solved.

Neighborhood Solutions

Have volunteers read aloud the remaining three paragraphs.

- Point out that several churches of many denominations are active in this organization.
- Ask students why the group has been successful. Possible responses: The people truly cared about the neighborhood; the people worked cooperatively.

❓ **How did ECCO members show that they took responsibility for their community?** Tell students about any similar community groups in your area.

Serve Your Community

An Ideal Community

Ask students to describe their ideal community. List their ideas on the board or on chart paper.

- Explain to students that they will be community designers.
- Students may work individually or in pairs to sketch a local area on the diagram.
- Circulate throughout the room to observe student activity and to praise innovative thinking.

Reaching Out

Provide a roll of butcher paper or tape together several sheets of poster board or chart paper for the activity.

- Encourage students to contribute and discuss their ideas for a community plan.

Faith in Action!
CATHOLIC SOCIAL TEACHING

Option for the Poor and Vulnerable

In this expression, *option* means that when people have a choice, they must choose to serve the needs of the weakest first. This principle requires humans to set aside bureaucratic definitions and program goals and to focus on distributing resources to those who need them most. People must focus public policy on making the riches of our nations, including food, medical care, and education, available to all.

The Catholic Church calls us

- to share what we have with others.
- to be active advocates for those who are less fortunate.
- to know that our efforts for others will be rewarded when we are judged by God.

Reflect   How am I preparing my students for a life of service to the poor and vulnerable?

Catholic Social Teaching Document

"In teaching us charity, the Gospel instructs us in the preferential respect due to the poor and the special situation they have in society: the more fortunate should renounce some of their rights so as to place their goods more generously at the services of others."

From *A Call to Action*, #23

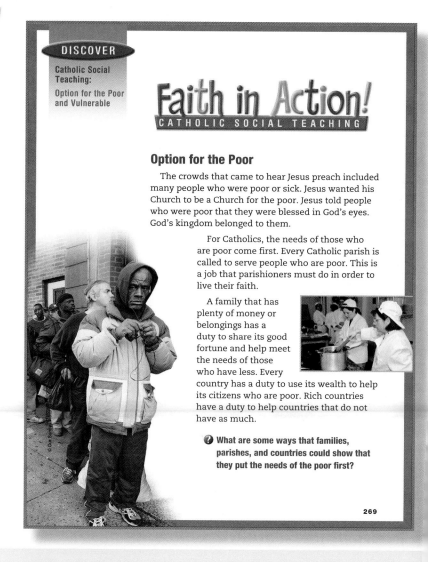

DISCOVER

Catholic Social Teaching: Option for the Poor and Vulnerable

Faith in Action!
CATHOLIC SOCIAL TEACHING

Option for the Poor

The crowds that came to hear Jesus preach included many people who were poor or sick. Jesus wanted his Church to be a Church for the poor. Jesus told people who were poor that they were blessed in God's eyes. God's kingdom belonged to them.

For Catholics, the needs of those who are poor come first. Every Catholic parish is called to serve people who are poor. This is a job that parishioners must do in order to live their faith.

A family that has plenty of money or belongings has a duty to share its good fortune and help meet the needs of those who have less. Every country has a duty to use its wealth to help its citizens who are poor. Rich countries have a duty to help countries that do not have as much.

❷ What are some ways that families, parishes, and countries could show that they put the needs of the poor first?

269

Discover Catholic Social Teaching

👐 **Let Us Pray**   God, thank you for giving us the opportunity to serve those who are poor.

Option for the Poor

Read aloud the name of the Catholic social teaching principle in the left column.

- Explain that an option is a choice, and that vulnerable people have few resources to help them live. This teaching means that Christians should choose to do what is most helpful for those who are poor.

- Read aloud the first paragraph. Help students recall Gospel stories in which Jesus cured or fed people who were poor.

- Have students read the next two paragraphs silently.

❷ **What are some ways that families, parishes, and countries could show that they put the needs of the poor first?** Accept all responses.

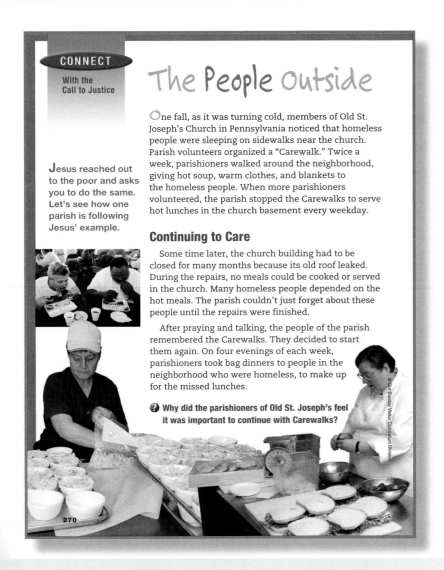

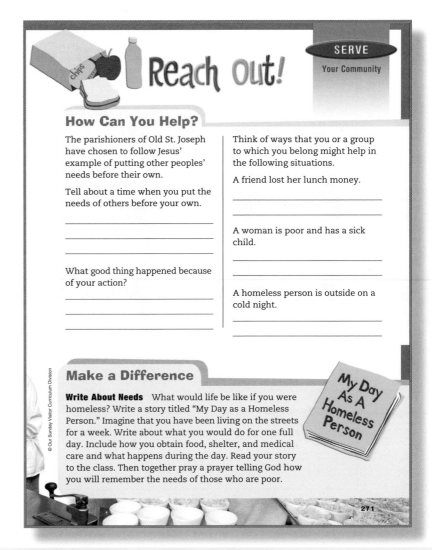

Connect with the Call to Justice

The People Outside

Ask several students to preview the text and act it out silently as you read it.

• Ask students why the Carewalks were started.

Continuing to Care

Continue to have students act out the text as you read aloud.

• Ask why the parishioners started the Carewalks again. The parish building was being repaired.

❷ **Why did the parishioners of Old St. Joseph's feel it was important to continue with Carewalks?** Discuss how the homeless would have felt if the Carewalks had stopped.

• Have students summarize how the people of Old St. Joseph's Church showed that they understood Jesus' teachings. They saw that other people were in need and helped them.

Serve Your Community

How Can You Help?

Read the first paragraph.

• Ask students how the parishioners of Old St. Joseph's put others' needs before their own.

• Have students write answers to the text questions in their books.

• Beginning with student answers to the questions, lead a discussion about how Christians can best serve those in need.

Make a Difference

Encourage students to write a story.

• Allow time for them to work independently.

• Ask volunteers to share their stories with the class. Praise the insights that students reveal.

• Invite students to pray spontaneously for the needs of those who are poor.

WORDS OF FAITH

A

absolution Words spoken by the priest during the Sacrament of Reconciliation. *(191)*

authority The power and the responsibility to lead others. *(136)*

B

Beatitudes Teachings of Jesus that show the way to true happiness and tell the way to live in God's kingdom now and always. *(97)*

blasphemy The sin of showing contempt for the name of God, Jesus Christ, Mary, or the saints in words or action. *(113)*

C

canonized Officially proclaimed a saint by the Church. Canonized saints have special feast days or memorials in the Church's calendar. *(128)*

capital punishment Taking the life of a person as punishment for a serious crime, such as murder. It is also called the death penalty. *(156)*

charity The virtue of love. It directs people to love God above all things and their neighbor as themselves, for the love of God. *(105)*

community A group of people who hold certain beliefs, hopes, and goals in common. *(77)*

conscience The gift from God that helps us know the difference between right and wrong and helps us choose what is right. *(87)*

conversion The process of turning our lives away from sin and toward the love of God and others. *(189)*

Corporal Works of Mercy Actions that meet the physical needs of others. *(105)*

covenant Sacred promise or agreement between God and humans. *(53)*

D

dignity Is self-worth. Every human is worthy of respect because he or she is made in the image of God. *(69)*

diversity means variety, especially among people. *(209)*

E

envy To resent or be sad from wanting for yourself what belongs to others. *(201)*

Eucharist The Sacrament through which Catholics are united with the life, death, and Resurrection of Jesus. *(183)*

F

faithful To be steadfast and loyal in your commitment to God, just as he is faithful to you. *(53)*

false witness A misrepresentation of the truth. *(164)*

forgiveness An act of welcoming someone back after he or she has done wrong. Forgiveness includes accepting the person, even though you do not approve of the wrong behavior. *(189)*

free will The God-given ability to choose between good and evil. *(85)*

G

gifts of the Holy Spirit Seven powerful gifts we receive in Baptism and Confirmation. These gifts help us grow in our relationship with God and others. *(214–215)*

grace The gift of God's life in you. *(85)*

Great Commandment The two-fold command to love God above all and your neighbor as yourself. *(103)*

greed The desire to acquire earthly goods without limits or beyond one's needs. *(201)*

H

heaven The state of eternal happiness with God. *(215)*

holiness Being what God created you to be. You become holy, or Godlike, by sharing God's life of grace. *(128)*

I

idolatry The sin of worshiping an object or a person instead of God. It is letting anything or anyone become more important than God. *(111)*

Immaculate Conception The title for Mary that recognizes that God preserved her from sin from the first moment of her life. *(131)*

J

justice The virtue of giving to God and people what is due them. *(209)*

K

kingdom of God God's rule of peace, justice, and love that is here now, but has not yet come in its fullness. *(121)*

L

laity Name for all of the baptized people in the Church who share in God's mission but are not priests or consecrated sisters and brothers. *(123)*

last judgment The judgment that will occur at the end of time when Jesus returns to judge all who have ever lived. Then, all will fully see and understand God's plan for creation. *(217)*

liturgical year The cycle of feasts and seasons that makes up the Church's year of worship. *(173)*

M

magisterium The Church's teaching authority to interpret the word of God found in Scripture and Tradition. *(139)*

martyr A person who gives up his or her life to witness to the truth of the faith. *(163)*

mission To be sent to share the good news of Jesus and the kingdom of God. *(209)*

modesty The virtue that helps people dress, talk, and act in appropriate ways. *(149)*

morality Living in right relationship with God, yourself and others. It is putting your beliefs into action. *(79)*

mortal sin A serious sin that destroys your relationship with God. *(70)*

murder The deliberate killing of an innocent person. *(157)*

O

obey To do things or act in certain ways that are requested by those in authority. *(149)*

Original Sin The choice of the first humans to disobey God. *(51)*

P

parish A Catholic community with shared spiritual beliefs and worship. *(79)*

particular judgment The individual judgment by God at the time of your death. *(217)*

Paschal mystery The mystery of Jesus' suffering, death, Resurrection, and Ascension. *(173)*

patron saint A model of faith and protector for you. *(131)*

penance The name for the prayer, offering, or good work the priest gives you in the Sacrament of Reconciliation. *(191)*

perjury A lie that is told in a court of law. *(164)*

precepts of the Church Some of the minimum requirements given by Church leaders for deepening your relationship with God and the Church. *(139)*

providence God's loving care for all things; God's will and plan for creation. *(45)*

R

reparation The action taken to repair the damage done through a sin. *(165)*

revelation The way God tells humans about himself and makes his plan known. *(45)*

S

Sacrament of the Anointing of the Sick Brings Jesus' healing touch to strengthen, comfort, and forgive the sins of those who are seriously ill or close to death. *(191)*

Sacrament of Reconciliation The Sacrament that celebrates God's mercy and forgiveness and a sinner's reconciliation with God and the Church through the absolution of the priest. *(189)*

Sacraments Signs that give grace. Sacraments were instituted by Christ and are celebrated by his Church. *(181)*

saint A person whom the Church declares has led a holy life and is enjoying eternal life with God in heaven. *(129)*

Scripture Another name for the Bible. Scripture is the word of God written in human words. *(45)*

sin The deliberate thought, word, deed, or omission contrary to the law of God. *(71)*

social sin A sinful social structure or institution that builds up over time so that it affects the whole society. *(71)*

soul The spiritual part of a human that lives forever. *(69)*

stewardship The human responsibility to care for God's creation and to respect all life as a gift from God. *(201)*

suicide The taking of one's own life. *(156)*

T

Ten Commandments The summary of laws that God gave to Moses on Mount Sinai. They tell us what is necessary in order to love God and others. *(60)*

Triduum The celebration of the passion, death and Resurrection of Christ. The Triduum begins on Holy Thursday evening and concludes on Easter Sunday night. *(175)*

V

venial sin A less serious sin that weakens your relationship with God. *(70)*

vocation God's call to love and serve him and others. *(121)*

vows Solemn promises that are made to or before God. *(149)*

W

worship To adore and praise God especially in prayer and in liturgy. *(111)*

titles of, 19, 31, 32
Triduum and, 231
as Truth, 165
works of, 121, 180–181, 191, 209
Jewish people, 58–61, 110–111, 224
Joachim, Saint, 152
Joan of Arc, Saint, 168
John, Saint, 224
John the Baptist, Saint, 15
John of God, Saint, 82
John XXIII, Pope, 129, 236
Jonah and the Big Fish, 44–45
Joseph, husband of Mary, 147
Joseph, son of Jacob, 58
Judah, 58
judgment, 39, 214, 216–217, 229
justice, **209**, 228, **273**

Kateri Tekakwitha, Blessed, 134
Katharine Drexel, Saint, 108
kingdom of God, 78, **121**, 216–217, 226, **273**
knowledge, 39, 215, 237

laity, 122–**123**, **273**
last judgment, 216–**217**, 229, **273**
Last Supper, 180, 182–183
  See also Eucharist
leadership, 20–23
Lent, 24–27, 174, 175, 230, 231
light, 32, 35
Litany of St. Joseph, 274
liturgical year, **173**–175, 230, **273**
Liturgy of the Word, 231
Lord's Day, 113
Lord's Prayer, 239
Lord's Supper, 231
love
  connection to God through, 68, 70–71
  of enemies, 157
  of family, 145–149
  as Great Commandment, 102–105
  of others, 76–79, 86–87, 120–123
  signs of, 180–181
  Ten Commandments and, 60–61
Luke, Saint, 224
lying, 164–165

Magi, 16, 19
magisterium, 138–**139**, 228, **273**
Margaret Mary Alacoque, Saint, 186
Mark, Saint, 224
Mark Chong, Saint, 220
marriage, 148, 181, 232
Martin de Porres, Saint, 100
martyrs, 90, 162–**163**, 168, 220, **273**
Mary, Mother of God, 8–11, 48, 130–131, 147, 226, 227
Mary Magdalen Postel, Saint, 142
Mass, 182–183
material possessions, 102–103, 197–201
Matrimony, Sacrament of, 148, 181, 232
Matthew, Saint, 224
Maximilian Kolbe, Saint, 160
Memorare, 240
Miriam, 64
mission, 206–**209**, 228, **274**
missionaries, 206–209
modesty, **149**, **274**
morality, 78–79, 86–87, 234–238, **274**
mortal sin, **70**, 190, 238, **274**
Moses, 59–61, 64, 110–112, 155, 225
Mount Sinai, 60, 110, 225
murder, 70, 156–**157**, **274**

Naomi, 56
natural moral law, **236**
New Testament, 45, 223, 224
Noah, 51, 225
Nobel, Alfred, 154–155

obey, 53, 148–**149**, **274**
Old Testament, 45, 222–223, 224
Ordinary Time, 8, 20–23, 174, 175, 230
Original Sin, 50–**51**, 227, 238, **274**

Palm Sunday, 231
Paraguay, 227
parish, **79**, **274**
Parks, Rosa, 68–69, 71
particular judgment, 216–**217**, 229, **274**
Paschal mystery, **173**–175, 225, 231, **274**
patron saint, **131**, **274**
Paul, Saint, 20–23
peace, 227
penance, 139, 181, 189–**191**, 231, 233, **274**
Pentateuch, 222, **224**
Pentecost, 36–39, 138, 175, 230
perjury, **164**, **274**
Peter, Saint, 136–138, 180
Peter Yu Tae-chol, Saint, 220
piety (reverence), 39, 215, 227, 237
pope, 138, 228
prayer, 24, 85, 231, 239–241 *See also prayers at the beginning and end of each lesson*
Prayer for Our Lady of Guadalupe Day, 243
precepts of the Church, **139**, 236, **274**
prophet, 224
Prophetic books, 223
providence, 44–**45**, **274**
pruning, **24**
psalms, 46, 62
purgatory, **229**

reconciliation, 139, 181, 188–191, 233
Reconciliation, Sacrament of, 139, 181, **189**–190, 232, 233, 275
reign of God, 121–123
reparation (satisfaction), 164–**165**, **274**
respect
  for God, 102–103, 110–113
  for life, 154–157
  for others, 70–72, 79, 112, 113, 237
revelation, **45**, **274**
reverence (piety), 39, 215, 227, 237
rich young man, 102
right judgment (counsel), 39, 214, 237
Rosary,
  How to Pray the Rosary, 246
  The Mysteries of the Rosary, 245
Ruth, 56

sacramental seal, 233
sacraments, 85, 173, **181**–183, 189–191, 232–233, **275**
saint, 128–**129**, 229, **275**
  See also individual saint by name
salvation, 173, 188
sanctifying grace, **237**
Sarah, 53
Satan, 50
satisfaction (reparation), 164–165, 233
Saul, 20–23
Scripture, **45**, 87, 222–225, **275**
  See also Bible; New Testament; Old Testament

seal of confession, 233
Second Coming of Christ, 216–217, 229
Sermon on the Mount, 96–97, 226
Service, Sacraments of, 232
service/serving, 36–39, 121–123
Sign of the Cross, 112, 239
sin, 70–**71**, **275**
  forgiveness for, 28, 32, 180, 183, 188–191
  freedom from, 31, 173
  results of, 87, 238
  types of, 50–51, 71, 238
social sin, **71**, 238, **275**
Solomon, King, 76–77
soul, **69**, **275**
Stepanek, Mattie, 123
stewardship, 201, **275**
suffering, 8, 11, 28, 31
suicide, **156**, **275**
Sunday, 113, 139, 173
symbols, 224, 226

Talbot, Matt, Venerable, 194
teacher, 135–139
temple, 76, 156
Ten Commandments, **275**
  Eighth, 164–165
  Fifth, 155–156
  First, 111
  Fourth, Sixth and Ninth, 147–149
  giving of, **60**–61
  Great Commandment and, 102–103
  meaning of, 234
  obedience to, 85, 225
  Second, 112
  Seventh and Tenth, 200–201
  theft, 200
  Third, 113
Teresa Benedicta, Saint, 74
theological virtues, 238
Thomas More, Saint, 162–163
Torah, 224
Tradition, 45, 224
Triduum, 28–31, **175**, 231, **275**
truth, 161–165

understanding, 39, 214, 237
unity, 147, 209

Venerable, 229
Veneration of the Cross, 231
venial sin, **70**, 183, 238, **275**
virtue, **238**
vocation, 120–**121**, 122–123, **275**
vows, 148–**149**, **275**

Way of the Cross, 28, 244
widow's contribution, 201
wisdom, 39, 214, 224, 227, 237
Wisdom books, 222, 224
wonder and awe (fear of the Lord), 39, 215, 237
worship, **111**, **275**

Yi Sung-hun, Saint, 220

Zacchaeus, 180, 188–189

The Subcommittee on the Catechism, United States Conference of Catholic Bishops, has found this catechetical series, © 2009 Edition, to be in conformity with the *Catechism of the Catholic Church.*

Nihil Obstat
Rev. Richard L. Schaefer

Imprimatur
✠ Most Rev. Thomas Wenski
Bishop of Orlando
December 14, 2007

The Imprimatur is an official declaration that a book or pamphlet is free of doctrinal or moral error. No implication is contained therein that anyone who granted the Imprimatur agrees with the contents, opinions, or statements expressed.

Write:
Our Sunday Visitor Curriculum Division
Our Sunday Visitor, Inc.
200 Noll Plaza, Huntington, Indiana 46750

Call to Faith is a registered trademark of Our Sunday Visitor Curriculum Division, Our Sunday Visitor, 200 Noll Plaza, Huntington, Indiana 46750.

For permission to reprint copyrighted materials, grateful acknowledgment is made to the following sources:

Confraternity of Christian Doctrine, Washington, D.C.: Scriptures from the *New American Bible.* Text copyright © 1991, 1986, 1970 by the Confraternity of Christian Doctrine. All rights reserved. No part of the *New American Bible* may be used or reproduced in any form, without permission in writing from the copyright owner.

Hinshaw Music, Inc.: Lyrics from "Go Now in Peace" by Natalie Sleeth. Lyrics © 1976 by Hinshaw Music, Inc.

Hope Publishing Co., Carol Stream, IL 60188: Lyrics from "Jesu, Jesu" by Tom Colvin. Lyrics © 1969 by Hope Publishing Co. Lyrics from "Shout for Joy" by David Mowbray. Lyrics © 1982 by Jubilate Hymns, Ltd.

Hyperion: From "Peace of Patience" in *Journey Through Heartsongs* by Mattie Stepanek. Text copyright © 2001 by Mattie Stepanek.

The English translation of the "Come, Holy Spirit" (Retitled: "Prayer to the Holy Spirit"), Litany of Saint Joseph, *Angelus* and *Memorare* from *A Book of Prayers* © 1982, International Commission on English in the Liturgy Corporation (ICEL); excerpts from the English translation of *The Roman Missal* © 2010, ICEL; the English translation of "Psalm 117: Go Out to All the World" from *Lectionary for Mass* © 1969, 1981, 1997, ICEL; the English translation of the Act of Contrition from *Rite of Penance* © 1974, ICEL.

Additional acknowledgments appear on page 278.

Call to Faith Parish Grade 4 Student Edition
ISBN: 978-0-15-902277-1
Item Number: CU1373

8 9 10 11 12 13 014588 15 14 13 12 11
Courier, Kendallville, Indiana, USA, July 2011, Job# 359029

Illustration Credits
8-9 Frank Ordaz; 12-13 Maurie Manning; 16-17 Simone Boni; 20-21 Dan Brown; 28-29 Joel Spector; 32 Nick Harris; 36 Dennis Lyall. 42 (bkgd) Stacey Schuett; 44 (bl) James M. Effler; 45 (br) Judy Stead; 48 (bl) Lois Woolley; 50 (b) Dan Brown; 52 (bl) Michael Jaroszko; 53 (tr) Michael Jaroszko; 53 (br) Judy Stead; 56 (bl) Lois Woolley; 57 (b) Ezra Tucker; 58 (bl) Tom Newsom; 59 (cr) Mark Stevens; 60 (bl) Corey Wolfe; 61 (br) Judy Stead; 64 Lois Woolley. 71 (br) Judy Stead; 74 Lois Woolley; 76 (bl) Cathy Diefendorf; 81 (br) Judy Stead; 82 Lois Woolley; 84 (bl) Jeff Preston; 84 (br) Jeff Preston; 86 (bl) Jeff Spackman; 89 (br) Judy Stead; 90 (bl) Lois Woolley. 94 (b) Peter Church; 96 (br) Steve Adler; 100 (cr) Judy Stead; 100 (bl) Lois Woolley; 102 (bl) Roger Payne; 104 (bl) Karen Patkau; 107 (b) Judy Stead; 108 Lois Woolley; 110 (b) Adam Hook; 113 (br) Judy Stead; 116 (bl) Lois Woolley. 119 (br) Yvonne Gilbert; 120 (b) Mike Jaroszko; 121 (bl) Judy Stead; 126 (bl) Lois Woolley; 128 (bl) Philip Howe; 129 (cr) Philip Howe; 134 (cr) Judy Stead; 134 (bl) Lois Woolley; 136 (b) Dominick D'Andrea; 137 (cr) Dominick D'Andrea; 141 (br) Judy Stead; 142 (bl) Lois Woolley. 147 (tr) Philip Howe; 152 (bl) Lois Woolley; 155 (tr) Robert Sauber; 160 (bl) Lois Woolley; 162 (b) Jeff Preston; 168 (bl) Lois Woolley. 178 (bl) Lois Woolley; 179 (br) Philip Howe; 180 (b) Jeff Preston; 182 (b) Yuan Lee; 186 (bl) Lois Woolley; 188 (b) Doug Fryer; 191 (br) Adam Hook; 194 (bl) Lois Woolley. 198 (bl) Peter Church; 201 (cr) Kevin Torline; 204 (bl) Lois Woolley; 208 (b) Dean Kennedy; 212 (bl) Lois Woolley; 214 (bkgd) Kevin Torline; 220 (bl) Lois Woolley.

Photo Credits
iii Gabe Palmer/Corbis; 1 l Rubberball Productions; 1 r Comstock Images; 2 Richard Hutchings/PhotoEdit; 6-7 bg Photomondo/Getty Images; 7 inset Father Gene Plaisted, OSC; 10-11 bg PhotoAlto/Creatas; 10-11 fg Richard Hutchings; 11 c Richard Hutchings; 14-15 bg Don Farrall/Photodisc/Getty Images; 15 inset Ariel Skelley/Corbis; 18-19 Benelux Press/Index Stock/Photolibrary; 22-23 bg Fridmar Damm/Corbis; 23 c Richard Hutchings; 23 b Richard Hutchings; 24-25 Richard Hurtchings/PhotoEdit; 26-27 bg Jakob Helbig/cultura/Corbis; 27 inset C Squared Studios/Photodisc/Getty Images; 30-31 t Corel; 30-31 b Daryl Benson/Masterfile; 31 fg Richard Hutchings; 34-35 bg Rich Reid/Getty Images; 35 inset Tetra Images/Corbis; 38-39 bg Corel; 39 t Photodisc/Getty Images; 39 b Richard Hutchings; 40 l Eric Camden; 40 l Bob Davidson Photography/Getty Images; 40 c Brian Minnich; 41 fg Eric Camden; 41 bg Bob Davidson Photography/Getty Images; 45 Thinkstock/Comstock/Getty Images; 46 Ed McDonald; 49 Brian Minnich; 50 cl Jacqui Hurst; 51 t Katie S. Atkinson/Getty Images; 51 b Sonny Senser; 54 Bill Wittman; 59 Sonny Senser; 61 John Nakata/Corbis; 62 The Mazer Corporation; 64 Ed McDonald; 66 l Eric Camden; 66 l John Connell/Corbis; 66 c Ed McDonald; 66 r Royalty-Free/Getty Images; 66 r Amos Morgan/Photodisc/Getty Images; 66 r Fuse/Getty Images; 66 r Corbis/Fotosearch; 67 bg John Connell/Corbis; 67 fg Eric Camden; 68 Bettman/Corbis; 69 c Ariel Skelley/Corbis; 69 b Jim Whitmer; 70 LWA-Dann Tardif; 71 James W. Porter/Corbis; 72 Paul Vozdic/Stone/Getty Images; 74 Jack Holtel/Photographik Company; 75 Ed McDonald; 77 c Cleve Bryant/PhotoEdit; 77 b Jim Whitmer; 78 Portland Art Museum/Gift of the Samuel H. Kress Foundation; 79 Richard Hutchings/Photo Edit; 80 Tom & Dee Ann McCarthy/Corbis; 83 bg Royalty-Free/Getty Images; 83 t Amos Morgan/Photodisc/Getty Images; 83 c Fuse/Getty Images; 83 b Corbis/Fotosearch; 85 t Houghton Mifflin Harcourt; 85 b David Young-Wolffe/PhotoEdit; 87 Sonny Senser; 88 Jeff Grenberg/PhotoEdit; 90 Brian Leng/Corbis; 92 l Ed McDonald; 92 c Brian Minnich; 92 r Ed McDonald; 92-93 bg Ed McDonald; 95 Sonny Senser; 97 Ed McDonald; 98 Diane Macdonald/Stockbyte/Getty Images; 101 c Brian Minnich; 101 bg Ed McDonald; 101 bl Brian Minnich; 101 br Brian Minnich; 103 l Kwame Zikomo/SuperStock; 103 r Steve Skjold/Alamy; 105 Andrew Bret Wallis/Getty Images; 106 Father Gene Plaisted, OSC; 109 Ed McDonald; 111 c Bill Wittman; 111 b Jim Whitmer; 112 Myrleen Ferguson Cate/PhotoEdit; 113 Paul Barton/Corbis; 114 Eric Camden; 116 Ed McDonald; 118 c Culver Pictures, Inc./SuperStock; 118 cl Culver Pictures, Inc./SuperStock; 118 cr David Turnley/Corbis; 118 r Eric Camden; 121 Philippe Lissac/Godong/Corbis; 122 Father Gene Plaisted, OSC; 123 Muscular Dystrophy Association; 124 Eric Camden; 126 Jack Holtel/Photographik Company; 127 t Culver Pictures, Inc./SuperStock ; 127 c David Turnley/Corbis; 127 b Culver Pictures, Inc./SuperStock ; 130 Arte & Immagini srl/CORBIS; 131 Father Gene Plaisted, OSC; 132 t Father Gene Plaisted, OSC; 132 cl Father Gene Plaisted, OSC; 132 cr Father Gene Plaisted, OSC; 132 bl Father Gene Plaisted, OSC; 132 br Father Gene Plaisted, OSC; 135 Eric Camden; 137 Jim Whitmer; 138 KAI PFAFFENBACH/Reuters/Corbis; 139 Father Gene Plaisted, OSC; 140 SuperStock/SuperStock; 142 Brooklyn Productions/The Image Bank/Getty Images; 144 l Patrick Johns/Corbis; 144 l Ariel Skelley/Corbis; 144 c Eric Camden; 144 r Eric Camden; 144-145 bg Patrick Johns/Corbis; 145 b Ariel Skelley/Corbis; 146 Eric Camden; 147 Jim Whitmer; 148 Ken Reid; 149 Joel Sartore/National Geographic/Getty Images; 150 Frank Siteman/PhotoEdit; 152 Roy Morsch/Corbis; 153 Eric Camden; 154 t Bettman/Corbis; 154 c David Turnley/Corbis; 154 bl Pierre Perrin/Zoko/Sygma/Corbis; 154-155 br Bettman/Corbis; 155 c Royalty-Free/Getty Images; 156 Stephen Simpson/Taxi/Getty Images; 157 Jim Whitmer; 158 Andy Sacks/Stone/Getty Images; 161 Eric Camden; 163 l Bettman/Corbis; 163 r Bettman/Corbis; 164 Jose Luis Pelaez, Inc./Corbis; 165 Tony Freeman/PhotoEdit; 166 Photodisc/Getty Images; 167 Tom & Dee Ann McCarthy/CORBIS; 168 Ariel Skelley/Corbis; 170 l Frank Cezus/Taxi/Getty Images; 170 l Frank Cezus/Taxi/Getty Images; 170 l Frank Cezus/Taxi/Getty Images; 170 l Frank Cezus/Taxi/Getty Images; 170 l Eric Camden; 170 r Ed McDonald; 170-171 bg Keith Wood/Corbis; 171 tcl Frank Cezus/Taxi/Getty Images; 171 cl Frank Cezus/Taxi/Getty Images; 171 bl Eric Camden; 171 bcl Frank Cezus/Taxi/Getty Images; 171 br Frank Cezus/Taxi/Getty Images; 172 t Michael Keller; 172 c Tobi Corney/Stone/Getty Images; 172 bl Pascal Crapet/Stone/Getty Images; 172 br Sonny Senser; 175 Gene Plaisted/The Crosiers; 176 Eric Camden; 178 Sonny Senser; 181 cl Elio Ciol/Corbis; 181 c Ed McDonald; 181 cr Royalty-Free/Corbis; 181 bl Jim Whitmer; 181 bcr Royalty-Free/Corbis; 183 Myrleen Ferguson Cate/PhotoEdit; 184 Bill Wittman; 186 Ed McDonald; 187 Ed McDonald; 189 Jim Whitmer; 190 Father Gene Plaisted, OSC; 192 Tony Freeman/PhotoEdit; 196 l Brian Minnich; 196 c Brian Minnich; 196 r Ed McDonald; 196-197 bg Brian Minnich; 199 t George Disario/Corbis; 199 b Jim Whitmer; 200 Victoria Bowen; 202 David Young-Wolffe/PhotoEdit; 205 Brian Minnich; 206-207 bg Maryknoll Minstries; 206 c Maryknoll Bolivia Photos; 206 b Maryknoll Minstries; 207 t Maryknoll Minstries; 207 c Maryknoll Minstries; 207 b Jim Whitmer; 209 Jim Whitmer; 210 Sonny Senser; 212 Joe Carlson/Corbis; 213 bg Ed McDonald; 213 fg Ed McDonald; 215 Jim Whitmer; 216 t Michael Newman/PhotoEdit; 216 b Peter Frank/Corbis217 l Larry Mulvehill/Corbis; 217 r Guy Cali/Corbis; 218 Peter Burian/Corbis; 223 t Myrleen Ferguson Cate/PhotoEdit; 222-223 b Richard Hutchings; 224 Ingram Publishing; 225 Richard Hutchings; 226 Father Gene Plaisted, OSC; 228 t Osservatore Romano/POOL/Reuters/Corbis; 228 b Jupiter Images/Getty Images; 230 l Father Gene Plaisted, OSC; 230 r Photos.com; 231 l Corel; 231 r Corel; 235 rubberball/Getty Images; 236 t C Squared Studios/Photodisc/Getty Images; 236 c Photodisc/Getty Images; 236 bl Photodisc/Getty Images; 236 br Photodisc/Getty Images; 239 Thinkstock/Getty Images; 240-241 Thinkstock/Getty Images; 242-243 Thinkstock/Getty Images; 244-245 Thinkstock/Getty Images; 246-247 Thinkstock/Getty Images; 248-249 Thinkstock/Getty Images; 250 l David Young-Wolffe/PhotoEdit; 250 l St. George Church; 250 l Mobile Loaves & Fishes; 250 l Michael Newman/PhotoEdit; 250 l Mark Bradshaw; 250 1 A. Ramey/PhotoEdit; 250 l Jeff Grenberg/PhotoEdit; 251 tl Kurt Stier/Corbis; 251 bl Ivo Von Renner/Stone/Getty Images; 251 bc D. Falconer/PhotoLink/Getty Images; 251 br David Young-Wolffe/PhotoEdit; 252 t David Young-Wolffe/PhotoEdit; 252 c Jose Luis Pelaez, Inc./Corbis; 252-253 b Terrance Klassen/Ponka Wonka; 253 inset Sonny Senser; 254-255 bg Digital Vision/Getty Images; 254 c Our Sunday Visitor Curriculum Division; 254 bl St. George Church; 254 br St. George Church; 255 inset St. George Church; 256 Digital Vision/Getty Images; 257 c Mobile Loaves & Fishes; 257 bl Steve Skjold/Alamy; 257 bc Joseph Harnish; 257 br Joseph Harnish; 258 c Mobile Loaves & Fishes; 258 b Mobile Loaves & Fishes; 259 c Sonny Senser; 259 bl Myrleen Ferguson Cate/PhotoEdit; 259 bcl Joseph Harnish; 259 bcr Myrleen Ferguson Cate/PhotoEdit; 259 br Joseph Harnish; 260 bg Jack Hollingsworth/Photodisc/Getty Images; 260 bl Michael Newman/PhotoEdit; 260 bc Norbert von der Groeben/The Image Works; 260 br Vince Streano/Corbis; 261 bg Jack Hollingsworth/Photodisc/Getty Images; 261 t Saint Charles Borromeo Catholic School; 261 c Saint Charles Borromeo Catholic School; 261 bl Saint Charles Borromeo Catholic School; 261 br Saint Charles Borromeo Catholic School; 262 bg Houghton Mifflin Harcourt; 262 br Sonny Senser; 263 c Mark Bradshaw; 263 bl Mark Bradshaw; 263 br Mark Anderson/Rubberball/Alamy; 264-265 bg Mark Anderson/Rubberball/Alamy; 264 c Mark Bradshaw; 264 bl Mark Bradshaw; 266 b Bob Daemmrich/PhotoEdit; 267 t A. Ramey/PhotoEdit; 267 b Billy Hustace/Stone/Getty Images; 268 David Young-Wolffe/PhotoEdit; 269 Mario Tama/Getty Images; 269 r Robert Brenner/PhotoEdit; 270 c Jeff Grenberg/PhotoEdit; 270 bl Dennis MacDonald/PhotoEdit; 270 br Lon C Dieh/PhotoEdit; 271 Dennis MacDonald/PhotoEdit

Acknowledgements
For permission to reprint copyrighted material, grateful acknowledgment is made to the following sources:

Liturgy Training Publications, 1800 North Hermitage Avenue, Chicago, IL 60622, 1-800-933-1800, www.ltp.org: From "Prayer for Our Lady of Guadalupe" (Retitled: "Prayer for Our Lady of Guadalupe Day") in *Blessings and Prayers through the Year: A Resource for School and Parish* by Elizabeth McMahon Jeep. Text © 2004 by Archdiocese of Chicago.

Jack Prelutsky: From "Me I Am!" in *The Random House Book of Poetry* by Jack Prelutsky. Text copyright © by Jack Prelutsky.

Patricia Joyce Shelly: Lyrics from "All Grownups, All Children" by Patricia Joyce Shelly. Lyrics © 1977 by Joyce Shelly.

Twenty-Third Publications, A Division of Bayard: "Grail Prayer" from *500 Prayers for Catholic Schools & Parish Youth Groups* by Filomena Tassi and Peter Tassi. Text copyright © 2004 by Filomena Tassi and Peter Tassi.

United States Conference of Catholic Bishops, Inc., Washington, D.C.: English translation of "Hail, Holy Queen" (*Salve, Regina*) from *Catholic Household Blessings and Prayers.* Translation copyright © 1989 by United States Catholic Conference, Inc.

Viking Penguin, a division of Penguin Group (USA) Inc.: "The Creation" from *God's Trombones* by James Weldon Johnson. Text copyright 1927 by The Viking Press, Inc.; text copyright renewed © 1955 by Grace Nail Johnson.

SE Acknowledgements

Activity Master Answer Key

Activity Master 1

1. –
2. –
3. +
4. +
5. +
6. –
7. –
8. –
9. +
10. +
11.–14. Responses will vary.

Activity Master 2

A	T	R	U	S	P
1	2	3	4	5	6

T	G	L	O	D	Y
7	8	9	10	11	12

Activity Master 3

1. (egasrtn) = strange; (dsog) = gods
2. (etka) = take; (aniv) = vain
3. (memReerb) = Remember; (ylho) = holy
4. (fteahr) = father; (tomhre) = mother
5. (llhsa) = shall; (ikll) = kill
6. (mocmit) = commit; (adtrulye) = adultery
7. (halls) = shall; (lstae) = steal
8. (flsae) = false; (tiwnses) = witness
9. (vocet) = covet; (weif) = wife
10. (cotve) = covet; (gdoos) = goods

Activity Master 4

Scripture	Whom did Jesus treat with dignity?	How did Jesus show that he respected the person?
1. Matthew 8:1–4	a man with leprosy	Jesus touched and healed him.
2. Mark 2:13–17	tax collectors and sinners	Jesus ate with them and spent time with them.
3. Luke 7:36–50	a sinful woman	Jesus allowed the woman to kiss and anoint his feet; he forgave her.
4. Luke 19:1–10	Zacchaeus	Jesus stayed at his house.
5. John 4:4–42	a Samaritan woman	Jesus spoke with her and promised her "living water."

Activity Master 6

1. GOOD
2. SIN
3. STUDY
4. RULE
5. BETTER
6. RELY
7. DECISIONS
8. CLOSER
9. INNER
10. DISCUSS

Puzzle Solution: LET YOUR CONSCIENCE
                  BE YOUR GUIDE

Activity Master 7

Section 1
1. I could help Mom with cooking dinner.
2. I could spend time with my younger brother.

Section 2
1. I could visit Mr. Hatsumi and ask him what he needs.
2. I could volunteer to walk Mr. Hatsumi's dog or take his trash to the curb.

Section 3
1. I could invite him to come to my house to play.
2. I could create a sympathy card for him.

Section 4
1. I could invite Bryn to my lunch table.
2. I could show Bryn where the buses are after school.

Activity Master 8

Answers will vary.

Activity Master 9

```
A   J   Y   O   Z   U   E   P   T   M   E
J   E   S   U   S   C   H   R   I   S   T
Q   F   A   D   K   M   O   N   Q   D   S
B   W   V   N   L   I   L   G   H   C   Y
C   P   I   R   O   L   Y   D   S   Z   D
M   G   O   Q   R   H   S   O   N   B   L
T   S   R   N   D   R   P   E   D   K   J
K   R   X   G   U   V   I   Z   U   T   N
P   F   A   T   H   E   R   L   W   O   Q
W   B   N   E   D   O   I   B   X   A   B
G   Z   C   R   E   A   T   O   R   J   I
```

Write one way you will use God's name with respect this week.
Responses will vary.

Activity Master 10

1. CAT E C HI S T
2. M US IC I A N
3. SE R V E R
4. D E A C O N
5. EU C H AR I STI C
   M I NI S T ER
6. Y O U TH
   MI N I ST E R
7. P R I ES T
8. RE L I GI O U S LIFE

1. Responses   2.
3. will vary.   4.
5.   6.
7.   8.

Activity Master 11

Saint Nicholas
December 6

Saint Blaise
February 2

Saint Peter
June 29

Saint Patrick
March 17

Blessed Kateri Tekakwitha
April 17

Saint Catherine of Siena
April 29

Saint Joseph
March 19

Saint Francis of Assisi
October 4

Saint Martha
July 29

Activity Master 16

Advent	Christmas
Immaculate Conception	Epiphany Holy Family Saint Nicholas

Lent	Triduum
Ash Wednesday	Holy Thursday Good Friday Holy Saturday

Easter	Ordinary Time
Pentecost Ascension	Assumption of Mary Baptism of Jesus Christ the King

Activity Master 12

Check students' coloring.

Activity Master 13

Check students' artwork.

Activity Master 14

Check students' artwork.

Activity Master 15

Check students' artwork.

Activity Master 17

Check students' artwork.

Activity Master 18

Check students' artwork.

Activity Master 19

Check students' work.

Activity Master 20

Answers will vary.

Activity Master 21

Gift	Description	I use this gift when I . . .
wisdom	Helps you see yourself as God sees you and act as God wants you to act	Responses will vary.
counsel	Helps you give good advice	
understanding	Helps you come to know God, yourself, and others	
knowledge	Helps you be open to God's loving communication	
fear of the Lord	Helps you recognize that God is greater and more wonderful than any created thing	
piety	Helps you show love and honor to God	
fortitude	Helps you stand up for what is right.	

Name _____ Date _____

God's Covenant

(A) Work with Words   Match each description in Column 1 with the correct term in Column 2.

Column 1

_e_ **1.** God's loving care

_a_ **2.** one who tried to avoid God's plan

_b_ **3.** the truth God has shown the world

_f_ **4.** the word of God in human words

_c_ **5.** one whose descendants are as numerous as the stars

_g_ **6.** being steadfast and loyal in commitments to God

_h_ **7.** the first humans' choice to disobey God

_d_ **8.** a sacred promise or agreement joining God and people

Column 2

a. Jonah

b. revelation

c. Abraham

d. covenant

e. providence

f. Scripture

g. faithful

h. original sin

(B) Check Understanding   Circle the letter that best completes the sentence or answers the question.

9. To live in a loving relationship with God and each other, the people of Israel followed the
- a. laws of Egypt.
- **(b.)** Ten Commandments.
- c. civil laws.
- d. laws of nature.

10. Which of the following did NOT come about as a result of sin?
- a. jealousy
- b. sadness
- c. fighting
- **(d.)** boredom

11. With her husband, Sarah is an ancestor to all of these faiths except
- a. Christianity.
- b. Islam.
- c. Judaism.
- **(d.)** Hinduism.

Name _____ Date _____

12. Which person was sold as a slave by his brothers?
- a. Abraham
- b. Jacob
- **(c.)** Joseph
- d. Aaron

13. Which leader of the chosen people parted the Red Sea?
- **(a.)** Moses
- b. Miriam
- c. Noah
- d. Nineveh

14. The first three commandments show people how to
- a. pray.
- **(b.)** be faithful to God.
- c. care for creation.
- d. work for love and justice.

15. God asked Abram and Sarai to journey to
- a. Egypt.
- **(b.)** Canaan.
- c. Eden.
- d. Jerusalem.

(C) Make Connections   Use the five terms below to write a one-paragraph answer.

plan   time   faith   sin   save

16–20. In this unit, you read scripture stories about creation and Adam and Eve, Jonah and the big fish, Abraham, Joseph, and Moses. Summarize one of these stories, and tell what it teaches you about God.

Sample response: By reading the story of Moses, I learned that God sometimes takes years and years to fulfill his plans. Moses was saved from being killed because his mother put him in a basket and the Pharoah's daughter found the basket and adopted Moses. When Moses grew up, he led the people out of Egypt and across the Red Sea. Moses kept his faith during the time that he spent leading the people through the desert. Moses received the Ten Commandments which showed the people how they could live without sin. These stories show us that God sends us strong leaders and will show us how to get along with one another.

Notes

_____
_____
_____
_____
_____
_____
_____
_____
_____
_____
_____
_____
_____
_____
_____

Name _____ Date _____

A Faithful People

(A) Work with Words Match each description in Column 1 with the correct term in Column 2.

Column 1

<u>c</u> **1.** A group of people who share beliefs, activities, and goals

<u>a</u> **2.** Working for this helps a community become the best it can be.

<u>e</u> **3.** An act that is seriously wrong and chosen freely

<u>f</u> **4.** Saying "yes" to what God teaches

<u>h</u> **5.** Another term for dignity

<u>b</u> **6.** The spiritual part of a person

<u>g</u> **7.** All of these are made in God's image.

<u>d</u> **8.** Putting belief into action, living in right relationships

Column 2

a. common good

b. soul

c. community

d. morality

e. mortal sin

f. faith

g. humans

h. self-worth

(B) Check Understanding Circle the letter of the choice that best completes the sentence or answers the question.

9. One part of making a good moral decision, is thinking about _____.

   (**a.**) the consequences of my choices
   b. what my friends would do
   c. what I can gain from my decision
   d. how to please my parents

10. Rosa Parks is most known for _____.

   a. becoming a saint
   b. feeding the poor
   c. writing poetry
   (**d.**) working for human rights

11. Which is a sin of omission? _____.

   a. taking things from a store
   b. talking in class during study time
   c. lying about a friend
   (**d.**) not helping someone in need

Name _____ Date _____

12. Which of these is a social sin?

   a. murder
   (**b.**) hurting people of a certain race
   c. lying to avoid punishment
   d. being lazy

13. Christians grow in grace through all of the following except

   a. the sacraments.
   b. thoughtful choices.
   c. prayer.
   (**d.**) being selfish.

14. Which is not a venial sin?

   a. lying
   b. being lazy
   (**c.**) murder
   d. cheating

15. Jesus' story of the Good Samaritan teaches people

   a. how to pray.
   b. the Ten Commandments.
   (**c.**) to help others.
   d. to forgive.

(C) Make Connections Write a response to each question or statement.

16. How does respecting the dignity of others keep the commandments and honor God?

   Possible response: It honors God because God created all human life. The commandments tell how God wants people to treat one another.

17. What is one thing you can do to reflect the love of Christ?

   Possible responses: help other people, forgive others

18. Why are all people worthy of respect?

   All people are made in the image and likeness of God.

19. Describe one way in which your class community might work for the common good.

   Responses will vary, but may include helping neighbors, collecting donations for charity, or welcoming newcomers.

20. Why is it important to live in community?

   Possible responses: God made people to live in community so they can help and support one another.

Notes

_____

_____

_____

_____

_____

_____

_____

_____

_____

_____

_____

_____

_____

_____

_____

Name _____ Date _____

Life in Christ

A **Work with Words**   Match each description in Column 1 with the correct term in Column 2.

Column 1

_e_   **1.** the law of love taught by Jesus

_a_   **2.** seven acts of kindness

_f_   **3.** how Christians show honor and respect to God

_b_   **4.** using God's name disrespectfully

_g_   **5.** another name for Sunday

_d_   **6.** a blessing

_c_   **7.** a prayer said for someone else

Column 2

a. Corporal Works of Mercy

b. blasphemy

c. intercession

d. Beatitude

e. Great Commandment

f. worship

g. Lord's Day

B **Check Understanding**   Circle the letter of the choice that best completes the sentence or answers the question.

8. Charity is the virtue of _____.

   a. trust
   b. forgiveness
   (c.) love
   d. happiness

9. According to Jesus' law of love, you must love others as _____.

   (a.) Jesus loves you
   b. your friends love you
   c. the Church loves you
   d. your teachers love you

10. Where did Moses receive the Ten Commandments?

   (a.) Mount Sinai
   b. Jerusalem
   c. Heaven
   d. Egypt

Name _____ Date _____

11. I perform a Corporal Work of Mercy when I

   a. help wash the dishes.
   b. make good grades in school.
   (c.) give clothes to a charity.
   d. use water sparingly.

12. The golden calf was a problem because

   a. Aaron made it incorrectly.
   (b.) Moses' people worshiped it.
   c. it was made of everyone's riches.
   d. it didn't look like God.

Fill in each blank with the correct term from the Word Bank.

13. I asked Jesus what I needed to do to enter heaven. ___rich young man___

14. "I am the Lord your God. You shall not have strange gods before me." ___first commandment___

15. "Remember to keep holy the Lord's day." ___third commandment___

16. "You shall not take the name of the Lord in vain." ___second commandment___

WORD BANK
first commandment
second commandment
third commandment
rich young man

C **Make Connections**   Use the four terms below to write a one-paragraph response to the question.

Great Commandment   charity
kindness   works of mercy

17–20. How does Jesus want you to live?

___Possible response: Jesus wants us to live according to the great commandment:___
___Love God above everything else and love other people as we love ourselves. If we___
___do this, we will automatically act with charity to other people. If we love God, we will___
___show others kindness. We will perform works of mercy to be certain that everyone___
___will have all that is needed to live comfortable lives.___

Notes _____

_____

_____

_____

_____

_____

_____

_____

_____

_____

_____

_____

_____

_____

Answer Key for Unit 3 Test   A9

Name _____ Date _____

The Church Teaches

(A) Work with Words   Match each description in Column 1 with the correct word in Column 2.

Column 1

_a_ **1.** the teaching authority of the Church

_h_ **2.** assists the priest at Mass

_d_ **3.** some of the duties of Catholics

_e_ **4.** person who called the Second Vatican Council

_b_ **5.** an ordained minister who proclaims God's word and does works of charity

_g_ **6.** God's kingdom of peace, justice, and love

_c_ **7.** baptized Church members who have not received Holy Orders or consecrated their lives to God

_f_ **8.** belief that Mary was free from all sin from the first moment of her life

Column 2

a. magisterium

b. deacon

c. laity

d. precepts of the Church

e. Pope John XXIII

f. Immaculate Conception

g. reign of God

h. altar server

(B) Check Understanding   Circle the letter of the choice that best completes the sentence.

9. Saint Catherine of Siena is an example to all _____.

   a. that writing letters is useful
   b. of how hard life can be
   c. of how women were treated
   (d.) that every Church member can contribute

10. A way for me to carry out the precepts of the Church is by _____.

   a. attending religion class
   b. completing my homework
   (c.) participating in Sunday Mass
   d. taking care of my pet

11. The Second Vatican Council was a special type of Church _____.

   a. teaching
   b. leader
   (c.) meeting
   d. office

Name _____ Date _____

12. A person and his or her patron saint share a _____.

   (a.) name
   b. country
   c. virtue
   d. birthday

13. The perfect model of holiness is _____.

   a. Peter
   (b.) Mary, Mother of the Church
   c. Jeremiah
   d. the Bible

14. When God calls a person to do good, he is showing that person his or her _____.

   a. reign
   b. authority
   (c.) vocation
   d. precepts

15. The title *Blessed* in front of a name means that the person _____.

   (a.) is on the way to being a canonized saint
   b. was ordained to the deaconate or priesthood
   c. preached to and blessed many people
   d. prayed every day for special blessings

(C) Make Connections   Use the five terms below to write a one-paragraph response to the question.

   parish   sisters   vocation   Church   peace

16–20. What choices will you face as an adult when you want to make choices about serving God?

Possible response: When we are adults, we can choose between serving God as deacons or priests or having other active roles in the Church. We can serve on parish committees or help with reading at Mass. We can be in religious orders as brothers or sisters. There are many ways to serve that are not directly part of the Church, too. We can be good to other people and share what we have. We can work for justice and peace as lawyers or judges or politicians. Almost any job, if done well, will be a good way to serve God.

Notes _____

_____

_____

_____

_____

_____

_____

_____

_____

_____

_____

_____

_____

_____

Name _____ Date _____

Faithful Living

(A) Work with Words Circle the letter of the choice that best completes the sentence.

1. The virtue that helps people dress, talk, and act properly is _____.
   - a. thrift
   - **b. modesty**
   - c. obedience
   - d. truthfulness

2. A martyr is a person who _____.
   - a. asks God for help in difficult times
   - b. tries to be a peacemaker
   - **c. gives up his or her life for the faith**
   - d. gives advice to Church officials

3. Lying under oath is called _____.
   - a. testimony
   - b. gossip
   - c. prejudice
   - **d. perjury**

4. Gossip harms people _____.
   - **a. whether it is true or untrue**
   - b. only if the story is about them
   - c. who do not pray
   - d. who show respect for creation

5. Truthfulness leads to _____.
   - a. pride
   - b. good grades
   - c. forgiveness
   - **d. trust**

6. The fourth through the tenth commandments guide people in loving _____.
   - a. themselves
   - b. the saints
   - **c. their neighbor**
   - d. God

7. I fail to obey the fifth commandment when I _____.
   - a. let go of harmful anger
   - **b. use tobacco or drugs**
   - c. eat healthful foods and exercise
   - d. avoid violence

Name _____ Date _____

Complete each sentence with the correct word from the Word Bank.

8–11. One of the major messages of the commandments is that life is God's gift and that humans are to treasure it. This is why __murder__, intentionally killing an innocent person, is wrong. For the same reason, __hatred__ is sinful when it leads you to wishing serious harm to another person. Because God loves humans, he will grant them __forgiveness__. People must also remember to make __reparation__ for their sins against life.

> **WORD BANK**
> reparation
> forgiveness
> hatred
> murder

(B) Check Understanding Match each description in Column 1 with the correct term in Column 2.

Column 1

- __c__ 12. remind people to honor marriage
- __d__ 13. sacred promises
- __a__ 14. one who wanted to be remembered for good works
- __f__ 15. says that life is sacred
- __b__ 16. encourages people to tell the truth
- __e__ 17. a martyr who remained true to his beliefs

Column 2

- a. Alfred Nobel
- b. eighth commandment
- c. sixth and ninth commandments
- d. vows
- e. Thomas More
- f. fifth commandment

(C) Make Connections Use the three terms below to write a one-paragraph response.

parents   authority   respect

18–20. Explain what the fourth commandment means for children and how you live it out.

Sample response: The fourth commandment tells us to honor our parents. This means that we should do what they tell us to do, as long as it is not sinful. This commandment also applies to anyone in authority. This means that we must obey teachers, babysitters, and other people who are in charge of us. I live out this commandment by doing work at home and following directions at school. I also live it out when I pay attention to the school crossing guards and other people who give me directions.

Notes _____

_____

_____

_____

_____

_____

_____

_____

_____

_____

_____

_____

_____

_____

Answer Key for Unit 5 Test   A11

Name _____ Date _____

The Paschal Mystery

(A) Work with Words Match each description in Column 1 with the correct term in Column 2.

Column 1

_f_ **1.** the cycle of Church feasts and seasons

_c_ **2.** strengthens the sick and reminds them of God's love

_e_ **3.** the first season of the Church year

_a_ **4.** sacramental covenant that a man and a woman celebrate

_d_ **5.** forgives sins confessed to a priest

_b_ **6.** liturgical season whose colors are white and gold

Column 2

a. Matrimony

b. Christmas

c. Sacrament of the Anointing of the Sick

d. Sacrament of Reconciliation

e. Advent

f. liturgical year

(B) Check Understanding Circle the letter of the choice that best completes the sentence or answers the question.

7. Which of the following is **NOT** part of the Paschal mystery?
- (a.) Jesus' birth
- b. Jesus' death
- c. Jesus' Resurrection
- d. Jesus' Ascension

8. Which statement is **NOT** true of the sacraments?
- a. They were given by Jesus.
- b. The Holy Spirit works within them.
- c. They are a sign that Jesus is still with us
- (d.) They are private prayers

9. The Sacrament of Penance and Reconciliation celebrates our _____.
- a. baptismal anointing
- b. original sin
- c. kinship and priesthood
- (d.) conversion and forgiveness through Christ

10. The word *Eucharist* literally means _____.
- a. bread and wine
- b. Body and Blood of Jesus
- (c.) thanksgiving
- d. sacrifice

Name _____ Date _____

11. The first Christians called the Eucharist the _____.
- (a.) breaking of the bread
- b. cutting of the loaf
- c. distributing of the food
- d. dinner for Christians

12. Which of these is an example of penance?
- a. remembering a friend's birthday
- (b.) apologizing to someone I have hurt
- c. keeping my room clean
- d. reading a story to a child

Complete each sentence with the correct term from the Word Bank.

13. The period from Holy Thursday to Easter Sunday is the __Triduum__.

14. Two separate periods of the Church year are called __Ordinary Time__.

15. __Lent__ is the season from Ash Wednesday to Holy Thursday.

16. In the Sacrament of Reconciliation, a person receives __absolution__, and his or her personal sins are forgiven.

17. __Easter__ celebrates Jesus' rising from the dead to new life.

WORD BANK

Lent
Triduum
Easter
absolution
Ordinary Time

(C) Make Connections Use the three terms below to write a paragraph that describes how you celebrate the Eucharist on Sunday.

participate   meal   give

18–20. Responses will vary, but may include the following. It is important for me to participate during Mass by singing and praying. My family shares a meal like the disciples did. The Eucharist is a special meal of bread and wine that becomes the body and blood of Jesus. The Eucharist calls me not only to share this meal but to serve others who have less than I do and give them what they need.

© Our Sunday Visitor Curriculum Division

Notes _____

Name _____ Date _____

Judged on Love

(A) Work with Words Match each description in Column 1 with the correct term in Column 2.

Column 1

___b___ **1.** helps you give good advice to others

___d___ **2.** helps you show love and honor to God

___a___ **3.** helps you see yourself as God sees you

___c___ **4.** helps you be open to God's revelations

___e___ **5.** helps you be aware of God's power

Column 2

a. wisdom

b. counsel

c. knowledge

d. piety

e. fear of the Lord

(B) Check Understanding Circle the letter of the choice that best completes the sentence.

6. Thinking of the last judgment should remind people to _____.
- a. fear the unknown
- (b.) work for justice and peace
- c. compete with others
- d. spend time in church

7. One sin against the seventh commandment is _____.
- (a.) theft
- b. murder
- c. idolatry
- d. lying

8. One sin against the tenth commandment is _____.
- a. adultery
- (b.) envy
- c. disobeying one's parents
- d. lying

9. A virtue that helps you follow the seventh commandment is _____.
- a. humility
- b. obedience
- c. trust
- (d.) both a and c

10. One virtue that helps you follow the tenth commandment is _____.
- a. honesty
- b. obedience
- (c.) generosity
- d. peace

Name _____ Date _____

11. Jesus' mission for Christians is to _____.
- (a.) make disciples of all nations
- b. have everyone be happy always
- c. give everyone a Bible
- d. teach themselves about him

12. Justice is _____.
- a. found only in courts
- b. a work of mercy
- c. a virtue for adults
- (d.) giving people what is due them

13. An example of appreciating diversity is _____.
- a. eating a well-balanced meal
- b. sharing school supplies
- (c.) learning about another culture
- d. writing a letter to your grandmother

14–17. Complete the paragraph with the correct terms from the Word Bank.

After humans die, they meet God and have their lives judged. This is the _particular judgment_. Then their souls will go to ___heaven___, where they will be with God always, or to ___hell___, where they will never see him. At the end of time, all souls will meet for the last judgment, when Jesus will come again in glory. This will be the fulfillment of _God's kingdom_.

| **WORD BANK** |
| particular judgment |
| God's kingdom |
| hell |
| heaven |

(C) Make Connections Write a brief response to the statement.

18–20. Describe three specific ways in which you are preparing for your mission in life.

Possible response: I am trying to get ready to be an adult by being a good steward and taking care of things that I am in charge of. This means that I take good care of my room and treat my brother and sister with justice. I also try to prepare myself for my mission in life by studying and using my talents to learn as much as I can so that I will be ready to do adult work when I am old enough.

_____

_____

_____

Notes _____

_____

_____

_____

_____

_____

_____

_____

_____

_____

_____

_____

_____

_____

_____

_____

Illustration Credits

(b) 8A Frank Ordaz; (b)12A Maurie Manning; (b) 16A Simone Boni; (b) 20A Dan Brown; (b) 24A Dan Brown; (b) 28A Joel Spector; (br) 32A Nick Harris;(b) 36A Dennis Lyall; (br) 41A James M. Effler; (br) 49A Michael Jaroszko; (br) 57A Tom Newsom; (br) 83A Jeff Spackman; (br) 93A Steve Adler; (bl) 101A Roger Payne; (br) 109A Adam Hook; (br) 119A Mike Jaroszko; (br) 127A Philip Howe; (b) 135A Dominick D'Andrea; (br) 145A Philip Howe; (br) 179A Jeff Preston; (b) 187A Doug Fryer; (br) 197A Peter Church;

Photo Credits

iv Ryan McVay/Digital Vision/Getty Images; v Eric Camden; vi (tr) Jim Whitmer; vi (br) Digital Vision/Getty Images; vii Myrleen Pearson/Alamy; viii (b) Tony Freeman/PhotoEdit; ix Image Source/Corbis; x Sonny Senser; xiv Blend Images/SuperStock; xviii Amos Morgan/Photodisc/Getty Images; xix Our Sunday Visitor Curriculum Division; xx (t) Blend Images/SuperStock; xxi Photodisc/Punchstock; xxii Ryan McVay/Photodisc/Getty Images; xxiii (b) Eric Camden; 1 (b) D. Berry/PhotoLink/Photodisc/Getty Images; 3 (b) D. Berry/PhotoLink/Photodisc/Getty Images; 4 (b) Our Sunday Visitor Curriculum Division; 5 (b) Corbis; 6A (t) Father Gene Plaisted, OSC; 6A (b) Photomondo/Getty Images; 6B (t) Father Gene Plaisted, OSC; 6B–6C (b) Photomondo/Getty Images; 8 (b) Corbis; 10 (b) Rim Light/PhotoLink/Stockbyte/Getty Images; 12 (b) Don Hammond/Design Pics/Corbis; 15 (b) Lawrence Manning/Corbis; 17 (bc) Squared Studios/Photodisc/Getty Images; 19 (bc) Squared Studios/Photodisc/Getty Images; 21 (b) PhotoLink/Stockbyte/Getty Images; 23 (bc) Squared Studios/Photodisc/Getty Images; 24A Richard Hurtchings/PhotoEdit; 25 (b) Matt Meadows; 28 (b) PhotoLink/Photodisc/Getty Images; 30 (b) Robert Marien/Corbis; 33 (b) Tony Freeman/PhotoEdit; 35 (b) Jack Hollingsworth/Corbis; 36 (b) Ryan McVay/Digital Vision/Getty Images; 38 (b) Corbis; 40 Our Sunday Visitor Curriculum Division; 41B (l) PhotoLink/Photodisc/Getty Images; 41B (r) Mazer Corporation; 41 (b) Jack Holtel/Photographik Company; 45 (b) Jack Holtel/Photographik Company; 46 (b) Fisher Litwin/Getty Images; 49B (l) Corbis; 49B (r) Getty Images; 49 (b) Jack Holtel/Photographik Company; 51 (b) Lawrence Manning/Corbis; 53 (b) Glen Allison/Photodisc/Getty Images; 57B (l) PhotoLink/Photodisc/Getty Images; 57B (r) Photodisc/Getty Images; 62 (b) Jack Holtel/Photographik Company; 63 (b) Jack Holtel/Photographik Company; 66 Houghton Mifflin Harcourt; 67A (bg) John Connell/Corbis; 67A (fg) Eric Camden; 67B (l) Corbis; 67B (r) Corbis; 67 (b) Jack Holtel/Photographik Company; 71 (b) Jack Holtel/Photographik Company; 72 (b) Nicola Sutton/Life File/Photodisc/Getty Images; 73 (b) Houghton Mifflin Harcourt; 75A Ed McDonald; 75B (l) Flying Colours Ltd/Digital Vision/Getty Images; 77 (b) Jack Holtel/Photographik Company; 80 (b) Jack Holtel/Photographik Company; 83B (r) Rubberball Productions/Getty Images; 83 (b) Gary John Norman/The Image Bank/Getty Images; 86 (b) Rubberball Productions/Getty Images; 92 Vico Collective/Blend Images/Getty Images; 93B (l) Nicola Sutton/Life File/Photodisc/Getty Images; 93 (b) Jack Holtel/Photographik Company; 94 (b) Photodisc/Getty Images; 96 (b) Jack Holtel/Photographik Company; 98 (b) Getty Images; 101B (r) Ryan McVay/Digital Vision/Getty Images; 101 (b) Lawrence Manning/Corbis; 104 (b) Jack Holtel/Photographik Company; 109B (l) Doug Menuez/Photodisc/Getty Images; 109B (r) Corbis; 109 (l) Jack Holtel/Photographik Company; 109 (r) Richard Hutchings; 110 (b) M. Freeman/PhotoLink/Photodisc/Getty Images; 111 (b) Jack Holtel/Photographik Company; 114 (b) Jack Holtel/Photographik Company; 115 (b) Jack Holtel/Photographik Company; 118 Our Sunday Visitor Curriculum Division; 119B (l) Corbis; 119B (r) Jack Holtel/Photographik Company; 120 (b) H. Wiesenhofer/PhotoLink/Stockbyte/Getty Images; 121 (b) Jack Holtel/Photographik Company; 124 (b) Eyewire/Getty Images; 125 (b) Jack Holtel/Photographik Company; 127B (l) S. Meltzer/PhotoLink/Getty Images; 127 (b) Jack Holtel/Photographik Company; 128 (b) M. Freeman/PhotoLink/Getty Images; 129 (b) Houghton Mifflin Harcourt; 130 (b) Reed Kaestner/Corbis; 132 (b) Corbis; 133 (b) Corbis; 135B (l) Our Sunday Visitor Curriculum Division; 135 (b) Digital Vision/Getty Images; 136 (b) Tracy Montana/PhotoLink/Getty Images; 137 (b) Jack Holtel/Photographik Company; 139 (b) Getty Images; 140 (b) Jack Holtel/Photographik Company; 144 Jose Luis Pelaez Inc/Blend Images/Getty Images; 145B (r) Ryan McVay/Photodisc/Getty Images; 146 (b) Scott T. Baxter/Photodisc/Getty Images; 147 (b) PhotoLink/Stockbyte/Getty Images; 151 (b) Corbis; 153A Ed McDonald; 153B (l) Corbis; 153 (b) Photodisc/Getty Images; 159 (l) Jack Holtel/Photographik Company; 161A Eric Camden; 161B (l) Radius/SuperStock; 161B (r) Radius/SuperStock; 161 (b) Houghton Mifflin Harcourt; 162 (b) Lawrence Manning/Corbis; 163 (b) Steve Cole/Photodisc/Getty Images; 165 (b) Jack Holtel/Photographik Company; 166 (b) Jack Holtel/Photographik Company; 170 Our Sunday Visitor Curriculum Division; 171B (l) PhotoLink/Photodisc/Getty Images; 171B (r) Amos Morgan/Photodisc/Getty Images; 174 (b) John Nakata/Corbis; 176 (b) Jack Holtel/Photographik Company; 179B (l) Jose Luis Pelaez, Inc./CORBIS; 180 (b) Jack Holtel/Photographik Company; 181 (b) Jack Holtel/Photographik Company; 183 (b) Jack Holtel/Photographik Company; 184 (b) Artville/Getty Images; 187B (l) Digital Vision/Getty Images; 187B (r) Harald Sund/Photographer's Choice/Getty Images; 187 (b) Clark Dunbar/Corbis; 188 (b) Photodisc/Getty Images; 189 (b) Jack Holtel/Photographik Company; 192 (b) Lawrence Manning/Corbis; 193 (b) Jack Holtel/Photographik Company; 196 Our Sunday Visitor Curriculum Division; 197B (lc) Squared Studios/Photodisc/Getty Images; 199 (b) Photodisc/Getty Images; 200 (b) Philip Harvey/Corbis; 203 (b) Lawrence Manning/Corbis; 205A Brian Minnich; 205B (r) Jim Whitmer; 207 Jack Holtel/Photographik Company; 208 (b) D. Berry/PhotoLink/Photodisc/Getty Images; 210 (b) Jack Holtel/Photographik Company; 213A Peter Burian/Corbis; 213B (r) David Buffington/Photodisc/Getty Images; 214 (b) Jack Holtel/Photographik Company; 219 (b) Jack Holtel/Photographik Company; 222A rubberball/Getty Images

Acknowledgements

Catechist's Notes

Catechist's Notes

_____
_____
_____
_____
_____
_____
_____
_____
_____
_____
_____
_____
_____
_____
_____
_____
_____
_____
_____

Catechist's Notes

Catechist's Notes

_____

_____

_____

_____

_____

_____

_____

_____

_____

_____

_____

_____

_____

_____

_____

_____

_____

_____